LOUIS XIII, THE JUST

LOUIS XIII, THE JUST

A. LLOYD MOOTE

UNIVERSITY OF CALIFORNIA PRESS
BERKELEY   LOS ANGELES   LONDON

University of California Press
Berkeley and Los Angeles, California

University of California Press, Ltd.
London, England

© 1989 by
The Regents of the University of California
First Paperback Printing 1991

Library of Congress Cataloging-in-Publication Data

Moote, A. Lloyd.
  Louis XIII, the Just / A. Lloyd Moote.
     p.   cm.
  Bibliography: p.
  Includes index.
  ISBN 0-520-06485-2 (alk. paper)
  ISBN 0-520-07546-3 (ppb.)
  1. France—Kings and rulers—Biography   2. France—History—Louis XIII, 1610–1643.   [1. Louis, XIII, King of France, 1601–1643.]
I. Title.
DC123.8.M66   1989
944'.032'0924—dc19
[B]   88-17344
                                                                              CIP

Printed in the United States of America

The paper used in this publication meets the minimum
Requirements of ANSI/NISO Z39.48-1992 (R 1997)
                    (Permanence of Paper)

For
Karen, Peter, Daphne, Bob

Contents

List of Plates   *ix*
Preface   *xi*
Introduction: Interpreting Louis XIII   1

PART I   THE FORMATION OF A KING, 1601–15

1   A Dauphin's World   19
2   The Boy King   39
3   King, Estates, and State   61

PART II   LOUIS THE JUST COMES OF AGE, 1615–24

4   Royal Marriage and Coup d'Etat   79
5   Seeking an Effective Mode of Governance   97
6   Fighting for Just Causes   116
7   Growing Up in Public   137

PART III   FRENCH ABSOLUTISM IN THE MAKING, 1624–35

8   Partnership of King and Cardinal   155
9   Ordering Priorities   175
10   Alais, Mantua, and the Day of Dupes   199
11   Governmental Revolution   220

PART IV   THE LEGACY OF LOUIS XIII, 1635–43

12   Warfare King, State, and Society   239
13   King and Culture   256
14   The Intimate Louis   273

Conclusion: Louis XIII Beyond the Grave   291
Appendix   299
  Map 1   Louis XIII's France   301
  Map 2   Two early royal campaigns, 1614 and 1620   302
  Map 3   The Huguenot challenge, 1621–29   303
  Map 4   The Thirty Years' War and the Habsburg challenge, 1618–43   304
  Map 5   Popular/Elite opposition and royal repression, 1617–43   305
Notes   307
Bibliography   359
Index   383

Plates

Following page 178

1 The boy king Louis XIII
2 Louis XIII around twenty-one years
3 Anne of Austria as queen of France, around her mid twenties
4 The prematurely aged Louis XIII
5 Cardinal Richelieu
6 Charles d'Albert, duke and constable of Luynes
7 Claude de Rouvroy, duke of Saint-Simon
8 Louis XIII accepting the surrender of La Rochelle
9 Louis XIII and the siege works of La Rochelle
10 A triumphal arch at Paris: the fall of La Rochelle
11 Medallion of 1618: the fall of Concini
12 Medallion of 1631: the Mantuan campaign
13 Medallion of 1635: declaration of war against Spain
14 Louise de La Fayette
15 The frontispiece of Guez de Balzac's *The Prince*
16 Louis XIII's daily occupations: evening (with Gaston d'Orléans, Anne of Austria, and the future Louis XIV)

Preface

During my graduate studies in the 1950s, my mentor said with a twinkle in his eye that Louis XIII had the reputation of not having the brains to come in from the rain, but had recently become intelligent enough to do that, and could be expected to become even brighter in the future. Little did this wonderful friend and teacher or I know that one day I would be taking up his challenge seriously. I hereby thank John B. Wolf for gently leading me toward the present work, which assumes that Louis XIII, called Louis the Just by his contemporaries, was not only an intelligent human being but also central to his reign. The convergence of that monarch's unique personality with the assumptions, problems, and wishes of his age created the Louis the Just of history and what I call the "Age of Louis XIII." That is the theme of this biography; hence the title *Louis XIII, the Just*.

The path I have taken has been exciting right from the start in the mid 1970s when I shifted from the subject of the minister-favorite in early-seventeenth-century France, under a National Endowment for the Humanities grant, to the monarch most of those favorites were associated with. I thank Alain Hénon of the University of California Press for getting me involved in what was then a French Monarchs series (the individual biographies of which have had their own publishing history and publishers), and for his warm and gracious backing ever since. Thanks are also in order to Ragnhild Hatton for her enthusiastic support of this book, and for the editors along the way at three publishing houses in two continents involved with the series.

It is a delight and honor to acknowledge institutional help: my own University of Southern California, for granting me sabbaticals plus a one-semester release from teaching, arranged by Jack Marburger and John Schutz following a three year stint chairing the university's restructuring of its General Education program; the Guggenheim Foundation, for making possible an enormously productive semester of archival research; and the National Endowment for the Humanities, for a semester's archival research which found its way unexpectedly into this book instead of one on the minister-favorite.

Let me also record my thanks to three librarians: to Marion Schulman at USC for laying her hands on every new publication about Louis XIII and informing me immediately; to Mary Jane Parrine of Stanford University Libraries, who did precisely the same thing during her years as Western European bibliographer at UCLA; and finally, to a wonderfully resourceful and modest official at the then Archives des Affaires Etrangères in Paris, who simply signs herself Mme Guyot, for retrieving one of the crucial volumes of Louis XIII correspondence which all the other staff members were convinced was lost! I also continue to marvel at the availability of manuscript and published sources at the Bibliothèque Nationale, Archives des Affaires Etrangères, and Bibliothèque de l'Institut de France, thanks to courteous staffs. Finally, institutional support has been given by Martha Rothermel, who printed out the results of my word processing with her inimitable combination of warmth and efficiency.

Several audiences and many persons of various walks of life in the United States, Canada, the United Kingdom, and France have heard me out on the "King of the Three Musketeers." Let me single out those who have been most important in those interchanges. First, I thank Edwin Perkins for what can only be described as the greatest act of friendship in going over the entire typescript with an editor's sharp eye at the stage where one-third of the text had to be eliminated; his advice was judicious, gentle, and enthusiastic. Orest Ranum and Mike Hayden read the pre-cut version, and made shrewd organizational and thematic suggestions. Dare I note another, anonymous, reader, who was so critical of the original text that he angered me into sharpening my thesis in a way that I hope will be debated rather than dismissed.

I cannot easily express my appreciation to Jeanne-Françoise Rouffianges (who played a vital role as listener and commentator and supporter at an important stage in the emergence of this biography, as well as providing me ever since with a number of current works related to Louis XIII). My gratitude goes to Andrew Lossky (whose gen-

tle comments muted some of my assertions and sharpened others);
to Madeleine Foisil (for her graceful erudition on the pleasant side of
Louis's childhood); to Olwen Huften (who challenged me to prove
that Louis was more important than the history of his humblest subjects); and to Elizabeth Marvick (probably the greatest influence on my
Louis XIII through her insight, which has helped me see a different
king from previous interpretations, as well as one different from her
viewpoint). I want to thank this last author also for letting me read
her biography of the young Louis XIII while it was still in typescript.

Friends have given me several forums for discussing Louis, in the
setting of their academic and family homes. Richard Bonney brought
me over from Paris to Reading University to speak on the Age of Louis
XIII. George Rothrock brought me to the University of Alberta twice
for intellectually stimulating encounters on my king, the second time
involving a remarkable *colloque* between Madeleine Foisil and Elizabeth Marvick on our king's childhood. Donald Bailey brought me to
the University of Winnipeg for talks on Louis and Richelieu, Louis as
a child, and—as it turned out—Canadian TV and radio discussions
of "the great historical person as a child." My former student Edwin
Ehmke made it possible for me to be part of a one-day Symposium on
Literary and Historical Biography at Stanford University with fifteen
other biographers; and Boots and George Liddle opened their home
to me for that weekend. My colleagues at USC have listened to me at
seminars and colloquium series, with Jack Wills providing much of
the organizational setting, and Dick Dales always prodding my conscience by asking how Louis was doing. I have even tested Louis XIII's
sex life with a delightful audience of seventy-, eighty-, and ninety-
year-old ladies called the Friday Reading Club; and had the temerity
to use Louis's often criticized style of governance as the foil for discussing President Ronald Reagan and political leadership before the
staunchly liberal Severance Club. It has all been fun.

The production side of readying a manuscript for publication,
which is not such a pleasurable experience for authors, has been
handled with such efficiency, thoughtfulness, and warmth by the
University of California Press staff that I have actually enjoyed some
of that taxing process. It has been a pleasure to work with Rose Ve-
kony as project editor, from the very first moment when we discussed
crucial punctuation and wording of book and chapter titles. Anne
Geissman Canright's copyediting combined a much-appreciated po-
liteness with a most helpful search for the clearest expression of what

I wished to say about Louis XIII. More than one *mot juste* from her pencil has also given my central arguments a forcefulness that I could not find on my own.

My children were still growing up when I started working on Louis; it is a delight to dedicate the finished product to them as adults. Their mother, Barbara Moote, helped in the formation of Louis; and I wish to thank her here for that help as well as for being a vital part of my previous professional formation and work.

After recording these many debts, I am happy to rest my case for Louis the Just and the Age of Louis XIII. None of us are self-made, professionally or personally; but the author is the one to answer for what he or she creates. I, like all those who have written on Louis's life and reign—and from whom I have learned so much—will have errors of fact or debatable inferences; one hopes there are also some contributions that would not have come from another person's perspective.

In turning this book over to my publisher and its readers, it is my greatest delight to record my gratitude for the emotional and intellectual support given to me constantly by Dorothy Carter Moote.

Introduction:
Interpreting Louis XIII

A perplexed historian once wrote: "Louis XIII was one of those persons whom we do not know how to judge; it is not possible to make pronouncements about him if one wishes to be scrupulously accurate and fair."[1] What perplexed that scholar makes this seventeenth-century Bourbon king of France an engrossing challenge for a historical biographer. For Louis XIII was driven by the contrary impulses of personal insecurity and determination to rule; and by an exalted sense of royal authority that was undermined by unkingly tendencies to be taciturn, morose, suspicious of others, and backbiting. He was known to his age by the sobriquet "Louis the Just"; but a few historians have called him sadistic, and even some contemporaries thought him a bit cruel. These personal contradictions and paradoxes would be sufficient cause to investigate his life even if his reign had not been important.

But his reign *was* important; and, not surprisingly, it contains paradoxes stemming from his baffling personality that beg to be resolved. How do we reconcile Louis's habitual dependence on others with his decisive acts against those persons when they thwarted his authority? Surely this man—who sprang a coup d'état against his mother that ended in the assassination of her political favorite, then fought two wars against her, and eventually humiliated her into fleeing from his realm—was not a weak monarch. Nor does he appear so dependent on others when we learn that as his reign wore on he dismissed every successive personal favorite who interfered with his

1

policies. And could a royal weakling rebuff his mother, wife, and brother in standing by the best minister of his reign?

More fundamentally still, how do we explain the fact that a ruler deemed by his contemporaries and historians incapable of holding sophisticated goals presided over basic political changes in his French state? Is it enough simply to assume that these were the doing of the celebrated chief minister of Louis's mature years, Cardinal Richelieu? If one pauses to reflect for a moment, it must seem odd that this monarch so jealous of his authority had little or nothing to do with the great authoritarian acts of his personal rule. So we ask: what role did this bundle of personal and political contradictions play in his own government's severe disciplining of the French nobility and other social and institutional elements of his realm, the destruction of the Protestant "state within the state," and the breaking of the encirclement of Bourbon France by the Austrian and Spanish branches of the rival House of Habsburg?

The strangest paradox of all is that Louis XIII has had only one full-dress biography, and few scholarly studies of specific aspects of his life.[2] While his reign is one of the best-known periods of French history, he is almost terra incognita in his own land. Indeed, when I began work on his life history I had to introduce him to acquaintances with a witticism: "Louis XIII was best known as the father of Louis XIV"; or, worse still, link him to the work of fiction most critical of him, with the remark "He was the king in *The Three Musketeers*."

This biography is designed to make Louis XIII sufficiently intelligible that we will no longer have to consider him an enigma, or an anomaly in his own reign. Rather than assuming that there was little connection between his person and his reign, I will pursue the theme of their intimate connection. My thesis is that, far from being the do-nothing king ridiculed in Alexandre Dumas's *Three Musketeers* or, as recent serious scholarship has reinterpreted him to be, the shadowy "collaborator" of his great minister Richelieu, Louis XIII was a highly effective monarch. Louis's sternly moralizing but hesitant nature, which earned him the lifelong sobriquet Louis the Just, led him inexorably to a very particular mode of governing that both suited his personality and worked. This same personality, moreover, lay behind the specific policies he formulated and implemented with his ministers, especially Richelieu. Ironically, however, the king's mode of governing made him look personally weak, thereby misleading both his contemporaries and later historians about his real political role. Equally ironically, his determined stand on principled policies was at the sacrifice of his own feelings, and gradually of his physical and emotional health, making him look even less attractive to his age and later scholars.

To do justice to both Louis's life and my interpretation, I have allowed his life history to unfold chronologically, while keeping my eye on the connections between Louis's personality, governing style, and policy making. Part One centers on the "formation" of the young Louis's personality from birth to age thirteen (1601–15); Part Two concerns the adolescent king's search for a mode of governing as he overthrew his mother and began his personal rule (1615–24); Part Three is on the adult ruler's policy making in collaboration with his chief minister, Richelieu, down to the formal outbreak of the war with the Habsburgs (1624–35); and finally, Part Four looks topically at the political, cultural, and personal legacy of Louis's reign by focusing on the last years of his life, the period of open war and what I call the warfare state (1635–43).

Many readers will be as impatient as I am to launch immediately into this royal life history. But in the case of a life as difficult to interpret as Louis XIII's, it is important first to say something about the way I have gone about that task. In the course of the biography I will refer to relevant work by other historians, noting where I agree and disagree. Here in the introduction it is appropriate to focus on the way primary sources, secondary accounts, and general assumptions by the historical profession and society in general have shaped my study, both as catalysts and as challenges and obstacles to this reinterpretation.

My greatest problem stemmed from the sources that Louis and his age left behind. For one thing, Louis was normally reticent to say anything, and what he did communicate by pen (sometimes pencil!) and voice was brief and cryptic.[3] Moreover, when he did speak or write, we are apt to wonder whether he was speaking his mind or saying what came to him from others, since he was notorious for leaning on others: first his mother, Marie de' Medici; then his political favorite Luynes; and finally his chief minister Richelieu. Third, there is a crucial absence of minutes for royal council meetings, so we rarely know Louis's role in formal decision making. Fourth, although Louis and Richelieu met or corresponded almost daily, their correspondence reveals precious few clues as to exactly how they interacted in the give and take of policy formulation. Finally, since Louis's comments were brief and largely made in response to Richelieu's memos, scholars have generally been tempted to assume that Richelieu was totally in charge.[4]

Other well-known sources have traps of their own for the unwary historical detective. I am thinking primarily, for Louis's early years, of the famous manuscript diary by Louis's physician, Héroard, and its nineteenth-century abridged published version[5] and, for the later years, of Richelieu's papers, notably his *Mémoires*, and his voluminous letters (in their nineteenth-century edition by Avenel, as well as the twentieth-century Grillon compilation, which also includes other ministerial correspondence).[6]

Elizabeth Marvick has written about some of the dangers posed by too ready reliance on Héroard, who did not merely record Louis's actions and words but interjected himself continually into his royal patient's life. Héroard also left exasperating gaps, both because he did not keep his diary all the time and because even when he did, some things escaped his notice or interest. Yet many an unwary scholar has taken Héroard as an objective and complete source for the life of the young Louis for, as Marvick notes, "in Western literature there is no document that gives us as complete a record of the development of an individual."[7]

As for Richelieu's papers, they are so carefully and powerfully ordered that one might easily be overpowered by them. Yet that ordering is a clue to be wary. Richelieu's *Mémoires* are not the objective history of the time that they appear to be, but a very particular narrative order, with distortions of his rivals' achievements when he was out of power and singular omissions of others' proposals and roles when he was in power. And his letters are only one-half of what Orest Ranum calls a "telephone conversation."[8]

I have used a number of devices to control these sources rather than let them control me. My first conscious strategy was to begin my research with the years when Louis was least under the influence of others, so that I could judge for myself the way he thought, felt, and acted. And my tactic was to look for situations that would betray his innermost thoughts, as well as those that revealed what he thought he "ought" to say. This part of my research was something like a controlled experiment in scientific research.[9]

From that vantage point I looked back into Louis XIII's childhood, to see how the person with whom I was now familiar had come into being. This involved confirming what Louis's physician had to say with evidence from other well-informed sources. Frequently a close reading of Héroard and his contemporaries led to unexpected conclusions. Rather than being simply manipulated by his entourage, young Louis appeared to have deeply ingrained, indeed innate traits that interacted with his environment. I also looked for clues to Louis's formation from known but overlooked sources—pamphlets, contemporary histories, even medallions and triumphal arches—which told me what royal virtues Louis's subjects sought to bring out in his character.[10]

Now it became possible to tread with some confidence on the most treacherous ground of my research; the period of "two-headed monarchy," when Richelieu dominates both in histories and in the sources—at least as usually read.[11] From his pre-Richelieu days I brought the king's penchant for standing on principle (his particular moralizing stand of tolerating Protestant Huguenot worship while opposing Huguenot rebellion, for example; and his dislike of Spaniards) and his interactions with and emotional reactions to other human beings. Knowing these factors about Louis allowed me to read the Louis-Richelieu correspondence in a way different from that of all the great Richelieu scholars, who rarely "knew" Louis.

Like a detective, I sought out political acts previously attributed by historians to the chief minister which looked suspiciously like acts the king himself might have approved or undertaken. Of course, I always looked for direct proofs of Louis's involvement and precise role to confirm my indirect, inferential suspicions. I was likewise willing to be surprised by aberrations or alterations in Louis's behavior that did not fit what I was sure I knew about him. Then finally, after looking at every other source, I consulted Richelieu's *Mémoires*. By keeping that source in reserve until the end, I could use it to complement other sources and thereby determine the ordering of events on my own, rather than using it as a chart of the course of history as so many others have.

Like the problem-ridden sources just discussed, the work of historians and fiction writers related to Louis XIII has often proved as much a challenge as an aid to understanding his life and rule. Yet every past interpreter of Louis has helped shape my own interpretation. I would like to record these intellectual debts, including some to friends whose work has stimulated me to differ and to others personally known and unknown who have led me to ideas that would startle the authors who acted as their catalysts.

I have learned much, first of all, from Dumas's half-historical, half-fictional view of Louis as a flawed man and a do-nothing king, and from the modification of it by nineteenth- and twentieth-century scholars of Louis's government and society who see the king as Richelieu's weak collaborator. Equally important in forcing me to think creatively have been the few biographical reexaminations of Louis, ranging from conventional studies to medical and psychological analyses. These have tended to make Louis XIII look either intellectually and emotionally too "normal" to be true or emotionally and physically very "abnormal." Finally, I have had to respond to the most popular kind of professional historical writing of the late twentieth century, which sees political elites, events, and change as relatively unimportant in the general scheme of history. One can conveniently divide that approach to history into two categories: one focusing on the popular culture of ordinary people; and the other—represented by the most influential historical "school" of our day, the Annales—working from the belief that political leaders are controlled largely by underlying economic, social, and mental "forces," which in turn provide historical continuity.

As I read about Louis XIII, the ghost of Alexandre Dumas was always at my shoulder. Dumas was not only a prolific writer of historical novels, but also a competent historian who knew the standard sources and even wrote a half-serious history of Henry IV and Louis XIII. Furthermore, his writings were part of an interpretive tradition, going back to Tallemant des Réaux just after Louis's demise, that drew on the king's well-known flaws in character to paint the picture of a pathetic incompetent.

Many readers will recall Dumas's clever caricature of Louis in *The Three Musketeers*. In his historical work *Great Men in Their Bath Robes*, Dumas openly declared his wish "to force history to call kings by their true names, and instead of saying Louis the Chaste or Louis the Just, to say Louis the Idiot or Louis the Miserable."[12] According to Tallemant's earlier version,

> the late king did not lack sense; but as I have remarked elsewhere, his mind bent in the direction of backbiting; he had difficulty in speaking, and, being timid, that caused him to act even less on his own. . . . He was a good horseman, could endure fatigue if called upon, and was good at arranging an army for battle. . . . He was a little cruel, as is the habit of most dissemblers and those with little heart, for the good sire was not valiant, although he wished it appear so. At times he reasoned passably well in a council meeting, and even appeared to have the advantage over the Cardinal. Perhaps the latter was shrewdly giving him this little satisfaction. 'Do-nothingness' [la fainéantise] was his undo-

ing. P[u]isieux governed for a while, then La Vieuville, superintendent of finances, acted as a sort of minister, before the great power of Cardinal Richelieu, destined to outrage everyone.[13]

I began to reflect: if the Tallemant-Dumas interpretation was based on one-sided evidence (showing only the king's flaws) and a shaky assumption (that a flawed royal character necessarily produced a weak ruler), a closer look at the evidence might lead to a different interpretation. Perhaps I could find that Louis's strong traits canceled out his weak ones and made him a stronger king than was assumed or, alternatively, that his character flaws themselves gave the reign some of its strengths.

Two scholars living in the late seventeenth and mid eighteenth centuries hinted at those two alternatives only to dismiss them. Pierre Bayle mused about Louis's weaknesses in a footnote of his famous *Critical and Historical Dictionary*: "What a remarkable thing that under a prince who exercised neither authority himself nor full freedom, royal power was more firmly established than it had been under the monarchs who were least dependent on their ministers and the most adept in the art of governing." In the end, Bayle's addiction to the prejudice of his times against kings ruling with the aid of favorites (unlike his own monarch, Louis XIV) prevented his skepticism from turning Louis XIII's personal liabilities into political assets.[14]

Father Griffet's scholarly three-volume history of Louis's reign went farther in historical revisionism, for he saw genuine strengths in the king's character. That eighteenth-century Enlightenment historian did not, however, feel that Louis's most positive quality, his will, was sufficient to offset his flaws:

> He was not capable of forming grand designs, or of thinking of the ways to make them succeed. . . . [Yet] if he sometimes lacked insight and ability [*de génie et de capacité*], at least in the affairs of state he had resolve and the will of a great king. . . . While the all but unlimited authority, which he let Cardinal Richelieu usurp, was the crowing glory of his reign, it obscured at the same time the merit of his person. He was never viewed as a great king, because he had a great minister; . . . content to let [the latter] know from time to time that he was the master, he yielded almost always to the superiority of his insight.[15]

In the last hundred years, serious scholars of Louis XIII's government and society have made Louis look even more appealing than Griffet thought possible. But while encouraging me that I was on the right track in focusing on Louis's character, even the finest political historians did not prove that the king's good points in themselves explained major developments of his reign.

In large part, political history today remains wedded to the partial revisions drawn by Marius Topin in his 1876 edition of Louis-Richelieu correspondence. Topin proved once and for all that Louis not only expressed his will to uphold his authority but also paid continuous attention to the details of policy making, and actually insisted on military decisions at variance with Richelieu's recommendations.[16] Unfortunately, these discoveries tell us little of the king's political ideas, or of the interacting of king and minister in major political matters.

Michel Carmona's 1984 revisionist summation of Louis's role retains Topin's mixed message. This distinguished biographer of Richelieu and Marie de' Medici takes Louis's will one stage further than Topin by breaking it down into the twin categories of authority and grandeur. But those grand-sounding themes turn out be nothing more than the vague royal aims of being obeyed at home and respected abroad. We are still left with Louis having a will without a way of his own. As Carmona admits,

> it is certain that Louis XIII did not find in himself the moral resources necessary to satisfy his double ambition of authority and grandeur. Too inconstant and lacking tragically in perseverance, he would require strong personalities around him in order to impose a continuity of views and a coherence of action in governmental policy, to face obstacles and adversity, and to translate expansive and vague aspirations into precise, concrete steps.[17]

Orest Ranum's seminal *Richelieu and the Councillors of Louis XIII* shows us how difficult it is to get beyond the old picture of a weak monarch by studying his government directly. Ranum blazed a new trail by examining unpublished correspondence between Richelieu, his fellow ministers, and Louis, and he concluded that Richelieu was the initiator of policy and Louis in essence the reviewer, whose moods had to be watched for the favorable moment to secure his approval.[18] Similarly, all the other premier scholars of Louis's reign, from Tapié to Carmona and Pagès to Treasure and Méthivier, speak of Louis and Richelieu as collaborators, of their work as an association, of a two-headed monarchy and a duumvirate; but they continue to assume that this was the "Age of Richelieu."[19]

Thus, in political studies, Louis XIII still appears more as an intruder in his own government than as a head of state central to its working. More than willpower on Louis's part must be found if a causal relationship between the ruler's positive qualities and the reign's achievements is to be established; and it is equally essential to grapple more creatively with his unseemly characteristics if the negative Tallemant-Dumas inferences from them are to be overturned. Political historians are premature in announcing the death of the "myth of the *roi-fainéant*," as Carmona does in citing Pierre Grillon's magnificent new edition of Richelieu's state papers. Grillon repeats a familiar litany: Louis XIII had a strong conscience about his obligations as a sovereign, was scrupulous in informing himself on policy issues, and did not hide his irritation at ministerial negligence. Yet Grillon concludes mildly and almost negatively: "Such a sovereign was surely not a master who could be easily manipulated"—implying that he could be manipulated, and perhaps had to be if anything of major importance was to be accomplished.[20]

In my quest for more convincing positive qualities in Louis XIII than direct studies of his government provide, I turned to biographical analyses of his personality. But biographers of the king, like sympathetic biographers in general, have tended to gloss over the weak points of their hero and to exaggerate more appealing characteristics. Thus, although Louis Batiffol brought to his several studies of Louis XIII an erudition that may never be surpassed, that early-twentieth-century scholar resembles his interpretive opposite, Dumas, in his selective use of undifferentiated sources. Batiffol's monumental *Louis XIII at Twenty* and other studies make the king too normal and strong to be convincing. Charles Romain's briefer *A Great Misunderstood King* suffers from the same weakness; and in addition it does not say enough about the king's person to prove that he was either misunderstood or great. Vaunois's year-by-year account of Louis's life is more careful in its positive pronouncements, but it flattens the king's life like an appointment book.[21]

The one genuinely comprehensive biography of Louis, by Pierre Chevallier, uses the unpublished dispatches of foreign ambassadors at the French court to show both the strong and the weak points of the king in great detail. But Chevallier's *Louis XIII* is essentially the same blend of contradictions that we have seen in other revisionist interpretations of the reign. He calls Louis a "Corneillian king," meaning that Louis resembled the characters of the contemporary playwright Corneille in his will to live up to his station, but he needed Richelieu to help him find the way: "Thus neither his relatives, nor the Huguenots, nor the *grands* of the robe and sword . . . could ever divert Louis XIII from his determination to be obeyed. . . . Most certainly, it was the good fortune of this king, who had more willpower and resolve than political capacity, to meet on his path Cardinal Richelieu."[22]

The most promising reinterpretation of Louis XIII's personality comes not from explaining away his blemishes but from exposing them to a searching analysis. The author Elizabeth Marvick brings to the study of her royal patient the techniques of Freudian psychology. To date she has emphasized Louis's first years, the period of his life on which we have the greatest information about the conflicts at work within his person. She is also the first scholar to make extensive use of the diary of Louis's physician in its original massive manuscript volumes.

Other historians have anticipated Marvick's work by assuming that the young Louis was a bright child with potential for ruling, but that he lost his abilities somewhere between childhood and adulthood.[23] Marvick, however, has gone deeply into that childhood to see precisely what happened to that potential. Marvick's analysis is far more penetrating than Philippe Ariès's celebrated *Centuries of Childhood* and the lesser known *Parents and Children in History* by David Hunt, both of which examine Louis's early experiences out of context in their eagerness to generalize about childhood in early modern France and Europe.[24] Her work also towers above earlier analyses of Louis's medical history whose authors did not know how to proceed after calling him "neurasthenic" and "susceptible to hating coldly to the point of criminal intent, incapable of affection, and absolutely without sufficient willpower to be his own master."[25]

In Marvick's view, Louis began life intelligent and healthy, only to have his natural growth emotionally and physically stunted by the manipulations of his parents, physician, nurse, and governess. The product of that unhealthy formation was a very unattractive adult Louis. He not only was both willful and dependent, as other historians had discovered, but he also had a malevolent side, with a "capacity to cruelty" devoid of "the horror many of his contemporaries felt at the bloody destruction" his French armies inflicted on other Christian populations.

For Marvick, the person whom contemporaries called Louis the Just was closer to what we might call Louis the Sadist. His was a personality devoid of conscience; his behavior leaned toward emotional solutions involving destructive and self-gratifying acts against others. Intellect and principle, whether personal or societal, seem to be singularly lacking in Marvick's provocatively somber recasting of the Tallemant-Dumas Louis XIII.[26]

This does not mean that Marvick draws the same inferences as Tallemant and Dumas about Louis's rule. On the contrary, she stands those authors on their head: in her hands their flawed Louis XIII has been reshaped into an abnormal person whose very abnormalities contributed to significant acts of state. Dumas and Tallemant would have been stunned by such a conclusion. And so will be all of Louis's reinterpreters, who never thought that that king could have been so influential—even through his most attractive qualities, let alone his darker traits. Yet here is Marvick's Louis, who injects into his government's policies a uniquely harsh tone.

While Marvick's work to date concentrates on the early years of Louis's life and rule, this latest biographer of the king also draws examples from the years of his collaboration with Richelieu. Here she focuses on Louis's active involvement in the unusual number of state executions during his personal reign, asserting that he took great pleasure in those undertakings. She shows also that Louis was emotionally involved in aspects of policy making, noting that he contributed to his government's stand against Spanish pretensions based on his own long-standing antipathy to Spain that owed nothing to Richelieu's influence.

Because Marvick's full examination of Louis XIII's statecraft is reserved for a future book on his adult life, our curiosity is aroused as to what she thinks were the precise nature and extent of Louis's participation in his government. In the meantime, her current work contains hints that he was not a full-fledged partner of his famous chief minister. Marvick stresses Louis's emotional involvement in policy making (his dislike of the Spaniards, for example) rather than his political ideas or developed principles. And, in line with other interpreters of Louis, she underscores the king's fretful dependence on Richelieu. In her version, Louis seems at times to have needed Richelieu's emotional support to give full vent even to his feelings. Conversely, her Louis was just as backbiting as previous portraitists have rendered him: he deeply resented his dependency on Richelieu. In Marvick's words, Louis "could be a brutal master but he was also a fractious slave."[27]

Marvick's focus on Louis XIII's most unflattering character traits requires careful reflection, for it is the most plausible explanation to date of the paradox of an apparently weak ruler and a strong reign. One has merely to look at Louis's behavior to agree with Marvick that, nasty at times, it was an element in his reign's statecraft. Yet such a paradoxical man as Louis had more to his person than can be explained away by emphasizing his dark side; and his involvement in statecraft was also wrought of more than emotional input. I am, furthermore, unwilling to judge him by our own standards—in Marvick's case, by assuming that what we would call sadistic behavior was judged that way in his own times. Hence, while being impressed with Marvick's technical prowess and command of her material, my reservations about her interpretation parallel my similar questioning of political analyses focusing on Louis's more attractive side.

Unease with the way the paradoxes of Louis XIII's rule were resolved by self-contained political and psychological analyses led me to the Annales historians' famous "structures," "conjunctures," and "*mentalité.*" To omit those external elements in studying the making of a monarch would be as one-sided as to ignore the ruler's inner ragings. While I was aware that the Annales scholars and allied historians of popular culture were hostile to the study of elite politics and persons, I also knew that the things they studied, from society and economy to belief systems, played a role in shaping the lives and actions of political leaders.[28]

How did Louis XIII look from the Annales perspective? First of all, he was born into a particular social structure: the deep-seated late-medieval and early-modern hierarchical "society of orders," in which not only the king but every sociopolitical order in his realm, from the great nobility to the peasantry, had its privileged place by law, custom, and sheer power. Second, Louis's accession to the throne coincided with a short-run trend, or conjuncture, in the faltering post-sixteenth-century economy, which cast its shadow across his reign, adding to the traditional problems of an economy not far removed from medieval subsistence. Finally, he inherited from his father's time a political mentalité, or mindset, which the French people had developed as they emerged from the anarchical French Wars of Religion. This mindset favored both the institution of monarchy and the person of the monarch, thus offsetting some of the weaknesses inherent in the monarchy's organs of government.[29]

At first I intended simply to use these Annales findings to frame the outer societal limits of what Louis could do as king, somewhat as Marvick used psychoanalysis to determine the inner psychical limits controlling Louis. This meant that as king, Louis could neither change the basic social structure of France nor do much to alter the economic base of either his subjects' existence or the state's treasury. At the same time, however, observant French people might have expected some increase in royal authority in both areas as a result of popular support for monarchy.

As I looked further into the subject, I saw that the Annales approach, far from merely setting the outer limits of what Louis XIII could do, could also shed light on the sort of person he was and what he actually did as ruler. The mentalité, in particular, of Louis's time included ideals, values, beliefs and ideas that were as much a part of Louis's formation as the emotional influences of his immediate entourage studied by Marvick.

In my efforts to discover the precise ideological elements that had influenced Louis but escaped the attention of scholars focusing on his emotions and policies, I took heart from the successes of historians of early-modern popular culture. If a scholar like Carlo Ginzburg could show how an obscure heretical Italian miller adapted the culture of the elite to his way of thinking,[30] why could I not do the same thing for an overlooked ruler at the top of the same early modern world? So I looked at Louis not as someone who was simply warped by a manipulative entourage into behaving nastily. Instead, he appeared to me as a particular human being with innate characteristics, into which he fitted not only hostile human influences (and other, more benign human influences studied by Héroard's current editor, Madeleine Foisil)[31] but also his reading of the political values he was exposed to. Of the latter, I focused on the contemporary royal virtues which French society at court and elsewhere asked him to emulate, in their pamphlets, histories, speeches, medallions, triumphal arches and other didactic sources. Here, to answer a biographer's questions, was a wealth of material relevant to Louis's mind and emotions that historians had never looked at.

Looking at Louis in this broader formative setting, I came to conclusions quite different from those held by either the Tallemant-Dumas tradition or its political and psychological reinterpreters. I began to see Louis XIII as someone with not just the will to rule but a sense of principles that served him both in his council chamber and in tête-à-têtes with Richelieu. I saw him not as a hesitantly self-indulgent inflicter of pain on others but as someone who normally put principle ahead of his own feelings. Piece after piece of the puzzle came together as Louis's willpower and his principles combined with his ideas on a whole host of issues.

The puzzle took shape still more rapidly when I turned to the key piece: Louis's sobriquet "the Just." Here was the most obvious way to find out what his principles were, as seen by his subjects as well as by himself. Yet no scholar had given the sobriquet anything more than a passing reference. This singular oversight can be explained partly by scholars' narrow documentary focus on purely political sources. A hidden underlying reason, however, is the fact that the early-seventeenth-century term *just* simply did not make sense to historians. From the modern vantage point, Louis's harsh disciplining of subjects bore no relation to our interpretation of justice, that is, with giving citizens the full protection of the law. Scholarly superimposition of psychological frameworks rooted in nineteenth- and twentieth-century culture on the post-religious-war world is also bound to confuse us about the mentalité of Louis XIII and his age, no matter how brilliant the analyst or alluring the analysis.[32]

Once I traced the use of Louis's sobriquet "the Just" by himself and his subjects throughout his personal reign, what had seemed an impossible puzzle now became a clear picture. The reader will have an opportunity to follow that journey via everything from triumphal royal entrances into rebel towns all the way to doggerel verses.

I must add that, after working through this maze by myself, I encountered in the work of a brilliant historian of early modern popular culture an apt way of expressing what I had done. Robert Darnton says that when we fail to get the point of a joke or an attitude from early modern times, we know we are on to something very important.[33] How are we to interpret Louis's being hailed as Louis the Just when he inaugurates his personal reign by allowing his friends to kill his mother's "tyrannical" political favorite, Concini? Sadism? Weak-willed act? Or rather the hesitant but principled acting out of the supreme royal virtue of justice! We may not see Louis's acts as just ones, or his statecraft as being principled; but his age saw them that way, and that is the only way we can understand the man—and the king—Louis XIII, called "the Just."

Once we see him that way, his personality looks quite different from the Tallemant-Dumas caricature or any of its variations by historian-interpreters. And once we fit this personality into the king's day-to-day interactions with Richelieu, that relationship changes too. It becomes clear that although Richelieu continually made policy suggestions, these went nowhere unless they fitted his monarch's inner moral world of principles and ideals—indeed, that the clever minister not only looked for the right psychological moment to make suggestions, but he also made the sorts of suggestions Louis himself wanted. The bare documents may tell us only that Louis "reviewed" policy; the hidden facts of his intellectual-emotional makeup indicate that he was very much involved in formulating and deciding political undertakings, even when he appeared to play a passive role.

This brings me to the last aspect of this interpretive history of Louis XIII: his role in history. My biographical research began with the knowledge that current historical circles either avoid or do not value the study of political elites and the importance of their decisions; it concluded with the satisfaction of knowing that what follows in the chapters ahead proposes quite a different view of things. I use the life history of Louis XIII as a test case of the theory that political leaders do indeed shape their worlds. These leaders are, of course, formed in part by their own societies as well as by their immediate entourage, but they begin life with unique innate characteristics, and the subsequent interchange between them and their environment is decidedly two-way.

Those leaders who ruled as early-modern monarchs governed within a framework well known to recent historical research: one of commonplace patron-client networks, evolving political superstructures, set social structures, and immutable economic conjunctures.[34] Yet they acted with some freedom and individuality. In the case of Louis XIII, I will argue that, far from being the prisoner of contemporary structures and conjunctures, he was more influential than they on the process of state building; indeed, it can be argued that in raising taxes to unbelievable heights, he defied the economic conjunctures, just as in eroding the power of individual social orders he worked against the concept of privilege that was one of the mainstays of the social structure.

There is an apt contrast here with the "antibiography" par excellence of the Annalistes. Fernand Braudel's monumental study of the Mediterranean world in the Age of Philip II contains brilliant character sketches of that supremely cautious late-sixteenth-century Spanish ruler, known appropriately as Philip the Prudent. Had the author wished, he could have used his insight into Philip's personality to craft a stunning biography, focusing on prudence as the driving force of the reign. Yet Braudel's Annaliste assumptions made his Philip the Prudent little more than a Polybian-Machiavellian swimmer moving with the tide of Mediterranean socioeconomic trends. This study of Louis XIII is designed to invert the Braudelian scheme by making Louis's own sobriquet "the Just" central to an understanding of his character and his age.[35]

In making Louis XIII a test case of the idea that political leaders shape their world, I not only invert the paradigm of the Annales and radically alter the normal use of popular culture, but I also challenge a time-honored Western cultural assumption about political leadership—that is, that only one basic type of political leader substantially shapes history, the so-called great person in history. That person is a charismatic individual in total charge of his or her government, with a clear political vision and well-thought-out policies. The reality, however, is far different, for in fact all heads of state influence their age, whether positively or negatively, by their strengths as well as their weaknesses. Within the ranks of effective leaders, several alternative modes of governing are more common than the charismatic leadership type. Those alternative modes, moreover, are just as strong, even though the leader adopting them lacks the qualities of the "great person in history." The Louis XIII of the rest of this book was such a person.

PART I

The Formation of a King 1601–15

1

A DAUPHIN'S WORLD

S hortly after 10:00 P.M. on 27 September 1601, in the oval chamber of the royal palace at Fontainebleau, the king and queen of France celebrated the birth of their first child. It was a boy, the first dauphin to be born to a reigning French monarch in fifty-eight years. Within nine years he would mount his father's throne, the only firstborn French royal son in over eighty years to become king.

Henry IV, first Bourbon king of France, was so excited over the prospect of a male heir to continue his dynasty that he scarcely left his wife during the twenty-two hours of difficult labor. Queen Marie de' Medici, brought ten months before from her native Florence to succeed the childless, divorced Queen Marguerite of Valois, was undoubtedly even more anxious to produce a live boy. With her first quickening contractions, the prospective parents and midwife were joined by the three ranking Bourbon princes, Henry's own sister, Marie's leading attendants, and five physicians. On finally being convinced by the midwife that the baby was indeed a boy, Henry thrust open the chamber's doors to let some two hundred courtiers stream in. Queen Marie, weak after hours of labor and attacks of colic, was gently told the news by her husband, where-upon she praised God and fainted. Meanwhile, the baby who had occasioned all the excitement rallied from the tiring ordeal of child-birth with the aid of a spoonful of wine, and was handed over to his future governess, Françoise de Longuejoue, baroness of Montglat, and his physician, Jehan Héroard, author of a famous book on the bone structure of horses, *Hippostologie.*[1]

The birth of the future King Louis XIII was justifiably celebrated throughout France with bonfires and songs of thanksgiving. What a relief it must have been for war-weary subjects to look forward to the perpetuation of the policies and personal qualities of the likable Gallic Hercules, Henry IV! In 1589 Henry had mounted a shaky throne, around which swirled a blood-drenched religious conflict between France's Catholic majority and its Protestant Huguenot minority. In little more than a decade he achieved spectacular successes denied the last three, childless Valois monarchs, whose court debaucheries, inept handling of religious conflict, and murders of political opponents had culminated in the assassination of Henry's immediate predecessor, Henry III. By contrast, the first Bourbon monarch of France ended the forty-year Wars of Religion in 1598 through his delicately crafted Edict of Nantes, which guaranteed limited religious rights for the Huguenots. Moreover, this charismatic "restorer of France" also contributed greatly to the accompanying shift in popular and elite mentalité from the Valois climate of violence and regicide to one that worshiped monarchs and focused national hopes on monarchy.[2]

Yet much remained to be done to restore political order and bind the religious wounds. Many French Catholics disapproved of Henry IV's toleration of Huguenots and chafed at his alliances with Protestant states against fellow Catholic monarchs in Spain and Austria. Twenty disgruntled extremists actually tried to kill their king. The Huguenot minority, some 10 percent of the population, were equally dangerous. Their right to worship in the southern mountains and on the western seaboard where they predominated, guaranteed by the Edict of Nantes, was also protected by royally subsidized Huguenot garrisons in 150 fortified towns. This Protestant "state within the state" was bound to rekindle religious animosity between Catholics and Huguenots, just as it stood as a reminder that the French king was far from sovereign in his state.[3]

The hopes and fears accompanying the birth of the future second Bourbon ruler of France ensured that he would be brought up in a demanding political climate. Henry indicated just how public the dauphin's world would be by allowing the horde of courtiers to gaze on the newborn infant, telling a horrified midwife: "Don't get angry. This child belongs to everyone." Later in his childhood, when caught in the middle of an argument between his governess

and governor concerning whom he belonged to, Louis would ruefully comment: "Some day I hope I will belong to myself."[4]

The dauphin entered the world of politics, courtiers, and personal servants not as a blank slate to be written on by others at will
but with distinct physical, emotional, and intellectual traits. Dr.
Héroard described the infant heir as large boned, muscular, and
vigorous, with a large, well formed head, brown eyes, small lips a
little turned up, very powerful lungs, large arms, straight legs, and
long feet. Later painted or drawn portraits show a chubby-faced,
well-proportioned boy, with a disconcertingly suspicious look in
his penetrating eyes and narrow, pursed lips. More attractive
than either his haughty, austere, full-faced mother, or his playful-
looking father whose breath reeked and beard was always dishev-
eled, the future Louis XIII gained many compliments on his deportment. A discerning ex-Queen Marguerite, on first seeing him
with his governor and riding master, exclaimed: "Oh! How handsome he is! Oh! How well built he is! How lucky the Chiron who
teaches this Achilles!"[5]

The heir needed all his native stamina to withstand the enormous physical and emotional self-punishment that would drag
down his health and cause a premature death in his forty-second
year. One physical problem appeared at birth. While not born with
the legendary teeth that his father, Henry IV, and his son Louis XIV
reputedly inflicted on their nurses, the dauphin had an appetite
greater than his ability to feed. An attending surgeon tried to help
by cutting the membrane under his tongue when he was two days
old. That physical handicap contributed to a dangling royal tongue
and, through emotional tensions, to a frustrating lifelong stammer
that appeared by his third year.

Inborn hyperactivity signaled an emotionally difficult person.
Piercing infant cries gave way to headstrong childish reaction
against discipline and violent outbreaks of temper. Many scholars
have attributed the dauphin's temper tantrums to bad handling by
his supervisors and parents. Yet time and time again we can trace
his psychical history from apparent external triggers back to unprovoked outbursts. Routinely, the physician Héroard referred to the
boy as a "stubborn child."[6]

Héroard's constant references to the dauphin as "very gay" are
a curious commentary on this pattern of mood swings. As the baby
approached his first birthday he was observed pulling hard on his
father's beard and tugging playfully on nobles' mustaches. He be-

came fond of playing hide-and-seek and of chasing after courtiers while laughing uproariously. We read of his being "impatient" to be taken by carriage to watch his father hunt in the forest. And we discover a young boy who would become very angry when tricked into looking in his mother's bed for his father and not finding him. The pattern also emerged of a dauphin crying out loudly, then suddenly becoming composed and laughing.

How intelligent was this physically strong but high-strung boy? We can discount Héroard's anecdotes of the infant Louis's advanced language, Marie's somewhat dry observation that her growing son was "doing well," and the good impression he made in carefully staged audiences on the constant stream of foreign ambassadors and native dignitaries. Nevertheless, Héroard's early observation of the boy's acute powers of observation and memory has a ring of truth. As both a child and an adult he was able to recall with stunning accuracy things that interested him, from the habits of courtiers to the names of his French and Swiss guards. Louis's official historiographer and close companion, Charles Bernard, later recalled that at a tender age Louis anticipated questions and replied aptly before the questioner finished speaking. According to Bernard, he could penetrate a person's innermost thoughts unless the individual was extremely careful. There are also indications that he could learn rapidly; Bernard, in speaking of Louis's aptitude for handling firearms, noted that "he showed an equal skill in everything else he wanted to apply himself to."[7]

The young prince's intellectual weakness was not that he lacked ability, but that he was naturally drawn to concrete, mechanical subjects. Even in the fine arts he leaned toward the practical side, despite an early creative flair for sketching and later for composing music. As a child he was proud to dance, play the lute, and perform the correct drumroll for a variety of martial situations. Music was one of the few things that calmed him down at night after a childhood rage. His first halting drawings can still be viewed in Héroard's diary, as can a later tracing of his mother's profile—in pencil, right over his physician's handwriting![8]

What influences did this gifted but willful child experience? Until he was seven he lived in the old royal château of St-Germain-en-Laye outside Paris, with all his father's other children (including several by Henry's mistresses) and attendants, largely female, from nurse to governess. This protective environment, a few miles from the full Parisian court and his own parents, was a mixed blessing.

On the one hand, the prince could avoid some of the heavy court etiquette and political jockeying that he later frowned upon. He could enjoy his spacious living quarters, the "new" château close by, and the royal gardens with their terraces, grottoes, and pathways down to the Seine river. He was also free to roam in the vast open meadows and in the forest with its teeming game that presaged a lifelong passion for hunting.

On the other hand, the heir was not isolated from court life or his parents; long before he moved to Paris and a predominantly male entourage, he absorbed many political lessons. Likewise, his emotional development was shaped by the interplay of his volatile nature and an entourage that tried its best to make him behave. Historical judgments on the influence of that human environment differ; but the consensus is that his family, attendants, and educators scarred him for life.[9]

Let us begin our foray into that difficult field with Henry IV, a father quite different from the son. Henry always retained the free-spirited spontaneity of his boyhood days at the court of his mother, the Huguenot Queen Jeanne d'Albret of the Franco-Spanish border ministate of Navarre. He was not one to remember past wrongs or bear grudges. When he added the French crown to his mother's Navarrese one, he forgave the Catholic royalist nobles whom he had fought as the Huguenots' leader. And he was magnanimous to the more militant Catholic League, led by the Guise family, even though in fighting to the bitter end of the religious wars they had ignored his crown and his subsequent conversion to the Catholic faith. Henry of Bourbon was also a lively companion, affable courtier, and flattering lover, although far from a model husband. Subjects and foreigners could not have missed the sharp differences in personality between this winsome, earthy, open king and the serious, intense, temperamental dauphin. Queen Marie once remarked to Henry about the gravity of their son's speech; and the entire court could tell that at times the father acted more like a child than did the son.

Still, there was a great deal of affection between father and son. Louis was transported with joy whenever Henry visited St-Germain. The father, his face flushed with excitement, held his son's hand as they walked and played, or as he conducted free-wheeling discussions with his ministers. The young prince, in turn, made a hero of his royal father. His interest in war and the hunt, in emulation of his father, gave them a natural bond. They were also alike in their distaste for ceremony and flattery.

Henry reputedly placed a sword in Louis's hand at birth. The dauphin's ecstasy knew no bounds at the age of three, when he was booted and spurred for riding; he could not wait for the day when he would mount a horse like his father. In time the prince was presented with firearms, toy soldiers, drums, and noble boys his own age to play with and form into miniature armies. By the time he was ten and king, Louis had an impressive collection of muskets, harquebuses, and even cannon. On attaining his official majority at thirteen in 1614 he had fifty-five harquebuses and a "cabinet of arms" that would follow him faithfully on the endless political-military travels of his personal reign.

The dauphin's interest in the hunt and other pastimes also bore the stamp of the royal father, though there were some marked differences reflecting a quite different personality. At an early age the boy mimicked his father's practice of stalking deer, right down to the last detail of bringing home a portion of the prize to show proudly to others. But young Louis had his own unique passion for falconry, first at St-Germain and then in the palace grounds of the Louvre in Paris. He began by observing birds and then turned to collecting birds of prey, passing the time of day by letting these predators loose among neighborhood starlings. He was equally attached to his pet dogs, all of whose names, tricks, and potential for stalking game at the hunt he knew intimately.

The heir fitted right in at court with his enjoyment of card games, chess, a form of croquet, and tennis. Like his father he hated to lose; at age eight he threw chess pieces at a courtier's head on being checkmated. Unlike his father, he acquired an intense dislike of gambling and cheating at it.

Louis not only adapted his beloved father's martial and hunting interests to his own desires, but he also began to form his own severe view of politics from hearing about his father's political problems. Very early on the dauphin developed an elementary prejudice in foreign affairs, calling the Spaniards "papa's enemies." This was natural, for his father's state was in constant danger of being encircled by the Habsburg dynasty's Spanish and Austrian branches. Spain ruled over Portugal, Northern Italy, Franche Comté, and the Spanish Netherlands; the head of the Austrian branch customarily ruled Bohemia and Hungary in addition to be-

ing elected Holy Roman Emperor of the German Nation. Perhaps Louis also heard that Philip II of Spain had tried to keep Henry IV off the French throne.

On internal politics, the young heir showed a keen appreciation of the importance of deference to royal authority. This was partly in line with his father's brand of royal authoritarianism, for Henry IV was fond of saying "I intend to be king." Yet there were clear differences also. Henry could maintain an aura of authority and still emphasize clemency more than implacable justice. He lectured the judges of the Parlement of Paris when they avoided registering new laws, but he was inclined to clemency for duelers who flagrantly broke the ban against the noble custom of settling points of honor with the sword. By contrast, when Henry's forgiving nature was stressed to the heir, Louis responded with the one example of Henry's strict justice: the execution of Marshal Biron, who had refused to be repentant after treasonous negotiations with Spain, Savoy, and England. Similarly, on learning that the French duke of Bouillon's conspiracy on the eastern border against Henry had ended in surrender in the duke's adjoining vassal state at Sedan, Louis exclaimed icily, "I will cut his head off." [10]

The one place where the heir balked at authority concerned his own ambiguous position in the social and political hierarchy of the realm. Henry IV tried to instill in the headstrong dauphin and his future courtiers a sense of young Louis's dual role as deferential son and regal heir. By the time Louis was three, the inevitable explosive scene occurred between them.

On 1 September 1604 the royal family arrived at the palace of Fontainebleau, south of Paris. For four days king and dauphin were inseparable. On the fifth Louis resisted Henry's efforts to extract a filial kiss and got into such a bad mood that his father and governess whipped him. This scene of less than an hour ended on a happy note. The dauphin scratched and pulled the king's beard; the king jokingly asked who the birch rods were for, and laughed uproariously at the child's lisping response: "fo you." After feigning a mock retreat from filial vengeance, Henry ran to kiss Louis when the boy said, "I want papa."

In the succeeding days, Louis alternated between trying to avoid a mandatory walk with his father on the mere threat of rain (which frightened him) and joining happily in impromptu adaptations of the royal *lever*: the monarch stopped his early-morning dressing when the heir was brought to him and handed his shirt to Louis, who obligingly handed it back. The tension built to a new crisis in October. On the twelfth, Louis would not take his father's hand, and he kept his cap on in defiance of the rule that a subject's hat must be removed in the king's presence. Henry impulsively threw the son's hat on the ground.

The morning of the twenty-third found the dauphin in a particularly foul mood. He resisted being dressed by his staff and was totally out of control by the time he was dragged to his father instead of being allowed to play. In retaliation for Louis's refusal to defer to the regal command "Take off your hat," Henry forcibly removed it himself, took the boy's drum and drumsticks, and placed the cap on his own head after swatting the child with it for good measure. Father and son became furious with each other. Neither the queen's returning of the hat and drumsticks nor the heir's prolonged confinement to his nurse's room, or even a belated, half-hearted whipping by his governess, calmed him down. Eventually the dauphin was placated by being allowed to play in his "pottery," dine, and be sung to sleep by his nurse.[11]

Was Henry IV a bad father in engaging in acts like this? I have described the famous "hat scene" in some detail to let the reader judge. Certainly he was not blameless in his handling of the difficult child. During the succeeding days the dauphin became so submissive to father and mother that he even let himself be called his father's "valet," a description that previously was anathema to him. The cost to Louis's self-esteem and autonomy must have been great.

Yet how *could* one deal with such a son? We can detect no less than three conflicting therapies that young Louis's baffled father and the rest of his entourage resorted to. For every overreaction to his bursts of temper we can find examples of gingerly indulgence. Henry, Marie, Héroard, "Mamanga" (Louis's name for his governess, Madame de Montglat), and his nurse "Doundoun" all plied Louis with gifts and treats, laughed when they should have punished him, and even played up to his sense of self-importance. In addition to overreaction and permissiveness, Henry and others often acted caringly to redirect the heir from self-centeredness toward respect for others. The throwing of chess pieces brought swift corporal punishment; vindictiveness was countered by suggestions that it was better to be magnanimous. Through it all, the future king of France learned about royal authority and its responsibilities the hard way.[12]

While contemporaries thought that Louis inherited his father's "spirit" and intellect, his mother may have had a greater influence on the dauphin's political outlook. Henry sensed a central component of this: the striking resemblance of Louis's stubbornness and displays of temper to the emotional makeup of Marie. He even predicted that they would clash some day. This mother-son connection has been generally overlooked by historians, who have seen Marie de' Medici as a mother in name only, lacking in affection toward her firstborn. Scholars often dismiss Marie's role in Louis's early formation with the erroneous statement that she never kissed him, or did so irregularly.[13]

The fact is, the queen did embrace the heir with regularity, if not exuberance, during his initial years. She also showed care for him in her letters, although these always had a practical bent in contrast to Henry's letters to the royal children's governess, which expressed a sense of joy in the children's very existence. Marie's letters remind one of the adult Louis's correctly concerned letters of condolence to subjects and his properly paternalistic communications with his sisters, surviving brother, and other close relatives.

The queen meticulously held out gifts as rewards for good behavior, while advocating inexorable punishment for "stubbornness." Still, she wrote to the dauphin's governess about the need to avoid whippings during the summer heat if possible, because the temperamental child "could get agitated"; and any beating should be administered "with such caution that the anger he might feel would not cause any illness." After 1609, when Louis's governess was replaced by a governor, the marquis de Souvré, Marie wrote to her son: "I am at ease in knowing that you are well and to learn that you very well behaved, and that you are studying and doing your exercises. Keep it up and obey what M. de Souvré tells you so he will be able to confirm me always in that good opinion."

Marie's letters to her other children, notably the girls, confirm our impressions of the sort of indoctrination she was giving her firstborn. To Henriette, Louis's youngest sister, she wrote that nothing was more pleasing than her "little exercises." To the middle girl, Christine or Chrétienne, came an admonishment to be compliant like the oldest sister, Elisabeth. The mother's displeasure with the news of Christine's illness, we read with some astonishment, "would be greater if I didn't think of the example of your older sister who has been so well-behaved and obedient in doing what the doctors ordered for her. . . . So that is what I want from you and urge you to do if you wish to be always well loved by Your very good mother Marie."[14]

Louis continued to look for maternal affection, despite Marie's cool demeanor. He was drawn to her also by an acquired filial deference, something that he could never fully shake later on in life, even when breaking with her spectacularly as a teenage king and again as an adult. His early childhood rages and pouting against her were no different from those he displayed so often toward his father, nurse, governess, and physician. Indeed, he could be so excited at the prospect of seeing his mother that he would help make her bed, be impatient if she did not come when expected, and race to kiss her when she finally arrived.[15]

In addition to filial obedience and spontaneous hope, Louis was bonded to his mother by their peculiar positions in the royal family. Although she was clearly queen, and he just as surely dauphin, there was always competition for both of them from the same source—Henry's love affairs. Henry had a habit of acquiring longtime liaisons, in addition to indulging in casual sexual encounters. Furthermore, he somehow always managed to get his current lady friend pregnant in tandem with his wife's regular pregnancies. And he insisted that his legitimate and natural offspring live together at St-Germain under the common care of Louis's governess! This was mortifying enough for Marie, who alternated between fighting with her husband and accepting his affection and concern for her well-being, but it was downright confusing and unnerving for a proud, young heir.[16]

The sons of the deceased Gabrielle d'Estrées, César and Alexandre de Vendôme, together with their sister, Catherine-Marie, were in a special category: they were born before their half brother Louis. King Henry favored César to the point of giving him special ceremonial functions and sumptuously marrying him off when the dauphin was nine. The Vendôme-Louis rivalry was not only a childhood torment for the dauphin, but it led to conspiracy and rebellion by his half brothers when he became their king.

Equally troublesome was the existence of Gaston-Henri and Gabrielle de Verneuil, children of Henry IV's favorite mistress for most of the period Louis was dauphin, Henriette d'Entragues. Before Marie de' Medici's appearance on the scene, the Verneuils' mother had wrung from her browbeaten royal lover a written promise of marriage. The impetuous offer was, of course, no longer in question after Henry's second marriage; however, its existence continued to poison family relations. Four years later, when Henriette was compromised by rumors of her family's involvement in a plot supposedly aimed at deposing Louis as heir, Henry got the worthless written document back. But the ensuing family scene set the court abuzz, and had the dauphin all ears.

What Louis heard was that even in defeat Henriette had wrung from his father a full pardon, plus the reduction of her brother's death sentence for treason to mere imprisonment. An embarrassed king held his wife's hand, while trying to explain to his glowering girlfriend that to exonerate her family further would be tantamount to declaring the queen a whore and the dauphin a bastard. Alas, Entragues continued to scold Henry for going back on his word, and she drove Marie to tears by branding her the king's "fat banker," the dauphin a bastard, and her own offspring the kingdom's legitimate heirs.

Henry shared in this emotional undermining of his son and wife. On the birth of the first Verneuil baby just weeks after the dauphin's arrival, the doubly "blessed" father declared expansively that the illegitimate baby was much prettier than the dauphin, whom he likened to the Medicis because he seemed dark and fat.[17] To add insult to injury, Henry named the Verneuil son after himself and Gaston de Foix, a famous Bourbon warrior. Henry and Gaston were precisely the names that the dauphin most coveted for his own person!

Queen Marie fought back against King Henry with tears and tongue-lashings. Dauphin Louis occasionally lashed out at the king, too: the "hat scene" came right after the king had gathered his entire "little brood" at Fontainebleau. But normally the heir took his wrath out on more vulnerable objects, notably his half brothers, with a series of childlike stratagems.

There was intellectual as well as emotional inspiration for these defense mechanisms. Behaviorally, the lad was mirroring both the fiery, proud temper of the queen and what Henry's biographer, David Buisseret, calls "the dark side" of the king's wit: "he sometimes let his tongue run away with him."[18] Intellectually, the heir's strategy was grounded in the ritual interplay of authority and deference at Henry IV's court.

Daily royal rituals were everywhere at hand, from the king's ceremonial rising (*lever*) and retiring (*coucher*) to presenting the king his napkin at meals and taking off one's hat in his presence.

All the dauphin needed to do was substitute himself for the king. Henry IV provided the justification for doing this by always maintaining Louis's special position in the sociopolitical hierarchy of the realm. One example will suffice. On leaving for his eastern military campaign against the duke of Bouillon in 1606, the king brought his four-and-a-half-year-old heir to the assembled Parlement at the Louvre and declared proudly: "I leave behind with you my dauphin, whom I have brought from St-Germain expressly for this; his person, after mine, should be the most cherished in the realm for you." [19]

Before he was two, Louis began to turn royal rituals against his unwanted siblings. In his sixteenth month he was holding his own *lever*, just like his father. His half brother Alexandre de Vendôme, called "Alexandre Monsieur" in imitation of the title of Monsieur for the king's or dauphin's legitimate brother, dutifully brought in the dauphin's shirt. Suddenly, without provocation, the dauphin grabbed the shirt and struck his half brother. Héroard dryly jotted down in his journal on Louis's life: "He couldn't stand him."

Two months later the heir was struggling with another ritual, driven by opposite impulses to play with the reigning mistress and to respect his mother's order that she stay away from the legitimate royal children. When Henriette offered to kiss Louis's hand he pulled it back, only to engage a moment later in mock sexual caresses while his mother regarded the scene disapprovingly. At times Louis would trick Gaston-Henri de Verneuil into saying he was the dauphin, then compel him to admit Louis held that title. On other occasions he ran from one room to another, laughing here and "going berserk" there (*comme un désespéré*) by hurling aside a rival's toy.

Gradually this self-protective brattiness led Louis unconsciously to a rigid conception of how a ruler kept his subjects in check. Family members or personal servants were "imprisoned" for "treasonous" activities, as when Louis's governess was placed in a corner for kissing César de Vendôme. If someone, even the king, dared to step out of his allotted position on the sociopolitical scale, that individual was in for a tongue-lashing. When the king angered his heir by kissing Alexandre too ardently, Louis ordered Henry out of the dauphin's seat at chapel with the words "He is in my seat; get out of there." The king went along with this game, not only getting up but taking off his hat as well!

At times these very practical jokes had a playful tone. Once the heir got revenge on his father for some minor "transgression" by turning the St-Germain sprinkler system on and soaking His Majesty. On other occasions it turned more serious. Thus Louis had a page take his place when punishment was meted out for the dauphin's disobeying his parents. When Marie could not help giggling at the seriousness with which her son took on his authoritarian role, he had her "beaten" by his governess.[20]

So Louis's little world evolved into a realm of hierarchical relationships, with his servants and relatives as his valets, Louis the valet of his royal master, and God sovereign over the king. There were mock musterings of soldiers, with the prince in command of his half brothers, and mock council meetings, where great nobles and royal bastards met with the dauphin—while his sister was excluded because she was a girl. Louis wrote to his parents that he was trying to overcome his obstinacy and be "well behaved"; and he likewise pardoned undisciplined "soldiers" (in reality, his unruly mock troops) with the stern admonition that they be wiser in the future. We will see him repeat these themes, and these very words, when he becomes king.

Along with the formative influences of his parents and extended family, the dauphin experienced a great deal of molding by servitors in charge of his physical, moral, and intellectual upbringing. Historians have been horrified by some aspects of that education. By any standards, including those of the time, Louis's medical care was particularly unorthodox. Dr. Héroard not only kept a meticulous record of his charge's meals and toilet habits, but from the outset substituted forced evacuations and other "remedies" for the natural princely intake and outgo.

Louis's preceptor and rival to Héroard, Nicolas Vauquelin des Yveteaux, was not far from the mark in suggesting that this regimen had a disastrous effect on the future monarch's physical health. The preceptor's criticism focused on the physical side: "I rarely saw him spit, sweat, or sniffle." A modern psychoanalysis by Elizabeth Marvick suggests that Héroard's remedies also stunted the growth of the dauphin's personality.[21]

Beyond sheer physical manipulation, young Louis's doctor, nurse, governess, and many male and female courtiers focused inordinate attention on his procreative equipment. Undoubtedly they shared Henry IV's concern with perpetuating the Bourbon dynasty; however, this proved far too much for the sensitive child. Louis was all too aware of sex from his father's open liaisons and his own

forced cohabitation with relations who, as he said so often, did not
come from his mother's stomach.

Until his third year the dauphin went along with this "hands-
on" education, laughing when the king's mistress put her hand under his skirt and inviting his nurse to play with him on his bed.
Courtiers found it amusing that he would invite them to kiss his
guillery instead of his hand, in homage. But gradually the prince
became ambivalent about sex. As he neared his third birthday,
Mme de Montglat and Dr. Héroard tested him, with the governess
asking what brides did and the physician reassuring him, "Please
say it; there isn't any danger." Whereupon the dauphin "put his
pike between his legs, raised one end, and rubbed it underneath."

Ambivalence went hand in hand with fear. Louis's nurse
warned him that if he let people touch his *tétons* or *guillery*, he
risked having them cut off! His doctor declared ominously, "Monsieur, your *guillery* is gone." He responded by ceasing to swear like
his father. When he invoked the weapon of penis chopping, it was
to threaten his nurse's husband with retribution for abusing her.

The heir was barely able to reconcile his growing prudery with
the ritual incantation of his destiny to marry the Spanish Infanta,
who was four days older and would in fact become his bride when
they reached fourteen. Here is a typical dialogue at age three and a
half: The king said, "My son, I want you to make a little child with
the Infanta." The dauphin replied, "Ho! No, Papa." The queen
added, "I want you to make with her a little dauphin just like you."
The dauphin responded, "No, please, Papa," putting his hand on
his hat and bowing. Then Mme de Montglat joined in the dialogue,
with Dr. Héroard noting, "[He] could not be persuaded." When the
child could be brought to admit the procreative purpose of his future marriage, there was the additional hurdle of accepting the fact
his "little darling" was a Spaniard.[22]

Fortunately, Louis's education was not entirely manipulative,
controlling, and disastrous. Just as in his complicated relations
with his parents, there were bonds between the dauphin and his
servitors. The future king of France was very attached to those who
were closest to him: his nurse, governess, and physician-diarist.
In particular, we know from Héroard's current editor, Madeleine
Foisil, that Mme de Montglat was very close to the dauphin as the
real director of his early life and a more constant support than Héroard, who usually gets the credit or blame from historians for
molding the future Louis XIII.[23] The very thought of leaving St-

Germain and Mamanga made Louis grow silent over a year before he actually left with Héroard for Paris.

In the years immediately following the big move in 1609, Louis kept in touch with Mamanga through visits to his brothers and sisters back at St-Germain. They corresponded frequently and with affection into his adulthood. We can look at what he felt, in a letter written in his own hand and signed "Ludovicus," shortly after he became king in his tenth year: "Mamanga, I am feeling better since I had my bowel movement; you can always be sure of my love [*amitié*], A Dieu Mamanga." It was probably in his early teens that Louis acknowledged, in his stilted way, her gift of some treats: "Mamanga, thank you for the nice cherries which you sent me. In return [*récompense*], I will love you much. LOUIS." Much later, at the agonizing siege of Huguenot Montauban in 1621, he wrote: "Mamanga, . . . you will always be in my good favor for I know you will always give me reason; the sieur de Roches will tell you the news of my health." [24]

It was much the same with Héroard. As king, long after there was a need to retain his chief physician, Louis did so. It was symbolic that this old Huguenot servitor and friend, born around 1550, would die in the king's quarters at the royal siege of Protestant La Rochelle in 1628. Louis visited the dying man and, according to an assisting physician, said ruefully, "I still needed him very much." [25]

That lifelong attachment to an older man, coupled with the equally strong friendship Louis continued to cultivate with his former governess, is proof that the young Louis XIII was not deadened emotionally or warped into becoming a hatemonger, as the Dumas legend and some of its reinterpreters suggest. [26] He kept on craving affection, even when he turned suspicious. And he kept on feeling, even when his attachment to principle sacrificed his emotional health. Had it been otherwise, he could not have had a ten-year relationship with a male courtier, or an idyllic interlude with an innocent lady-in-waiting. Nor could he have developed the increasingly warm personal and political bond that he forged with Richelieu over an eighteen-year period.

Montglat and Héroard were also Louis's earliest formal instructors. His physician's manuscript diary records his first childish letters, his mastery of the alphabet at age three and a half, printing and writing his ABCs just short of his sixth birthday, and the tracing and writing of first letters to his parents. [27] He learned (reluctantly) to read, and translated some Latin. There was a steady diet of wise sayings from philosophers and history lessons about France and ancient empires, as well as a host of other sources for a sound personal and political morality.

Mamanga started him with Solomon when he was three, and he particularly liked the proverb "Happy is the man who has found a virtuous wife." He learned similarly uplifting sayings such as "Humility is the path of glory that leads to honor." Obviously Louis was not simply memorizing lines, although he did that with ease. When he recited from Pibrac, "Whoever holds his tongue is wise," the boy added with the wry biting humor that became his trademark: "So whoever lets it run on is mad." [28]

Louis was no mere cipher in his early religious education, either. The Lord's Prayer, in his childish, lisping version, was rendered as "Pater Noter, who is. Why is this plate white . . . ?" More seriously, when learning the Ten Commandments in his sixth year, the dauphin questioned his lesson that one should not kill Spaniards. On being told that the people of Spain were fellow Christians, the boy compromised by deciding it was right to fight Turks to the death since they were non-Christian. When a representative of the Ottoman Porte inconveniently appeared in the flesh to test this assumption, the future "Most Christian King" decided (on Héroard's prompt that the ambassador came as a friend) to settle for a forced conversion. [29]

While Montglat's tutorial influence halted with Louis' departure for Paris and all-male company, Héroard continued to instruct the growing boy in company with his new governor, deputy governors, and a succession of formal tutors. The changeover was a gradual one, beginning when Louis was six. First Henry IV's boon companion, courtier, and future marshal, Gilles de Souvré, began to administer some of the dauphin's lessons as his governor. The presence of the king's new confessor, Father Coton, became a regular feature, with absolutions and sermons, as well as a short catechism composed by the priest at the urging of Mme de Montglat. It included the question "Who are our enemies?" and the response "The world, Satan, and the flesh." That catechism's outlines can be found in Héroard's own pedagogical dialogue between himself and Souvré, published as *On the Institution of the Prince* and presented to his young charge on New Year's Day 1609. [30]

Part of this transition period involved courtly grooming befitting a future monarch. Louis began to go regularly on hunts, first in a carriage, then on horseback. On special occasions, such as his festive entry to the capital on Leap Year Day 1608, he enjoyed full ceremonial honors: the dauphin was met by all the princes and seigneurs of the French court, five hundred horsemen in all! In June 1608 the boy was dressed in pourpoint and boots, definitively shedding his child's skirts. And in the fall and winter Henry began to gather around his heir a number of noble boys the same age as Louis, to instill deference in them and a regal posture in their future monarch.

Even Louis's letters, although surely dictated, took on a regal style: "Papa, I did not wish to dispatch M. de Frontenac without [entrusting him with] bidding you bonjour." In his actions, too, the heir shifted more and more from being a recalcitrant charge to acting like a dignified prince. For example, after complaining to Mamanga and Héroard that his noble companions did nothing but pester and push him around so that he did not know what to do other than have them caned, he was brought around to the position of chastising them gently and teaching them thereby to love and serve him as their gracious "master." [31]

On 24 January 1609, the seven-year-old dauphin finally experienced the formal rite of passage to a full court and male company, by taking the short ride from St-Germain to the Louvre in central Paris. In succeeding days the prince dined with the king, was served "from behind" by a nervous young noble companion, and began to take charge of his own staff, which now numbered some 175.

His new functions ranged from signing requests for staff pay to administering his first official acts of justice. Louis tried to settle fights by ordering Souvré to whip recalcitrant young courtiers, although he bristled when others suggested such punishment for these *enfants d'honneur*. Equally proudly, he exercised his power of "grace" by having his governor release from jail one of Souvré's lackeys. Louis also pursued his normal attention to detail by drawing up the roll of his little *gentilshommes* in precisely the order of their entry to his "military" service.

Louis's male educators were criticized later for neglecting everything but the "unregal" activities he was most fond of, and Louis himself complained that his governor kept him a child. In reality, these servitors were well suited for taming, grooming, and educating the very difficult royal heir. Souvré was a far better candidate for governor than Henry IV's licentious boon companion Bassompierre. One deputy governor, Pluvinel, was the top equestrian teacher in all France and had trained Richelieu. The other deputy, des Préaux, assisted the dauphin's chief preceptor, Vauquelin, another able man.

Vauquelin was a worldly Epicurean who had written love poetry for King Henry's amorous needs, tutored Henry's oldest natural son, and offended both Queen Marie and a staunchly Catholic group at court by his intellectual freethinking. Yet even a jealous Héroard recognized Vauquelin's attempts to imbue the heir with conventional morality. The preceptor began his first lesson with a discourse on Louis's heritage as a Catholic and son of a great monarch. He admonished the boy to "love and fear God, [and] make himself truthful and just," and to "love and honor the king and queen, [first] as having superior authority over him, and then as his father and mother." Finally, he told the dauphin that "virtues were learned through books."[32] Marie's dismissal of Vauquelin in 1611, following her husband's death, removed a tutor who might have softened Louis's lifelong aversion to reading.

The tension between Louis's wanting to get his own way and his being taught to give in to duty involved his own name. He yearned to be christened Henry after his father, and Gaston after his ancestral hero, Gaston de Foix. Yet he was baptized Louis in September 1606 and soon was signing himself "Loys." He also had to participate in the baptismal ceremony that named his half brother Gaston-Henri. As a final insult, following the death of Louis's sickly younger brother in 1611, Marie de' Medici had the baby of the family and her favorite son christened as Gaston in 1614.[33]

Louis made the best of his given name, and its historical associations helped to shape his political ideals. Louis was an appropriate name for a Bourbon, for the family traced its origins to the great thirteenth-century king of France Louis IX, called St. Louis. Long before the dauphin was baptized, people around the heir emphasized the connection. When Louis balked at his half-brother being called Henry, Héroard shrewdly stressed St. Louis's most famous virtues of piety and equity. And the prince's physician-tutor alluded to a third great virtue of monarchs—valor—as he expounded on Louis IX's Crusade against the Muslims. Young Louis de Bourbon listened with rapt attention.

When Louis made a ritual visit to the French monarchy's necropolis in the basilica at St-Denis, north of the capital, he proudly noted that no less than six royal tombs there bore his own name. Did he also understand that he was being deliberately directed toward those royal virtues of past kings that his entourage wanted him to emulate? Certainly his own innate character and early upbringing prefigured his embodiment of several cardinal royal virtues emphasized in contemporary histories, pamphlets, and sermons, as well as his private tutorials. His distaste for the sexually charged atmosphere of his father's life and court was leading to piety and chastity. His innate intelligence presaged wisdom. His fierce willfulness and pride were being tempered into a quiet determination that could lead to valor. And prudence was latent in his growing habit of observing everything around him.

Two other royal virtues were very much in the air: clemency and justice. Henry IV was clement to a fault. Louis XIII, born as chance would have it under the sign of Libra—the balance scales of justice—was inclined by nature and upbringing toward being just. What did that mean in the France of the early 1600s? On the surface the contemporary royal virtue of justice was the opposite of clemency, for it stressed punishment rather than forgiveness. Yet it called for a ruler to exercise his full judicial authority as the kingdom's "font of justice," and this meant that he should not only correct subjects when they failed to do their duty but also be magnanimous when they repented. If it was easier for the willful young dauphin to insist on the obligations of others to him, we have seen him being educated to exercise his princely authority in a responsible way. That duality was apparent in a newsletter by the court poet, Malherbe, written just before Louis was unexpectedly placed on his father's throne. Malherbe praised the dauphin for being "extremely good by nature, but [wanting] to be respected, as is reasonable." [34]

As dauphin, Louis was still far from focusing clearly on justice, or any other royal virtue. We can, in fact, see him casting about with great expectations in several directions, for some time after he ascended the throne of St. Louis and Henry the Great. In an undated letter to his old governess, he wrote:

> For piety Saint Louis
> For clemency Henry IIII [IV]
> For justice Louis XII
> For love of truth Pharamont
> For valor Charlemagne
> And for temperance Charles V
> And Louis XIII will surpass all these Kings by the grace of
>   God. [35]

It is appropriate to take leave of Louis XIII's early childhood years on this uncertain, but hopeful, note. Historians have, of course, tried to make definitive judgments on the battle between nature and nurture that went on in the dauphin's world, but their assessments, right down to the present, have been as divided as his inner being must have been. Madeleine Foisil, following the Batiffol interpretation, sees Louis's early childhood as a happy experience in a supportive environment. Elizabeth Marvick, in reinterpreting the Tallemant-Dumas tradition, views Louis's early life experiences as disastrous for his personal development: it left him at the Freudian anal stage, in a state of dependence, obstinacy, sadism, and masochism; vulnerable to the gastroenteric ailments that would eventually kill him; and with exaggerated defenses against a seductively abusive father.[36]

Can I suggest that the complex truth contains elements of both these opposing interpretations without mirroring either one? Louis was a difficult child, and his well-intentioned entourage employed remedies that both stunted him physically and emotionally and channeled his impossible willfulness into the making of a person with very strong principles, principles that eventually would find an outlet. He bent, but he did not break.

2

THE BOY KING

At mid afternoon on Friday, 14 May 1610, the dauphin of France was enjoying a short carriage ride and the chance to practice with his firearms near the Louvre. The king was headed in a separate carriage for the home of his favorite advisor, the duke of Sully, his thoughts concentrated on a projected military campaign in the German borderlands. The queen remained behind at the Louvre, basking in the glow of her recent coronation and preparing for her "inaugural" parade on Sunday past the specially erected triumphal arches, theaters, and banners which her husband and son were now viewing. The mood of the capital was one of excited expectation.

Henry IV had arranged for his wife's coronation so that she could act as regent while he joined his army of fifty thousand in Champagne. His immediate objective was to dislodge the Holy Roman Emperor and Spanish troops from the cluster of Rhineland territories known as Jülich-Cleves. That principality, like the other "states" within the Germanic Empire, was virtually independent of the Austrian Habsburg emperor; but unlike the others, Jülich-Cleves had lost its duke, and in the ensuing succession dispute among rival German princes the Habsburgs had simply occupied it.

Whether Henry would have quickly intimidated the rival Habsburg dynasty, or triggered a long foreign war and brought back instability to his own France, will never be known.[1] At a bottleneck on the king's route, a muscular man jumped on the wheel of his carriage. With the aim of ridding France of the "tyrant" who was waging war on fellow Catholics, François Ravaillac stabbed the monarch three times in the chest. The duke of Epernon had the presence of mind to act as if Henry were only wounded; after seeing that the assassin was seized alive, he turned the carriage around and raced for the Louvre.

Henry IV's body was carried upstairs to his first floor apartment. Marie de' Medici cried hysterically on discovering the cause of the commotion next to her apartment. And Louis was spirited back from the play of a dauphin to the reality of being an eight-year-old king. In keeping with his personality, Louis XIII exclaimed: "Ha! If I had been there with my sword, I would have killed him." Of course, emotions other than bravery and justice soon vied with those royal virtues for control of his inner being. For several days following Henry IV's murder, Louis retired at night to the safety of his mother's bedroom, and still slept fitfully out of fear that he too would be killed. Momentarily, the boy king may also have expressed a wish that his younger brother (his favorite, who died soon after) take his place.[2]

Remarkably enough, the minor king's accession to the French throne, through a terrifyingly violent act, caused no political cataclysm. The royal court of two thousand, the twenty thousand governmental officials in Paris and the provinces, the capital city of four hundred thousand, and the rest of France's sixteen million souls were spared that turmoil. (See Appendix, map 1.) Instead, the royal succession process, which had become smoother and smoother over the centuries, worked to perfection, even though the circumstances were far from perfect. It gave France a four-year royal minority and allowed a caretaker regency-government of Henry's aging ministers, headed by the queen mother, to cope with a series of problems for a full seven years.

The immediate transition played on two universally accepted myths: that the French monarchy was a never-dying institution, and that the monarch was the "true image of God." It was also most fortunate that the dead king had a male heir; Louis XIII could never be challenged as Henry IV had been following the demise of the Valois dynasty. When the queen mother shrieked out on seeing her husband's body, "Alas! the king is dead," Chancellor Brûlart de Sillery replied coolly, "Your Majesty, excuse me. Kings do *not* die in France," pointing to Louis as the living monarch. Contemporary pamphlets underscored the belief in the divine right of monarchs with the powerful warning that "he resists God who, madman that he is, contravenes the power of kings."[3]

Marie acted quickly to turn theory into fact. Within two hours she and her late husband's ministers undertook three practical measures: Louis and his siblings were placed under the close guard of an intrepid captain of the king's bodyguards, Vitry; the streets around the Louvre were patrolled to calm the populace and break up any large gathering; and the queen mother's advisor, Epernon, and her late husband's erstwhile rival, Guise, went to the nearby high court of the Parlement of Paris to secure the judges' acknowledgment that Marie was regent for her son.[4] These three immediate acts were followed in the succeeding days, weeks, and months, by three important rituals. Each served the dual purpose of strengthening the authority of the queen mother and boy king and shaping the political philosophy that Louis had begun to adopt as dauphin.

The first of these rituals was a special royal session of the Parlement of Paris, held the day after Louis XIII's accession. Dressed in the traditional violet of royal mourning, the young monarch came to the high court and mounted a violet dais embroidered with gold fleurs de lis. In literal terms, he was lying on his bed of justice, hence the term for the ceremony, *lit de justice*. Symbolically, he came as the chief justiciar of the realm to take back the judges' delegated judicial authority, just as as his namesake and Bourbon founder, St. Louis, had dispensed direct royal justice under the oak trees of Vincennes. And politically, he was recording before an expanded parlement of judges, great nobles, and royal officials his granting of regency powers to his mother until, at age thirteen, he reached his official majority.[5]

The lit de justice of 15 May 1610 undercut any possible claims by the parlementary judges that they had already "made" Marie regent.[6] In return, the judges gave their new monarch some not so subtle political lessons. Louis uttered in an inaudible voice the lines he had memorized, then tried to absorb the responsibilities that the deadly serious jurists laid before him. One judge thought he should learn to imitate the biblical Solomon, the Roman emperor Alexander Severus, and the previous king of his name, Louis XII, called the "father of his people." Of course the judge also called on the magic name of St. Louis, both to inspire the royal minor and to flatter the regent by comparing her with St. Louis's famous mother and regent, Blanche of Castile. Another judge repeated these themes and then conjured up an even more intimidating figure, Henry IV. Young Louis was admonished to imitate Henry's virtues, which ranged from moderation and clemency to justice.

The ritual of Henry IV's funeral was a much more deliberate process than the lit de justice. Custom dictated that the monarchy honor the late king, camouflage the fact that he was dead, and play up the new monarch. Marie ordered two years of official court mourning and had the palace draped in black. Week after week, the late king's body, together with a lifelike effigy, lay in state in the great hall of the Louvre, guarded by clerical and military guards and surrounded by flaming torches. Finally, after rounds of religious service, the body was taken to join Henry IV's ancestors at the basilica of St-Denis on 1 July.

The grand master of ceremonies intoned, "The king is dead," and everyone fell to their knees crying genuine tears of grief for "Henri le Grand, par la grace de Dieu Roy de France et de Navarre, très-Chrestien, très-Auguste, très-Victorieux, incomparable en Magnanimité et Clémence." Then the grand master retrieved his baton from the grave and shouted, "Vive le Roy." The king of arms called out in turn, "Vive le Roy Louys XIII de Nom, par la grace de Dieu Roy de France et de Navarre, très-Chrestien, nostre très-souverain seigneur et bon maistre, auquel Dieu doint très-heureuse et très-longue vie." Finally, back at the great hall of the Louvre, in the presence of high court judges, representatives of the civic government of Paris, and the late king's household officials, the grand master ceremoniously broke his baton to symbolize the end of the royal household's allegiance to Henry IV and its re-formation as part of Louis XIII's personal household.[7]

Louis XIII's last inaugural rite, his coronation or *sacre*, was delayed until the fall of 1610. In part, the delay mirrored the shift of the French coronation rite from its medieval function of validating a new ruler's authority to its more modest early-modern ceremonial role of celebrating the king's special place above his subjects. In addition, it reflected Marie de' Medici's concern for sparing her son an exhausting rite in an unusually hot summer. She also wanted to avoid playing out this festive ceremony on the morrow of her husband's assassination.[8]

In October, King Louis slowly and deliberately proceeded from the capital to the coronation city of Reims. His official entrée suited the occasion: he entered Reims on a white horse beneath triumphal arches and received the city's key from a "nymph" in a chariot. He could hardly wait out the next three days. On the morning of the seventeenth he awoke on his own at five o'clock, then had to wait hours for ceremonial knocks on his door by the peers of the realm. With a large escort, the fledgling ruler reached Notre Dame of Reims at 9:30 A.M. The sacre lasted until 2:15 P.M.

The sacre was naturally an emotionally draining experience for the nine-year-old, although his physician wrote that he "bore with extreme virtue all the fatigue of that ceremony." The little boy came out in him when he playfully slapped the young duke of Elbeuf for giving him too wet a kiss. More seriously, he swore a series of solemn oaths: to conserve the French Catholic clergy's canonical privileges and churches; to try "in good faith to banish from my jurisdiction and lands under my rule all heretics denounced by the [Catholic] Church"; to help the "Christian people" live peacefully; and to prevent all "rapine" and "iniquities," as well as render justice with "equity" and "mercy."

The rest of the sacre dramatized the divine right of monarchs, both in its sophisticated version as held by clergy, nobles, and officials and with imagery that made sense to ordinary folk.The serious boy king, too, could grasp the responsibility and power implicit in the symbols of his coronation. The ring on his finger represented the sacred trust of his "marriage" to his realm. His awesome power was embodied in the crown, scepter, hand of justice, sword, and various garments that were placed on the altar and then presented to the monarch. And his role as a priest-king who could do miraculous things was illustrated by his taking wine as well as bread at communion, just like the clergy, rather than bread alone, as the rest of the laity did.

At the sacre's conclusion, the assembled crowd shouted, "Vive le Roy," and Notre Dame of Reims rang with the sound of bugles, oboes, trumpets, and drums. Outside, souvenir hunters scrambled for medallions bearing the king's effigy. Without a break, the king went to the local archbishop's palace for a sumptuous dinner, surrounded by the lay and ecclesiastical peers of his realm (all seated a step below his level). Only at the very end of this longest of days could the Anointed of God revert to a simple boy's pleasure, the methodical arrangement of toy soldiers on his bed.[9]

There was a popular postscript to the sacre of 1610. The royal personage depicted in contemporary pamphlets as "the true image of God" was crowned and anointed to cure the realm of physical as well as political ills. Henry IV had disliked emulating Jesus by ceremonially washing the feet of the poor every Maundy Thursday or "healing" his subjects' scrofula at Easter, Pentecost, Christmas, New Years, and other high holy days. Louis XIII did his duty, first as dauphin in place of his father, and then routinely throughout his own reign. It began officially with a rite of passage at the shrine of St. Marcoul in Corbeny, where French kings since time immemorial had stopped on their way back to Paris from their sacres. Louis XIII visited the shrine and spent over an hour touching some nine hundred scrofulous subjects and foreigners. Though flushed and famished, he refused any relief as the magical words were repeated: "The king touches you; God heals you."[10]

Louis's central role in the rituals of his royal minority was naturally not duplicated in the political realm. In fact as well as by law, his mother governed on his behalf. Yet the young monarch had to be formally involved, since everything was done in his name. At first, this meant that ambassadors saw him briefly but regularly, some royal correspondence came before his eyes, and ministers and courtiers kept him somewhat informed. That was enough in itself to intensify the political molding of a boy king who, even as dauphin, had taken in everything around him and insisted on having his authority recognized. In addition, as he approached his formal majority in 1614, he could not be kept out of council meetings and political actions. This spelled trouble for Marie, who never knew when her son might immaturely try to inject his strong feelings about a particular issue into the governing process. It also spelled frustration for Louis when he was hushed up or ignored. While his feelings were in accord with most of what the regent did, and his ingrained deference contributed to a harmonious relationship on the surface, the mother and son began to drift apart as the minority progressed. (See plate 1.)

Marie de' Medici's regency was devoted to the task of avoiding internal turmoil and external danger. Her success in achieving those twin aims must, in the immediate setting, be considered a major achievement, for contemporary opinion held that a regent did not have a major king's full authority to innovate. Yet in absolute terms her regency looked weak; she was forever placating interest groups within France and acting as a junior partner in nonaggression pacts with the most powerful neighboring states. She ruled with Henry IV's able ministerial team of septuagenarians, who had gained much wisdom from the Wars of Religion—but that searing experience of the 1580s and 1590s made Chancellor Brûlart and Superintendent of Finances Jeannin cautious in the 1610s. Furthermore, Marie became overly attached to her close Italian friend, Leonora Galigaï, and Leonora's adventurer-husband, Concino Concini, who were more interested in protecting their own growing political influence and shady financial dealings than in suggesting bold royal actions. After Marie dismissed the financial wizard of Henry IV's era, Sully, in 1611, there were only two counselors who consistently advocated political firmness to the regent: her friend Epernon and her wise secretary of state for foreign affairs, Villeroy. So Louis XIII grew up knowing that all was not well in his realm and that his crown was becoming tarnished.[11]

Marie was faced with three basic problems: religious tensions, foreign dangers, and noble unrest. The most pressing issue was religion, for Ravaillac's murder of Henry IV brought to the surface deep-seated prejudices and fears within Catholic and Huguenot circles. On the Catholic side, two militant groups were suspected of being behind Ravaillac's individual act. One was the international Society of Jesus, spawned by the sixteenth-century Catholic Reformation to combat Protestantism; the other comprised former members of the French Catholic League left over from the religious wars. Huguenots and moderate Catholics were quick to recall that French Jesuits and Leaguers had been implicated in previous attempts on Henry's life. Indeed, the Jesuit order had been so closely identified with some of its individual members' advocacy of tyrannicide—killing a king who "tyrannically" opposed the Pope and Catholic church—that Henry had banished the order for a time from his realm. Both groups had been associated also, during the Wars of Religion, with the foreign power of Spain.

Behind mixed perceptions of Jesuits and ex-Leaguers in 1610 lay sharp divisions of national opinion over the principles espoused by these and other Catholic conservatives. The very vocabulary of this militantly conservative wing of French Catholicism bristled with terms like *ultramontane* and *dévot*, and called forth equally inflammatory terms like *bon Français* and *Gallican* from their French opponents. To be ultramontanist meant to be loyal to the Pope, "beyond the mountains." To be dévot meant devout commitment to the twin causes of the sixteenth-century Catholic Reformation: reform within the church and combatting Protestant churches and states in the outside world.

But for every dévot who thought that, in praising the Spanish monarchy's mission of leading international Catholicism against Protestantism, he or she was being principled there was a bon Français who feared Habsburg encirclement of France. Likewise, for every ultramontanist there was a Gallican who worried lest papal authority undermine the power of the French monarchy (royal Gallicanism) or the traditions of the Catholic church in France (clerical Gallicanism). Similarly, royal and clerical Gallicans fretted about what would happen to church and state if well-intentioned ultramontanist and dévot influences brought into France the church reforms promulgated a half century before at the Council of Trent.

At the opposite end of the religious spectrum from the ultramontanist dévots were the kingdom's dangerously apprehensive Huguenot minority. Those French Protestants knew the Catholic Reformation was gathering momentum, not just at the grass-roots level of clergy and concerned laity, but in the government as well. Unlike Henry IV, Louis XIII had been raised a Catholic, had a Jesuit confessor, and at his coronation swore an oath to extirpate Protestantism from France. In fearful reaction to that menace, the Huguenots began to think of expanding their military defenses and of using their periodic national assemblies as a vehicle for turning Protestant France into a quasi republic modeled on the Dutch Netherlands.

Marie acted quickly to pacify everyone. The trial of Ravaillac was sufficiently swift, impartial, and thorough to show that he had no Jesuit or Leaguer accomplices. His ritual death—which ended in his body being torn apart by horses and the public carrying away his remains from the public fire to neighborhood bonfires—placated an emotion-drained Parisian public. The festering animosity between Gallican and ultramontane, dévot and bon Français, never had a chance to become a general infection, as Marie curbed inflammatory language on all sides. Similarly, the volatile Huguenots were mollified by the reissuing of the Edict of Nantes eight days after Louis's accession. Marie let it be known that the special coronation oath to extirpate Protestantism was not binding on her son. She republished the agreement of Nantes in 1612, 1614, and twice in 1615. To be sure, the wary Huguenots held national political assemblies every year or so, but these dissolved as soon as the regency made symbolic concessions.[12]

Where did young Louis XIII stand on religion? Though surrounded by Catholic preceptors and accustomed to a daily round of vespers, mass, and confession, the boy king was more attached to the principle of loyalty to his state and person than to church theology or organization. We find him listening intently enough to a long debate at the Dominican order's international assembly in 1611, and he even sided with the orthodox position in holding that the Pope possessed authority over a general council of the church. But he bristled at talk against the Huguenots as a group, for he had a deep attachment to his *premier valet de chambre*, Beringhen, and his physician, Héroard. His tolerationist stand, in general, mirrored his mother's domestic policy on religion, but it was much more deeply felt.

Despite disliking the Huguenot finance minister Sully for being the intermediary for Henry IV and his amours, Louis responded with "astonishment" and disbelief in 1611 when told that his mother had dismissed the minister "for good reason." Years later Louis was always delighted to see Sully when he came to court from Poitou, where he was governor, for he knew this subject was staunchly opposed to all royal foes, whether they be Spaniards, rebel Huguenots, or conspiring Catholics. Equally revealing is the sight of Louis at eleven, feigning a toothache and then adamantly resisting his governor's attempt to take him to hear an intolerant priest's sermon: "No, Monsieur de Souvré, I don't want at all to go to Valadier. He only cries out against Pouillan [Louis's Huguenot boon companion Montpouillan] and against Beringuan and the Huguenots."[13]

Marie tried to mold the minor king's Catholicism through three different preceptors. In 1611, she replaced the freethinking Vauquelin with the "good Catholic" and skilled litterateur Nicolas Le Fèvre. On Le Fèvre's death the following year, her choice as assistant preceptor, David Rivault de Fleurance, took over the post. Vauquelin bitterly criticized his successors in an educational tract for Louis XIII's son, but we can discount much of what he said about them as self serving. Other judgments of Le Fèvre and Fleurance are equally partial. Le Fèvre and the king's confessor, Father Coton, for instance, have been given too much credit for Louis's increasing tendency toward chastity and justice, whereas Fleurance has been blamed too much for the monarch's obsession with military minutiae and mechanical trades thought to be beneath the dignity of a king of France. In general, all three tutors were most successful when they stressed the things young Louis deemed worthy—and when they avoided antagonizing him.

Fleurance was especially adept at bringing out the best in his pupil. Author of *Elements of Artillery* (1605), he cleverly linked mathematics with gunnery, and the travels of Julius Caesar with the pilgrimage of St. Louis. The preceptor knew how to capture his royal charge's attention by discussing proper regal deportment in military adversity and success, after which he alluded moralistically to the ninth-century Emperor Basil, who believed that monarchs were human and owed everything to God. He also wrote an edifying history for Louis, *Remonstrances of Basil, Emperor of the Romans, to Leon his dear Son . . . to serve as the Education [of Louis XIII]* (1612, translated into French at Louis XIII's request), as well as a religious treatise, *Discourse to the King in the Form of a Catechism on the Ninth Article of Faith: "Sanctam ecclesiam catholicam, sanctorum communionem"* (1614).[14]

Closely linked to religion was the regency's second major concern, foreign relations. In her quest for external security during her son's minority, Marie decided on a cautious policy. Henry had guarded against Catholic Habsburg aggression by allying with the Catholic duke of Savoy in northern Italy, and with Protestant states ranging from the Dutch Republic and Rhineland principalities to Swiss cantons and the adjacent Grisons, or Grey Leagues. By contrast, Marie simply sought harmony with the Habsburgs.

The regent escaped a possible war with the Imperialists and Spaniards by humbly scaling down Henry IV's campaign over Jülich-Cleves to a mere token military demonstration. She was most fortunate that this strategic German principality was subsequently divided among small German princes without Habsburg power being increased in the Rhineland. Meanwhile, however, she lost influence in northern Italy when she directed Henry's Savoyard ally to give up his territorial designs on Spanish Milan. And she alienated the Protestant powers of the Netherlands, Rhineland, and Switzerland by her one diplomatic coup: a double marriage alliance with the Spanish royal family, involving Louis and his sister Elisabeth.

The Franco-Spanish pact of 1612, on which Marie placed all her hopes, accommodated both dévot and bon Français outlooks. Clearly in line with dévot wishes for a pro-Spanish, pro-Catholic foreign policy, the pact seemed to fit bon Français aims too with its aim of neutralizing Spain until 1621, when the Spaniards' truce with the breakaway Netherlands provinces, the new Dutch Republic, would expire.

Louis XIII was still too young to grasp the full import of this accommodation. How could anyone have known that within that ten-year span Marie's disengagement from Europe would bring about dramatic Spanish expansion in Italy and the Rhineland? Even more inconceivable was the spectacular increase of the emperor's power not only in his family domains of Bohemia and Hungary but also in the Germanic Empire, all in the same ten-year period. Since both phenomena were at the expense of France's erstwhile Protestant allies, Marie's agreement of 1612 would ultimately place a grown-up Louis XIII in an extraordinarily difficult position when he came to grapple with Catholic Habsburg successes all around his state.[15]

Meanwhile, the minor king managed to retain his childhood prejudices against Spaniards and still support his mother's current alliance, his own future marriage to the Spanish infanta Anna, and his favorite sister's betrothal to the future Philip IV of Spain. When Marie asked whether he preferred an English or a Spanish bride,

Louis whispered excitedly to a courtier, "Spain! Spain!" Then, when the Spanish ambassador came to negotiate the settlement, the king was courteous, despite disliking the man—both personally and as a Spaniard.

At the same time, young Louis not only retained his aversion to Spaniards but also began to link "papa's enemies" abroad with French Leaguers, and even with his Jesuit confessor, Coton. Here was a bon Français in the making! The first incident took place soon after Henry IV's assassination. Although Louis undoubtedly heard rumors that Jesuits and Leaguers were involved, his judgmentalism did not stop there. He got into a nasty confrontation with Father Coton, refusing to tell his confessor why he was lost in thought, "because you will immediately write it to Spain."

Coton and Marie attributed such ideas to the "enemies of the Jesuits who pushed him into using that language," and Louis's nurse fell in jeopardy of losing her position. Yet the stubborn boy king held his ground. In response to his mother's tongue-lashing for linking Coton and the Spaniards pejoratively, Louis reportedly retorted "that he would not always be so young, and that [one day] they would remember having scolded him." Clearly, the Day of Dupes in 1630, when Louis broke cleanly with the French dévot support for the Habsburgs as the leaders of international Catholicism, had much deeper roots than historians have assumed.[16]

Marie's negotiation of the Franco-Spanish marriages culminated in a three-day extravaganza in 1612 at the Place Royale (today's Place des Vosges), an arcaded square of brick and stone apartments erected by Henry IV in the newest fashionable quarter of Paris. A contemporary snapshot illustration of the scene, in which floats, fireworks, and a tournament of "running at the ring" on horseback captivated court and capital, was so striking that it has found its way anachronistically into books extolling the splendors of Louis's famous son, the Sun King!

The celebration of the future Bourbon-Habsburg marriages in 1612 could not hide the third great problem of the regency: noble restiveness. Gradually the air of goodwill following Henry IV's assassination had given way to normal court tensions. The current generation of royal princes and great nobles (called *les grands*) included young men only a decade older than King Louis, and too young to have been sobered by the Wars of Religion. They began to jostle and intrigue for France's most desirable military, royal-household, and ecclesiastical posts, as well as for pensions, hoping to take advantage of both the royal minority and the huge treasury surplus Sully had amassed. Marie defended the royal minority by being generous to those who complained the most.

The leading troublemaker was Louis's cousin, Henri de Condé. In 1610 Condé was a brash twenty-one-year-old. Within three years he was spoiling for a fight, puffed up by the fact that the recent deaths of two older Bourbon princes and one of the king's brothers made him second in line for Louis's throne. Condé made ostentatious entrées to Paris with escorts of a thousand horsemen, forged coalitions with other princes and great nobles, and then had the effrontery to offer loyalty to the regent in return for money and positions. Early in 1614 the prince went one step further as he and his noble allies and clients took up residence in eastern France, where they held many of the royal military governorships of towns and provinces. Marie temporarily detained the second most dangerous prince, Louis's half brother César de Vendôme, to prevent him "from doing something that will irritate the king";[17] but that rival sibling escaped to the western province of Brittany, where he was military governor.

This was the first challenge to Louis XIII's authority as king, and he was very involved, even though the malcontents' open letter of complaint in February was addressed to Marie and impugned her administration. How could Louis not be piqued? The petitioners were attacking his own mother and the government that ruled in his name. They even suggested that their "just and good king" would listen to their "good instruction" and "overthrow" the "pernicious authority" of his mother's evil advisors.

While Louis disliked Marie's most objectionable advisor, the Italian adventurer Concini, he was bound to react against the manifesto's suggestion that the regent's team be replaced by the monarchy's "natural advisors." The term *natural advisors* signified a different view of the state from that held by the early modern French monarchy. Louis XIII had been raised in the belief that all subjects owed him obeisance, and that the kingdom's three social orders, or estates, of clergy, nobility, and commoners all had a subordinate place in society. Yet here were the highest members of the noble second estate claiming that the king *had* to rule with their assistance.

The malcontents of 1614 even demanded in their manifesto that the regent convoke the seldom assembled elective body of the three estates, known as the Estates General. Through that consultative body they meant to complement their "natural" authority in the government with sweeping changes in the regency's internal and foreign policies. Their manifesto declared that the Estates General would "reform" the state—a vague but ominous threat to shift power and wealth from the monarchy to the social orders. The impending marriages of Louis and his sister were to be postponed by the regent until the assembled Estates made their recommendation on the "utility" of the Franco-Spanish pact. Finally, the grandees insisted that Marie meet the Estates before 27 September 1614. This would allow the opposition to pressure the monarchy to give in to its wishes while Louis was still a minor; after that date he would officially assume full royal authority, and his mother would be in a much more powerful position to resist their demands.[18]

As the crisis unfolded, Louis's response differed considerably from Marie's. From start to finish he was impatient to pursue his renegade subjects. Some of this impetuosity can be explained by his youth and political naïveté, but it was also true to his character. Louis was driven to think that subjects should be made to obey their ruler, regardless of the political and military risks to the king of forcing a fight during his minority and without a large royal army. So he watched impatiently as his regent mother, postponing plans to take Louis and Elisabeth southward for the exchange of brides, relied on the traditional weapons available to see her regency through the crisis.

Lacking a large peacetime army, Marie fell back on the first line of royalty's defense: letters went out to the military governors and lieutenants in the provinces and fortified towns, asking them to use their authority and local militias to keep order. Since all governorships and lieutenancies were removable posts held by princes and great nobles, Marie felt she could rely on the loyalty and prestige of the group as a whole to keep in check the few governors who had joined the malcontent faction.

At the same time, Marie appealed directly to Louis's subjects with a widely disseminated rebuttal of the rebels' manifesto. This document welcomed the call for an Estates General, while testily stating that the qualities she had instilled in her son allowed him to "recognize" who his true servitors were.[19] Marie also mobilized her son's peacetime guards and recruited some Swiss mercenaries. But she lacked the nerve to follow the advice of the hard-liners in her council to strike at rebel headquarters in the east before their movement could spread. Instead she negotiated.

The result was predictable. Her negotiating team arranged the Treaty of Ste-Ménehould, signed on 15 May 1614, which conceded the requests for an Estates General and postponement of the Franco-

Spanish marriages in return for the dismantling of rebel forces and strongholds. Louis's half brother César, however, defied the agreement by expanding his military hold over Brittany; and Condé's clients tried to seize Poitiers, which was on the route the royal family would eventually take to exchange the French and Spanish princesses. Marie now had no choice but to brush aside the reservations of her closest confidants, Concini and Galigaï, and side with her pro-war advisors, Villeroy and Epernon. In the summer of 1614, Marie and Louis headed with a sizable force for the provinces of Poitou and Brittany in western France.[20]

Louis not only kept up with this shifting political scene, but he also spoke his mind time and again. He needed no urging to be suspicious of two particular offenders, his cousin Henry de Condé, and his half brother César de Vendôme. There had already been one especially disagreeable altercation with his cousin since becoming king. In 1611 Condé had entered the regent's cabinet "brusquely and with no respect," covered his head, and sat down without acknowledging his sovereign. Louis had exclaimed, "Mousseu de Souvré, look, look at Mousseu le Prince; he is sitting in front of me, he is insolent."

The effect of Condé's defiance in 1614 on Louis is recorded in the dispatches of the well-informed Venetian ambassador. The king began to display such "bad will" toward his cousin that Marie and the ministers postponed her son's inevitable entry to the royal council as long as they could, fearing that he might ruin peace negotiations. Finally, in April, when Louis was within six months of attaining his majority, they had no choice but to grant him occasional entry and to hope his strong sense of right and wrong could be kept in check.[21]

Louis XIII had good reason to be angrier still with César de Vendôme. A sibling rivalry from Louis's years as dauphin had been long simmering. Then there was the immediate provocation of his mother lashing out at César for escaping preventive detention, fleeing to Brittany, and intercepting a royal letter that asked the Breton lieutenant governor Montbazon to keep the province loyal. Young Louis listened as Marie exploded over César's having "made himself a criminal of high treason for a scrap of paper." The boy king put his mother's reaction into his own frame of reference; his valet Beringhen heard him mutter in his sleep about "brother Vendôme": "He opened my letters which I sent to M. de Montbazon! He opened them!"[22]

Louis was delighted that the regency council was considering military action. He took his firearms from the closet, laid his equipment out on his bed, and fought a losing battle to be allowed to sleep with his helmet rather than his nightcap.[23] When his mother turned timidly to negotiations, the king struck as stern a pose as he thought appropriate, telling a departing royal envoy: "Go, and tell these messieurs to behave themselves [*qu'ils soient bien sages*]." This admonition to behave—or, literally, "be wiser"—was much on the king's lips those days. A few weeks before, ex-Queen Marguerite had persuaded Louis to request a reprieve for a courtier, guilty of the crime of quarreling in the queen mother's antechamber. The shaken man came on bended knee to king and regent. Marie told him curtly, "Another time be wiser." And Louis added "gravely," in words "said on his very own": "The queen my mother has granted you the pardon. You wouldn't have it without me; but another time be wiser."[24]

We also know how Louis felt about the Treaty of Ste-Ménehould. When word of the princes' signing reached him he masked his feelings, revealing "neither joy nor sadness." Evidently he did not want to question what his mother had done, after the fact. But this precocious twelve-year-old had vehemently opposed some of her key concessions during the bargaining. At a council meeting to finalize the treaty, Marie had been pressed to give Condé the key Loire river town of Amboise as a guarantee until the Estates General met. Suddenly Louis burst in on the meeting. With tears of "regret and anger" the boy begged his mother not to have him "despoiled" that way. Stupefied by her son's audacity, the regent could only exclaim in amazement: "Sire, who gave you that advice?" Nothing could budge him from his stubborn stand, even though his opinion fell on deaf ears.[25]

When the royal council turned from diplomacy to the policy of seeking out the enemy in the western provinces, Louis was overjoyed. He could hardly wait for the council session at which the decision to attack was made. The lad exclaimed that he wanted to go to Poitou and Brittany "to deliver these provinces from the evils they were suffering." To make sure everyone understood, he added that he wished to go there in person.[26]

The summer offensive of 1614 not only made young Louis XIII happy, but it showed him off at his very best. It revealed as a lie the rebels' propaganda that the young monarch was a weak, sickly creature, barely kept alive by the medicines, purges, and enemas his overprotective mother and physician regularly prescribed. It educated subjects in the knowledge that the young king strongly desired that royal authority be respected, and that he displayed magnanimity when errant subjects repented. It furthered the king's own character development as well by blending his troublesome childhood stubbornness and judgmentalism with uplifting royal virtues suitable to the times.

Mother and child responded to the princely propaganda about the boy's health in ways reflecting their stations. The king was testy about either being called sickly or taking prescribed cures to maintain his health. Unable to avoid the preoccupation of others with his body, he used the princes' views to avoid the family's medicines: "No! No, madame. It isn't good for me to take them at this time," he exclaimed to his mother while the rebels plotted at Soissons before the Treaty of Ste-Ménehould. "The men of Soissons will say I am sick."[27]

Marie was naturally uneasy at the slightest suggestion that her son's rule or life was doomed. One such suggestion had come in an almanac for 1614, with "predictions" by its author Morgard: in January, "plottings"; in March, "arms will be fired"; in April, "great sedition"; and in August, a change in the head of state! No early modern ruler could afford to let troublemakers play on the popular mentalité of that age, which dreaded uncertainties in nature and society alike and looked for any sure "signs" of the future. Marie counterattacked as part of her antirebel pamphlet war of 1614, with tracts ranging from *L'anti-Morgard* to *Réfutation de l'astrologie judiciaire*. All told, some 120 royalist tracts were unleashed between January and September, and Morgard and other seditious pamphleteers were jailed.[28]

As the king and his mother set out for western France with a large retinue, subjects were overjoyed to see a living monarch riding with the best of his huntsmen after wild animals, presiding over shooting contests, fishing, and practicing his firearms as he rafted down the river. Humble folk shouted "Vive le Roy!" with tears in their eyes, and women waded into the Loire river knee deep to gaze at their divinely anointed seigneur. Louis patiently endured interminable church services, long-winded welcoming speeches, the touching of six hundred scrofulous subjects on Ascension Day, and a variety of beds and sleeping accommodations. More pleasant was his royal role at local Breton dances, and a shopping tour to buy toys and jewelry for his brother and sisters back at St-Germain.

What had first been billed as a short visit to Orléans introduced Louis and his subjects to the royal "campaign" technique of an extended journey. (See Appendix, map 2.) This was to become a trademark of his reign, making him the most traveled and most accessible ruler within France of any French king. Wherever he went in 1614, rebels fell in line. Wavering subjects remained obedient. And one

electoral district after another was influenced, by the king's presence
and royal negotiators, to elect representatives for the coming Estates
General who were committed to royal authority.

As the king's party swung southwest to Blois, Tours, and Poitiers,
Condé gave up his attempt to seize Poitou. Amboise, which Condé
had earlier received as a warranty that the Estates General would
meet, sent its keys to the king. The major future leaders and strongholds of the Huguenot wars against Louis XIII, from the duke of Rohan to the proud Atlantic port of La Rochelle, shunned rebels' over-
tures in proclaiming their loyalty to King Louis. The only resistance
came from César, who wrote disarmingly to Louis of his "fidelity"
and "affection" while remaining in arms in Brittany. Louis understood perfectly. "Ho! What obedience! He hasn't yet disarmed," he
exclaimed, handing the letter to his governor. And so the royal party
headed northwest to Saumur, Angers, and Nantes.

At Nantes, Louis made an impressive showing before the Provincial Estates of Brittany, speaking his own words instead of a speech
prepared by his governor. Going straight to the point, he said that he
had come for the "relief and repose" of the three local estates—which
translated into the tearing down of rebel fortifications, selection of
royalist delegates to the Estates General, and submission by local
rebel leaders. The most troublesome submission for Louis was his
own half brother's. The Breton governor greeted the king with the lie
that he had come as a "most humble and obedient subject" at Louis's
"first" command. Héroard records the scene faithfully: "With his
voice trembling and his face flushed with anger, the king replied,
'Serve me better in future than you have in the past, and understand that the greatest honor you possess in the world is being my
brother.' " Vendôme could only reply, lamely, "I believe it's true."[29]

We can pause here and reflect on the state of the realm and its boy
king in September 1614, as the court made its way back to Paris for
the celebration of Louis's majority and the Estates General. For the
moment, France was loyal to the queen mother, who had managed to
rally subjects to their king and at the same time put off the meeting
of the three estates until after her son's formal majority. Reflecting
this success was a 50 percent drop in prorebel pamphlets between
May and September from their high point earlier in 1614, and a dramatic increase of pamphlets extolling the virtues of peace—from 3
percent to 20 percent of all tracts published.[30]

The youthful monarch had also profited from the challenge of

1614. Ex-Queen Marguerite informed a not too repentent Condé: "It is incredible how the king is grown in body and spirit on this trip . . . , a prince determined to make himself strongly absolute, and [one] who promises to have himself truly obeyed. It won't do to toy with him from now on." Condé had his own taste of what was in store for future challengers of royal authority when he returned to court and offered the olive branch of peace. The prince blithely told his young liege lord that he had grown enormously since their last meeting, only to draw the proud royal reply "that he had grown in body, and even more in courage."[31]

Louis's public bravura was genuine, but it also masked the boy's discomfort over personal confrontations. As dauphin, Louis had experienced many frustrations in his efforts to assert himself before others, including his father and mother. Being king placed him in a position of being "right" more often, and consequently he could be more gracious in lording it over his subordinates and advisors. Being in the right also tended to give Louis XIII a sense of purpose. This would eventually help to shape his political decisions and enable him and his estranged wife to provide France with a royal heir. What it could not prevent were side effects, in the form of psychosomatic ills and illnesses.

While unable to prevent inner conflict, Louis was able to balance his external comportment by means of the royal virtues he had been taught to embody. As the royal minority proceeded, the virtue of justice came to be stressed above the others. Louis felt comfortable with being just, and others thought it suited him and his needs as well. Even the archrebel Vendôme alluded to this consensus in asking the king to live up to his "reputation for justice." Some people went so far as to call him Louis the Just. In the midst of the troubles of 1614, and frustrated by his wayward tongue, Louis noted this sobriquet, commenting wryly that he wanted people to call him Louis the Just and not Louis the Stammerer.[32]

What did this "justice" mean to a generation at one remove from bloody civil-religious strife? To view the royal medallions and scan the poems of 1614 is to face the bewildering reality that justice had several shades of meaning. Louis felt most comfortable with its strictest rendition: justice meant punishment of wrongdoing. But contemporaries, while at one moment speaking of justice in that sense, would in the next breath refer to the royal justice of standing above punishment for the sake of a broader good such as peace. That latter meaning was close to Vendôme's view of justice as the fair-minded treatment of subjects' grievances. Finally there was the idea that justice meant simply to forgive. This interpretation placed justice very close to clemency, but with one important difference: just forgiveness, rather than being merely the condoning of wrong acts, involved the recognition that a wrongdoer had repented. These high-minded forgiving sides to the contemporary concept of royal justice were important in two respects: they made a conflict-ridden age more humane, and they educated the youthful king to feel as regal in accepting obedience by wayward subjects as in imposing it on them.

The various meanings of justice were all around the observant Louis XIII in 1614, as he savored the outward submission of the princes. The most dramatic display of that indoctrination came with the king's and queen mother's festive entrée to Paris from Nantes. As thousands of happy subjects cheered, Louis passed through arches of triumph that bore references to all the royal virtues. But the most striking message was emblazoned on an immense tableau depicting Louis in full regalia at the bow of the ship of state and Marie at its helm as it triumphed over the storms of political turmoil. For those who might miss the message, the accompanying mottoes proclaimed Louis XIII a "peaceful" and "most just" king, and the queen regent as "moderate in peace and war."[33]

For subjects eager to memorialize the exciting events of 1614, there was also a goodly supply of royal medallions. These propaganda pieces had their usual share of soaring eagles and rising suns, but we also find a newcomer to medallion symbolism: the balance scales of justice. Whether the image makers knew that Louis had been born under the sign of Libra, they and everyone else associated his mother's acts and his own deportment with the royal virtue of justice. One such medallion featured the royal sword, a crown, the balance scales, and a hand of justice. A second displayed two globes on parallel lines, beneath a balance in equilibrium. The motto, *occasus aequat et ortus*, is accompanied by an explanation that the rising sun of France "never deludes itself, preferring clemency to victories, and will forget the faults of rebels who submit to [the king], and even share his good fortune with them."

A somewhat more stern royal message comes from a poem entitled *On the Subject of Peace*. The accompanying illustration balances the regal figures of fidelity, justice, and peace on the left against the bad figures of blasphemies, murders, and "other impieties" on the right. The poem elaborates on that theme by likening Louis XIII to the medieval king most associated with justice, St. Louis:

> Look ye at King Louis, regard his youthful image.
> . . . .
> God has brought him forth with generous courage!
> Has wished to create him of nature fully sage,
> Balancing Justice for all equally.
> France! See who makes you live so happily,
> New Saint Louis, whose heart so generously
> Thwarts all the schemes of those who live perniciously.[34]

Of course, it was not easy for King Louis to think of himself as a powerful and just Father of his People while his mother continued to supervise his every act. It mattered not that she gave him presents, provided him with a variety of entertainment that ranged from foreign comedies to dancing and playacting with his siblings, and indulged his taste for falconry and playing soldiers with his "army" of young noble playmates. He had freedom to indulge in crushes on little girls and attachments to older father figures, including an innocuous but handsome and attentive keeper of his falcons (who would some day help Louis throw off his mother's yoke). But Marie kept Louis on such a short leash that he was upbraided when he played with nonnoble boys, beneath his station.

Marie did stop his corporal punishment, after Louis expressed the wish that she defer to him more and have him whipped less now that he was king. She brought his formal lessons to an end, except for Spanish, and, reluctantly, introduced him to royal council debates. Yet Louis kept losing arguments with his mother over the slightest object of his desire, whether it was having his father's religious book for his chapel or having a picture for his living quarters. Marie was so controlling of Louis's life at court that she banished the younger Vendôme half brother Alexandre to Malta, thus nipping in the bud a friendship she thought dangerous.

To be sure, the king was oversensitive in saying, "Everyone is against me." He also expected more than could be given to a boy who was, after all, only thirteen in September 1614. But Marie and her ministers were thinking more of protecting their present power than of Louis's future requirements—as the Venetian ambassador noted. That shrewd observer pointed to the queen mother's solution: keeping her son "away from affairs" and estranged from anyone with "spirit" who could "enlighten" him. In the envoy's words, Marie's coterie wished simply to maintain Louis "in the habit of the greatest respect and obedience toward his mother."[35]

Unable to deal with his frustrations, Louis continued to respect his mother and to bridle at anyone (like Condé) who treated her with too little deference, but all the while simmering inside. He began to mask his feelings in a tight-lipped and expressionless manner, occasionally relieving the tension by blurting out a cutting remark or muttering a wry aside. When he did speak his mind, it could be damningly judgmental and pyschosomatically harmful. We frequently catch him sick with fear that an insolent remark he made to his preceptor or governor would get back to his mother.[36]

On 2 October 1614, Louis XIII went to the Parlement of Paris to proclaim formally the end of his minority. Yet he was fully aware that at age thirteen he was too young and immature to rule. Thus, reading his lines boldly and without stuttering, Louis told his mother before the assembled judges and peers that he wished to have her continue as regent. A leading judge, with more foresight than he realized, suggested in one of the ceremonial speeches that Louis XIII emulate St. Louis and thereby live up to his own title of "Just Prince."

The day before the ceremony there came proof positive that this "just king" already had principles of his own, whether he was really king or not. Presiding over the royal council for the first time as a major, Louis stunned his cousin Condé and the other "great ones" by siding with finance minister Jeannin's plea that court pensions be slashed to balance the budget. When Condé objected, Louis cut him off, saying: "Don't speak a word about it! I will put everything in good order when the Parlement reconvenes."[37]

Marie was shrewd enough to understand her son's intense desire not to be affronted, but she never realized that he could turn his authority against her. Shortly after Louis's majority, the queen mother was confronted by a tearful king. Louis wanted to upbraid Condé for letting one of his retainers enter the royal palace of the Louvre while under penalty of death, "to the scorn of the king's authority and of justice." Marie tactfully told Louis that she would speak to the prince herself. And she did warn Condé never to anger the king that way again, "because, despite his youth, he bore with great impatience whatever offended his authority." Perhaps thinking she had smoothed over the bad blood between the king and all the rebel leaders, Marie foolishly insisted a week later that Louis greet another of the princely malcontents of 1614, Bouillon, "with good cheer." The king dutifully presented a "good face" to the duke, but could not help saying suspiciously, "You are welcome if you come with good intentions." Furious at these "very rude words," Bouillon went straight to the royal governor Souvré, then to Marie. The queen mother passed it off lightly, telling Bouillon to pay no attention and to take his place at the coming Estates General.[38]

3

KING, ESTATES, AND STATE

What is it like to be thirteen and legally responsible for a country's destiny? For King Louis XIII in September 1614, it meant a considerably increased involvement in state affairs, although not enough to make him content. From the moment of Louis's majority, Marie de' Medici ruled his state not as duly authorized regent but only at his continued "pleasure" as "head of council." This meant that the legality of all state acts depended on Louis's validation, however automatic that was for this dutiful son. Henceforth, official communications were directed to him, the royal council met in his presence, and the affairs of his state were conducted in his name. Marie signaled the change by sending instructions to France's ambassadors, telling them to address all future official correspondence to the king.[1]

Beyond these mechanical changes, Louis was introduced to ruling in a way that very few monarchs have experienced on coming to power. On 27 October 1614, barely one month after his majority, some 474 representatives of the realm's three estates assembled for the formal opening of the Estates General. They continued to meet until 23 February 1615, giving the teenage king a dramatic and graphic view of his state. Heretofore he had been virtually restricted to influences from his immediate entourage and the royal court. Now he heard speeches by orators from each estate, listened to delegations tell him both sides of disputes between the estates, and received their grievance lists, or *cahiers de doléances*, at the assembly's conclusion. All this took place in a highly charged political atmosphere that included personal duels and political beatings, the printing of some two hundred pamphlets urging a variety of state reforms on the king and delegates, and numerous handwritten proposals addressed to Louis by both sages and cranks.

On the surface, the Estates General of 1614–15 was neither a good nor a powerful influence on the teenage king. It has gone down in history as an ineffectual gathering devoid of purpose and rent by internal divisions. Hence, historians have been content with two conclusions: on the one hand, that it was so weak yet so bothersome to Marie de' Medici that no ruler called another meeting of the estates until the beginning of the French Revolution 175 years later, and on the other, that it was useful only in allowing a clever Marie de' Medici to secure the delegates' approval of her past policies and the indefinite prolongation of her rule.[2] An undercurrent to these two views even suggests that the failure of the Estates General in 1614–15 "ensured the triumph of royal absolutism in France."[3]

If we look at the France of 1614–15 as its contemporaries saw it, we get a rather different picture. What historians call absolute monarchy was anything but a foregone conclusion at the end of the Estates General in 1615.[4] Louis XIII, during his personal rule after 1617, would need all the emotional energy and principled determination he could summon to impose substantial controls on the three estates and the political society they represented. Nevertheless, and in a far more personal way than historical specialists have noted, the Estates General of 1614–15 did pave the way for the future, by providing Louis XIII with powerful political lessons. In effect, the estates' meetings and the political climate in which they were held completed the formation of the king that had begun while he was dauphin and then was accelerated during the four years of his royal minority.

Looking back on this encounter between king and estates, we can see no less than five ways in which it shaped the monarch. First, it revealed to Louis the social foundations of his state. Second, the squabbles that divided the three estates told him a great deal about the fractiousness he would have to deal with when he seized the reins of power from his mother two years later. A third influence came in speeches to Louis by the most discerning leaders of the estates, which laid down guidelines for the impressionable young king and hinted that he should be more vigorous in his rule than his mother had been during his minority. This moralizing was accompanied by a fourth factor, namely specific proposals by the three estates for the reform of Louis's state. These reforms were to remain a hidden agenda for

Louis throughout his reign. Finally, the estates' approval of Marie de' Medici's past and continued rule constituted a fifth powerful legacy for Louis XIII, one that set the stage for the king's dramatic challenge of her power.

Louis XIII's most immediate lesson from the Estates General concerned France's social organization, intact since the Middle Ages, into three estates or orders. The First Estate was composed of Catholic clergy. The Second Estate was reserved for the nobility, and specifically for families with long-standing noble lineage. This "old" nobility was called alternately *noblesse de race* (nobles of race) for their hereditary origins or *noblesse d'épée* (nobles of the sword) for their prime function as military defenders of the realm. Third Estate status was relegated to what we would call the middle and lower classes, although it included state servants in major judicial and financial offices whose entry to government posts technically made them "new" nobles, called *noblesse de robe* for their official robes.

The three estates did not officially participate in state decision making, since the monarch had the right to rule absolutely with advice from his council. In practice, however, the royal government reflected each estate's traditions and interests.[5] Louis, in his recent entry into council proceedings, had already seen how thoroughly the tripartite organization of French society was represented at the highest level of government. Marie ruled with a formal council plus informal advisors featuring bishops, cardinals, and the papal nuncio; grandees like Epernon (and, when in favor, princes like Condé); and nobles of the robe, whose talents were needed for the council's specialized posts of chancellor (Brûlart), superintendent of finance (Jeannin), and secretaries of state (notably Villeroy).

Louis also had a nodding acquaintance with the estates' influence below the conciliar level, notably through his lit de justice at the Parlement, and contact at court with provincial governors. By custom, the monarchy routinely appointed princes and great nobles to provincial and town military governorships, just as it did for the great honorific positions in the royal household. While a Second Estate incumbent could be removed at will by the ruler, his successors would come from the same high noble ranks. The high military officers, including the marshals of France, constable of the army, grand master of the artillery, and admiral of the fleet, were also always noblemen.[6]

Meanwhile, the Third Estate had come to dominate the judicial and fiscal hierarchies of the government—at the lower echelons by commoners, and at the highest levels by robe nobility. There were primary civil-criminal courts of bailiffs and seneschals, intermediate presidial courts, and regional sovereign courts (*parlements*) led by the prestigious Parlement of Paris for north-central France. A parallel financial structure featured local tax collectors and tax administrators (*élus*) in districts called *élections*, so-called treasurers of France in the intermediate *généralités*, and, at the highest level, regional accounting courts (*chambres des comptes*) and tax courts (*cours des aides*).

The Third Estate, or *Tiers*, owned these judicial and fiscal posts just as surely as the noble "natural advisors" of the crown did the military ranks. Indeed, the Tiers had turned civil offices into private property, thanks to the French monarchy's century-old custom of selling those positions. More recently, in 1604 Henry IV had guaranteed that families could keep an office in their possession on the death of the incumbent, through the privilege known as the *paulette*. This seven-year, renewable contract allowed the officeholder to name his successor, but only at the price of a fixed annual fee.

In social terms, for any specific high judicial or fiscal post, venality of office and the paulette transformed the officeholding personal nobility into hereditary robe nobility by the third generation. Politically, this practice made the robe nobility guardians of royal laws; they could shape the administration of royal justice and interpret the king's laws independently of a monarch's wishes. While the ruler could overrule his officials through lits de justice or royal commands called *lettres de jussion*, he could not resort to the ultimate weapon of dismissing venal officials without reimbursement. Even temporary exiling or imprisonment of an official for alleged acts against state interest risked massive demonstrations by his outraged colleagues. The reductio ad absurdum of this situation was that a theoretically absolute monarchy had to employ the risky tactic of threatening to abolish the paulette or punitively raise its fees at the end of a contract period, just to keep its officials politically in line![7]

The First Estate also had a unique political role, even though most clerics had no formal governmental functions. Individual archbishops and bishops had enormous public influence as administrators of their territorial archdioceses and dioceses. The periodic General Assembly of the French Clergy, representing all Catholic clerics in the realm, had a more direct impact on state policy and government. These assemblies always discussed political issues relevant to their estate, and approved the so-called free gift, or *don gratuit*, which the French clergy gave to the monarchy in lieu of regular taxes. Yet the monarchy, by regularly controlling high ecclesiastical nominations and appointing loyal clerics to key government posts, likewise had a strong influence on church affairs.[8]

The assembling of the three orders in the Estates General of 1614–15 reinforced Louis XIII's boyish understanding of all these things. Perhaps the easiest point for him to grasp in 1614 was that the estates were ranked in accord with the importance that monarchy and society placed on their respective functions. As a priest-king who was anointed by God and healed the scrofulous, Louis knew that the clergy were the First Estate of his kingdom because the soul was more important than the body; their praying for the king and preparing his subjects' souls for heaven were obviously the greatest services that could be rendered the state. As a lad molded in his father's image as a soldier-king, Louis could tell that his Second Estate nobility were only a degree less important than the clergy, for they defended the kingdom with their arms at risk to their lives. And as the descendant of St. Louis and royal "font of justice," the king could also appreciate the role of the Third Estate, with its range of subjects from high and low officeholders to professional persons and merchants, and finally mere artisans and peasants. The Tiers had the least exalted but most vital dual function of working and paying the bulk of the taxes, for the clergy's prayers and the nobles' military service left them virtually tax exempt. Throughout his life, Louis XIII was to act on the assumption that his society was made up of separate orders and estates, and that each should be treated according to its distinctive role.

Louis must also have noticed that beneath the surface of this neat tripartite division within the Estates General there existed a complex hierarchical reality. Although some of that complexity was camouflaged in the meetings of 1614 by the uneven representation of groups within each estate, the reality still showed through. Despite the fact that almost half of the clerical delegates were bishops and archbishops—the most politically adept element within the clergy—there was also a scattering of cathedral canons, some representatives from the regular monastic orders, and thirteen parish priests. Nor was Louis misled by the absence in 1614 of most of *les grands* from the Second Estate's ranks. Condé and his princely friends were still very much in evidence at court, with Condé serving in the government itself as a prince of the blood. Louis may have initially been puzzled that the bulk of the noble deputies were obscure country gentilshommes, but this lesser nobility quickly let him know that most within its ranks boasted noble ancestry going back at least three centuries, and that their families had provided persons of the stature of a Sully to Henry IV. Finally, although the Third Estate was overrepresented in 1614 by its most influential subgroup, venal officials, Louis also was aware that there were several functionaries from towns, some merchants, and even a few individuals representing the peasants, who constituted 85 percent of the population.[9]

This complex world of subgroups and corporations within the estates was far from orderly. Historians have tried to make sense of it by calling it a society of orders. In such an arrangement, a myriad of corporate bodies, or orders, were supposedly given a social rank and political importance according to the value society placed on their function. And in fact this describes Louis XIII's France better than the term *class society*, with its emphasis on wealth and social mobility, or *caste society*, where mobility is virtually ruled out.

What the term *society of orders* does not explain is that an order could be a social group like the peasantry, a political unit like a town, or an institutional unit like a parlement—and that individuals could fit into more than one group. At the Estates General of 1614, over half the bishops were nobles, and there were families with brothers in two, and in one case all three, estates. Nor does the concept of orders explain the constant bickering between corporations at the same level. It does not do full justice, for that matter, to the intense jockeying between levels, as corporations grasped for a higher rank or maneuvered to avoid being overtaken in public esteem or royal favor by rival bodies beneath them.[10]

Both the neat theoretical ranking of estates and orders, and the bickering that went on in practice placed Louis XIII in an excellent position to be arbiter of his subjects' fate.[11] In addition, the Estates General gave the king an excellent schooling in that art. As the formal opening in the great hall of the Hôtel de Bourbon gave way to conclaves of the individual estates at three separate locations in the heart of Paris, three stormy issues divided the estates. Two of these greatly agitated the king; one did not. Significantly, his emotional response was not simply a parroting of his mother's views, nor a following of the priorities of his council. Far from that, his ranking of the three disputes was peculiarly his own, and it remained with him throughout his personal reign.

The queen mother barely escaped the wrath of First and Third Estate alike on the famous first reform proposal of the Tiers. This proposal, although officially nothing more than a call for the monarchy to reaffirm its divine-right principle that the king was not beholden to any powers on earth but to God alone, was in reality a thinly veiled Gallican principle against papal intervention in French affairs. The Third Estate members—themselves the guardians of law and order—could not imagine the regent opposing their divine-right article, since it sought to counter the doctrine of regicide, which, four years after Henry IV's assassination, they felt still stalked the land.

For its part, the First Estate was dominated by zealously reformist bishops who outnumbered the monastic representation, which feared church reform and defended their old ways under the principle of Gallican traditions. The reformist clerics could see nothing good in the Gallican article, and they pushed their ultramontanist support of the Pope to the point of demanding that the queen mother utterly suppress the religiously offensive declaration of the Third Estate. Moreover, the clergy wished to bring the bogeyman of the Gallican judges—the decrees of the Council of Trent—into the French kingdom. This was not an innocuous issue: several Tridentine reforms called for juridical discipline which would automatically give the French clerical courts control over secular matters. To sanction such a constitutional change was anathema to the French monarchy as well as to its courts of justice headed by the Parlement of Paris.

The queen mother and her advisors deftly avoided both strident Gallicanism and extreme ultramontanism. Marie persuaded the Tiers, against their better judgment, to leave a blank space in their cahier where the Gallican article should have been, thereby avoiding the outright suppression the clerics wanted. And she innocently suggested that the clergy themselves introduce the reform of faith and morals into their dioceses in the spirit of the Council of Trent. In point of fact, the General Assembly of the French Clergy did approve the Tridentine decrees in 1615.

Louis XIII was more strongly principled and less diplomatic than his mother in this dispute. While we do not know where he stood on the famous Gallican article or whether he said anything in the council debates directly on it, he did enter into the debate on the more general issues of clerical impartiality and deference to royal authority. Perhaps there was an underlying royal bias against ultramontanism here; in any case, it is noteworthy that the determined king took a stand on precisely the values that were most ingrained in him, which allowed him to venture an opinion without fear of being "in the wrong."

The young ruler became irritated when Cardinals Du Perron and Sourdis tried to muzzle Condé and his Protestant ally, Bouillon, at a council discussion of the Third Estate's divine-right article. We are a long way already from the Louis XIII of 1611 who was terrified of a whipping from Souvré following their disagreement on what he should say to a Huguenot delegation. Now, early in 1615, Louis firmly kept Condé from exploding by saying, "Monsieur, I beg you, don't say anything more," whereupon he turned defiantly to the group and said, "Since they challenge Monsieur le Prince [as a valid witness], they mean to challenge me also."

Obviously the king could change his personal loyalties while holding firmly to principles he believed in. Forgotten for the moment was Condé's recent insubordination; now it was not Condé but Sourdis who, in the measured words of a career bureaucrat, spoke before the king with "unbelievable insolence." As the cardinal and prince continued their verbal sparring, Condé said with steely control that only his respect for the king and the fact that Sourdis was a priest prevented him from having his lackeys beat the cleric. Touched by this display of princely loyalty against the insolence of a fellow subject, Louis XIII embraced Condé twice before his entire council, thanked him for being concerned for his person, and begged the prince not to leave him.[12]

This temporary siding with Condé did not prevent Louis from opposing the same prince and other nobles a month later, on a second divisive issue: the grandees' flaunting of their own mores in the face of royal law and authority. Just as the clergy valued their attachment to the Pope, the great nobles prided themselves on their "right" to uphold their individual honor in duels with fellow nobles or have their lackeys beat up mere commoners who dared to question the nobles' stature or status. This was just a part of the endemic anarchical spirit within the proud old nobility, and Louis would fight many legal and military battles against their lawlessness. In 1614–15, their lawlessness flared up in abundance. The queen's own close advisor, the duke of Epernon, had the effrontery not only to free a royal guard who had been jailed for killing another guard but also to swagger into the Parlement of Paris in boots and spurs in a foolhardy effort to prevent sentencing of the murderer.

The most dramatic incident pitted Condé against Marie de' Medici, with Louis XIII being drawn into the confrontation by his mother. Condé had stubbornly defended his chamberlain, who had beaten another noble client of the prince for telling Marie some of Condé's secret schemes in return for a new post in the king's guards. When Condé arrogantly refused to back down, Marie tauntingly told her son, "Mon fils, come and see the effrontery and insolence of Monsieur le Prince who admits ordering the caning of a gentilhomme in your employ." No doubt Marie was vindictively seizing the first chance to punish Condé for his recent revolt. But she also was challenging Condé's anarchical insinuation that Henry IV would have upheld noble honor in such a case by letting the prince impose his own brand of justice, rather than trying the case in the hostile Parlement of Paris, as Marie was doing.

Louis XIII needed little urging from his mother to turn once more against his cousin. At issue was an implicit affront to royal authority, which the king deeply resented. For Condé had humiliated one of Louis's personal *serviteurs*—a far more serious matter in a hierarchical society than a prince's effort to maintain preferential judicial treatment for his own servitor. Louis was further offended when Condé tried to stop him from speaking his own mind, with the remark "Sire, I beg you most humbly not to speak on that case." The king's cousin even made a third error: after treating his sovereign lord like a juvenile bystander, Condé tried to play on the youth's regal vanity by making a distinction between loyalty to the king (whom he would "never affront"), and his disagreement with the queen mother (whom he told directly that "her animosity and anger would not prevent him from serving the king").

Marie de' Medici set the stage for a spectacular denouement of the scene by informing all three estates as well as the Parlement of the caning incident. Louis then played out his appointed role, including receiving a large delegation from the Estates General, thanking them for their fidelity, and dutifully forgiving Condé when the prince made a grudging display of contrition at a special audience in the queen mother's cabinet. But what was best remembered was Louis XIII's emotional reaction during the initial clash with Condé. The official *Mercure français*, published later, noted that the monarch did not like having his mother stop him from talking back to the prince. The *Mercure* added that when Condé left the Louvre, Louis cried out, "Ha! Madame, you did me a great wrong in stopping me from speaking." If Condé's recent rival, Cardinal Sourdis, can be credited with truthful reporting (in a conversation with the Florentine ambassador), the young monarch even added the angry boast "If I had had my sword, I would have thrust it through his body."[13]

The third explosive issue of the Estates General period involved the rivalry between the old nobility of the Second Estate and members of the Third Estate who were working their way into the new nobility of the robe. The old nobles of race and sword were doubly frustrated by the effects of the dramatic sixteenth-century rise in prices, which had left many fixed-income Second Estate families in a precarious economic position while enabling wealthy Third Estate individuals to monopolize the state's venal offices of justice and finance. The Second Estate deputies took out their frustrations both individually and collectively. One noble deputy went so far as to have a Tiers representative from his province beaten. When the Third Estate insinuated that the nobles had sold their loyalty to the monarchy in exchange for pensions, the Second Estate retorted that the Tiers were as far removed from true gentilshommes as valets from their masters, whatever their technical status as nobles of the robe. In the end, the old nobles clamored for the abolition of venality and the opening of judicial and financial offices to their own kind. The Third Estate deputies, torn between their own interests as venal officials and the instructions of their largely nonofficial electors back home to attack venality, finally opted for asking the monarchy to combine the abolition of venality with deep cuts in noble pensions.

Despite acrimonious debates by the estates, a raging pamphlet war in the local press, and occasional violence in the streets, Marie de' Medici did nothing more than promise abolition of the paulette, and then postponed the implementation of that reform as soon as the Parlement of Paris objected. As for her young son, he apparently did not react at all. This lack of response seems odd for a person who later gained the reputation for a parsimonious court and opposed the sale of offices in his personal household. Louis XIII's unconcern seems, however, to have mirrored his social values. He may very well have sensed that deserving Second Estate nobles should be allowed to maintain their rank at court through state help; and that venality was acceptable in civil offices staffed by Third Estate members, but not for noble-dominated positions in his own household. Above all, no issue over pensions or venality could arouse Louis's righteous indignation the way the Gallican article and Condé's insubordination had.

Divisiveness among the estates during the winter of 1614–15 went hand in hand with public yearning for a strong, firm royal hand and an implicit impatience with the perpetuation of the ex-regent's temporizing on political squabbles. Each estate had its own recipe for future national order. The dévot clerics called for a pious, religious atmosphere that would unite France, Spain, and all of Catholic Europe; and their orator at the assembly's closure, the bishop of Luçon and future Cardinal Richelieu, stressed the importance of having ecclesiastical members in the royal council. The nobles, in turn, had their vision of an ideal hierarchical France with every order in its place and the nobles restored to their pristine luster with their valor properly rewarded. Finally, the stern judicial and financial officials of the Tiers quested for evenhanded justice against noble lawlessness, clerical laxity, and the plundering of poor commoners by corrupt state fiscal practices. For all the differences in their emphases, the three estates agreed in seeing state "reform" as a return to an ideal earlier age, generally centered in the reign of Louis XII a century earlier and antedating the contemporary evils of war, venality, high taxes, and injustice.

While many of these pious hopes were aimed at the queen mother's ears, some assembly orators had the vision—and nerve—to appeal to the future in the person of their young king. The general message was clear, despite flattering allusions to the queen mother's past good intentions: her son was asked to break with the monarchy's tolerance of the cancer of public disorder that had marred his minority. No one was more direct than Robert Miron, mayor of Paris and orator for the Tiers at the opening of the Estates General. Speaking to both Marie and Louis, Miron declared: "Virtue has engendered vice; and the excess of Your Majesties' bounty, openness, and clemency has inadvertently fostered audaciousness, impunity, impiety, and in their train an infinity of ills, public disregard for all divine and human ordinances, and finally a general relaxing of all rules in every order and profession of the realm." [14]

This theme of royal order replacing indulgence captured the imagination of clerical deputies as well as officials. When dueling and other lawless acts grew to excess in the streets of Paris, the bishop of Montpellier told Louis XIII to his face: "I implore Your Majesty to see how the mounting ills are beginning to render you guilty, even though your age should still favor your innocence." The bishop continued with a dark warning and a bright hope. While God visited the iniquity of kings on subjects for their own sins, he could just as easily "chastise" princes for their own "crimes." The solution was for Louis "to arm his hand of justice with the rigor of divine and human ordinances," since "in these extreme maladies, it is an extreme cruelty to be forgiving." Louis XIII and Marie de' Medici reportedly listened to this speech with rapt attention. [15]

The king and his mother were further moved by the celebrated speech at the assembly's close by the bishop of Luçon, spokesman of the First Estate. Historians still quote that speech because it marked the political debut of Richelieu, but it was more important to contemporaries in setting a tone for Louis XIII's early majority years. More adept politically than his fellow episcopal orator, and already known to Louis through court sermons the king had been taken to hear as a child, Luçon knew how to touch on every reform proposal and please everyone—including the queen mother—while still challenging the young ruler to greater things. The charismatic cleric called for discipline instead of innovation. It was a stirring rallying cry for the age.

Luçon bluntly stated that the maintenance of past laws was more effective than the passing of new ones—even the Estates' would-be reform proposals! Yet he wooed Marie by singling out what he called the young king's worthiest act so far on behalf of the "restoration of the state": entrusting royal affairs to his mother! With equal diplomacy, the teenage monarch was "humbly and ardently supplicated" to continue that delegation of authority. Then the future cardinal and minister deftly cut across the lines dividing the Third Estate's divine-right article and the clergy's ultramontanism by saying that the First Estate would play its part in teaching subjects to revere their ruler.

In a metaphor dear to the future chief minister's heart, Luçon proclaimed his order's desire "to see the royal dignity asserted through you, so that it will be like a sure rock which breaks everything that strikes against it."[16] Whether the thirteen-year-old ruler consciously absorbed this lesson of the thirty-year-old Luçon or not, the speech had its effect as part of the ongoing call by Louis's subjects for him to restore order to his estates and state. We can also be certain that this future minister of Louis XIII was already, in 1615, practicing the psychological techniques he would later employ during their years of collaboration.[17]

The pleas of men like Miron and Luçon for royal firmness were punctuated with constant references to the king's virtues, both real and hoped for. Speech after speech called on Louis to emulate his heroic father, good mother, and pious ancestor, St. Louis. The royal trait of justice was also a constant theme, in addresses by clergy, nobles, and judicial officials as well as in pamphlet form. The most eloquent tract came from the pen of Jean Savaron, the same controversial member of the Tiers delegation whose insulting of the nobility for "selling" their loyalty in return for pensions had triggered a round of noble retorts and Third Estate rejoinders that reached the ears of both the king and the queen mother.

Savaron lashed out against venality and allied evils such as pensions and rapacious taxes, challenging the king more tellingly than the bishops of Luçon and Montpellier did. "Kings with the name of

Louis have loved the law," the pamphleteer began disarmingly, and then lulled Louis with flattering news: "If you have chanced to sample the writings dedicated and addressed to Your Majesty, you will note there the name Just. Your actions, having followed your wishes, have already acquired for you the wonderful title of Louys le JUSTE." Then, invoking this magic sobriquet in the service of a blood-chilling warning, the delegate concluded: "Sire, it is impossible for you to keep it, unless you banish venality." [18]

The detailed reform cahiers of the Estates General look anticlimactic when compared with this rousing oratory. Indeed, hopes were high enough at the opening of the Estates General. Louis XIII told the assembled delegates and packed galleries that he had convoked "this great and notable assembly at the beginning of my majority to let you hear the present state of affairs; and to establish good order by means of which God will be served and honored, my people comforted, and each person conserved in that which is his, under my protection and authority." [19] But soon after, the deputies became divided over what they wanted from the monarchy; and the queen mother tried her best to hurry them toward an early dissolution.

Louis XIII was not important in that cat-and-mouse game, except for revealing a seriousness of purpose beneath the official rhetoric he engaged in at his mother's side. When the Estates presented piecemeal suggestions, he politely thanked them for their concern and admonished them to concentrate on completing their comprehensive cahiers so that he could act on their suggestions for state reform. Similarly, when a delegation of the three estates came to press for an investigation of government finances, Louis curtly replied: "I understood what you were telling me. I beg you to work fast on the cahier." Marie, by contrast, praised the delegates' zeal and in the same breath diplomatically suggested that their lingering over individual issues delayed the presentation of the cahiers and the royal response to them. [20]

In February 1615, the Estates General officially ended with the presentation of the reform cahiers to Louis XIII. The litany of proposals included the abolition of the paulette and venality, reduction of court pensions, lower taxes, and the hope of an investigation of financial irregularities in the government (surely an allusion to influence peddling by Marie's friends Concino Concini and his wife, Leonora Galigaï). Each estate also wanted to strengthen its own special position in the society of orders. Paradoxically, as historians have noted, the estates coupled a "desire for more provincial and local self-government" with the wish for "a centralized state with clearly defined organs of government led by a strong monarchy."[21]

The reform proposals of the Estates General combined an ambiguous legacy with a confusion of aims. In the end the reforms were stillborn, as the monarchy did nothing more than acknowledge receipt of the cahiers' proposals when they were presented. Yet the reforms remained throughout Louis XIII's personal reign as an ideal that subjects yearned for and that the king himself thought desirable because of his concern for his subjects' welfare and his estates' well-being. That future ambiguity was already evident in Louis XIII's confrontation with the handful of delegates who met illegally after the dissolution of the Estates General in the hope that their lobbying would force the monarchy to implement the reform proposals. When the stragglers were summoned to the Louvre on 24 March 1615, their king sternly forbade them to continue meeting. Then he read these carefully crafted lines, which he had memorized for the occasion: "I wish to relieve my people as much as I can. I have listened to you very carefully. I will communicate [your wishes] to the queen my mother and to my council."[22]

The adolescent Louis XIII's dutiful blend of idealism and realism on the matter of state reform received a final lesson in statecraft barely four days after the confrontation of 24 March. Filling the vacuum left in the wake of the demise of the Estates General, the Parlement of Paris invited the "princes, dukes and peers, and officials of the crown" to join it in discussing "propositions to be made for the service of the king, relief of his subjects, and welfare of his state."[23]

Of all the corporate groups within the society of orders, the Parlement of Paris was probably the most difficult for the monarchy to control. This supreme court in criminal and civil affairs for north-central France was a unique institution in early modern Europe. In its capacity as the kingdom's sole court of peers, it judged the greatest of the nobility, called the "dukes and peers"; as the guardian of royal laws, it registered all new legislation in the realm, and by custom used that judicial review to amend or even reject laws that its members believed clashed with unwritten "fundamental laws." It had time and again supported the monarchy against internal rebellion and external challenges from the Papacy; it had been the first official body to declare Henry IV as rightful heir and monarch after Henry III's successorless death; and we have already seen Henry's widow turn to the Parliament to ease her son Louis XIII's unexpected accession to the French throne.[24]

During a political crisis, the parlementary judges could be the key to maintaining the French people's obedience and reverence toward their anointed ruler; conversely, they could, through their acts or words, encourage dissent or even trigger rebellion. In March 1615 they combined a genuine desire to secure royal enactment of the Third Estate's moribund reform suggestions with opposition to the one change Marie de' Medici was interested in—abolition of the paulette. Some of these jurists were also clients or friends of Condé, willing to embarrass Marie by using the rallying cry of "reform" to attack the queen mother's disliked Italian favorites, Concini and Galigaï.

We need not follow every step of the confrontation between monarchy and the Parlement. Suffice it to say that Marie de' Medici blunted the parlementary attack by postponing the abolition of the paulette until its normal renewal date at the end of 1617, and by the hollow concession of letting the judges draft and present to the king their own proposals for improving the French state. In the process, Louis XIII learned to dislike the judges' meddling in state affairs and to believe that he had every right, as the head of justice, to decide for himself what was good for his people. To be sure, it was obviously the king's mother in council who laid down the strategy employed against the parlementarians, and just as surely Louis was told what to say. Yet the experience of playing a properly regal role and injecting some of his own personality into the fray gave Louis a taste of his forthcoming personal reign.

Let us allow Louis XIII to reveal his feelings through the royal words and visage of March, April, and May 1615. At an initial conference with the parlementary delegates on 30 March, the king humiliated the judges by insisting that they, and not his agents, forbid their tribunal to meet in special assembly. With a look of indignation, Louis resisted all their appeals against this inglorious act, while Marie shrieked, "You can glory in obeying the king." When the Parlement kept pressing for the assembly, its leaders were called to the king's cabinet on 9 April to hear the chancellor say that the king was greatly offended, and would remember the wise older judges who had voted against their junior colleagues on this issue. Louis added, spontaneously, "Messieurs, it is I who say what the chancellor has told you."

The judges quickly retreated from the untenable ground of an expanded "great parlement" to the purely judicial act of the Parlement proposing its own "remonstrances." The king in turn dutifully shifted his responses as the queen mother took a harder line. While his former governor and speaking coach beamed approvingly, Louis ordered the judges not to "meddle in state affairs." His mother added: "He is your king, your master, who will use his authority if anyone goes against his interdictions." And Louis ad-libbed: "That is my will; as your king and your master I forbid this of you."[25]

The queen mother then fell back on Chancellor Brûlart's diplomatic device of allowing the remonstrances as a harmless outlet for the parlementarians' frustrations.[26] At a royal audience on 22 May, the remonstrating judges tested Marie one last time by criticizing her pro-Habsburg foreign policy and alluding to "foreigners" (Concini) and "sorcerers" (Galigaï and her physicians) as "evil advisors." Brûlart replied that the king was a major accountable only to God and could choose for advisors whomever he wished. Jeannin defended the government's fiscal policies. Marie choked with anger as she defended her regency years. And Louis XIII said very simply that he was *"mal satisfait"* with the parlementarians' audacity. The remonstrances fell on deaf ears just as had the Estates General's cahiers; and the experience left the king suspicious both of the judges as an insubordinate lot and of reforms demanded by his subjects rather than granted by royal "grace."[27]

As restive subjects groped for a new way to alter public policy in the face of these setbacks, Louis XIII's mother confidently basked in the glory of seeing her power officially approved by the divided estates. This was the last and most ironic legacy bequeathed to her son by the Estates General of 1614. The irony lay in the fact that the very things Marie wrung from the assembled estates led directly to her son's real accession to and her own ouster from power. The Estates General authorized Marie to go ahead with the Franco-Spanish marriages, which thrust Louis abruptly into personal adulthood. It also approved Marie's perpetuation of her rule, thus compelling the frustrated Louis to turn to his only way of attaining political adulthood: a coup d'état against his mother.

No one expected this. Yet what we have seen of Louis's thoughts, feelings, and actions during the course of the Estates General points to an explosive political awakening for the king in the making. The Florentine ambassador tells us all we need to know about Louis XIII's personality during this time, writing that the king was extremely secretive, capable of being overcome with indignation, a "lover of all that is properly done," and someone who "wants justice." Bartolini concluded, ominously: "Despite his youth, he shows well in advance what one can expect of him."[28]

PART II

Louis the Just Comes of Age 1615–24

4

ROYAL MARRIAGE
AND COUP D'ETAT

B y 1615, Louis XIII was marked for life as a highly emotional
person with strong principles. He also had a worrisome
tendency to seek out someone to lean on. And he had difficulty
expressing differences with others, resorting instead to studied silence and occasional, sharply worded retorts. This royal teenager
was not ideally equipped to handle his ambiguous position as a
formal head of state who was under the control of a strong-willed
mother. There was bound to be inner torment and eventually an
open explosion as the king approached manhood.

Nevertheless, Louis's rites of passage to personal and royal
adulthood were more hair-raising than any novelist could invent: a
wedding-night humiliation on 28 November 1615; and hesitant plotting with friends that sent his mother's Italian favorite to a violent
death on 24 April 1617 and herself into political exile shortly after.
The former event set the tone for an unhappy life, torn between
personal inadequacy and the principle of doing right. The latter
experience inaugurated a public reign of principled severity, so violent that we recoil in disbelief; yet ironically, the exile and murder
made the king's reputation as Louis the Just.

For those readers raised on Alexandre Dumas's picture of an
adult Louis XIII bereft of will and wit, it will take some persuasion
to show how the teenage king, however principled, could challenge
his mother and her favorite before he was sixteen years of age. Even
for those specialists of the reign who know Louis XIII had both wit

and will, there remains some mystery in that act, for what fifteen-year-old in any age or place has done such a thing? To show how it came to pass, we need to look first at the king's life during his early majority years, then examine the unfolding of the nuptial experience, and finally turn to the setting for the events of 1617.

At the conclusion of the Estates General in February 1615, the youthful monarch told his subjects that "he was a major in relationship to everyone and everything except the queen, his mother."[1] Marie, misled by her son's external behavior and her own desire to wield power, believed him. The boy had crushes on the most unassuming males at court, surely not the sign of a great future ruler. And he carried his childhood preoccupation with mechanical trades into his teens: making omelets (they became famous), devising special desserts, casting toy cannon, shoeing horses, and building miniature forts. These activities seemed the mark of someone who felt secure only in foolproof and trivial pursuits. Even the Venetian envoy, hopeful of anti-Habsburg and antipapal tendencies in the king, wrote resignedly: "He would promise much if only his education had been better, and his mind more inclined to serious things."[2]

But the royal pursuits were not so trivial, and Louis's commitments were serious. This was true especially of his friendships. Condé feared that the king would become the tool of a nonentity or coquette, but it did not enter his head that the monarch could use the crutch of a friendship to realize his own political goals. Marie was even less astute, reportedly devising the strategy of surrounding him with persons of "mediocre capacity and little spirit."[3] Among these was the man who would help Louis overthrow his mother and her favorite.

His name was Charles d'Albert, sieur de Luynes. (See plate 6.) Stories circulated that Luynes and his two younger brothers shared the same best suit, and that a hare could quickly jump across their family lands. Yet they were of the same lesser nobility that had predominated at the Estates General. Henry IV's friendship for Luynes's father, a soldier of fortune, caused him to place the younger Luynes among the dauphin Louis's noble comrades. The gentilhomme began to look after the heir's birds of prey; and the young boy's fondness for the gentle, handsome, and supportive middle-aged man grew.[4]

By the end of 1614, Louis's attachment was so strong that it bothered Queen Mother Marie, her Italian favorite, Concini, and the king's former governor, Souvré. Yet Luynes remained in Louis's favor and his brothers also gained easy access to the king. How did the king prevent a sequel to his mother's earlier banishment of Alexandre de Vendôme? We need follow only one example. In October 1614, Souvré made the Albert brothers stay away from the royal bedchamber, even during the ceremonial *lever* and *coucher*, hoping to supplant the gentleman-favorite with his own son, Courtenvaux. Someone told the king that his former governor was responsible, and Louis countered by treating Souvré with silence and dark looks, until the mortified man got the queen mother to negotiate an accommodation.

In employing passive resistance here, Louis had discovered the only way he could assert himself, considering the queen mother's imperiousness and his own timidity. The son also held his ground in refusing to tell his mother who had told him of Souvré's maneuver against Luynes, until she promised not to punish that individual. Equally revealing was the fact that Louis did not bear a grudge against Souvré or Courtenvaux, both of whom he actually liked. He paid for all this agitation with a soaring pulse and symptoms of illness. This powerful combination of indirect strategy, fierce loyalty, forgiveness, and sacrifice of personal health, then, separates the real adolescent Louis XIII from both the weakling and the vindictive Louis of historical fiction and scholarship.[5]

If the court was baffled by the dynamics of Louis's friendships, it was equally unaware that his interests always had a serious element, even when they appeared frivolous. When he sketched with pen and ink, it was of horses pulling cannon, although incongruously placed in a child's setting of trees, churches, and village brides. Louis dutifully took part in court masques and ballets; however, his dislike of elaborate protocol and showing off caused him to refuse outright to lead his sister Elisabeth in a dance before the Spanish ambassador. The Spaniards were disconcerted by this affront so close to the marriages of Louis and Elisabeth to the children of King Philip III of Spain, Anne of Austria and the future Philip IV. The French court poet, Malherbe, could only comment: "If age and love don't change his ways, he will be inquisitive only of things that are *solide*."[6]

Louis was all seriousness in preparing for his marriage. He took Spanish lessons, and learned to ride so quickly and well that ladies and soldiers alike gave him rave reviews. Sketches have come down to us of a full-faced, chubby adolescent proudly astride his favorite horse, Le Couchon. The teenager continued to rub shoulders with his boyhood noble companions and feel at ease with these Second Estate scions, now young men: Courtenvaux, Blainville, Montpouillan, Candale, and others. He picnicked with Souvré's older generation, now resplendent with high military rank: the marshal Souvré; the inimitable Bassompierre, who was courtier, soldier, and lover combined; and captain of the guard Vitry and his brother du Hallier, who would play lead roles in the assassination of Concini. These men drank to Louis's health and he to theirs; then he lay down on a portable bed to listen to their serious talk and to play with fireworks.[7]

Fortified by that military camaraderie, the king was all set to ride south to Bordeaux to meet his bride. He was unperturbed by the last-ditch schemes of anti-Habsburg grandees led by Condé to place armies astride his path and publish manifestoes against Marie's "evil" ministers and foreign favorite. When asked by a countess whether he was serious about his marriage plans, Louis replied: "Yes, I'm so set on it that if I found the devil in my path trying to stop me, I'd run him through the throat."[8]

Marie de' Medici contained Condé's northern rebel forces by mobilizing an army of ten thousand infantry and fifteen hundred cavalry under the French marshal Bois-dauphin. The second in command was Concini, now known as Marshal Ancre thanks to his and his wife's favor with the queen mother, who had made him marquis of Ancre, governor of key places to the northeast of Paris in Picardy, and then a marshal in the armed forces. The royal party then proceeded southward in August 1615, escorted by a second army, led by the duke of Guise, numbering three thousand foot and one thousand mounted soldiers. This show of force was enough to keep restive southwestern Huguenot nobles from carrying out their threat to join the princely rebellion. Luckily, too, the staunchly loyal Huguenot governor of Dauphiné, Lesdiguières, held southeastern France for the royal cause.

The most excited person on the journey was the king himself. On 15 August, Assumption Day, he dutifully confessed his sins to his confessor, Father Coton, then gave the royal touch to three thousand ailing subjects. The next night Louis set his alarm for 3:30 A.M., but anticipation aroused him half an hour early, at 3:00. Eventually he aroused Souvré, heard mass at 5:00, and was on the road by 6:45. Contrary to pessimistic predictions that the royal group would not get past Orléans, the king reached that town on the twentieth; and by the twenty-fourth the cortege was already at Amboise, where Luynes entertained the king's party in a style for which royal favorites were famous.

Amboise was an important symbolic stop. Marie had awarded temporary control of the château there to Condé in 1614 as a guarantee that the Estates General would meet. When the château reverted to the crown in 1615, Louis wanted to give it to Luynes, but hesitated to approach his mother. Finally, he was able to make the request in the presence of his first keeper of the wardrobe, who helped him by alluding to his wish. Someone commented that the king "was still not accustomed to interfering with anything." It would have been more astute to emphasize Louis's ability to find a way to gain what he wanted.[9]

Louis also displayed a fearlessness that at times bordered on impetuosity. The king moved along their route so quickly that his mother and ministers were often left far behind. Only Elisabeth's bout with smallpox in September delayed her brother's arrival at his destination, Bordeaux. At the journey's end, Louis showed his true colors when a false report of an imminent rebel attack reached him. Without flinching, he put on his military dress, which he adorned with a bright scarf, and, on 7 October, dramatically entered Bordeaux as he had wanted to—informally and with his soldiers.[10]

The marriages between the French and Spanish crowns were solemnized by two sets of ceremonies at Bordeaux and Burgos, first by proxy and then with formal nuptials following the exchanging of princesses at the border. Louis's parting with his sister Elisabeth was emotional, for she was his favorite sibling. In contrast to the queen mother who had said her adieus the day before to avoid last-minute tears, the king went through the final ritual and was so overcome that three hours later he was still in tears. On top of this, Louis was admonished to act like a king. Not surprisingly, he developed a headache, and remained upset well into the night.[11]

Louis also injected his personality into the arrangements for the arrival of his bride, Anne of Austria. While Marie chose her close friend, the duke of Guise, to accompany Elisabeth to the exchange spot in the middle of the Bidossa River and to escort Anne back to Bordeaux, Louis insisted that the moment his bride set foot on French soil she be met by his own best friend, Luynes, with a personal letter from her groom. More dramatically, as Anne neared Bordeaux on 21 November, Louis rode out to observe her secretly from his carriage, saying loudly to her and his coachman in his best

Spanish and impatient French: "Yo son incognito, yo son incognito! Touche, cocher, touche!" On Anne's arrival in Bordeaux, she was greeted first by her mother-in-law's close friend, the princess of Conti, then by Marie, and finally, through Marie's introduction, by Louis. How different these scenes were from the uninhibited Henry IV's brusque incognito entry to Marie de' Medici's bedroom before they were officially married! The son of that womanizing *vert galant* was not giving any sign that *he* would be "father of his people" in the literal sense.

There were charming moments during Anne and Louis's nuptial celebrations, during the following week. When they exchanged love gifts, he gave her a plume from his cap, asking for a bow from her hair in return. The formal wedding on 28 November was impressive. Anne wore a flowing velvet gown of royal purple and fine gold fleurs-de-lis. Louis was in gold-embroidered white satin, with an enormous ruff around his neck. Everyone remarked that they looked like brother and sister as they made their formal entry to Bordeaux four days after their marriage was solemnized.

Compliments could not camouflage the fact that this young couple was rushed into a serious personal and political commitment that was beyond their years and temperaments. They were barely fourteen years old, Anne having been born four days before Louis. Despite Queen Anne's pretty face, rosy cheeks, and celebrated white hands, which were to be the toast of European royalty, she was too fun-loving, even frivolous, to suit her royal husband's serious, martial tastes. It made no difference that she intended to please her lord and king, or that she was already knowledgeable about the roles of royal favorites in Spain and hence could adapt to Louis's favoring of Luynes—and many other favorites after him.

As for Louis, that chubby faced, tousle haired person of stammering tongue and few words, given to talking of falconry, deer hunting, and fort building, he was insufficiently open and self-assured to meet his bride half way. His shy, semi-public first encounter, "incognito," symbolized it all, although no one could have known how difficult their marriage would be. They had their Catholic religion and their regal upbringing in common—not enough for two persons so incompatible in character.

The first real contact between Anne and Louis, on their marriage night, was a trying experience for both. King Louis, scared to death and fatigued by the wedding ceremonies—right down to the blessing of the marriage bed—retired to his own bed at 5:30 P.M.

Noble courtiers attending the monarch tried manfully to assuage his fears and counter his sense of shame about sex by telling him promiscuous tales. Sharp at eight, the groom's mother appeared at his bedside, saying before the king's male companions: "My son, it's not all done in getting married; you have to come to see the queen your wife, who awaits you." Louis dutifully replied: "Madame, I was only waiting for your command. I'm happy to set out with you to find her." Mother and son went to the bride's bedroom for Anne's introduction to Marie's peremptory ways. The mother-in-law admonished: "My daughter, here is your husband whom I bring to you; receive him into your bosom and love him well, I beseech you." The daughter-in-law replied dutifully that her only wish was to please "Your Majesties."

Marie waved away all but two royal nurses, leaving the young couple behind the curtains of the state bed, in a room suggestively decorated with gold and silver tapestries depicting the life of Artemis, virgin goddess of nature and protector of women. At 10:15 the king asked the nurses to bring his robe and slippers, and retired to his own suite and bedroom, saying that he had done his duty two times. Of course, this official consummation was simply for the record: it was of crucial importance for French foreign and domestic policy that the marriage bond between France and Spain be irrevocably forged.

Though there had in fact been no sexual consummation, Marie de' Medici was sufficiently legal and crude to display the bedsheets the next morning. And, to be sure, something *had* taken place at the marriage bed rite. For Louis retired with a *"glande rouge"*; and Anne accepted a painful, unconsummated entry as if this was normal nuptial behavior. The embarrassment of the first night was reinforced by the common rumor that the king had not been able to perform his duty: "He produced nothing but clear water."

Tallemant added the hearsay of Louis exclaiming, "Look out! I'm about to go and piss in her body." That supposed quip is not easily squared with Louis's hesitant words to Anne, as he relayed them to his mother and doctor: "I asked her if she really wanted to; she said she really did." Far from being brash on his marriage night, he lost his nerve and did not recover it for four long years. He continued his habit of sleeping alone, visiting his wife ritualistically during the day and for a brief goodnight parting, just as he visited his mother ritualistically for council meetings in her chamber. Six months passed before the newlyweds ate a meal together.[12]

The wedding celebrations were scarcely complete before Louis was drawn into the equally nightmarish scenario of a fierce power struggle over who should control his government. The main contenders were the prince of Condé and Marshal Ancre. Marie de' Medici, as the real head of government and Ancre's patron, supported her unpopular foreign favorite with reckless abandon. This placed Louis XIII in the unenviable position of balancing loyalty to his mother, disapproval of princely rebelliousness, and mounting personal outrage at Ancre's arrogance.

Sparring between the king's cousin and the queen mother's favorite began during the first months of 1616 as the royal wedding party, on its way back to Paris, lingered in the environs of Luynes's political base at Amboise. A silent Louis witnessed the prince's initial success at the ratification of the Treaty of Loudun on 3 May. This agreement by the queen mother with the noble rebels of 1615 bought temporary peace at the price of royal concessions to the Catholic grandees Condé, Longueville, and Maine, their most intransigent Huguenot allies led by the duke of Rohan, and such Huguenot moderates as Bouillon and La Trémouille. Condé emerged with the greatest spoils. He was made head of the council of state and of specialized councils for justice and finance, which gave him the power to sign all financial disbursements.

Condé's influence on government was a disaster. Throughout the summer of 1616, he made impossible personal demands and wandered aimlessly in and out of court. State affairs were neglected while Marie showered her son's cousin with favors, then enlisted the diplomatic skills of the bishop of Luçon to get Condé to accept Marshal Ancre as her favorite and confidant. But the pact between prince and favorite only caused Condé's friends to turn to fantasies of killing Ancre, placing Marie in a nunnery, and seizing Louis. It was rumored that the queen mother's marriage to Henry IV might be nullified, Louis XIII and his brother Gaston declared illegitimate, and Condé awarded the throne of France by default!

When the honorable prince told Ancre he could not protect him against irresponsible acts by Condé's friends, Marie panicked, and Louis went along with her reflex action. On 1 September 1616, Louis coolly led an innocent Condé into Marie's chamber at the Louvre while engaging in small talk, then left "to go hunting." To the prince's consternation and disbelief, he was immediately arrested by the king's personal guards. It was a perfectly executed royal act, much like Louis XIV's arrest of his own would-be chief minister, Fouquet, a half century later.

Louis XIII would declare afterwards that he had been opposed to Condé's arrest. Was he? He certainly hid his feelings well. The king told the arresters to try to avoid violence, and then assured the seized man that his life would be protected just like his own. Only when Condé refused to eat Louis's food for fear of being poisoned did the king reveal any emotion: he was furious that this cowering subject would question his word.

Toward Condé's followers, who fled for their lives, as guilty as their leader was innocent, Louis displayed an interesting blend of moralizing and restraint. When he mistakenly thought his old archrival César had come to the Louvre instead of disappearing, he remarked: "Good! So here is that son of a whore captured." Yet when the flight turned into armed fighting, and false rumors reached court that Vendôme and Bouillon had been slain, the monarch cut short a rejoicing courtier with the words: "I do not rejoice in the death of another person." The remark is telling, especially in conjunction with Condé's exclamation that Bouillon should have been killed for his treasonous thoughts.[13]

Condé's incarceration intensified the power struggle between two factions equally marred by political self-seeking. The rebels' new rallying cry of avenging their leader's arrest could not overcome their moral bankruptcy as a party aimed at transferring to themselves the power and patronage enjoyed by the queen mother's Italian favorites. On the royal side, the arrest was part of a new state policy of firmly resisting rebel demands. That policy shift stemmed from the appointment during the last months of 1616 of a vigorous ministerial triumvirate: Claude Barbin, Claude Mangot, and Armand-Jean du Plessis, bishop of Luçon. The triumvirs' effectiveness was hampered, however, by popular antipathy toward the couple who had put them in power, Concini and his wife, Galigaï.

Of the three "creatures" of the Ancres, Barbin had the most influence, and eventually suffered most severely from the king's wrath after the royal coup d'état of 1617. A shrewd manipulator of money and people, this private financier had advanced his career by leasing the collection of state fees to the profit of his friend, Leonora Galigaï, then became Marie's personal financial director and finally royal superintendent of finance. Barbin took the lead among the new ministers in boldly urging Marie to oppose princely disorder.

Mangot's background was somewhat less controversial. He had parlayed a brilliant law career and legal assistance to Concino Concini into acquisition of the top post in the Parlement of Bordeaux, then briefly served as a secretary of state, and finally as keeper of the seals, thereby assuming the judicial functions—but not the office itself—of chancellor, which post was always for life.

The minister who signed his name Lusson at this time was the last of the three to enter the council, and owed a great deal of his influence with the queen mother and her Italian favorites to the patronage of Barbin. Armand-Jean du Plessis, sieur de Richelieu, was the ambitious scion on his father's side of the petty noble Richelieu–du Plessis family, which had been prone to dueling and overspending, and on his mother's side of the hardworking La Porte–Meilleraye family of robe lineage. He had already come far as bishop of Luçon, orator of the clergy at the Estates General, almoner of young Queen Anne, and personal secretary to the queen mother. In November 1616, he became secretary of state for foreign affairs.

Sympathetic biographers have read more into the future cardinal-minister Richelieu's brief conciliar career of 1616–17 than the hard evidence proves. All we can say with certainty is that he showed himself to be bright and energetic in internal and external affairs. His surviving letters to Ancre were embarrassingly fawning, even for an era that assumed the way to become a favorite at court and stay there included a large dose of flattery and obsequiousness. Luçon also revealed his driving ambition and authoritarian bent to such an extent that, at his fall in 1617, the keenly observant young Louis XIII expressed relief to be rid of his tyranny.[14]

The triumvirate was able to hold the military edge for the royal side against Condé's followers in the desultory fighting of the last months of 1616 and the beginning of 1617, but without finding a moral cause that would definitively tip the balance in this latest miniwar. To the contrary, the ever-escalating level of the Ancre couple's conspicuous privilege and power undermined everything Barbin was attempting to accomplish, and served also to make the queen mother more vulnerable as the Ancres' patroness.

This unseemly situation gave the timid Louis XIII his first opportunity to make his ideas and will prevail in the royal government. There was no one else to break the political deadlock and halt the realm's descent into chaos. The favorites' arrogant display of political influence, plus their tarnishing of royal authority, proved powerful enough moral issues to overcome the sternly principled fifteen-year-old's inhibitions against challenging his mother's ruinous hold on his government.

The king began giving strong signals of his resolve to be fully involved in state affairs. One day in 1616, when his passion for hunting caused him to lose track of the time, Louis became angry at his entourage for lying: "You tell me it's only one o'clock so it won't cut short my fun; it's more than a half hour since the hour has sounded. I have to go! I have to be at council by 2." [15] Louis also gave fair warning of how he would intervene in the political process. The best example is an incident, also in 1616, when he reacted to his dogs' differing degrees of obedience, while pulling his toy cannon. Louis praised the animal which had done his duty, scolded the recalcitrant one, and then said to his entourage: "One must treat human beings like that. Punishments and rewards maintain states." [16] That governing style could be applied against the queen mother's favorites, just as it had been invoked against a king's overmighty cousin.

It was customary in early modern Europe for heads of state to reward liberally persons they liked. The path from personal favorite to minister-favorite was also well trodden in those times, for in order to maintain favor, individuals with some power wanted to see their clients appointed to high office, to suggest policies that would protect their interests, and eventually to hold high office themselves. Lerma had already gone down that path in Spain, and Spain's Olivares and England's Buckingham were soon to embark on the same route to power. It was a treacherous path, however, inviting vilification by the envious. A favorite who became ostentatious or overbearing in wielding influence could drag down the reputation of his royal patron, thus ending his own career and perhaps life. In the current instance, the Ancre couple were widely perceived to have strayed across the line that separated permissible conduct from scandalous. [17]

The behavior of Concini and Galigaï not only kept the grandee rebellion alive, but it also inspired a flurry of scurrilous pamphlets against them and Marie de' Medici, and aroused popular wrath as well. Marshal Ancre's primary residence next to the Louvre, and his deliberately suggestive straightening of his clothes after tête-à-têtes in Marie's apartments, led the populace to dub his route of access to the queen mother the bridge of love. Punsters said that Marie was never without her anchor.[18]

More ominously, in retaliation for what was perceived as Ancre's primary role in provoking Condé's arrest, a Parisian crowd ranging from poor workers to noble adventurers vandalized the marshal's secondary residence in the *faubourg* St-Germain, near Marie de' Medici's emerging new Palais du Luxembourg. The rioters knew exactly what they were attacking: Concini's and Galigaï's portraits were destroyed, Marie de' Medici's likenesses tossed from the windows, and only Louis XIII's image left unscathed. [19] Yet despite this grass-roots movement, Louis found himself in the eerie position of being virtually ignored at court, while the throngs who had lionized Condé at the height of his influence a few months before were now falling all over themselves to curry favor with Marshal Ancre. He had every reason to be upset.

Louis XIII was less vocal about Concini's secretive wife than about the swaggering marshal. No doubt he was inhibited by Leonora Galigaï's intense friendship with Marie de' Medici, which went back to their infancy in Florence and had blossomed when the fellow expatriates were transplanted to the French court. Leonora was head of Marie's household, her constant companion and confidante. Evil-tongued courtiers whispered about the woman's fits of depression, her Jewish physicians, and her dependence on astrologers and "black magic." Even Louis occasionally let his own feelings be known. When Galigaï complained about his pet dogs' noise reaching her quarters in the Louvre, he retorted that she could easily find lodgings outside the palace.[20]

Concino Concini was a more obvious object of the king's indignation, going back to the previous reign when Henry IV rewarded the glib courtier's ability to make Marie forget her husband's infidelities by making him first equerry. Now, thanks to Marie's favor, the man's unsavory character was combined with a flaunting of power through his governorship of key places in Picardy, a post as first gentleman of the king's chamber (in tandem with three French grandees), and a marshal's baton. After the Treaty of Loudun, he dropped his Picard connections, only to build a more substantial power base as lieutenant general to the governor of Normandy.

Ancre's arrogance and licentiousness were exactly the formula to cause the worst reaction in the king's emotional system. Louis XIII was offended right from the beginning by this first gentleman of the chamber's autocratic infusion of dignity into the haphazard royal *lever, coucher,* and audiences. The Italian favorite even had the nerve to dismiss from the royal chamber, in the king's name, Louis's favorite preceptors, Rivault and Pluvinel. Louis also reacted to Concini placing his hand on the royal nurse and punning: "Sire, the women at your *coucher* should *coucher* with M. d'Aiguillon, who is a grand chamberlain, and with me as first gentleman of your chamber." Louis stared in anger, turned his back, and murmured, "Oui les vilains."[21]

Concini spent most of the fall and winter of 1616 establishing his Norman power base, yet visited the court often enough to keep Louis XIII's anger focused on the favorite, who threw his political weight around and acted as if the ministerial triumvirate were his lackeys. Concini, Galigaï, Marie, Barbin, and Luçon all sensed danger from the king's quarters, but acted ineffectually. Galigaï experienced bouts of mental illness which diminished her effectiveness as Marie's emotional support. Barbin steadied the queen mother's nerves when she became panicky, yet he and Luçon were torn between fears that Ancre would get Marie to dismiss them for being too independent and the growing suspicion that their future lay with the young king. Just before the coup d'état of 1617, the two ministers discreetly passed word to the young monarch of their loyalty to him, but to no avail.

Sometimes the queen mother encouraged her son to participate more in his government (which meant defending Ancre's behavior in public!).[22] On other occasions she tested his restiveness by offering to abdicate authority to him at a parlementary session. According to Luçon's reflections much later, Louis declined because he sensed Marie's insincerity. In the end, Marie and Ancre nervously tightened control over the monarch's itinerary—which merely intensified his frustrations.[23]

Word filtered through to the rebel army that their monarch was opposed to Ancre.[24] But what could the king do? He stated his dilemma squarely not long before his coup d'état, exclaiming, "The marshal wants to ruin my kingdom, but my mother can't be told that because she will just get mad."[25] That dilemma caused one bout of illness after another, from September 1616 to April 1617.

After Ancre's suburban residence was destroyed, Louis uttered an enigmatic "Didn't you hear clearly what I told you?" when Ancre demanded reimbursement at a council meeting. On learning that Barbin had arrangement payment, he said, bitterly: "They say there isn't any money at all in the treasury when I want to give chits for thirty *livres*; but they easily find one hundred and fifty thousand for Marshal Ancre." That incident alone made the king sick, though he hid his illness for four days to avoid taking medicine.

In October, Ancre attempted his most brazen act of all when he began legal proceedings designed to make him a duke and peer. The king's shock was so great that he suffered convulsions and lost consciousness. His aides had to pry his teeth open with a knife. He was finally revived with enemas and his first bleeding.

Was there no end to the insensitivity of the man who, in 1615, had kept his hat on at a solemn parlementary audience with the king? Apparently not. On 22 November, Ancre strode with a retinue of a hundred men into the Louvre's grand gallery, without so much as acknowledging his sovereign's presence. Then he allowed his own entourage to pay him homage by removing their hats. Dr. Héroard remarked that Louis XIII withdrew to the Tuilleries, "his heart bursting with displeasure."

More than raw, naked hatred of Marshal Ancre was in question here. The king's psychic reaction also stemmed from disturbing advice he was beginning to receive on how to rid himself of the source of his misery. As Christmas 1616 approached, Louis performed a royal ballet, danced the *branle* with his queen, and showed her the military training-ground of the noble boyhood friends he planned to send into battle against the rebel grandees. But he also had a dream in which he brandished his sword against Abimilech, the biblical usurper of royal authority in ancient Israel. During ritual visits to his wife and mother he was flushed in the face and close to swooning. What inner turmoil the sensitive teenager must have experienced as principle and close friends drew him against the Ancres and his own mother![26]

Three, perhaps four main persons were urging him on. The most obvious was Luynes, whom Ancre and Marie periodically viewed with suspicion without knowing what to do about him. Luynes was a complex individual whom the troubled monarch could totally trust, yet who liked to please everyone and was ambitious enough to eye with envy Ancre's honors and power. Here was the ideal person to draw from the hesitant king his innermost thoughts and wishes as they sat night after night talking in the king's suite or in Luynes's chambers directly overhead.

There was also a man of action, Louis d'Hôpital de Vitry. This son-in-law of Louis's old governess, admired by the king for his utter lack of fear, was well positioned as the captain of the king's guards who would be in charge during the spring quarter of 1617. Vitry let Louis know that he would execute any command against Ancre. As the king hesitated, along came another person crucial to the undertaking. Guichard de Déageant was an aide to Barbin and hence able to tell the king all about Ancre's ambitions and projects. His diplomatic finesse was instrumental in bringing a conscience-stricken but determined king, a gentle king's favorite, and a hit man around to agreeing tacitly on the means toward a desired end—the destruction of Marshal Ancre's power. A fourth person, Jean de Caumont de Montpouillan, for whom the king had an extreme fondness, was perhaps also equally involved.

The conspirators' initial plan seems to have been to take advantage of a council decision to place the king at the head of his troops for their spring 1617 offensive against the rebels. Once at the front, Louis would rally both sides against Ancre. But Marie kept him in the capital, even guarding his hunting trails; so the would-be soldier king had to forego that route. Then Louis settled on his friends' suggestion to arrest Ancre and have the Parlement of Paris try him for abuse of authority.

The plotters got their opportunity in April 1617. Ancre was making one of his periodic visits from Normandy to Paris; Vitry was in charge of the king's guards; and the mild-mannered Luynes was driven to act out of fear that his ouster from the king's company by Marie and Ancre was imminent. They had to move quickly before the suspicious queen mother and her favorite got wind of the plot. As it was, the paranoid Ancre began lashing out against anyone who was not blindly loyal. He erected a gallows in the capital, drew up a purge list, and planted spies everywhere. Louis XIII had to clap his hand over a conspirator's mouth for fear a Concinian spy would hear incriminating words. Even Louis's close companion, Montpouillan, was approached with a bribe.[27]

There were several false starts, and four sleepless nights for Louis. Vitry was judged the surest person to take the lead; the king need give but the slightest word, and the captain of the guards would arrest Marshal Ancre. But the king's friends hesitated. What if, after Ancre's arrest, Marie played on her son's filial deference? She might wring from him the release of her favorite, and the death of the king's followers. It was therefore crucial to get their monarch to authorize some form of death sentence for the hated Concini. But what would this principled ruler allow?

Let us eavesdrop on the contest for the king's conscience, as Vitry returned to Louis XIII for last minute confirmation. With his brother and brother-in-law as witnesses to this royal command, the captain came straight to the point: "Sire, if he defends himself, what does His Majesty wish me to do?" Louis remained speechless. Luynes and his two brothers were too timid to open their mouths. Finally Déageant (or possibly Montpouillan, who was almost as close to Louis as Luynes, and certainly as fearless as Vitry, and thus doubly respected by the monarch) clinched the point: "The king intends that he be killed." Déageant's account states that the king still said nothing, while Montpouillan's version adds that, after a long royal pause, there followed this curious exchange between Vitry and Louis: Vitry, "Sire, do you so command me?"; Louis, "Yes, I so command you." In any case, the conspiratorial session ended with the captain of the guards saying, "Very well, then, Sire; I will carry out your command."[28]

What did Louis XIII intend? The overwhelming consensus of historians is that he ordered an assassination. But was that fully in keeping with the young king's complex makeup? The Louis XIII whom we have encountered thus far did not rejoice at the death of another, yet he wanted "justice" to be meted out to wrongdoers. Such a person could *allow* the execution of Concino Concini, without being able to *command* a cold-blooded murder. We are not splitting hairs here in making that distinction, but simply acknowledging the complicated way in which a fifteen-year-old king inaugurated his personal reign. In his own contorted way, Louis XIII reconciled proper respect for his mother, the urge to kill, and a principled sense of duty to allow what he felt was an act of justice for his realm.[29]

On 24 April 1617, Marshal Ancre entered the huge outer gate of the old east wing in the half-medieval, half-renaissance palace of the Louvre, while King Louis was playing billiards upstairs in the new wing. The gate closed behind the Italian adventurer in the face of most of his armed retinue. The doomed man stood trapped before a second closed gate. At first Vitry missed Ancre in the milling courtyard crowd, but he was quickly directed to his man. The captain arrested the queen mother's favorite in the name of the king, grasping his shoulder roughly. The poor devil cried out in disbelief,

"Against me?" It was the end. Vitry's relatives and friends drew their pistols, shot the favorite on the spot, and then stabbed him for good measure and kicked his slumping body aside.

Thunderous shouts of "Vive le Roy" greeted the king from the crowded courtyard. A moment earlier, Louis had bravely drawn his sword when he and a timid Luynes thought the shots signaled Ancre's triumph. Now he was hoisted to window level, shouting his thanks to his subjects. Contemporary memoirs, newsletters, pamphlets, and medallions dramatically told this story in several different versions, but they all agreed in hailing the result as an act of justice. Only a few memoir writers, reflecting later on unseemly favors acquired by the coup's originator, Luynes, censured the shedding of Concini's blood.[30]

The hastily summoned Parlement of Paris called the act such a clear expression of the king's justice that it had the force of law, and required no posthumous legal proceedings against the obviously "guilty" Ancre.[31] Royal medallions reflected that legal opinion. The medallions of 1616 had allegorized the newlywed king battling his grandees as a person wielding a sword and a balance, or fighting back with the virtues of prudence, force, temperance, and justice. After Ancre's demise, Louis became Apollo slaying a dragon, or an ancient Roman fending off the serpent with his pike. The metallic motif of a female justice on a cloud, grasping a sword and a balance, blended nicely with royal ballets featuring a strong but good Louis as David, fighting against Goliath or Python.[32] (See plate 11.)

Pamphlets, too, proclaimed the message of *David's battle with Goliath: to the Most Christian King Louis the Just.* In *The Wondrous First Blow of Louis the Just*, we run across a typical example of contemporary assertions that this was not a premeditated murder, but a just royal deliverance of the realm from a tyrant's clutches:

> In April *le vingt et quatorziesme*
> Our very great *Louis Treiziesme*
> Cast down a monster, sent him to the grave;
> A monster ruined with arrogance,
> Showered with honors from all over France,
> And never seen among the fighting brave.
>
> Louis, of Jupiter the Living Image,
> Surpassing the wisdom of his youthful age,
> Silent and prudent with care so exemplary;
> With anguish for subjects searing his soul,

> A mortal displeasure deep in his bowel,
> He bides his time to punish the haughty!

Equating justice with the recognition of virtue and the punishment of vice, the author concluded that "our Gallic Hercules" had shown his resolve never to suffer injustice again.[33]

Like the author of *The Wondrous First Blow*, Louis XIII's historiographer and others later attributed Louis's acquisition of his sobriquet "the Just" to the coup d'état of 1617.[34] That is an exaggeration, for the term had been applied to him earlier. Yet the event did cause the sobriquet to last for life as Louis's most distinguishing trademark. Today, it seems odd that such a bloodcurdling punishment of vice should have made Louis XIII's reputation as a just ruler. But to an age that had known religious wars, the assassination of kings, and a babble of tongues at the Estates General, it must have made perfectly good sense to look for a stern version of royal justice to restore the realm to the order subjects remembered from the distant past.

5

SEEKING AN EFFECTIVE
MODE OF GOVERNANCE

Moments after Concini's demise, Colonel Ornano proudly told his sovereign: "Sire, at this hour you are king, for Marshal Ancre is dead."[1] Many fifteen-year-olds would have cringed at the way this turn of events had come about and shrunk from its consequences. Louis XIII did neither. This determined youth managed immediately to arrive at a stopgap way of making decisions. Then, as he grew from adolescence to adulthood between 1617 and 1624, the king profited from sobering experiences with the grasping minion Luynes, ambitious ministers, and a manipulative mother. Through trial and error, Louis worked his way by his early twenties to what would become his unique mode of governance.

Contemporaries and later scholars viewed this governmental experimentation and its evolution with skepticism, because Louis neither took full charge himself nor seemed to delegate wisely during those seven years. Seeing no pattern in Louis's governing other than a groping for advice and a reliance on others, scholars have done little more than damn him with faint praise for completing his political apprenticeship and finally realizing his own inadequacies, thereby paving the way for an effective minister to rule for him.[2]

Even as gifted a historian as Tapié has reasoned in this vein. He alludes to the period of Luynes's favor, 1617–21, as one with "a weak ruler unable to overcome the inertia and addiction to routine of his ministers, and beside him a favorite . . . who in the eyes of the public bore the responsibility for every source of weakness." Of the succeeding period of political drift, 1621–24, Tapié says: "The most alarming thing of all was the absence of a guiding hand to direct the affairs of the realm as a whole. . . . Louis XIII was conscious of this deficiency and felt it keenly. Around him he saw only men who were mediocre, men with limited ideas."[3]

Yet before we scoff once more at the adolescent Louis XIII's mode of governance, we should examine it in the light of what rulership is in practice rather than in theory. Given the frailty of human nature in general, and the reality that few heads of state fit the ideal of brilliant, charismatic leadership, it is instructive to follow the beginnings of an uncharismatic leader's governing style, a style that later became extraordinarily effective. Let us not be blinded by the young Louis XIII's weaknesses. The mode of governance that Louis arrived at by his early twenties had the potential of greatness because it drew on the strengths in his personality and—equally significantly—took into account his weaknesses. My only regret, in sketching this argument of the adolescent Louis XIII as being something more than the tool of his minion, ministers, and mother, is that a brief chapter on governance cannot do full justice to the subject, even in conjunction with the succeeding chapters on his policies and life-style during these years. Yet it is a start in the process of fitting the king's life history together with the history of his reign.

The immediate postassassination scene at the Louvre showed that it would not be easy for the teenage ruler to control the process of governmental reorganization. Following in Ornano's footsteps, Vitry's friends rushed to the victorious king's side to give an account that not only protected them from any possible criminal guilt but also placed them in line for handsome rewards. Leaving nothing to chance, the wily conspirators reminded Louis of his order to have Concini arrested, and they embellished their report by saying that the tyrant's armed retinue and his willingness to defend himself had forced Vitry to kill him.[4]

The king was as grateful as they had hoped. Barbin's former assistant and a key figure in the assassination strategy, Guichard Déageant, gained the second spot in the new finance ministry and became a major government figure. The fearless executioner Vitry was given Concini's post as a marshal, and he and his brother, du Hallier, along with Colonel Ornano, took charge of the king's military orders in the capital. Still greater spoils of victory were given to the royal falconer as Luynes succeeded Concini as first gentleman of the king's chamber and lieutenant general of Normandy. Like Buckingham in England and Olivares in Spain, Luynes's closeness to the king in his chambers and on the hunt placed him in a strong position to become a minister-favorite.

Fortunately for Louis's independence, he and his supporters had decided in advance of the coup to recall the aging ministers who had served during his minority. The return of these seasoned councillors kept Luynes, Vitry, and others from completely dominating the inner circles of Louis's coalition government. The cautious Chancellor Brû-lart returned as head of the king's council, with his judicial functions being given to the former keeper of the seals, Guillaume du Vair, a man of strong principles who replaced the pliable Mangot. Brûlart's son, Puysieux, assisted the old man of the council, Villeroy, who replaced Luçon as secretary of state for foreign affairs. Barbin gave way to President Jeannin as superintendent of finances.

Along with these conspirators and graybeards, the king's hand can be seen at work as the government assumed the task of transferring power. Take, for example, the ruler's greetings to individuals and corporations as they came to the palace to pledge their allegiance. The Parlement's judges, who had remained loyal during the current princely revolt, were proudly told by their monarch, "Serve me well; I will be a good king for you." By contrast, the delegation of Chambre des Comptes, which included many paid clients of Concini and some friends of Barbin, was sternly told by the king that if Chambre members promised to serve him "alone," he would forgive them. Leaving nothing to chance, Louis also grilled the governor of the Bastille about his past and future "fidelity," then administered a new oath of office, saying, "Go then and do your duty at the Bastille, and answer to me alone." Finally, like the inexperienced teenager he was, the ruler greeted the venerable Villeroy on his return to the Louvre with the salutation "My father, I am king now; don't abandon me in any way."[5]

As Louis XIII deliberated on the larger issue of what to do with his mother's fallen regime, he was guided by high public expectations as well as recommendations from his entourage. In eastern France, civil war had ended abruptly with Louis's blanket amnesty, and the beleaguered dukes of Maine, Nevers, and Bouillon joined the royal forces to eat and drink with wild enthusiasm. Parisians, closer to the coup, acted out their joy in an orgy of popular justice. Not content with knowing Concini dead, a crowd bypassed the Parlement's overruling of Louis's wish to have the Italian's body strung up on a gibbet. The people stole the marshal's body from its resting place beneath the church opposite the Louvre. Crying "Here's the enemy of the king and his state," the mob displayed the body upside down, tore it apart and burned various portions, offered morsels to dogs, and hung pieces on gibbets. The Ancres' son barely escaped a "horrible carnage."[6]

This popular justice was mirrored in the official royal treatment of the fallen favorite and his widow. On being informed of Concini's death, the king is supposed to have said, "God be praised; my enemy is dead."[7] Then, in council and against the recommendation of the parlementary judges, he decided to try not just Leonora Galigaï but her dead husband as well! Considering that Louis had joined with courtiers in celebrating Concini's death and had wanted to have the body strung up, it would appear that the idea of a dual trial was Louis's own rather than the suggestion of his supporters.

The English ambassador even hinted that the king was acting with too much enthusiasm in his pursuit of royal justice. And it is tempting for a twentieth-century historian to become judgmental about what today looks more like royal vindictiveness bordering on sadism than mere punitive justice. We should resist this temptation, however; otherwise we would have to condemn an entire society for rejoicing with the king in the fall and ritual trial of a universally condemned tyrant.[8]

As the parlementary judges deliberated over the fate of Concini's widow, the king showed by his nervousness that he wanted Leonora condemned, and by staying away from Paris that he wished to distance himself from his feelings. On the day that, ten weeks after her husband's death, Galigaï was decapitated and burned at the Place de Grève, Louis's physician recorded that "people had talked to him so often and at such length that he was in continual apprehension, not being able to sleep until 3:30 A.M."[9] Ironically, the Paris crowd had come to feel sorry for the emotionally disturbed woman during her brave defense against the convenient charge of "sorcery."[10]

Louis's most difficult decision concerned his mother's fate. The facts are simple enough: immediately after Concini's death, Vitry placed the king's guards around Marie de' Medici's living quarters, and Louis refused to see her except for a formal farewell when she finally departed for a glorified exile at the royal château of Blois. The explanation is more complicated. Louis's behavior was such a departure from the norm of filial deference, and his own past practice of it, that some contemporaries could only conclude it was not the king's will. The royal historiographer Bernard pointed his accusing finger at Luynes's coterie. Marie's reaction, while multifaceted, gives us a better clue. The queen mother fumed about Louis's ungrateful behavior, and tried to blame Luynes for it. But when the Florentine ambassador cheerfully suggested that the king would have a change of heart, "she replied that she held out no hope, and that she knew only too well the king's nature." [11]

As Louis's historiographer Bernard surmised, Luynes's band undoubtedly made the decision easier for Louis by suggesting Marie would be happier in provincial Blois than in a hostile capital. But surely Louis knew on his own that there was no other way to deal with his mother. The suspicious monarch could not have believed Marie's repeated self-denying messages from the captivity of her Louvre apartment that she wanted to renounce power utterly to him. Far better to place her where he could not feel her presence, and hope she would become reconciled to being excluded from his council.

The parting of mother and son on 3 May 1617 tells us much about Louis's relations with Marie at this time. Straying from her prepared farewell speech approved by the royal council, the queen mother requested flexibility in the location of her exiled residence. Louis replied as a dutiful son that she could go where she wanted. Seeing him falter, Marie then asked her "last" request as a mother: for the freedom of the fallen minister closest to her, Claude Barbin. Misinterpreting the king's embarrassed, unclear reply as a capitulation, she then called Luynes over to ask his good offices.

Not Marie or Luynes, but Louis had the last word, calling impatiently in his choppy, repetitive speech, "Loynes, Loynes." As the queen mother rode away with her large retinue, the king stared from his wife's window until Marie's carriage crossed the Pont Neuf. This was not the last time that Marie would interpret her son's polite, evasive words incorrectly. It was a dress rehearsal for the most famous of all Louis XIII's confrontations with his mother on the Day of Dupes in 1630, when the political triangle of Louis, Marie, and Luynes would be replaced by that of Louis, Marie, and Richelieu.

Louis XIII dealt with Marie's and Concini's ministerial creatures exactly the way he wanted: according to his scale of political crimes and punishments. Mangot was the most innocuous of the triumvirs; hence, he was merely ordered peremptorily by the king's messenger to hand over the seals of his office, and was not allowed to see his monarch. In sharp contrast, Barbin was immediately jailed and his financial records seized. Ostensibly this action was to facilitate the trial against the Ancres, but it clearly reflected the king's belief that he was guilty of criminal negligence. Marie tried to intercede with Louis, first through Luçon, then at her own leave-taking with her son, and finally by letter from Blois.[12] Barbin was kept in prison for sixteen months, then banished forever from France. Neither his own later appeals to Louis, nor those of Déageant and Luçon, succeeded in restoring his reputation and confiscated assets.[13]

Luçon's fate was more complicated than that of the other triumvirs, reflecting a contest of wills between a hostile Louis XIII and a temporizing Luynes. From the king's perspective, the future cardinal-minister Richelieu had three strikes against him: his closeness to Barbin, his indebtedness to Concini for his office, and his terrifyingly bright, authoritarian manner. The monarch revealed all his adolescent distrust on seeing the bishop of Luçon try to join the other secretaries of state after Concini's fall: "So! Luçon! I've finally escaped your tyranny."[14]

Luynes immediately objected that Luçon was not all bad, pointing out the bishop's offer of loyalty before the coup. The king's favorite seems also to have suggested that the cleric's diplomatic skills and influence with the queen mother could help to keep her under control. Louis was sufficiently impressed to let Luçon act as Marie's temporary bargaining agent while she was incarcerated in the Louvre, and to let him accompany her to Blois. The bishop, however, departed soon after for his diocesan residence, probably in anticipation of royal disfavor. Explicit royal orders then sent him further away to the papal territory of Avignon.

These successive exiles undoubtedly reflected Luynes's second thoughts that Luçon was too dangerous a rival to leave with Marie. But they also bear the mark of a suspicious young Louis XIII, terrified of double manipulation by an imperious priest and an irrepressible mother. For his part, Luçon put the best face on his fall from secular grace in his memoirs, doctoring the sequence of events to suggest that the king bore him only good will.[15]

Once Louis XIII completed the transfer of power to his own governing coalition, he settled into a pattern of making decisions by formal council vote and devoting long hours and most of his energy to ruling. The meteoric rise of Charles d'Albert de Luynes to the informal position of minister-favorite, however, made contemporaries skeptical about the importance of either the council or the king in the decision-making process. To understand how Louis XIII governed from 1617 until Luynes's death of scarlet fever in 1621, we must start with that favorite's role.[16]

Louis XIII's infatuation for this forty-year-old father figure may have been sufficient cause for the falconer's quick outstripping of his rivals for the king's ear in 1617. Although Louis had promised the post of first gentleman of the chamber to his friend and fellow conspirator Montpouillan, he reversed himself and gave it to Luynes. Then Vitry, who very much wanted to become the king's right-hand man, was shunted off into political obscurity. And Louis could not seem to hold back from showering Luynes with offices, titles, and money.

Without quite realizing it, the king had soon given away more than he wanted to. He made Luynes not only a member of his council, but also a duke and peer, and constable over the entire army. In his last days, following the death of du Vair, Luynes even took on the role of sealing state documents. This power base in the central government was complemented by a powerful provincial fiefdom. In one fell swoop, Louis awarded Luynes the entire territorial base that Concini had so painstakingly accumulated in Normandy. The opportunistic provincial nobleman-turned-courtier quickly bartered his Norman holdings for a surer base as governor of Ile de France, centered in Paris. Still not content, Luynes negotiated another exchange, giving up that governorship for an even greater power cluster in Picardy, that all-important northeastern province facing Spanish troops amassed in the neighboring Spanish Netherlands. Luynes ended up holding the governorship of Picardy and its capital at Amiens, and acquiring that province's lieutenancy for his brother Cadenet. (See Appendix, map 1.)

The duke and constable of Luynes also developed a powerful clientage of family and friends, placing them strategically around the royal family and in high society. Besides being first gentleman of the chamber and royal falconer, he thrust his own confessor, Father Arnoux, into the key post of royal confessor—and in 1621 had Arnoux dismissed when that priest stopped speaking on his behalf in the royal confessional. He married the young and vibrant Marie de Montbazon of the wealthy Protestant Rohan family, then persuaded the king to make Mme de Luynes the head of Queen Anne's household. His two brothers married well, with Cadenet acquiring the titles of duke and marshal of Chaulnes, while Brantes became duke of Luxembourg-Piney and acquired lesser military and courtly posts. Even the king's younger brother, Gaston, was placed in the charge of a sequence of personal governors loyal to Luynes, first the count of Lude, and then the baron of Ornano.

Luynes was but one step removed from the sheer arrogance and bravado of a favorite-turned-autocrat like Ancre and Buckingham—both of whom paid for their brand of favoritism by being assassinated.

Instead, the Frenchman epitomized an equally common but milder minister-favorite type that suavely courted and played off rivals, and used the monarch's favor in his own interest as well as the public's. Luynes was a cross between Philip III's cautious Lerma and Philip IV's ambitious Olivares, in contemporary Spain. Handsome, charming, the author of self-deprecating letters written in a childlike hand, he had the reputation of being able to win over an enemy if they ever came face to face. Yet he was envied and criticized for combining inordinate favor with far greater political influence than Concini-Ancre had ever dreamed of.

What exactly was the extent of that political power? Public opinion, focusing on the teenage king's emotional dependence on his middle-aged favorite, leaped to the conclusion that the servitor controlled his master's government, despite his lack of political vision. The courtier-soldier-diplomat Fontenay-Mareuil wrote of Luynes: "He was intellectually mediocre, and wasn't much better suited for administration than for war; nevertheless, he governed both as long as he lived with an absolute power." Luynes's obsessively jealous rival, Luçon, could not imagine how the person he characterized as a grasping, pusillanimous mediocrity could be running the state.[17]

In truth, Luynes's role was greatest in state appointments, where his influence on the king was at times excessive. Control over patronage was closely linked to the favorite's overall political style of wheeling and dealing, rather than confronting underlying issues directly. Time and time again that style colored, and sometimes shaped, the ruler's responses to crises. Thus, when Marie de' Medici fled from Blois in 1619, we see Luynes getting Louis to bring Luçon out of political oblivion to act as a moderating influence on the queen mother; and when that tactic failed, we find him persuading Louis to bring Prince Condé out of prison into the royal council to counter Marie's ambitions. Luynes also influenced the course of council debates, thanks to his conciliar faction. Nevertheless, Louis XIII's statecraft was the product of many influences. In general, the favorite's closeness to his sovereign had to vie with the give-and-take of council debate, the crises of the day, which determined much of the council's agenda, and the king's personality.[18]

This last factor cannot be stressed too much. Louis read dispatches, held long and well-informed meetings with foreign ambassadors, and, above all, listened closely to the debates of his council. To be sure, Héroard's marginal notation about Louis just before Luynes's death, "N[ot]a his pleasure for the council," can be interpreted in two ways: either as showing the king's zeal as being exemplary or as suggesting that it was worth noting because it was so rare.[19] I cannot, however, conclude from Louis XIII's frequent lack of enthusiasm about work that he ever actually shied away from working. As in other things, Louis had progressed during his formative years from a position of giving in to his feelings to one of sacrificing them to what he thought was his—and others'—duty.

Fontenay-Mareuil, in looking back on the Luynes period, blamed Louis XIII "for letting his favorites take too much authority," but then noted that "he devoted to his affairs all the time that was necessary; so that he was often seen returning from hunting, which was his greatest diversion, if the hour set for the council arrived before he was finished." The observant courtier could not help but editorialize about his sovereign "treating the former matter as the principal one, and the latter as the accessory; wishing always, young as he was, that affairs went well."[20]

There were certainly enough contrasting views in the royal council to give Louis XIII ample opportunity to make up his own mind. The hard-line Keeper of the Seals du Vair clashed with the temporizing father-and-son combination of Chancellor Brûlart and Secretary of State for Foreign Affairs Puysieux. From 1619 on this was intensified by heated debates between Prince Condé and Marshal Lesdiguières. Fresh from a humiliating prison term, Louis's cousin was eager to show himself a fearless, loyal subject; he was spoiling for a military-religious crusade against the French Huguenots who had once been his allies. He ran headlong into the moderate Huguenot Lesdiguières, who came to court from time to time in order to plead for royal reconciliation with his fellow Protestants and for war with Spain.

Financial policy was shaped and presented to the council by a sequence of finance ministers. First came the venerable Jeannin, and then Luynes's forceful ally Déageant. He was succeeded by Henri de Schomberg, who became a close associate of Louis in the last months of Luynes's life.

The inner governing body was rounded out with a strong, but by no means preponderant, favorite's "party." At one time or another this clientage included Luynes's brother Cadenet and his cousin Modène; the ex-advisor of the queen mother turned royal agent Ruccellaï; the king's confessor, Father Arnoux; and the titular head of the council, the weak-willed Cardinal Retz.

In council, Louis usually sided with the majority. One has the impression, however, that a majority vote merely fortified his own instincts or beliefs. We will see this most dramatically in his wars against recalcitrant Huguenots from 1620 to 1622. On some crucial matters, such as his shooting war against Marie's supporters in 1620, he acted bravely and surely when his favorite leaned toward diplomatic compromise and his council was torn with misgivings. As time went on, the royal teenager grew more confident about pursuing his instincts, and when he embarked on a course of action it was all but impossible to get him to back down from the commitment of every nerve in his body. Foreign diplomats, courtiers, and government correspondents all agreed that the maturing monarch was just as stubborn on public matters as he had been willful as a child over personal whims.[21]

Even with Louis XIII's serious commitment to govern and the injection of his principles into decision making, Luynes's influence remained an embarrassment to the king as well as to his subjects. Pamphleteers patronized by Louis and Luynes did their best to argue in print that a monarch had the right to dispense favors at will. But these defenses on paper could not hold their own against popular broadsides with titles like *The Astonished Devil on the Ghost of the Marquis of Ancre and His Wife to Messieurs of Luynes* (1620), which urged the king to reward only meritorious princes, wise men, and the virtuous.[22]

Louis could have spared himself much pain by simply dismissing Luynes—and some courtiers thought that he was on the verge of doing just that when his favorite died. Yet even as the king's personal ardor cooled and he resorted to making sarcastic asides about "King Luynes," still he persisted in giving the man ever higher offices. Apparently the young ruler just could not bring himself to disgrace the man who had befriended, loved, and encouraged him to take hold of the reins of royal power.

Luynes's death finally broke the spell over the royal master, with profound repercussions for the king's governing style. Louis immediately vowed never again to let a personal favorite exercise political power, or even intervene in politics, thereby addressing his overwhelming tendency to lean on others. He kept that vow to his deathbed. That resolution, however, left the character flaw of dependence on others intact; the danger now was that the king would fill the void left by Luynes's demise by leaning on his career ministers. He understood. Indeed, in 1622 he was terrified by the thought that some minister, any minister, might gain control over him. The obvious solution was to divide his affection between a self-effacing favorite and a trustworthy minister. Yet in 1622 he could find neither!

Proud, suspicious, and bewildered, Louis divided his private favor among the courtiers Bassompierre, Esplan, and Toiras, while in the public realm he made even the pettiest decisions himself. Ministers had to report to him about everything, secretaries of state could not sign routine letters without his approval, and he sealed state documents himself. Naturally, the twenty-one-year-old quickly wearied of shouldering such responsibility. He complained for a time of his ministers badgering him at all hours, and he habitually took escapist recourse in exhausting hunting parties and equally enervating military campaigns against the Huguenots.[23]

Still, he could not run too far, for his sense of responsibility brought him quickly to heel. As he grappled between 1622 and 1624 with reconciling his personal weaknesses and the needs of his state, Louis continued his practice of making major decisions in his council and experimented with a variety of ministerial combinations to assist him in council deliberations. First he brought his mother back, although he relied most heavily on a feuding conciliar triumvirate composed of Schomberg, Condé, and Puysieux. These men checked each other so much that the king was able to steer the war against the Huguenots, and diplomatic moves against the Habsburgs, along the lines he wanted. A year later, royal dissatisfaction with conciliar bickering and the performances of Schomberg and Condé ended government by king plus three.

Within the triumvirate, Louis had leaned most of all on Schomberg. He could not help liking a man who was incorruptible and shared his own distaste for Huguenot rebellion and Habsburg aggression. Unfortunately, the superintendent's honesty was not matched by fiscal competence. Louis dismissed Schomberg with the assurance "that he would continue always to take care of him and his relations."[24] He was replaced by a courtier with excellent financial connections, Duke Charles de La Vieuville, a captain of the king's guards and grandnephew to a finance minister of Henry III and Henry IV, but also, and most crucially, son-in-law of an enormously wealthy state creditor.

Condé was treated more peremptorily than Schomberg. He had been too strident in pressing the king to fight the Huguenots to a finish, when Louis felt the Protestants were repentant enough to merit a peace treaty. Having lost the policy debate, the prince left the council angrily, with Louis's encouragement. This outburst amounted to a disgrace; nothing could persuade the king to allow Condé to return during this period.[25]

These ousters left the Brûlart family as the strongest force in the royal council during 1623. There were some appealing features to ruling with this family of multiple complementary talents. In addition to the venerable chancellor, who regained control of the seals, there was his son Puysieux, who had gradually worked his way in the foreign office to the top post as secretary of state. A kinsman, known as the Commandeur de Sillery, was well placed as French ambassador to the Pope in Rome. What could be more logical for Louis than to turn to the Brûlarts, at a time when peace with his Huguenot subjects freed him to concentrate on the growing Habsburg menace in Italy and elsewhere? Yet the new conciliar leaders lasted no longer than the triumvirate.

The Brûlarts might have withstood the intrigues of their conciliar rivals, even though they faced the combined opposition of La Vieuville and Marie de' Medici. But their behavior also alienated the king, and that proved fatal. Puysieux's inclination toward conciliation with Spain, going back to Marie's regime, made him suspect to the ruler. And Brûlart, once so efficient and honest that his dismissal by Marie and Concini had brought the king to tears, became hesitant and temporizing, thereby losing the king's good will. On 4 February 1624, Louis banished the family from court for three compelling reasons: pocketing money earmarked for foreigners who could aid the French cause against the Habsburgs in Germany, Flanders, and Italy; "hiding from me the best part of affairs passing through their hands"; and doing little to enhance royal power. Stung by Louis's message, via the royal secretary Tronçon, that his family had committed "abuse, injustice, and embezzlement," Brûlart died within the year. Puysieux lived another quarter century in ignominious exile.[26]

Louis XIII naively tried to prevent a repetition of the Brûlart experience by dividing foreign affairs among three secretaries of state and naming his own choice, the weak Etienne d'Aligre, as keeper of the seals. This merely gave Superintendent of Finances La Vieuville the opportunity to dominate in foreign and internal policy making alike. At first Louis approved, as La Vieuville suggested ways to slash the budget and began negotiations for a network of anti-Habsburg alliances. Soon, however, the new servitor became even more independent and tainted with financial scandal than the Brûlarts.

All of the ministers with whom Louis had begun his personal reign in 1617 were now dead or disgraced. Where could the twenty-two-year-old monarch find a new advisor whom he could lean on for strong advice compatible with his own beliefs yet also trust not to act behind his back? On 29 April 1624, the king succumbed to his mother's long-standing wish and appointed to his council the former bishop of Luçon, known since 1622 as Cardinal Richelieu following his elevation by the Pope to the cardinalate.

Within four months, Richelieu's whispering and pamphlet campaign against La Vieuville, plus deft maneuvering in the council, delivered the coup de grace to his tottering rival's career as, on 13 August 1624, Louis XIII's personal scale of justice found this latest leading minister wanting. The superintendent was imprisoned after being upbraided by his sovereign for "bad" service, and he was lucky to flee from France a year later. This latest act of royal justice left Richelieu and Marie de' Medici with no serious rivals in the council— except, of course, for the demanding king himself.[27]

Apart from the lack of obvious alternatives, why did Louis XIII allow himself to be faced in 1624 with the mother-and-minister combination he had so disdained in 1617? Did his submission signal a return to matriarchal and ministerial "tyranny"? Historians have tended to think so. But in view of the ruler's gradual political maturation and determination to allow no one to dominate him, this reasoning is not convincing. A more nuanced explanation seems in order.[28]

Between 1617 and 1624, Louis XIII had kept his ever-resourceful mother and her clerical servitor at bay, but at a high personal and political cost. Eventually some accommodation had to be worked out, both to ease the king's own guilt, and to use the energies of Marie and Richelieu for, rather than against, his state. We have already alluded to the stages of that triangular evolution: Marie's exile in 1617; her escape two years later, followed by Louis's decision to have the exiled Richelieu join Marie; the subsequent "Wars of the Mother and Son"; Marie's reentry to the king's council in 1622 and Louis's authorizing the Pope to make Richelieu a cardinal; and finally, in 1624, Richelieu's entry to the council, and the fall of his rival, La Vieuville. What logic did this curious series of steps follow?

From 1617 to 1619, a conscience-stricken Louis had failed to keep the queen mother content in exile. No matter how many letters and diplomatic missions he sent to Blois professing his filial devotion, she made him feel guilty for excluding her from royal decisions. The king's political marriage of his sister Christine to the heir of the duchy of Savoy, with only a perfunctory request for their mother's approval, was but the most inflammatory example. Marie's barrage of critical tracts embarrassed, shamed, and preoccupied the king so much that it is a wonder he could concentrate on anything else.[29]

Marie's dramatic escape to Angoulême on 22 February 1619, by way of a swaying ladder, magnified Louis's misery. The son now faced a mother's strident propaganda campaign, backed by her hastily assembled army of noble malcontents led by the Duke of Epernon, to "free" him from his "evil" favorite. So began the first of two campaigns dubbed the "Wars of the Mother and Son."[30]

Louis knew he did not want to fight his mother, as the hotheads in his council pressured him to do; yet he could not act as if she were blameless, as a devout court faction headed by his confessor and the papal nuncio urged. His solution, in line with the recommendation of his ministerial veterans Jeannin and Brûlart, was to advance slowly to Angoulême with an army, all the while hoping that an advance team of negotiators could avert a military clash.[31] Part of the price he paid for that compromise was in acceding to Luynes's suggestion that the bishop of Luçon be brought from Avignon into the queen mother's war council as a moderating influence. This would not be the last time the king sacrificed his personal feelings for state reasons.[32]

Once the king decided on his course of action, he had to cope with equally trying external assaults on his psyche. Despite his moderate response to maternal treason, Louis's own confessor tried to make him feel guilty. The king, Father Arnoux said in an angry sermon, "was not given the right to draw his sword against the person who had brought him into the world." Likening the royal military advance to the work of the devil, Arnoux cried out: "I beg Your Majesty, by the entrails of Jesus Christ, not to give birth to such a scandal."[33]

Louis avoided feeling guilty by focusing on his wayward mother's militant advisor, Epernon. The duke was a perfect target for the king's moral outrage, having already crossed his sovereign three times since 1617. First, during a court altercation, he had threatened to strike the keeper of the seals with his sword, in the king's presence. An incredulous Louis had exclaimed: "What? In my presence? And at the Louvre?" The second instance occurred when Epernon deserted his military post at Metz, across the border from uncertain war clouds in Germany, and the third when he went from Metz to Marie's rebel camp.

Louis wrote to Marie that he was advancing with troops to free her from the clutches of the man who was leading her "to the ruin of his people and the diminution of his authority." To the loyal Huguenot governor of Dauphiné, the monarch wrote in more explicit terms:

"I am resolved to give monsieur d'Epernon all the chastisement that he merits for an action of that nature, which I could never believe he would have the nerve to think of, let alone dare to undertake." These letters could not have been dictated by Luynes, as is generally assumed, for in the peace talks Luynes tried to convince Louis to forgive the duke.[34]

Even with his filial anger safely diverted, the king paid a heavy emotional price for his nonshooting war against a treasonous queen mother. The first night of the crisis, he slept from 8:30 until 6:00; the second, from 9:00 to 8:00; and on the third fitful night he could not unwind until 1:30 and slept until 8:30, well past his normal waking hour. Louis began to relieve his bowels at odd hours of the night. In March he became concerned about his health, waking with a start at 2:30 A.M. and asking his physician to check his body for measles. When he went to the Parlement of Paris to force the judges to register two fiscal edicts financing the mobilization of his armies, the monarch trembled so hard that his teeth rattled.[35]

Although Louis's strategy did bring his mother around to signing the Treaty of Angoulême on 30 April 1619, before a single shot was fired, his generous terms made Marie more of a problem than ever. The queen mother now had her personal freedom, a provincial governorship over Anjou, and the lust for still more power. Furthermore, by letting Luçon lead Marie's negotiating team, Louis unwittingly enabled the enterprising bishop to gain total control over the queen mother, leaving her former assistants Epernon and Ruccellaï out in the cold. Henceforth, the ruler would have to deal with Marie and Luçon in tandem! In reaping this bitter harvest, he also sacrificed to his mother's intransigence his deep personal commitment to strip Epernon and other turncoats of their royal offices.[36]

A belated reunion of the royal family and their allies at Tours in September 1619 was a sham. Concini's murderer, Vitry, courted Marie; Luynes and Luçon courted each other; and Louis looked happier than usual as his mother shed tears of joy and complimented her eighteen-year-old son on his stature.[37] But in the spring of 1620, Marie lured to her side the king's Vendôme half brothers and his cousin Soissons. So began the second War of the Mother and Son.

Chastened by the disastrous outcome of the first war, this king, with his uncanny memory, could not have forgotten his morose thoughts of two years before. In 1618, he had told his friend Bassompierre that the Valois king Charles IX's premature death stemmed from giving in to Queen Mother Catherine de' Medici.[38] In 1620, Louis

XIII was suffering from a strikingly similar reconciliation with Queen Mother Marie at Angoulême and Tours. This time he was determined to see that his mother gave in to him, rather than he to her.

After being talked out of a preventive arrest before the princes' flight, and into waiting in vain for the rebels to repent, the king sided with the hawkish conciliar minority led by Condé. Leaving the timidity of the council veterans and Luynes far behind, he said to the doubters in the capital: "You are not of my counsel; I have taken a more generous one. Be sure that even if the roads be all covered with arms I will go straight to the heart of my enemies. They have no cause to declare themselves against me, for I have offended no one."[39]

Within two weeks of the princely defections, Louis took the most immediate and dangerous rebel province, Normandy, by storm, with his small army of three thousand. (See Appendix, map 2.) At a war council deep in his half brother's territory, he replied regally to his ministerial purveyors of doom and gloom: "Perils here, perils there, perils on land, perils on sea. Let us go straight to Caen!" If the contemporary historian Matthieu can be believed, Louis added with a military flourish: "It is not good to dispute if we will go, because we have to. If those in Caen knew that we were haggling over our departure, they would close the gates."[40]

From there the king took dead aim at his mother's provincial stronghold of Anjou. While prepared to accept her capitulation through negotiation, as both hawks and doves in his council advised, Louis balked when Marie rejected unconditional surrender. Luynes pleaded with Louis to compromise; instead he led his army into battle. Luynes then advised Louis to avoid Angers and its strong defenses; he avoided it, all right, but on ethical, not military, grounds. Since Marie remained at Angers, while her army was camped at nearby Ponts-de-Cé, he could fight her forces without confronting her directly. Louis prepared the battle scene himself, stayed seventeen hours in the saddle, and carried the day. As a gesture of good will, he returned the defeated enemy's standards to his mother.[41]

The subsequent Treaty of Angers in August 1620 was founded on Marie's face-saving acknowledgment that she had taken up arms only out of fear of being oppressed by the royal government, and her humbling oath to renounce "forever" all cabals and factions. Her son acted very much like a paternal Louis the Just. Proudly declaring that "his justice and bounty were so well known that there was not a single man in his kingdom who had any grounds to complain of any oppression," the king refused to reinstate those who had deserted from his service. At long last he was heeding Secretary of State Villeroy's criticism of his blanket pardon following Concini's death: never allow princely rebels to return to favor as if they had never fought against their king.

Having made the point that he was the sovereign and his mother the subject, Louis decided to yield something for the sake of family peace. He piously declared that his mother's pleas had spared the count of St-Aignan from execution, a fate that was customarily delivered upon early modern royal commanders who took up arms against their sovereign. To sweeten the bitter taste of her defeat, Louis also promised to ask the Pope to make her advisor a cardinal. These concessions seemed to be worthwhile. One of the bitterest foes of the two wars, the papal nuncio Bentivoglio, found it appropriate to compare Louis to Henry IV in his "glory of arms," and to St. Louis in the "eminence of his piety." [42]

Still, Louis hesitated to capitalize fully on his victory at Ponts-de-Cé, as fear of his mother and her servitor continued to gnaw at him, and his own favorite played on those anxieties. The monarch kept posponing the day when Marie would be welcome at court, and he and Luynes also asked the Pope to delay making Luçon a cardinal. Then Luynes died, and in the void Louis found himself face to face with his conflicting emotions about his mother. Within six weeks he invited Marie to play the traditional role assigned to a monarch's closest relatives: she was made a member of his council. [43]

Many readers will see this act as Louis's way of getting rid of the guilt he felt over keeping his mother at arm's length—and it was that, in part. But it was also a courageous gamble that a defeated mother would be satisfied with the prestige of a council seat and cause him no more harm. Certainly, Louis remained on his guard. The new papal nuncio caught the royal mood of this time perfectly, writing that "the king is full of suspicion that [the queen mother] wishes to control him, just as she did during Concini's time." [44]

In the following months, Louis XIII followed Marie's recommendations on few issues, and fewer still that ran counter to his past views. We catch him making some personnel decisions, such as Schomberg's dismissal, in his mother's room, but always accompanied by the Brûlarts and La Vieuville. His appointment of his old nemesis and Marie's former servitor, Epernon, as governor of Guienne was on the recommendation of Marie's old enemy Condé. His dismissal of the Brûlarts pleased his mother, but it fitted his needs even more. He appointed Aligre as keeper of the seals independently of all court and council factions, and pointedly told the new minister so.[45] Marie might lapse into the fantasy that she could only increase her influence in the king's council, but Louis had already removed her once and defeated her in battle, and he could certainly overcome guilt feelings and exclude her again.[46]

The only decisions Louis made that we can identify as being on Marie's agenda and against his past wishes were the crucial ones advancing Richelieu's career. The withdrawal of the king's opposition to the bishop becoming a cardinal was a begrudging royal implementation of the Angers accord.[47] Richelieu's entry to the council, and La Vieuville's fall, were exactly what the queen mother and cardinal wanted. Yet all three acts were deliberate steps in Louis's quest for an effective mode of governance.

Whispers at court and political pamphlets of various persuasions had already exposed Louis to the obvious and painful question: if the king could not take full charge, why did he not have the sense to choose a strong and wise advisor who would help him?[48] As 1622 gave way to 1623, and 1623 to 1624, more and more attention was focused on Cardinal Richelieu as the obvious person to fill that role. He was extraordinarily bright, politically adept, and knowledgeable— so much so that, when Richelieu was about to be brought directly into the king's inner circle early in 1624, courtiers and political rivals sensed the inevitability of his rise to power. And Louis XIII seems to have been weighing the cardinal's talents even as he said, with characteristic suspiciousness, "There's a man who would dearly love to be in my council; but I can't agree to it after all he's done against me."[49]

Louis finally called Richelieu to his council in April 1624 with a mixture of fear, respect, and hope. Richelieu played his cards perfectly, avoiding the errors of the fallen ministers of the previous two years. Whether or not the king knew that his new minister was orchestrating a campaign to oust his strongest conciliar rival, the cardinal's partisan message was in tune with Louis's own values. The king pricked up his ears on hearing that La Vieuville was more arrogant and incompetent than his ousted colleagues, and that his wealthy father-in-law Beaumarchais—as state treasurer and, at the same time, loaner of massive sums to the state—was robbing the government blind. The king quickly saw that La Vieuville was not the best man to advise him.[50]

No one knew at the time that the circle of major ministerial changes was broken, still less that Louis XIII, through seven years of experimentation, had arrived at a system that could work for his particular personality. All that was clear was that the queen mother's servitor was now the only outstanding member of the king's councils, and just when the king had reached adulthood. We, of course, are privileged by hindsight. We also have before us Louis's letters from the years up to 1624, which reveal two things about the incipient Louis-Richelieu partnership. The first was the king's desire to be "a good master" and to have "good servitors." A wise minister like Richelieu could be encouraged by those premises, just as he was forewarned of the exact scale of punishments this particular master applied to "bad" advisors. The second revelation in the royal correspondence was that the king, while prone to look outside himself for political wisdom, had a very strong sense of self. His letters of that time bristle with the words *my affairs, my authority, my will,* and *my service.*[51]

Occasionally, the king's correspondence alludes to yet a third ingredient for an effective royal-ministerial relationship. This was a set of political notions held by the king, which bordered on political goals. Historians have doubted their existence; let us look next at what they were.

6

FIGHTING FOR JUST CAUSES

No one would describe Louis XIII as a great political leader with sophisticated goals and elaborate plans to achieve those goals. Throughout his personal reign he was stronger on principles than on policy, more of a reactor than an initiator. Yet as he reacted during his late teens and early twenties to the issues of the day, he took stands that amounted to state policy in embryonic form. Indeed, the three fundamental achievements that Louis and Richelieu realized together after 1624 were already anticipated by the king during the previous seven years.

In the area of internal state reform, the adolescent Louis XIII focused on disciplining his subjects more than on assisting them materially. On the subject of religious division within his realm, Louis scrupulously protected existing rights of worship, while at the same time curbing the power of the Huguenot "state within the state." Even in his response to growing Habsburg power on France's borders—the weakest aspect of royal policy during the first years of his personal reign—one can detect a toughening of Louis's stand that antedates the appearance of Richelieu.[1]

Of course, it is not enough simply to state what the pre-Richelieu Louis XIII decided. Skeptics about his independence of judgment will quite properly insist on proof that the adolescent monarch did more than go along with the recommendations of his most trusted, forceful, and articulate councillors of the moment. Fortunately, though, we know enough about what Louis said on crucial occasions to determine that he did have strong opinions of his own. On the question of internal reform and order, those opinions were so consistent during the first seven years of his personal rule that no one can doubt whose mind shaped policy. On religious division, he sorted his way through a myriad of conciliar recommendations, formulated his position quickly, and adhered to it with tenacity and conviction. Finally, on foreign affairs, we can spot distinct changes in the ruler's personal mood and aim that parallel exactly the evolution of his government's policies.

This initiative is striking in itself for a ruler who was supposedly incapable of making decisions himself. But in addition, all of the basic decisions by Louis XIII's government have a common moralistic theme, which also comes from the king. From the moment of Concini's demise to the appointment of Richelieu, Louis XIII was forever ready to fight for what he considered to be a just cause. In the law courts, he pressed his case against grandees who flaunted royal authority. At siege after siege of Huguenot towns, he struck out against those who had taken the law into their own hands. In diplomatic and military maneuvers on behalf of foreign allies and international treaties, he took a convincing stand against what he saw as Habsburg aggression. In short, the king who had inaugurated his personal reign as Louis the Just quickly made that sobriquet common coin throughout his realm.

In 1622, a moralizing Louis wrote to his mother: "The care of my person will never stand in the way of the relief that I can give to my subjects by the undoing of my enemies."[2] Of course, the adolescent Louis XIII intended "relief" to mean more than punishment of politically delinquent individuals and states. After all, he had heard the delegates to the Estates General of 1614–15 call for financial relief and economic regeneration as well as internal order. Responding to that wish, Louis summoned his own Assembly of Notables to meet in Normandy at the end of his inaugural year. But it quickly became clear that what this frugal young monarch wanted most from these delegates—and from his subjects at large—was the sacrifice of individual indulgence.

The agenda set by Louis's council for the handpicked gathering of fifty notable clerics, nobles, and judges in December 1617 stressed parsimony. Nobles were to cut back on their state pensions. Judicial and financial officials were to authorize the suspension of the paulette mechanism that had guaranteed heredity of offices. And the king was to reduce his household, council, and military personnel, not to mention conciliar intervention in the affairs of the regular law courts.

If Louis's subjects had shared his parsimonious tastes, he would have won everything he wanted from the notables. Each order, however, was jealous of its special interests. Nor did Louis help his cause by holding this reform assembly in a province held by his new minister-favorite: Luynes looked ridiculous posing as a reformist minister while amassing wealth and offices for his own clan. All that came from the royal reform program of 1617 was the abolition of some of Louis's own household and military posts, and temporary suspension of the paulette. Louis bristled as the parlementarians argued that the latter privilege was binding on the monarchy; but three years later he quietly let it be resumed in order to keep his judges focused on their role as enforcers of royal law and order.[3]

It has been aptly stated that the paulette's suspension "probably owes more to the simple assertion of Louis XIII's authority over his office-holders than any coherent political or financial policy."[4] Yet this is a good example of how, in fact, simple royal assertions *became* policy. Louis's unsuccessful diatribe against venality of judicial office had its successful parallel in an impromptu royal lecture on the buying and selling of military offices. His courtier-soldiers Vitry, La Vieuville, Vendôme, Ornano, and Montbazon discovered that the king was enunciating general policy when he suddenly told them that he would not "suffer any longer the selling of governments like houses." And he underscored his conviction by adding, "I would not be king if that happened, and I intend to be."[5] Such ad hoc moral pronouncements were quickly transformed into royal legislation that ranged from Louis's renewal of the traditional royal bans on noble dueling to new laws curbing subjects' excessive expenditures for luxury garments. Henry IV had promulgated similar laws, then ignored them. Louis began his personal reign by reenacting them, then pursued them with a vengeance.[6]

This single-mindedness was especially true with regard to dueling and similar acts of noble defiance against royal authority. To be sure, Louis scrupulously applied justice on behalf of subjects as well as against them. One of his first acts after his coup d'état in 1617 was to release all political prisoners except Condé—and to Condé he allowed fresh air and visitation rights (in his cell) with the princess of Condé. But subjects were far more impressed by the king's simultaneous punitive acts. As one dead dueler was being strung up by his feet, his opponent ran to save his life. Some observers attributed such acts to Luynes, but the most spectacular case of crime busting proves that these actions were merely Louis's way of reforming his state.[7]

The story of the lawless baron of Guémadeuc is interesting because it reveals a Louis XIII who held firmly to his principles and ignored appeals by his half brother César de Vendôme, Ancre's assassin Vitry, and the baron's swooning wife. The Breton noble first got into trouble when he killed a fellow nobleman over a question of ceremonial ranking at the Provincial Estates of Brittany—a typical early-modern jockeying for social position. Louis's immediate reaction was to send his own guards into a key fortress commanded by the baron. The hapless Guémadeuc then mortally offended the king by seizing the place from the royal guards.

In his mind Louis flashed back to a similar defiance of royal justice in 1611, when the noble patron of a salt-tax smuggling ring had arrested a royal tax collector for imprisoning his band. On that earlier occasion, the ten-year-old boy king had used the incident to challenge his preceptor's lesson that kings should always pardon their subjects. Young Louis had snapped back, "And Monsieur de Vatan?" and then whispered in his governor Souvré's ear: "The queen my mother says that if he is pardoned, there will be many others eager to do the same thing."[8] Now, in mid 1617, with neither parent nor preceptor around to influence him, Louis XIII said of Guémadeuc, "There's another Vatan."

Feeling comfortable about the political and moral issues, but fearful of the outcome, Louis remained tight-lipped as the hard-line du Vair and the temporizing Brûlart argued in council debate. Then the king ordered Vitry to seize Guémadeuc, and held Vendôme personally responsible, in his capacity as governor of Brittany, for facilitating the arrest. To Vendôme's lieutenant general, the ruler wrote: "I am so offended by [Guémadeuc's] slighting of my authority that I won't leave a stone unturned nor spare my own person in order to settle matters quickly by regaining possession of the place and properly punishing the one who has acted so brazenly." When the judges specially commissioned by Louis voted the death penalty, not even the widow-to-be's appeal swayed him. To her cries of mercy, he replied simply, "I owe justice to my subjects and in this instance I must prefer justice to mercy."[9]

The Guémadeuc case of 1617 reveals a Louis XIII making up his own mind, and keeping up his guard against the temptation to be merciful. He abruptly canceled an appearance at a lavish dinner at the

Vendômes to avoid an emotional plea, yet came down with colic anyway. With Vitry and Luynes still locked in a duel of their own for command of the king's heart, he had no overpowering emotional crutch to lean on in his hour of need.[10]

It is instructive to look at Louis's personal attitude toward dueling at two other times, one near the end of Luynes's years as minister-favorite and the other just before Richelieu's influence began to be felt. In 1621, Louis prevented a duel between Cardinal Guise and the duke of Nevers, in the process upholding state order against the rival interests of church and nobility. In 1624, he enunciated his position on dueling—which Richelieu would later find a practical way of implementing.

In the Guise-Nevers altercation, Louis came down hardest on the cardinal. The high cleric was promptly consigned to the Bastille for inciting a duel by insulting the duke. Then Louis curtly rejected the papal nuncio's demand that the king undergo absolution for the "sin" of imprisoning a man of God. Nevers's punishment, for the lesser crime of wanting to defend his honor with the sword, was an indefinite banishment to his estates. The entire matter was finally laid to rest when the cardinal died during the royal siege of a Huguenot town. Seizing the chance to be Louis the Just *and* Pious, the French monarch quickly informed Nevers that God had ended the duke's quarrel in his own way, asked him to rejoin the court, and assured him of royal protection against any further affronts to his honor and reputation.[11]

Undoubtedly Luynes brought his own brand of diplomatic compromise into this royal resolution of the courtly flare-up, for the king and his friend spent anxious midnight hours together while Guise was being apprehended.[12] Yet the overall royal solution reflected the monarch's own instinctive view of the intertwined world of royal, noble, and clerical values. This is clear from a letter written by Louis XIII to Constable of France Lesdiguières in 1624. After thanking the highest-ranking military personage in his state for enforcing yet another royal edict against duels, the king penned this conclusion: "And since it is important for the good of my service that it be inviolably observed, the first who disobey must serve as an example."[13]

By comparison with the adolescent Louis's stoically simple view of state reform, his approach to religious division was puzzling in its paradoxes. The French ruler was keen on persuading his Huguenot subjects to turn from religious "error" to the "true" faith. Yet his scruples about maintaining the rights of French Protestants, as laid down by the Edict of Nantes, prevented him from wanting forced conversions. Although he continued his childhood affection for individual Huguenots, he now followed common Catholic practice in referring to the minority religion condescendingly as *la religion prétendue réformée*. His desire to purge the royal court and army of blasphemous language and bawdy humor brought him close to hairshirt asceticism. Yet worldly materialism found its way into his counterreformatory zeal for expanding the property and other resources of the Catholic church at the expense of Huguenot temples.[14]

In trying to do justice to all these personal impulses, Louis XIII got France into a decade of religious strife. Strictly speaking, his virtually annual military campaigns from 1620 to 1629 against the Huguenot towns and armies of the eastern seaboard and southern mountains were not wars of religion, for the king's aim was simply to make his Huguenot subjects respect royal authority and Catholics' rights in the Protestant areas of the realm. By employing violence against the Huguenot "state within the state," however, he stripped peaceful and rebel Huguenots alike of their only sure line of defense on behalf of their religion.

At the commencement of his personal rule, Louis XIII announced that the Huguenot territory of Béarn, in his ancestral ministate of Navarre immediately southwest of France, would have to permit Catholic worship. This typical act of benevolent justice by Louis thus upheld the rights of Béarnais Catholics against the policy of exclusive Protestant worship laid down by his own grandmother, Queen Jeanne d'Albret of Navarre.[15]

Equally typical was Louis's spur-of-the-moment decision three years later to enforce his tolerationist decree on the Béarnais. Prior to that time, Louis had been preoccupied with more pressing challenges to state order. His top priority had been his mother's rebelliousness, and the Wars of the Mother and Son that had followed in 1619 and 1620. He had also been too busy keeping the peace between Catholics and Protestants in France proper to think of Béarn; his strategy had been to investigate every act of Catholic persecution alleged by the French Huguenots at their annual national assemblies of 1618, 1619, and 1620. Then his defeat of Marie de' Medici's army at Ponts-de-Cé in mid 1620 gave Louis the perfect opportunity to pursue justice in Béarn. He had an army, he was within marching distance of the Béarnais, and their officials were not enforcing his edict of restitution.

As during his Norman campaign, Louis refused to listen to timid councillors who talked of bad roads, worsening weather, the distance from his capital, and the deeply entrenched Béarnais Huguenots. Nor did he pay attention to the tears of his wife, or the hesitations of his favorite. He headed for the Pyrenees, exclaiming, as only this morally obsessed ruler could, "For three years I have put up with this contempt [by the Béarnais of his edict]. But I see that my presence is needed in Béarn, and I will set out to assure the repose of the province."[16]

The omnipresent Catholic dévots in Louis's camp thought they were seeing the reincarnation of a medieval crusading king. But their monarch was not St. Louis fighting a holy war against an "infidel" people, but Louis the Just, fighting for the religious rights of all subjects. To be sure, Louis XIII turned Louis IX's feast day into an annual religious celebration, made "St. Louis" the password for entry past his guards during dangerous times, and absorbed himself in a biography of that royal ancestor for a full half hour—a rare reading "spree" for a monarch who hated reading. He was more intensely religious than his father, who had been tossed to and fro by Catholic and Huguenot entourages before settling on Catholicism, first out of necessity, and eventually out of conviction. He was like his mother in adhering scrupulously to religious forms, yet more moved than she by edifying sermons. Indeed, both parents would have been taken aback by their eighteen-year-old son piously telling the worldly Prince Condé, "I don't ever want to hear people saying filthy or nasty things."[17] So we find Louis with as strong a dislike of the ungodly as of libertines.[18] Nevertheless, he balked when his confessor, Father Arnoux, tried to take Cardinal La Rochefoucauld's equation of intellectual libertinage with sexual license one stage further and call for a royal crusade against Huguenot heresy.

The religious lobby that Louis XIII diverted on behalf of the just cause *he* felt comfortable fighting was formidable. His grand almoner, La Rochefoucauld, the head of his council, Cardinal Retz, the papal nuncio Bentivoglio, possibly Secretary of State Puysieux, and future associates of Richelieu like the famous "Gray Eminence," Father Joseph, all fell short of bending the king's will to their zealotry. Nor did Father Arnoux succeed in influencing Louis, despite his capacity as confessor to both the king and Luynes. Arnoux's sermons in the king's chapel against heresy were wasted words. In vain, that confessor got Luynes to swear before God that he would take the monarch on a holy war, in thanksgiving for the king's favor. Yet Louis was simply not interested in fighting heresy with the sword. Only when Luynes spoke of the Huguenots being a menace to royal authority, or

Condé urged a military solution to the challenge of their state within the state, did Louis listen.[19]

As the king swept through southwestern France on his way to Béarn in 1620, he paid as much attention to cowing his mother's recently defeated Catholic supporters as to ensuring the loyalty of local Protestant governors. (See Appendix, map 2.) Thus the proud and staunchly Catholic governor of Guienne, Epernon, humbly went down on his knees before his sovereign lord. When the ex-rebel governor of Normandy, Longueville, greeted his monarch with the honeyed words "Sire, I see Your Majesty has grown a lot," the king retorted, "And I, my cousin, see that you have shrunk a lot!" At the same time, Louis upbraided the Huguenot town mayor and pastors of St-Jean-d'Angély for holding services during his entry to the town, and awarded the government of the key western port of Blaye to Luynes's brother, Brantes. Yet in other cases he simply replaced disloyal Huguenot governors with their royalist coreligionists.[20]

Louis did not intimidate his Béarnais Huguenots so quickly. As he came ever closer to his ancestral kingdom of Navarre, the local parlement at Pau was still debating his decree of 1617 to restore Catholic worship and church property. Louis also had to reckon with the wily Navarrese governor. The king obviously liked the duke of La Force, and doted on his son, Montpouillan; when the family had lost out to Luynes's influence at court, they had been granted power in Navarre. Now they were balancing loyalty and affection for Louis with the contrary interests of their Béarnais fellow Protestants. Characteristically, Luynes secretly bargained with La Force for token parlementary compliance. Equally characteristically, Louis XIII grew impatient with the governor's balancing act and the judges' procrastination.

On 9 October, Louis learned that the Pau judges had rejected his edict outright. Caught deep in southwestern France, with news of caballing in the capital on behalf of his mother and his cousin Soissons, and even more disturbing news of English and Spanish activities on the northeastern frontier, Louis did not hesitate for a moment. He told a delegation from Pau that although he normally did nothing without a council meeting, he had decided himself to complete the trip in order to force obedience. Despite an eleventh-hour parlementary capitulation, Louis told the anxious governor and a judicial envoy, "It is in your interest that I go, to firm up your weakness."[21]

On 14 October, the king entered Pau without ceremony, made a lightning, unexpected trip to Béarn's only fortified town, Navarreins, where he pensioned off the commander and replaced him with a loyal

Catholic, then returned to Pau for the formal imposition of his will. Béarn and the rest of the kingdom of Navarre were incorporated into the French state, and property was restored to the local Catholic authorities.

At the first Catholic service in fifty years, Father Arnoux gave the sermon, and the king proudly exclaimed, "Ah! How Cardinal La Rochefoucauld will be pleased! He strongly urged me to do all this." As their triumphant monarch returned to Paris at the end of 1620, contemporary writers were awestruck that within a period of four months he had subdued territories ranging from pro-Marie Normandy in the extreme north to Huguenot Béarn at the southwestern border, subdued his mother, humiliated great noble subjects, and crushed a quasi-independent Protestant state.[22]

Louis XIII's 1620 campaign against Protestant Béarn did not in itself trigger his campaigns of 1621 and 1622 against the Huguenots of France proper. Indeed, the king spent the winter and spring of 1620–21 trying to combine punitive and benevolent justice in the cause of religious peace. His council ordered the summary execution of some inhabitants of Tours for rioting and burning a temple to the ground; and he issued a royal declaration guaranteeing security for loyal Huguenot subjects.

Given more time, prompt acts like these might have controlled the endemic religious strife. Provincial French Protestants, however, were too jittery from Catholic assaults and the recent experience of their coreligionists in Béarn to let the king's justice take effect. Their national assembly of 1621, at the great Protestant seaport of La Rochelle, was an exceptionally belligerent gathering. Its delegates made a serious error in remaining assembled after Louis angrily refused to listen to their remonstrances and ordered the meeting to end. In the summer of 1621, the Huguenot assembly defiantly divided Protestant France into eight military circles under the greatest Huguenot nobles of the realm, raised troops with local public funds, and even threatened to block the Loire river at Saumur should their monarch march down the western coastline toward La Rochelle.

Louis XIII felt he had no choice but to take up the sword again. If the Huguenot nobility and townsfolk were turning their part of his kingdom into an armed camp, he would have to destroy their military power. Hence, in the summers of 1621 and 1622 the king himself led his army into the heart of Protestant France, past Poitou, Saintonge, and Guienne into the southern mountains of Languedoc. (See Appendix, map 3.) There was no complicated military strategy. Any Protestant walled town in his path was asked to surrender; if it refused, the town was taken by siege.

To be sure, Louis was not above using bribery to get town governors and local Huguenot army commanders to capitulate. But whereas Luynes was happy to hand out financial rewards to docile Protestant nobles, Louis declared that "one should reward nobility with honors, not money." The king was also not above trickery. Witness the Huguenot governor Duplessis-Mornay of Poitiers refusing to be won over with a marshal's baton, then "temporarily" surrendering his governorship only to see the post given permanently to the grandson of the royalist Huguenot Lesdiguières. Yet Louis respected the right of his Huguenot subjects to resist converting in exchange for special honors. When Lesdiguières refused Louis's initial offer in 1621 to make him constable over the entire army because the prerequisite was to convert, the king still gave him the rare title of field marshal general. The following year the proud Protestant decided he wanted to be constable and converted.[23]

Louis XIII's carefully balanced letter to his new marshal general in 1621 tells us more than anything else about royal motivations on the campaign trail. On the one hand, Louis pledged his protection of heretical, but loyal, subjects:

> I leave you in freedom, knowing that nothing should be freer than one's conscience, which God knows how to move when he wishes. It is also in His holy care that I leave the secret of your [religious] vocation and that of each and all of my subjects of the *religion prétendue* [*réformée*]. I will not allow any of them to be oppressed or harmed for their faith.

On the other hand, the ruler made his stand against rebel heretics equally clear: "It is true that if any use the mask of religion to undertake acts illicit or contrary to my edicts, I will know how to sort out the truth from the pretexts, punishing the latter and protecting those who remain in their duty." In the letter's conclusion, Louis came as close as he could to expressing his feelings about the personal bonds that cemented the hierarchical society of orders in the monarchical state—leaving no doubt that these views belonged to Louis XIII, and were not dictated by other persons. The ruler said that he was sure the new marshal general would give his "blood and life in the execution of a justice so necessary for the repose of the state. I give you my word that wherever disobedience and rebellion of any [subjects] force me to take up arms, you will have the principal command and the most honorable charges."[24]

The armor of these convictions stood the soldier-king in good stead during the summer heat and autumn rains of 1621. He was relaxed, focused, and almost happy. He showed off his technical military skill during a visit by his wife and mother, riding from eight in the morning until midnight as he situated cannon, tents, hospitals, and a chapel. He insisted on staying with his troops even as cannonballs felled soldiers at his side. Later he would admonish his entourage not to flee at the first enemy volley, saying that reloading the rebel cannon would take some time! He was forever conscious of the social status, military rank, and individual names of all his officers. He refused to let soldiers engage in the "ignoble" work of digging trenches, unless they accepted bonus pay. And when doctors' orders confined him to quarters because of the infected air caused by rotting animal carcasses, he insisted on being briefed at dawn, noon, mid-afternoon, and late at night. Finally, he turned his sieges and army camps into a model of religious discipline. He had public prayers offered up for success, punished soldiers for tempting God by taking his name in vain, and touched fourteen hundred subjects on Assumption Day in the searing heat without a canopy.[25]

And how did Louis XIII treat the other side? Towns handing over their keys and denouncing "republicanism" got off with a royal lecture to obey their sovereign better in future. Towns that resisted received a penalty measured to fit the crime. At St-Jean-d'Angély, where Louis had lectured Huguenots on respect for the monarchy in 1620, he spared the inhabitants and their noble leader Soubise; but he had the town walls torn down and made the townspeople swear never again to take up arms against their sovereign. When he reached Bergerac, the king celebrated the destruction of the town's walls by enunciating a royal policy later associated with Richelieu. In stern Louis XIII language, the ruler declared that "he wished to allow no fortified places at all except on the frontiers of his kingdom, so that his subjects' courage and fidelity would act as citadels and guardians of his person."[26]

The pattern established at St-Jean and Bergerac was repeated all down the west coast and into the southwestern mountains. But this unimaginative strategy bogged down in individual sieges that were costly, time-consuming, and frustrating for the impatient young king. In mid summer, before the gates of Clérac, Louis began to wonder whether harsher justice might not end the interminable series of individual sieges. From his war council came murmuring that if he did not start acting with greater severity he would become known as Louis *le Debonnaire* instead of Louis *le Juste*. And from the defiant Protestants at Clérac came the taunt in local dialect that Louis the Just should be renamed "Louiset Cassayre" (Louis the Hunter) because of his weakness for the chase.

Louis almost took the bait, exclaiming, "They have good reason to call me hunter, for I have indeed resolved not to leave the hunt I have begun against these savage and disobedient beasts until I have humbled and tamed them, and torn down their hedges and filled in their ditches and dens." Nevertheless, after storming the town with severe losses on both sides, Louis was mollified by one of the most emotional appeals of his military career. The town pastor pleaded with him "to acquire the title of Merciful along with the one he already had of Just" so that—unlike the people of Israel, who had lamented, "We have seen God and we die"—the Cléracians might say they had seen the "guardian God of this world" and lived.

In the end there were four hangings: a lawyer-father and minister-son, a consul from St-Jean who had broken his oath not to rebel again, and a shoemaker–turned–sergeant major. A doctor was given a royal reprieve when the noose was around his neck. Scrupulously fair, the king arranged for four livres of ransom to be paid to his soldiers in lieu of pillaging, with the royal treasury to be reimbursed by the town coffers. Thus Louis kept his promise not to harm the town's persons or goods.[27]

The long and unsuccessful royal siege of Montauban in the fall of 1621 proved that the siege-after-siege strategy would not bring about the collapse of Protestant France, long before Richelieu came on board to suggest alternatives. Both Louis and Luynes were to blame for the Montauban fiasco, in shunning advice to avoid that impregnable symbol of southern Huguenot independence. Towering over the Languedocian plain, led by the fiery oratory of Soubise's brother, the duke of Rohan, and defended by massive walls, towers, bastions, and a forbidding moat, this city of some twenty thousand souls defied an army on paper of thirty thousand which during the seige shrank to twelve thousand.

August, September, and October passed. Sixteen thousand cannon balls were fired at the city; returning volleys, exploding powder supplies, and raging scarlet fever carried away thousands of royal soldiers—sometimes two hundred at a single sortie. The dead included Keeper of the Seals du Vair, a secretary of state, the royal historiographer Matthieu, the duke of Maine, an archbishop, and two bishops. On 10 November, a tearful Louis gave up the siege, saying "he was in despair from experiencing this displeasure."[28]

As Luynes lay dying of scarlet fever, Louis took out his frustrations in the sacking of nearby Monheur on 13 December 1621. His personal justification was that the townsfolk had allowed neighboring soldiers to murder their Huguenot governor, just when the man was on the point of turning Catholic and royalist. With that in mind, he removed the garrison, women, and children, then in a fit of pique burned the town beyond recognition. Leveled Monheur, like defiant Montauban, was a telling symbol of royal failure.[29]

A winter respite back at Paris gave Louis the chance to rethink his military strategy—and the long campaign of 1622 showed evidence that he had listened to strategists of some intelligence. His campaign trail that year took him much farther, and he selected his sieges more carefully. He also came close, at the end, to turning his brand of justice into pure tit-for-tat revenge. Fortunately for his reputation, his subjects' lives, and the peace of his realm, he pulled back from the moral precipice in time to achieve a moderately successful general peace treaty with Huguenot France.

A brief look at the military campaign of 1622 will show us how Louis the Just measured up to his sobriquet under the strain of civil war. Accompanied by his mother and his cousin Condé, but not his expectant wife (whose pregnancy and miscarriage are part of the story to come), Louis set a dizzying pace. Before the campaign ended and the royal party returned to Paris in 1623, the king had gone westward to Nantes, waded through waters up to his belt at Rié, bypassed La Rochelle, seized Royan above Bordeaux, assaulted the interior of Languedoc, and reached the Mediterranean at Marseille.

At the Isle of Rié, Louis XIII braved the tide as it came in, placing himself in a position where he could either conquer or die, for to retreat would have meant drowning. Soubise fled to La Rochelle with four hundred men, leaving fifteen hundred dead and five to six hundred captured. When the king entered the southern mountains, he wisely avoided the graveyard of Montauban, drew a local map from his memory of the previous campaign, and then let his army wreak total vengeance on the neighboring small community of Nègrepelisse.

Taking smaller places as he made his way down the south-central mountain ranges, and demolishing or half dismantling fortifications, the king gained the defections of some of the greatest Huguenot military commanders, including Châtillon, grandson of the leading Protestant of the sixteenth-century Wars of Religion, Admiral Coligny. La Force handed over Ste-Foy in Guienne, in return for a marshal's baton. And once again, royal policy on fortifications was made clear: to the Norman inhabitants of Rouen, jittery over a fort at Quillebeuf that threatened shipping on the Seine River, Louis wrote of his design "to raze not only the fortification of Quillebeuf, but also those in all places in the kingdom's interior, sparing only those in frontier places."[30]

We cannot leave 1622 without dwelling momentarily on the sieges where Louis's military justice was at its best and worst. At Rié, Louis the Just showed his magnanimous side by heeding Schomberg and Vendôme, thus overriding Condé's argument that all the men at St-Jean who had broken their oath not to fight again deserved death. Reflecting the inegalitarian principles of his time, the monarch ransomed all the noble captives but hanged 13 commoners and sent 575 others to the horror chamber of Mediterranean galley service. The scene at Nègrepelisse was quite different, reflecting the king's position that greater punishment was warranted for a town that had killed royal troops in cold blood the year before. Defending soldiers and civilian men, women, and children alike were killed indiscriminately. The invading troops could hardly move through the carnage of bodies and blood.

Louis's official policy at Nègrepelisse lay somewhere between Cardinal Retz's plea for clemency and Condé's argument for severity, which was based on the biblical story of King Saul and his punishment for rejecting God's commandment to exterminate the evil Amalechites. Bedridden by a debilitating cough that kept him from the siege, the sovereign lord of France decided that the severe law of Moses had been superseded by Christ's grace. According to Bernard, the king exclaimed "that justice had to be exercised against such a self-willed rebellion, but it must be done through proper forms and against few persons, especially those who would be found most guilty." This explains why a few persons who had fought in 1621 were hanged *after* the assault on the town.

The fact remains, however, that Louis's justice triggered a massacre *during* the assault. He had made the horrible mistake of telling his soldiers they could sack the town, provided they not set fires or harm the women. Did Louis the Just really believe that his men would make those distinctions in the heat of battle? After the massacre, he either concealed his remorse or felt none when he wrote his mother that he had "exercised a little justice necessary for repressing the insolent temerity of these mutineers." He added darkly about rebels remaining in his path: "several who have not been brought around by my clemency will fall in line out of fear of a similar chastisement."[31]

Partisan royalist pamphleteers and the king's historiographer did what they could to make royal justice at Nègrepelisse look more virtuous than it was—but they wrote with a guilty conscience. Bernard stressed the king's official orders; pamphleteers extolled the glories of punishment. In contrast to the *True Portrait of Louis the Just* and *Panegyric of the Monarch* of 1618, which had proudly proclaimed the king's release of Condé as balancing punitive with benevolent justice, the *Laurel Wreaths of Louis the Just* and other tracts of 1621–22 had Louis XIII bestowing "glory" on subjects by forcing fidelity with the sword.[32]

The savage application of justice at Nègrepelisse took place in June. By October, Louis XIII's thoughts turned to mercy. To be sure, he was enticed by the Huguenot generalissimo Rohan's willingness to sign a compromise peace treaty encompassing all Protestant towns. He was also prompted by the urging of Constable Lesdiguières and Secretary Puysieux that he turn his attention to Habsburg aggression abroad. But there were also signs that Louis the Just was regaining his balance in deciding what justice to his subjects actually entailed. He bristled at Condé's insistence on a fight to the death. He began to pay attention to the moderate views of a rising conciliar specialist on diplomacy, justice, and finance, Claude Bullion. And he had indelibly fixed in his mind the elder statesman Jeannin's admonition of the previous year: royal victories were ruining his realm and killing his subjects.[33]

The Peace of Montpellier, in October 1622, brought all the terms Louis XIII had imposed on individual towns over the last two years into a comprehensive treaty. The French Huguenots retained their celebrated fortifications at Montpellier and La Rochelle, as well as the partially fortified towns of the eastern Cévennes Mountains near the Rhône River. But they had lost eighty "places of surety," and they agreed not to hold a national Huguenot assembly without royal approval. The king could be well satisfied with the progress he had made toward being fully king of his kingdom.[34]

Foreign affairs were another matter. Between 1617 and 1624 peace collapsed in several regions of Europe, leading to spectacular victories by the Austrian and Spanish Habsburgs. Yet Louis XIII was slow to respond, and even made some initial blunders that advanced the Habsburg cause. Why did he so act? Historians blame his behavior on lack of vision within his government—but that judgment comes from historical hindsight and modern assumptions of secular state interest, not the tangled web of conflicting urges that faced Louis XIII.[35]

While historians have assumed that Louis ought to have known that Habsburg victories posed the greatest threat to his state, he was in fact preoccupied by the more immediate danger he saw in his own mother and some of his Huguenot subjects. And when he did turn his thoughts more seriously to developments abroad, many subjects sharply criticized him for abandoning the twin causes of crown and church. He was, moreover, on treacherous foreign terrain that could not have been readily mastered by even the most experienced and clairvoyant of his subjects, including Richelieu.

Everywhere Louis XIII and his ministers turned, from central Europe northward to the Low Countries and south to the Swiss and Italian Alps, the Pax Hispanica that Marie de' Medici had enjoyed during her son's minority was disintegrating; and everywhere as well, both sides could argue a moral claim to French support. On the one side stood Henry IV's Protestant allies: the Dutch Republic, Elector Frederick of the Rhenish and Upper Palatinates in Germany, and the Grisons or Gray Leagues in the Alps. Could Louis abandon these old friends to a Habsburg absolutism that was bent on destroying their autonomy and tightening the circle of Habsburg territories surrounding France? Yet on the other side, the Spanish and Austrian Habsburgs could claim that they were fighting the same cause that Louis XIII was against his Béarnais and French Huguenots. Should he not strike a blow for monarchy and Catholicism abroad as well as at home?[36]

Since knowledgeable subjects were bewildered by the issues and fast-moving events, what could one expect of a young, inexperienced king, especially one who acted decisively only when he was sure he had a just cause to fight for? Under the circumstances, a certain amount of initial hesitation and experimentation was to be expected. Rather than be apalled at the fumbling of Louis XIII's government, we should be amazed that between the outbreak of the Thirty Years' War in 1618 and the entry of Richelieu to his councils in 1624, the king found his way through the maze of foreign policy traps and ministerial confusion to an embryonic policy that combined practicality and principle. Is it not ironic that an inexperienced young king, guided mainly by his sense of rectitude, reached that far?[37] (See Appendix, map 4.)

Louis was understandably puzzled by the first phase of the Thirty Years' War. A fellow Catholic ruler, Ferdinand of Habsburg, faced a revolt by his Protestant subjects in Bohemia and Hungary at exactly the same time that he was being elected Holy Roman Emperor of the German Nation. The French king had to decide. Should he support Ferdinand II's appeal for French military aid? Or would it be better to weaken the Bourbons' rival dynasty by siding with the Bohemian rebels and their German Calvinist ally, Elector Frederick, whom they had just elected king after deposing Ferdinand?

In the court-and-council debates of December 1619, Puysieux, Jeannin, Schomberg, and a later aide to Richelieu, Father Joseph, told Louis XIII that he should not aid the emperor but should instead offer to mediate a compromise settlement. The king of France seemed to go along with this cautious approach, for he cut short his wife's lobbying for her Habsburg relatives with the curt remark, "Madame, be satisfied with being Queen of France."[38] But obviously Louis's trait of wanting to do something on behalf of a good cause was gnawing inside. At the urging of his confessor in a Christmas Eve sermon, the king decided impulsively to send troops to the beleaguered Catholic Habsburg ruler in Vienna.[39]

Louis soon realized the folly of his moral impulse: by aiding the emperor's religious mission he would also be increasing that rival ruler's secular power. Yet he met with even greater disaster abroad in 1620 by falling back on his ministers' cautious mediation scheme. En route to Vienna, the French plenipotentiaries panicked at the sight of the rival Catholic and Protestant armies of the German principalities approaching Ulm. Quickly negotiating the Truce of Ulm, Louis's agents thought they were averting a double disaster in the Holy Roman Empire with a single stroke of the pen. As the French saw it, the Evangelical Union and Catholic League forces would leave each other alone, thereby preventing the Bohemian war from spreading to the German Empire; and Louis XIII, assured of a trouble-free eastern frontier, could employ his arms against his rebel mother and the Huguenots. The Ulm pact did, in fact, allow Louis to concentrate temporarily on domestic troubles. But, to the consternation of the French government, it also had the bizarre effect of destroying opposition to the Habsburgs in Bohemia and key parts of Germany.

Thanks to the German truce, Catholic League troops were free to march down the Danube to White Mountain, near Prague. On 8 November 1620, they joined Ferdinand's forces in crushing the armies of the Bohemian rebels, their Hungarian allies, and the elector Palatine. Emperor Ferdinand then imposed Austrian absolutism on Bohemia;

and in Germany, the duke of Bavaria occupied Elector Frederick's Upper Palatinate lands with his Catholic League forces.

Meanwhile, the Evangelical Union army rushed from Ulm in the opposite direction to save the Rhineland Palatinate, only to find Spanish troops from the Low Countries already in control. By playing the role of an impartial judge, Louis XIII had unwittingly destroyed his father's great Palatine ally in Germany. To cap the disaster, Habsburg Spain recalled most of its army from the Rhineland in time to use it against Henry's old Dutch allies in 1621, when the Spanish-Dutch Eleven Years' Truce expired.[40]

Disasters can have good side effects if the recipient is willing to learn from the experience. Louis XIII was observant enough to profit from two lessons implicit in the Bohemian-Palatinate debacle of 1618–20. First, he learned to balance pro-Catholic "reason of religion" arguments with pro-French "reason of state" ones in foreign affairs, making him a bon Français rather than a dévot.[41] Second, he sensed that he must be partisan rather than neutral in his pursuit of "reason of state." For a monarch as wedded to morality and justice as Louis XIII, this was hard, but far from impossible.

Thus began a quarter-century pursuit of foreign policy ventures that involved a degree of aggression but that Louis the Just could label defensive and fair.[42] The moralistic bon Français in Louis XIII did not of course emerge without preparation. We need only recall Louis's childhood diatribes against Leaguers, Jesuits, and Spaniards. There were also telltale signs of a spontaneous bon Français morality at the outset of Louis's personal rule. The occasion was a flare-up of hostilities between Savoy and Spain, during which the young French king sided verbally with France's old Savoyard ally, whom Marie had left to fend for itself against the Habsburgs.

On this occasion, Louis's morality was called into question when the Spanish ambassador insinuated that his entourage was manipulating him into an immorally aggressive stand. The king retorted that he was his own man and that he sincerely wanted a Savoyard-Spanish peace, but that if forced by Spain into war he would oblige:

> I would be very pleased for [the king of Spain] to know that my affairs are not in as sorry a state as he imagines. But even if everything should be undone in my absence, nothing will stop my going over the mountains and forcing the king, your master, to keep the word he has given me, and on which the duke of Savoy has relied out of consideration for me.[43]

In 1619, Louis forged a stronger link with Savoy by marrying his sister Christine to the duke's heir; he also put his garrison at Metz on alert against the threat of the Thirty Years' War coming too close to France. Then, in the winter of 1621–22, we find him racing at breakneck speed from Béarn to the opposite corner of his realm at Calais on the English Channel to guard against rumored invasions by England and Spain. At the same time, he used personal diplomacy to try to prevent the resumption of the Spanish-Dutch war and to plead for English military assistance to the Palatinate. This madcap personal diplomacy in the northeast was a dress rehearsal for Louis's repeated forays into the realm's frontiers and beyond during the next two decades.[44]

Madcap adventures and impromptu statements were one thing; consistent application of a moralistic bon Français position was another. No historians, to my knowledge, have believed that the pre-Richelieu Louis XIII achieved any such consistency. I believe that they are wrong, and that the crisis Louis faced over use of the Val Tellina Alpine passes from 1620 on provides the evidence.[45]

In mid 1620, while Louis XIII was campaigning against Huguenots and permitting the disastrous Treaty of Ulm, the Spanish governor of Milan sent troops northward into the Alps to protect the Catholic Val Telliners, who had overthrown their Protestant overlords, the Grisons. Henry IV had used his alliance with the Grisons to control four vital Val Tellina passes for France and its Italian allies. Now Spain could transport troops via the passes from Italy through Switzerland to the Rhineland, Low Countries, or the emperor's territories. The threat to France and its natural allies—Venice, Savoy, the Grisons, the Swiss cantons, and the Dutch republic—was obvious.

Louis XIII reacted personally with repeated demands to the Spanish ambassador that the passes be restored, backing his words with an escalating diplomatic offensive. In 1621, with the Spanish monarchy vulnerable on the death of Philip III and the accession of his teenage son, Philip IV, Louis's courtier friend Bassompierre arrived in Madrid to negotiate an Alpine accord. By the Treaty of Madrid, the Spanish government agreed to restore Grisons sovereignty over the Val Tellina rather than add an Italian front to its wars in the Low Countries and Germany.

The Habsburgs had not capitulated, however. Spain used the treaty's guarantee of Catholic worship for the Val Telliners as justification for staying in the area; and the emperor kept the Grisons from counterattacking, using his authority as their nominal sovereign. Early in 1622, Louis again played the role of bon Français by threatening armed intervention on behalf of Grisons rights. Yet Spain promptly held to its position with yet another act in the name of the Catholic faith; papal troops were brought in to protect the Val Telliners' religion; and Spanish forces blithely continued to use the local passes.[46]

Louis XIII's Peace of Montpellier with the Huguenots finally freed him to consider war with Philip IV and his manic-depressive minister-favorite, Olivares, as a serious option. Early in 1623 we find the French king telling Queen Anne, "Write to the king your brother, and tell the Spanish ambassador that I am resolved to have the Treaty of Madrid carried out, or, failing that, I will employ all my power." To the Venetian ambassador he promised, "The Spaniards will yield with grace or by force."[47]

Louis could well feel confident. On his way home from southeastern France he had met his sister Christine's Savoyard relations. From that meeting came an offensive-defensive alliance with Savoy and Venice in 1623. The three powers agreed on the common objective of driving the Spanish Habsburgs from the Val Tellina, and Emperor Ferdinand's forces from their Grisons vassal state. Louis added to the agreement a clause that encouraged the German princes to continue fighting the emperor in central Europe. He also stationed French troops near the Spanish Netherlands.[48]

The French monarch's increasingly aggressive stand was made all the easier by ministerial changes from 1622 to 1624, notably Schomberg's dismissal for fiscal incompetence, the disgrace of the Brûlarts after their hesitation to stand up to Spain, and the emergence of the aggressive La Vieuville. On La Vieuville's advice, Louis sent a special envoy, Coeuvres, to the Alps in 1624 to plan a clandestine military campaign aimed at clearing the Val Tellina and Grisons of Spanish, imperial, and papal forces. At the same time, La Vieuville arranged the Franco-Dutch Treaty of Compiègne, which helped finance Holland's war with Spain, and negotiations began for the marriage of Louis's youngest sister, Henriette, to the future King Charles I of Protestant England.

La Vieuville fell from favor later that year, but not because Louis disliked these policy recommendations. His mistake was in acting too independently and pursuing bon Français aims with such disregard of Catholic interests that he made Louis look unprincipled. The moral bon Français in Louis XIII thus looked immediately to Cardinal Richelieu to fine-tune a position the king already espoused and to suggest ways to guarantee its success within moral boundaries acceptable to the king—but not to change Louis the Just or his policies.[49]

At the end of his teens, Louis XIII said that he was "on the road to becoming truly king of France, and that whoever would try to set him off his course would never be his friend."[50] That random reflection aptly describes the serious commitment behind the king's remarkable political quest between 1617 and 1624. The other, personal side of that journey is equally revealing. In sacrificing self to state interest, Louis the Just profoundly affected not only his public persona, but also his private being.

7

GROWING UP IN PUBLIC

Louis XIII's childhood has attracted so much attention that we almost forget that he had an unusual adolescence. Here he was, married to a foreign princess at age fourteen, turning against his mother before he was sixteen, and caught in the grip of an embarrassing obsession with a middle-aged subject during his late teens—and all the while weighted down with ceremonial burdens and the awesome task of learning how to rule his kingdom. Living in those conditions would have been difficult enough for even the most self-confident and outgoing youngster; for the high-strung Louis XIII, it was almost impossible at times. Hence he escaped the oppressive court scene whenever he could with a clear conscience, notably by plunging into his military campaigns of 1619 through 1622. (See plate 2.)

When he had to stay at court, Louis turned necessity into a virtue. There was an endless train of audiences with foreign ambassadors (from papal nuncio and imperial ambassador to Venetian, Spanish, Savoyard, English, and Dutch envoys), the importuning of notable subjects for special favors, the protocol of the daily *lever* and *coucher*, and the royal touching of hundreds of scrofulous subjects (plus a few hopeful Spaniards, Portuguese, and Italians) on High Holy Days.

To these we must add the burden of endless council meetings and voluminous royal correspondence. Council sessions were a daily regimen, except during emergencies, when Louis conferred two or three times a day, or during a military campaign with its added war council sessions. For correspondence with domestic or foreign authorities, Louis relied on a secretary of state, although he always approved the contents and signed his name alongside that of the secretary of record. Then there were Louis's celebrated short notes in his own hand—cryptic commands or secret orders (authorizing a subject's banishment from court or arrest, for example) or personal guarantees that the contents of official notes were his will (as when he had Déageant write to the bishop of Luçon requesting him to leave Avignon for Marie's camp). Finally, Louis penned or had his personal secretary imitate his hand for letters of courtesy, congratulation, and condolence to all the members of great noble families—a staggering lot!

Amusingly, Louis personal secretaries were so accustomed to copying his hand that the king's correspondents occasionally thought his letters were forgeries even when he wrote them himself. There was also a hidden agenda in this correspondence, which escapes the modern historical researcher just as today unrecorded telephone conversations are lost for all time: whether Louis was sending a detailed campaign news report to his mother, letting his wife know he missed her, or exhorting his brother to be serious about his schoolwork and other exercises, the king always entrusted a verbal message with the letter bearer. And he always let the recipients know that they should consider everything the messenger said as coming directly from the king himself.[1]

Was there no time to enjoy life or grow into manhood naturally? Louis did have some pleasures along the way, for example Italian, French, and Spanish comedies, court masques, and tournaments featuring the king and male courtiers "running at the ring" on a horse with a lance. He danced well, practicing his court ballets over and over in his apartment (in the Luynes years, always with that favorite) and then giving a skilled performance before a packed, privileged audience in the Louvre. He liked moving from one residence to another, from St-Germain of fond boyhood memories to Madrid in the woods west of Paris, and also to Fontainebleau, which was conveniently located on the way to and from his southern campaigns. As he entered adulthood he discovered that the forests around Versailles teemed with game, and in 1624 he established a modest royal hunting lodge there. Whatever his residence, he never missed daily royal mass, vespers, private prayers, and confession to Father Arnoux and his fellow Jesuit successors. But he was happiest on horseback with his bosom friends, hunting down a stag or wolf or sending the falcons that always perched on his arm off in pursuit of winged prey.

Louis endured more than he enjoyed, and what he had to endure he ritualized in such a way as to avoid emotional experiences he found uncomfortable. The reader of Héroard's huge handwritten tomes becomes quickly accustomed to the formalized pattern of Louis's daily life. The most eyebrow-raising feature was the way he made contact with his immediate family. He ate and slept alone, saw his wife once or twice during the day, under circumstances that prevented any intimacy, then ritually visited her for an hour before retiring to his own room. When his mother returned from exile, Louis added a second daily round of perfunctory visits—usually to Marie's quarters. After her reentry to his council, Louis frequently discussed policy there, carefully accompanied by his ministers.

Louis's lifelong embarrassment with his stammering speech accounts in part for this awkward social formality. But his letters, whether dictated in private to a personal secretary or written by himself, are stilted too. It matters not whether he was writing to his brother, Gaston; to his sisters Elisabeth (now called Isabella by the Spaniards), Christine in Savoy, and, after 1625, Henrietta Maria (his youngest sister) in England; or to members of a noble family. He was most comfortable when commiserating over a family's tragedy or playing the role of a just father figure helping his subjects be good by praising and admonishing. Even then, the language is wooden. He was overly pleasant to brother Gaston, whose gifts "pleased" him, as did Gaston's "pleasure" with his studies. To the duke of Bellegarde, who had lost his brother, he called the loss "more painful to me than I can say, having lost in him a good servitor whom I loved."[2]

It is tempting to call some of this dutiful letter writing narcissistic. For example, when Luynes died Louis wrote with seeming self-centeredness to his widow of "knowing that your greatest consolation is in me." On reflection, however, this comment looks more like a typical example of Louis's struggle to overcome a proper kingly formula. The degree of stiffness in the king's letters also depended on the exact rank, merit, and feelings of the recipient. Stiff as he was to the duchess of Luynes, he warmed up as his letter progressed, expressing "the ennui I felt over the loss of my cousin . . . [and] the affection I bore him so keenly and strongly that it will remain undiminished after his death and be carried over to his [loved ones]." By contrast, Louis was glacial in announcing the death to his own mother, who had felt persecuted by the king's favorite. Then there is the warmest of all these condolence letters, to the duke of Montbazon, the widow Luynes's father and Louis's friend: "You who know how I loved him can best judge the ennui I have over it. If there is anything in the world that could sadden me, it is that accident which, coming from God's hand, must be received by the resignation of our will to His."[3]

When Louis tried to be spontaneous, the result was more likely than not simply the mirror opposite of his courtly ritualizations, and thus had the same effect. Or, worse still, it involved behavior that courtiers found unbecoming of a monarch. An example of the former was Louis's occasional balking at a formal royal entrée beneath temporary triumphal arches to a throne in the center of a town. He put up with the custom at Bordeaux, Toulouse, Montpellier, Lyon, and many other provincial centers, as well as on his return to Paris from military campaigns. He also took part in religious processions of thanksgiving for a happy event, such as the return of Catholic worship in Béarn, or to invoke divine assistance against heat waves and droughts. But he pointedly began his personal reign with an impromptu entry to Rouen for the Assembly of Notables. At Protestant Parthenay in 1621, he cermoniously refused to allow a raised dais, commenting that it was not needed to show the townspeople's *fidélité*. After that remark Héroard wrote dutifully in the margin of his journal, "He can't stand ceremony."[4]

Forced informality alternated with downright unregal behavior. On his travels, the king frequently bedded down on straw rather than await the arrival of his state bed. (Mattresses were rare, and were always transported with other belongings when the court was on the move, even from palace to palace.) On other occasions he would make do with the sleeping facilities of his host's town or country residence. When eager for a quick departure, the monarch would sleep fully clothed. Whether fighting or hunting, his pleasure increased with the worsening of the weather. The intense summer heat, the bitter cold of winter, and the driving rains of spring and fall were fond companions. He would refuse to take off his boots and dry himself on reaching the shelter of some hut that his historiographers could only describe as "miserable" (*méchant*).[5]

When Louis had to stay indoors because of the weather, he was unusually restless. He tried to while away the time playing cards or chess, painting or doing pencil sketches, beating out a drumroll, playing the hunting horn, singing psalms, or dancing to songs. But as his physician noted: "The heavy snowfall, the wind, the bad weather stop him from going out. He goes here and there, plays chess and billiards. None of this satisfies him in the least."[6]

Foreign envoys and native courtiers could not understand why the king squandered his nervous energy in ways that were unproductive to his state, damaging to his image, and dangerous to his health. Those closest to him, notably Héroard and Luynes, heard his increasingly common complaints of being fatigued, sick for days on end, or simply depressed. Along with his frequent head- and toothaches, stomach upsets, and fits of coughing up phlegm, the nosebleeds that had vanished with his father's death reappeared. His letters, too, began to betray this preoccupation with his health.

The hypochondria and psychosomatic illnesses indicated something still more tragic: Louis had failed to grow emotionally. Paradoxically, those personal traits that were fashioning him into Louis the Just, a king who was destined radically to alter his realm, were holding him back as a person. His childhood pattern of repressing his feelings, obsessing himself with minutiae, and focusing on safe tests of his judgment continued unabated. At eighteen we find him examining every nook and cranny of his half brother's captured château at Caen, and at twenty-one redrawing the map of Nègrepelisse from memory. He spent hours building a furnace to forge toy cannon, meticulously drew up plans for a day's hunting expedition, and proudly showed off a handmade toy fort to his wife. Similarly, he applied safe and simple rules to end court disputes over precedence. When his cousins Condé and Soissons fought over who should give him his napkin at mealtime, the king had his brother Gaston hold that honor and told the princes they were embarrassing each other in front of everyone.[7]

Other simple acts looked childish in a near adult with a crown. At the age of eighteen Louis absorbed himself in inventing miracles for the amusement of his confessor, and talked of St. Anthony seeing the Devil with a body but no head, and "a pipe up his ass." Occasionally, his feelings as well as his imagination got the better of him. Resentful of the favor he had bestowed on the duke of Luynes, and tired of the duchess's once-charming flirtatiousness, Louis maliciously told his favorite that the duke of Chevreuse was courting his wife. When the king's outspoken friend Bassompierre chided him for setting husband against wife, the king replied, "God will forgive me if it pleases him; but I had great pleasure in getting back at her, and in causing him [Luynes] displeasure."[8]

An equally disquieting incident involved a dispute between two enfants d'honneur in charge of the hunting birds in the royal chambers. To the astonishment of a nobleman observer, the monarch refused to pull the servitors apart, saying: "No! No! Don't stop them. Let them fight." Whereupon he added: "I'll certainly separate them—I'll have their heads cut off." Here was a reversion to some of the contorted humor of Louis's childhood. Is it surprising that the owner of the Dieppe inn Crown of Brittany, when introduced to the sixteen-year-old Louis, exclaimed: "God grant you a good and long life, Sire; In olden times I kissed your father, but I see clearly that I will not kiss you. May God bless you, Sire, and long protect you."[9]

Fortunately for his subjects, Louis normally kept that darker side of his personality in check; but unfortunately for him, he missed the chance to become more of an authentic, autonomous human being. The opportunities were at hand, especially in his closest relationships. I am not referring to his relations with his mother, for her own rigidity and imperiousness blocked his every effort to become more relaxed.[10] But his teenage marriage reached a crossroads where it could have blossomed and perhaps transformed his life in the process. His relationship with his minister-favorite, Luynes, also bore signs of genuine affection on the part of the king that went beyond purely physical and emotional attraction.[11]

Louis and Anne had an uphill struggle. First there was the disastrous wedding night in 1615, and the king's subsequent shrinking from any physical contact with the queen. Even the exiling of the meddlesome queen mother in 1617 did not make matters much easier. For the next two years Louis's reticence to consummate his marriage was stronger than statist arguments that the arrival of a dauphin would sharply decrease the endemic plotting by members of the king's extended family and their grandee associates by removing their hope of succeeding him if he were somehow overthrown, declared incompetent to rule, or died. As it was now, the Condés and Vendômes were free to cast aspersions on the king's manhood, his marriage, and his crown.

Louis admitted as a teenager to Héroard that Queen Anne "inflamed" him, but he recoiled out of fear of inadequacy and the sheer terror of losing control. Anne also became repugnant to Louis by allowing a number of dashing courtiers to play up to her—all quite innocently, but a stern husband disapproved. Young Anne's zest for life was encouraged by the duchess of Luynes, who became her head of household and inseparable friend after an initial cold reception upon succeeding the queen's Spanish chief attendant at Louis's insistence. The duchess had a partner in this crime, Mlle de Verneuil, a half sister to the king who in the monarch's coded correspondence was ominously called "sin" (*le péché*).

Graced by a natural beauty that offset an embarrassing teenage complexion and a prominent nose, Anne was attractive enough physically and could hold her own in witty court conversation. (See plate 3.) Yet her voice was shrill, her attachment to others more out of loyalty than affection, and she expressed her dislikes candidly. In Spain she had been impatient to be with her betrothed, despite a governess's admonition to be less impetuous and more ladylike. "Haven't you always told me to speak the truth, Madame?" she exclaimed. "I have spoken the truth and I shall not retreat."

We have a 1619 letter from Anne to Louis's governess Mamanga that is equally revealing. The queen wrote that she was in good health and that contrary rumors were "entirely false." Then, with sureness of both pen and feeling, she added her greeting to the governess's charges, but not to "my sister Verneuil, who is a lazy thing." Anne's character reveals itself equally well in a free-spirited letter to her sister-in-law, in which she says that she has had to go to bed with a toothache, that she enjoyed Christine's letter, and that she is sure her sister-in-law will be bored at her new home in Savoy.[12]

Young Anne managed to keep her pride, stubbornness, and temper under control, under trying conditions. She endured Louis's dismissal of most of her Spanish staff, as well as restrictions on entry to her chambers by the Spanish envoy. She accepted being excluded from politics, even though her husband's religious interests aroused her dévot feelings and his foreign policy concerned her father, Philip III of Spain. When the queen did dare to venture a comment, she was careful not to sound pro-Spanish. Congratulating her husband for halting Spanish aggression against Savoy in June 1617, she added with fiery determination: "Did people think that because I was born in Spain I am Spanish? They're wrong! I'm French, and don't wish to be anything else."[13] True to her word, she testily wrote to her father that she and her Spanish ladies of honor had become very French, even in their dress; his pleas for information about French policies (which she could never have had access to, in any case), were ignored.[14]

What more would it take? The problem was obviously largely Louis's, not Anne's. He could flirt with the duchess of Luynes and other ladies in Anne's household, but neither the papal nuncio nor the royal confessor could bring him to his wife's bed by religious arguments. Luynes's employment of romantically suggestive ballets at carnival season had no effect. The upright Louis also rejected the suggestion of making love to an inviting lady-in-waiting as a prelude to entering the queen's forbidding bed. It goes without saying that the Spanish government's fears of a total breakdown of the Franco-Spanish marriage pact and protests at the prolonged insult to their national honor made little impact on the king's anti-Spanish feelings.

By chance, Louis's sister Christine and his half sister Mlle de Vendôme were engaged to be married around the same time, early in 1619. Louis was stung by the suggestion that his sister might give birth to a child in line for the Savoyard succession before he could produce an heir to the French throne. Then he was aroused by the experience of witnessing the consummation of his half sister's marriage. The new duchess of Elbeuf arose from the embrace of her husband and exclaimed to a startled monarch: "Sire! You do the same thing with the queen, and you will do well." A week later, on the night of 25 January 1619, a determined Luynes seized his still-hesitant royal patron as he was retiring for the night and pushed him sobbing into Anne's bed. Luynes then locked the door, with only one female servant to verify the physical union.[15]

It was the beginning of a real honeymoon for the two lovers, a chance for Anne to come into her own as something more than a ceremonial queen, and an opportunity for Louis to blossom as a person. Louis looked contented, Anne simply radiant. The next few months flew by for the seventeen-year-olds. The royal physician recorded exactly when and how often they made love with a strange marginal symbol in his diary: +++ followed by "rts" or "r," or even by "r²" or "n²" (indicating lovemaking two times?). Louis lingered in his wife's bed for hours before retiring to his own chambers every night, and forsook his habit of rising early in the morning. So enraptured was the royal husband that his entourage became concerned about the effect on his health; they asked him to take fortnight breaks between their lovemaking.

Here is a sample of the new Louis XIII's daily living, as recorded by Héroard:

> *27 January:* at 10:30 went to the chapel of Bourbon; at 1:45 dined in the queen's chambers; to the Tuilleries via the gallery; to vespers at the Feuillant monastery; to Luynes's chambers; at 6:45 supped; to the queen; returned at 8:15; did his business; climbed to Luynes's chambers
> +++ for the comedy; undressed; went to the queen; put in bed; little sleep; at 6 slept until 8 A.M.

28 January: slept [without Anne] from 10:30 to 10:15

30 January: went to the queen's chambers from 7:00 to 7:15; [later] went to the queen's chambers and escorted her to the comedy; retired at 11:45; undressed, put in bed, purged; shortly after got up in his robe, went to the queen—at 1 A.M. slept until 3 A.M.

31 January: got up at 3; returned and slept until 6; went to the queen; to the chapel of the tower; later to the queen; via the gallery to the council; went to Luynes's chambers to practice the ballet; supped; to the queen; to the comedy; retired at 12:15, undressed, to bed; slept 1 A.M.–10 A.M.

10 February: [marriage of Princess Christine and the prince of Piedmont] went to the queen, and then to Luynes's chambers for supper; I was told he supped with great pleasure; at 10 P.M. he escorted Mme Christine to her room, was there when the Prince came to bed, and for some time after; then in his own bed at 11:45; at midnight with the queen; undressed, and to bed, without sleeping; retired at 2 A.M. until 8:30[16]

If only an heir had resulted from that blissful time. Louis became a devoted husband, taking Anne on his summer war campaigns and swearing never to touch another woman. On more than one occasion the queen blushed when asked how the "dauphin" was doing. Perhaps Anne did become pregnant late in 1619, only to abort early: the evidence shows that she underwent a debilitatingly weak period, when everyone gave up hope for her life. Louis helped her back to health with his presence, and also by siding with those doctors who said not to bleed her anymore.[17]

After the recovery, ecstasy. In May 1620, to the accolades of a packed audience in Henry IV's Place Royale, the royal sweethearts enacted a scene more spectacular than the famous carousel of 1612 honoring their engagement: Louis XIII challenged his most athletic courtiers in a competion of running at the ring with lance and horse. In a field of thirty lords, the king won twice, then broke a tie with three of his subjects by carrying the last ring. For once in his life joyously spontaneous, Louis looked proudly toward his riding master, Pluvinel, then leaped onto Queen Anne's bench to receive the prize of a ringed diamond, holding his glowing wife in his arms.[18]

The honeymoon lingered on through 1620 and into 1621. Louis kept in constant touch with Anne during the 1621 campaign by establishing her quarters near his sieges, and she probably fitted in well thanks to her past experiences riding with him up to twelve hours on horseback during his hunting expeditions. But the campaign of 1622 was a different story. Anne was planning to stay behind because she had just entered the second month of pregnancy. On 14 March 1622, running through the Louvre in her usual high spirits with her closest friends, Mme de Luynes and Mlle de Verneuil, she tripped and fell. Louis visited Anne after her miscarriage on the sixteenth, but he was preoccupied with his coming military campaign. On the twentieth he left for the south unaware of the circumstances behind the mishap.

Louis heard the facts a week after the accident. Immediately, he resorted to his usual way of dealing with feelings. He already had a mental dossier on Mme de Luynes, for the woman's own father had warned him about the libertine poetry of love she had been giving the queen. Louis conveniently blamed Anne's friends for her present political sin, stifling his anger toward her.

The king's mechanism did not serve either Louis or Anne well. His sanctimoniously worded order for the banishment of the queen's two friends was deflected both by her importunings and by the gallant intervention of the king's friend, the duke of Chevreuse, who married the newly widowed Mme de Luynes. Louis relented: the two ladies could see Anne occasionally. As for his marriage, a sense of duty to produce an heir compelled him to continue the physical aspect of the honeymoon period; but the passion, concern, and sharing were replaced by suspiciousness, resentment, and emotional distancing.[19]

For two more decades Louis XIII and Anne of Austria played out their nightly ritual: he went to her bed, they occasionally made love, and he always returned to his own chambers to sleep.[20] There were to be other pregnancies and miscarriages, and eventually the births of two sons. But circumstantial evidence shows that the pregnancies, and much of the lovemaking, occurred only in times of political crisis or distraction, when the king let down his guard or felt in control. So this single mistake by the queen in 1622, combined with the pride that kept her from groveling for pardon, and the king's addiction to what was proper, made a normal married life impossible. Rather than cast the blame on one or the other party, let us turn to the impact on their individual lives.

Louis may have lost more than Anne through their fall from marital grace. After three years of intimacy and emotional growth, his progress came to an abrupt halt. The difference between the pre-fall and post-fall Louis can be seen in his letters to his wife. At the peak of the honeymoon period, in 1620, the king had written from his army camp: "I passionately want to see you." In 1621 he was attentive enough to her needs to break the news of her father's death himself, albeit in brief, awkward language. But look at the pompous language of his order for the banishment of Anne's companions. "As I love nothing so much as you," he began stiffly; and he concluded, in patronizing fashion, "It is for the good of my service and yours that things transpire as I command." Although Louis tried thereafter to say and do the right thing, he might just as well have been preaching a homily. A message from his camp later in 1622 read: "I want so often to be near you that the absence is painful; but one has to give all the proper attention to the good of my affairs and the repose of my subjects." He concluded with the same apparently narcissistic turn of phrase we have seen elsewhere: "Since it is for a good cause, you will bear all the more patiently the absence of the one you wish to see."[21]

The queen suffered too—which only magnified their estrangement. She became isolated from her husband's feelings and thoughts, and lost what hope she had previously held of being allowed a meaningful role at court. To add insult to the injury, within a year of Anne's miscarriage, and weeks after Luynes's death, Louis admitted his mother into his political confidence.[22]

Fortunately, Louis's principles on upholding the sanctity of marriage and honoring the marriage pact of 1615 with Spain spared Anne the ultimate humiliation, although the pre-honeymoon rumors of her repudiation resurfaced and continued on and off throughout their marriage. She remained in a difficult position, nonetheless. Louis's ingrained dislike of Spaniards, not to mention his suspicious nature, was poised against the queen if she gave any appearance of stepping out of line, either politically or morally. And her boredom with a dull, barren life did lead her astray.[23]

Louis drove Anne to distraction by meticulously dictating all changes in her household staff and tightly controlling her personal budget. She responded by letting the dashing English minister-favorite, Buckingham, into her apartment in the spring of 1623, when he and Prince Charles were on their way to Spain in quest of a Spanish marriage for that English heir. Louis was offended and scandalized, and he quickly brought his political and moral justice to bear on Anne, by decreeing that henceforth no male could visit the queen's quarters unless he was present. Louis was within his rights, but his timing was bad, for just then Anne was recovering from an epileptiform seizure. Still worse was the tactless way he announced his wife's punishment: via his mother! The king's secretary confided his disbelief to his personal journal: could not the king have told Anne himself, and gently?

When the queen let it be known that the change in protocol "angered her," the breach widened. Relations deteriorated to the point that in 1624 Louis dismissed Anne's secretary Le Secq, and "became so angry that his chin trembled" when the man threatened the leading royal minister La Vieuville with Anne's wrath for not taking her side against the king. The wrathful monarch scolded Anne, jailed Le Secq for thirteen days, and then ordered him to stay away from the court and Paris whenever the king was in residence.[24]

This recoil from marital intimacy did not prevent the king from looking elsewhere for closeness. Indeed, he was capable of sustaining one or two relationships in addition to his marriage. People had already noticed Louis's childhood attraction to other little girls and boys, and by his early teens they had come to accept his need for some sort of friend to lean on. As he entered his mid teens there were limitless possibilities among the ladies and men at court. The only questions were: would it be a female *favorite* or a male *favori*? Who would the person be? And how long would it last?

Louis's chaste flirtations with young ladies at court failed to blossom during his late teens; nonetheless they made Anne jealous and were the prelude to two adult liaisons of some length. Meanwhile, the teenage Louis's interest focused on the male courtiers he saw so regularly at court, on the hunt, and in the army. His half brother and his governor's son had passed from the scene, just as ignoble boys of his childhood had. Then along came Charles d'Albert de Luynes, who attracted Louis's attention along with several other courtiers. The fact that this handsome middle-aged courtier was soft-spoken, caring, and concerned to make Louis a real king and man must have helped him outbid rivals like Vitry, who was fearless, and Bassompierre, who was honest. Luynes became an uncle figure, close to a surrogate father.

He was more than that, however. Louis could not bear to be apart from his courtier-servitor-friend; he even dreamed about him in his sleep. When Héroard mechanically reported the king climbing the stairs of the Louvre two and three times a day to Luynes's apartment above the royal chambers, we can be sure he was describing something far removed from a ritualized exercise. What Louis was experiencing was a prolonged, powerful infatuation: his physician's diary recorded the cryptic comment, "shameful."

Whether the king became sexually involved is impossible to say. Mme de Luynes, who was a stormy temptress in her own right and eventually the bête noire of Louis and Richelieu, never breathed a word of a sexual liaison between her husband and her monarch. Contemporaries, critical of the relationship, focused exclusively on the scandal of a monarch being unable to control his urge to be profligate with his favor. We will have to be content to state that this was the first of a series of long-term emotional involvements by Louis XIII with men.[25]

Louis's involvement with Luynes should have been easier than his marriage. After all, success as a lover and potential father was not at stake. Yet the problems inherent in the royal personality were laid bare by this male courtier–royal adolescent connection. The basic conflict was that Louis relied heavily on his friend for emotional support yet wanted desperately to be independent. Observers of his behavior were quick to note the inner conflict, as revealed by the king's inability to be separated from his *favori*, and his cutting remarks about "King Luynes" in the heat of the siege warfare of 1621.[26]

It was a pity that Louis's love for Luynes, which managed to transcend pure infatuation, never quite got him past the notion of loving the favorite as a reward for his support—almost as an act of justice. One would have thought the royal master had all the incentive in the world to give freely to one who gave so freely to him. The servitor had given his master the courage to seize the reins of power, selflessly pushed him into the queen's bed, and stayed up nights with him during political crises. Yet Louis could not bring himself to offer his own love with no strings attached. After his friend's death, he said with genuine feeling, but also with reservations: "I loved him because he loved me."[27]

Indeed, Louis the Just's ingrained judgmentalism led him momentarily to consider having Luynes tried posthumously for corrupt practices (just as he momentarily thought of bringing charges against Schomberg a year later). Fortunately, his learned sense of justice worked for Luynes's family. In gratitude for what his minister-favorite had done for him, the king allowed the widow Luynes to marry one of his friends, he kept one of Luynes's brothers on as governor of the Bastille until 1626, and he continued to rely on the other brother as an advisor.

This complicated ending to an important relationship certainly reveals anything but the indifference that some courtiers assumed their monarch felt about his favorite's death.[28] Above all, Louis expressed sadness—for how would he fill the void? Héroard's manuscript diary tells us what the nineteenth-century editors of the abridged journal gloss over: when Luynes fell ill, Louis visited him morning and afternoon, day after day, until forbidden by his doctors. A few hours before the minister-favorite's passing, Héroard wrote that Louis was "grief-stricken [*affligé*] by the extremity of M. le Connestable's illness."[29]

After Luynes's death and the marital debacle of 1622, Louis XIII had nowhere to turn for the emotional support and release he so badly needed. Would-be personal favorites were either shunned by the king or banished from court through the influence of his mother or ministers (as Toiras and d'Esplan were), just as potential rivals for favor had been in Luynes's day (Montpouillan) and during the era of Ancre and Marie (the Grand Prior Vendôme). For three months in the spring of 1623 Louis was reduced to escaping to the forests around Fontainebleau for hunting trips that lasted from three to eight days, "taking with him only [the servitors] of his little pleasures and his companies of mounted musketeers which he was extraordinarily fond of."[30]

So Louis XIII entered the Richelieu years as frustrated personally as he was hopeful politically. How the stunted growth of his personality would affect his reign was uncertain to those around him. Was his lack of spontaneity and joy going to darken the political landscape? Would his ritualized formulas for personal and public problems and his inability to develop healthy relationships mire his state in inertia? Or would the traits that served him so poorly in his personal life—and were already causing people to consider him a weak leader who needed a strong advisor—serve his state well?

We can find hints of answers to these questions in two radically different examples of the adolescent ruler's behavior and two similar reflections on his teenage personality. First we have the views of the Huguenot leader Rohan, who had fought and bargained with the king and was connected by blood to Marie de Rohan-Montbazon, better known first as Mme de Luynes and later as Mme de Chevreuse. Rohan described the fifteeen-year-old king of 1617 as "strongly jealous of his authority, which he could not realize, and inclined to believe the bad rather than the good." On Louis in 1624, at twenty-two, Rohan wrote that it was "rather [too] easy [for him] to believe bad of someone than to believe in their good." Similarly, the well-placed courtier Fontenay-Mareuil described the king at the outset of his personal reign as "wanting always, however young he might be, to have his affairs go well; and having nothing so likely to maintain or ruin a man in his eyes than that his advice should turn out well or badly."[31]

Clearly, both observers were wary of their sovereign's darker side, which presaged a harsh reign ahead. But their observations also assumed a royal sense of what was right, a trait that could mitigate the harsher tendency in their monarch. That inference was in keeping with the central message of contemporary proroyal pamphlets on Louis the Just.

Two incidents show this dual potential far more powerfully. Historians who see sadism dominating Louis's rule single out the campaign of 1622, when the apparently casual king pointed cannon at Huguenot peasants encroaching on his troops' emplacements, killing two of them. Yet a very different side of Louis was evident during the previous year's fighting, when the far from casual king granted a rebel nobleman safe-conduct to see his mortally wounded brother at the royal camp, and refused to go back on his word. To the royal confessor's objection "But Sire, he is a criminal of lèse-majesté!" Louis retorted, "It makes no difference; if he has made one mistake, I don't intend to make a hundred."[32]

What would happen if the protective and punitive sides of the king's character were combined in political matters? What sort of blend would that entail? But let us not rush ahead of our story. Instead, we can allow ourselves one last, fleeting glance at the adolescent who was being submerged by adult cares and weighty royal virtues, yet had not sacrificed all his feelings. At the end of his wars of 1620–22 with Huguenot rebels, a weary Louis entered the charming southern town of Arles to the welcoming cries of "Vive notre bon Roy Louys." Tears ran down the king's cheeks as he replied, "God bless you, my people! God bless you!"[33]

PART III

French Absolutism in the Making 1624–35

8

PARTNERSHIP OF KING AND CARDINAL

Historians have always been awed by the political changes in the France of Louis XIII during the decade 1624–35, for they marked a major stage in the development of what is called absolute monarchy. The monarch crushed family, court, and ministerial opposition more serious than the opposition he had met during the Wars of the Mother and Son—including plotting against his brother's forced marriage in 1626, flagrant dueling by the courtier Bouteville in 1627, and the Day of Dupes challenge of 1630 by Marie and his minister Marillac. The Huguenot state within the state, which Louis had been challenging piecemeal, vanished in 1629 after the fall of La Rochelle. Habsburg power, which Louis had previously dealt with diplomatically, was challenged by French military intervention in the Val Tellina in 1625–26, the Mantuan Succession War of 1629–30, and a steadily accelerating response elsewhere that culminated in open war with Spain in 1635. Finally, the intrusion of the monarchic institutions into subjects' lives during this period was extensive enough to be termed a governmental revolution.

Two individuals collaborated to achieve these things. Without Cardinal Richelieu's assistance, although the ruler of France would still have been known as Louis the Just, his brand of justice would surely have effected less sweeping changes. Without Louis XIII's trust, although the former bishop of Luçon might well have made a name for himself in church circles, his brilliant analytical powers and political pragmatism would not have been applied to the reallzation of his king's moralizing urges. Who knows what would have happened to Louis XIII's horror of noble dueling and revolt, his intent to raze all Huguenot town defenses while tolerating heresy, or his ingrained suspicion of everything Spanish?

How did these two men collaborate? To answer this question, we must surmount the barrier that caused Georges Pagès to declare, "It is impossible, because of the state of our sources, to know what was the precise role, within the government, of the king and Richelieu." The starting point is Ranum's general inference, from the royal-ministerial correspondence after 1635, that Louis was "primarily the reviewer of policy" and Richelieu "both the formulator and co-ordinator of it." To understand more of the earlier partnership of these two men, we must broaden our search to include their temperaments, working habits, social outlook, and ways of thinking, as well as the personal bonding that began as respect and developed into mutual affection and gratitude.[1]

In 1624, Armand-Jean du Plessis, Cardinal de Richelieu, was thirty-nine and a bundle of nervous energy, marred by migraine headaches and fits of crying. He exercised steely self-control over a wiry but frail constitution. On the surface, this fastidious, imperious-looking cardinal could not have been more different from Louis, as judged by the portraits we have of the boyish sovereign at age twenty-three. The king's uncertain royal look, curly hair, and temporary fuzz on the chin, had not yet given way to the sad dark eyes, black moustache, and center-parted hair that hung lower on the left side of the aging Louis XIII's emaciated visage. Yet for all the differences in appearance and age, the minister and master were fairly equal in afflictions of body and soul. (See plates 4, 5.)

The bad health of both Louis and Armand cast a shadow over their reactions to problems and crises. Richelieu was fond of applying negative medical metaphors to state affairs: an aging state cannot be truly reformed but only nursed through normal adversity, whereas a life-threatening situation for the state calls for radical measures. Personally, he could be expansive and charming, but his personality and position invited plots against his person. He reacted with understandable paranoia—and ruthlessness.

Louis XIII's medico-political view was less elaborate. As with his personal fevers and disorders, he lashed out at the political illness of the moment, then tried to put the irksome matter out of his mind. Unable to avoid the festering issue, he would brood over the rectitude of his response. Whenever personal and political malaise coincided, Louis slipped into his infamous *mauvaises humeurs*. During these dark moods he was virtually unapproachable, as down on himself as on his closest friends.[2]

Clearly this king stood to benefit from working with someone close enough in temperament to understand his moodiness and turn his liabilities into assets.[3] Louis's physician, Dr. Bouvard, noted in 1635: "Never has anyone experienced so swiftly an alteration in his health caused by strong passions as does His Majesty, something that His Eminence [Cardinal Richelieu] understands better than others." Richelieu went straight to the heart of the problem: "Your Majesty's emotions control his body so absolutely that the slightest passion seizes his heart and plays havoc with his whole system. . . . I have never seen you ill from any other cause."[4]

The servitor's solution? Urging the king to do what he often did anyway: sacrifice his feelings to state needs. In a typical ministerial *avis* of the late 1620s, the cardinal wrote with amazing frankness to his master: "The king is good, virtuous, secretive, courageous, and a lover of glory, but one can say candidly that he is extremely quick-tempered, suspicious, jealous, sometimes susceptible to diverse passing aversions, as well as to following the first impressions received to the neglect of the third or fourth opinion."[5] Charting a course through that emotional-moral labyrinth, Richelieu appealed to what he repeatedly called the king's "natural goodness" against two equally dangerous extremes: tit-for-tat justice that could verge on cruelty, and capricious clemency that bred permissiveness.

When Louis expressed satisfaction on learning that Emperor Ferdinand had ordered his turncoat generalissimo Wallenstein assassinated, Richelieu told him that such a feeling was unbecoming of a great king. The French monarch should be careful, his minister said, or people would start calling him Louis the Merciless rather than Louis the Just. Conversely, Richelieu was well aware that his master could impetuously favor friends caught in the web of his punitive justice. Despite Louis's prompt acts against flagrant duelers like Guémadeuc, he had looked the other way when an anguished Schomberg engaged in a duel after his dismissal in 1623; and in 1625 the king let his personal favorite Barradat off with mere banishment after the braggart proposed a duel.

Richelieu waged an unrelenting campaign to turn royal morality into a consistent policy. We have one example from the royal crackdown on dueling in 1627. Schomberg's son-in-law got into a duel over a minor but insulting provocation: someone had hurled a biscuit at his tormentor. The cardinal urged his king to consult the parlementary judges, royal confessor, and Cardinal La Rochefoucauld as to whether the seriousness of dueling outweighed the pettiness of the motive. His conscience cleared, Louis stripped the fleeing Schomberg relations of their state offices.

Consistency was not easy. Although he had the archdueler Bouteville executed for dueling, Louis later pardoned the Schombergs on the argument that "the justice we owe our subjects [has] inclined us to [their] pleas." The concerned servitor, who admitted his own conflict over the death penalty for fellow nobles, understood fully the inner demon he was helping his royal master to fight: "God has seen fit to give your Majesty the force of character necessary to act with firmness when confronted with business of the greatest importance. But as a balance to this noble quality He has allowed you to be sensitive to matters so small that no one in advance would suspect they might trouble you." [6]

Louis's ambivalent feelings on individual justice have to be placed in their social setting. He had grown up accepting the notion of hierarchy and the traditions of individual estates and orders; yet he wanted unqualified obedience to royal authority at every level. What the king had learned by association and upbringing was now complemented by the experience of an advisor whose outlook was remarkably similar.

Armand-Jean du Plessis de Richelieu's family background and personal career made him familiar with all three estates of the realm plus the royal court and government. [7] His father, François, had risen from the lesser nobility of Poitou to become grand provost at the Valois court. The elder Richelieu was in charge of maintaining order and provisions within the king's personal retinue and was ranked just below the great officers of the king's household (which included the masters of the stable, hunt, wardrobe, and king's chamber). François died serving as a captain of the guards for Henry IV when Armand, born in 1585, was not yet five.

Armand's eldest brother, Henri, was well positioned as a courtier-soldier during Louis XIII's minority; a second brother, Alphonse, decided on the monastic life. Armand was groomed by Louis XIII's riding master, Pluvinel, to be a courtier-soldier, but he was also inclined to theological studies. In 1607, Richelieu embarked on an

ecclesiastical career when he assumed the family's recently acquired ecclesiastical post at Luçon. Bishop of a poor diocese, almoner to Queen Anne, and finally a cardinal and holder of several
benefices, he was as committed a cleric as he was instinctively a
gentilhomme.

Through his mother, Suzanne de La Porte, Richelieu had another rich inheritance. Her Poitevin grandfather had been a tax
agent for a local prince, her father a celebrated parlementary lawyer
who helped frame the great sixteenth-century ordinances of royal
laws. The La Portes were as successful members of the robe nobility
as the Richelieus were typical nobles of the sword.

The Richelieu who served Louis XIII was a unique exemplar of
the values of the three estates.[8] As a cleric, he blended Catholic
reformationist zeal and reverence for the Papacy with an appreciation of the autonomy of the French monarchy. He had come to
court as a friend of such religious dévots as Pierre Bérulle, who
founded the second of his famous Oratory seminaries at Luçon;
however, bon Français leanings lay just beneath the surface. Unlike
the dévots, but like Louis XIII, Richelieu respected the Huguenots,
while wanting to see them convert peacefully. As bishop of Luçon,
he had written a polemic against Calvinism, fought off an attempt
by local Huguenots to build a temple adjacent to his cathedral, and
fretted about the Protestant state within the state, whose greatest
seaboard town of La Rochelle lay just down the road.

Richelieu came to the court with some of the style of a Second
Estate noble. He married his relatives into great families like the
Condés. He pursued personal wealth. He even used public funds
for private interests. Yet he saw the nobility's greatness not in independent lawless acts, but in service to the monarch. He earned
the title of duke and peer in that service. And he joined his king in
condemning noble violence, horrified by an uncle's dueling death,
his father's killing of the offender in a second duel, and his brother
Henri's demise in a duel over the spoils of the first War of the
Mother and Son.

When it came to the ways of the Third Estate, this descendant
of jurists was a curious blend of royal reformer and pragmatist.
Like his royal master, he was opposed on principle to venal officeholding and judicial obstruction of state laws; yet he knew how
crucial parlementary loyalty was to establishing a climate of submissiveness, by subjects both high and low. Louis had a habit of

lecturing judges for interfering with affairs of what he called "my state"; Richelieu saw the need to bring the judgmental ruler around to a compromise that advanced the cause of that state.

Differences in their social outlook were less significant than shared attitudes. Had it been otherwise, Richelieu would have quickly suffered the fate of Louis's previous advisors. The self-effacing monarch who was comfortable in the dress of a simple soldier could tolerate ostentatious tastes only in a cardinal who liked to lead his armies. The frugal king who talked benevolently of "my poor people" could understand the duke and peer who thought of the poor as beasts of burden, at their best when working hard.

Differences in work habits were much greater, though even there the two men complemented each other. The monarch knew his duty to apply himself, but he was restless at court and rarely looked beyond the immediate and the mechanical. The minister was a born workaholic who liked to concentrate on the whole problem, but he needed privacy to be at his best. Monarch and advisor came to each other's aid.

Rising early and retiring late, accustomed to sleeping alone, Louis could fully appreciate his chief minister's long days, his abhorrence of subjects intruding on his privacy asking for favors, and his passion for living and working away from the bad air, noise, and congestion of the court and capital. Together they arranged to work as much as possible outside Paris and near each other—first at Limours in the vicinity of Fontainebleau, and eventually at the king's childhood palace of St-Germain and the minister's nearby château of Ruel. They were in constant contact through Richelieu's daily letters and Louis's replies. At the king's side was always a secretary of state and personal secretaries (notably Louis Tronçon until his disgrace in 1626, and Michel Lucas thereafter). King and cardinal also met regularly, either at the royal residence or (thanks to the master's sensitivity for the stress on his servitor) at Richelieu's château. A special royal *brevet* of 1626 freed the cardinal-minister of "all the suits and importuning of individuals" so that he might save his health and energies for "the great affairs of state."[9]

In return, Richelieu praised his king's conscientiousness, and scolded him like a father for concentrating on incidental details. He knew just how far to press Louis "to apply his energy to the great important affairs of his state and to shun the petty issues as unworthy of his attention and thought," as he wrote in his *Testament politique*.[10] Richelieu's own example reinforced this admonition. Marvick notes the king's attraction to the "boldness, physical courage, tireless energy, orderliness, [and] self-discipline" of his servitor.[11]

Of course, that minister's influence did not turn the ruler into a formulator of elaborate schemes and the means to achieve them. Richelieu did, however, elicit from Louis the best use of the king's "good sense," or what Andrew Lossky has called his "direct intuitive perception of reality." This good sense was normally applied to judging the cardinal's written or oral suggestions, and to discovering the "wisest" opinion in council debates, a knack that both Bernard and Richelieu praised. For his part, Richelieu formulated policy suggestions in the lucid manner of contemporary scholastic reasoning by giving the pros and cons, then left the proper inference to be drawn by his monarch.[12] This style of advising progressed from the early years, when Richelieu dared not be too conclusive, to the later years when he was more comfortable driving the logic home.

Let us look at an example of this intellectual collaborating. As the 1620s came to a close and Louis was drawn toward a military showdown in northern Italy with the Habsburg rulers and the duke of Savoy, Richelieu penned a point-by-point memo, and Louis wrote precise answers in the margin.

Points that the king may be pleased to resolve before leaving

[Queries in Richelieu's secretary's hand]

[Answers in the king's hand]

What is to be done in case M. de Savoye denies the provisions necessary for the king's army? Clearly their arrival is being secretly blocked.

We will take by force what they won't turn over through reason, advancing through the duke's lands.

If he does not finish supplying the provisions, both those he is obligated to provide, and those coming from Provence?

In that case I will consider the treaty broken and we will go to war.

If in future the Spaniards prevent the passage of the said provisions to Casale, via either Genoa or other places, contrary to their obligations by the article signed by them and M. de Savoye?

M. de Savoye will be summoned to join my armies as he is obligated, and we will march against the Spaniards.

If the said duke absolutely won't come to reason concerning their passage . . . ?	We will send *commissaires* to examine the nature of places to be requested.
If he tries to stall indefinitely, giving the Spaniards time to fortify, and unites more closely with them?	We will prevent it.
If he stays perpetually in Veillane and orders the approach of [relief] troops, which would make us justifiably fearful?	The same.
What pay does the king wish to provide in his army?	In future the soldiers will be paid an advance of 40 sols a week . . . and they will have the muster owing them when they return to my kingdom.
If some officers retire without leave, whether the king wishes to fill their posts immediately after he is notified?	I will take care of it.[13]

Exchanges like this on basic policy matters gave Louis XIII the reputation of being a diffident ruler, led by the nose by Richelieu. But when viewed in the light of the ruler's previous history, it is clear that the king's answers reflected his own ideas, morality, and way of handling crises. Even when he scribbled in the margin or on the back of a memo "good" or "all that is very good," this is all he needed to say, for Richelieu routinely advanced ideas compatible with Louis's political views and sense of justice. Richelieu's gradually acquired habit of suggesting the wording of Louis's written and oral replies to subjects should be similarly understood: the master trusted his servitor's shrewd sense of the proper response, while reserving to himself the option of altering its tone or substance.[14] We should therefore not assume that Louis's views colored policies only when he made explicit recommendations on minute matters, as was his custom with military arrangements, law enforcement, finances, and appointments. It goes without saying that whenever Louis wrote, self deprecatingly, "All the same I leave [these thoughts] for you to judge what is appropriate," Richelieu wisely carried out his recommendations.[15]

Occasionally, we can uncover some of the hidden complexity

underlying this two-way exchange.[16] A good example is the capture, prosecution, and execution of Bouteville for defying the royal ban on dueling. The best known phase of that decision-making process is represented by Richelieu's memo, with his unequivocal recommendation: "It is a question of cutting the throat of dueling, or of the edicts of Your Majesty." The body of that memo was cautious, however, in case Louis decided on clemency. Richelieu let his principled king know that a Louis the Just would be acting equally honorably by either pardoning or punishing.[17] But in fact, Louis needed no urging to make the "right" response to Bouteville's flaunting of the law. After all, he had initiated Bouteville's arrest himself, and he later argued passionately against the pleas for clemency by the defendant's relative, the duke of Montmorency:

> I have been constrained to overcome my own feelings and the wish and inclination I have, as always, to respect whatever concerns you, in order not to bring down the wrath of God on my head, by wishing to save an individual [which would violate] the express oaths I made in His presence [on the subject of duels], and incur the blame of society for causing my edicts to be broken and my authority scorned. . . . What touches my heart even more is the loss of my nobility, whose blood and life are no less dear to me than my very own. . . . I have been compelled to let justice prevail, God knowing how much my whole being has been disturbed and afflicted.[18]

The complicated collaboration of king and cardinal was fortified by strong emotional bonding. The beginning, of course, was shaky. The royal master was suspicious of this suave and sophisticated appointee who had alarming elements of Luynes's winsomeness and La Vieuville's self-assurance. While Richelieu's bright, ingratiating manner had worked well with Concini, Marie, and Luynes, it was not foolproof in the presence of a sovereign opposed by nature to flattery and arrogance. As late as 1629, the cardinal-minister pleaded with the king to trust his advisors, to listen to them and not their detractors, to support them even when they were critical (in private) of royal conduct. He concluded wistfully, "Sometimes the king is extremely satisfied with me; sometimes he takes a dislike [to my service]."[19]

Fortunately, the master and servitor were able to build on their common ground and mutual needs. Although beholden for his entry to the council in 1624 to the good offices of the queen mother, Richelieu made it plain in a private meeting with Louis that he would serve king and state exclusively. This solemn vow, repeated throughout their long association, was backed constantly by his encouragement that Louis be a "great king." Richelieu was equally adept at playing the humble servitor who merely carried out his master's commands and would gladly resign if his services were longer helpful—an effective counter to Louis's past suspicions about the cardinal's overbearing manner.

The cardinal-minister's letters illustrate this ongoing campaign of mutual indoctrination. Shortly after Richelieu replaced La Vieuville as the king's major advisor, he thanked "the great king" for elevating "mediocrities," signing himself "the very humble and very obedient servitor, le Cardinal de Richelieu." Within a year this complimentary closing lengthened to "the very humble, very faithful, and very indebted subject and servitor." That same year, the servitor told his master he would "maintain with the little spirit and industry that God has given me a total fidelity with which I will be, right down to my last breath, [your very humble . . .]." In 1626 during the crisis surrounding Gaston's marriage, which appeared to threaten the cardinal's life and his sovereign's throne, Richelieu obeyed Louis's command to come to his side with the statement, "Your Majesty is so prudent and so wise that he cannot fail in his councils." The closing to this letter was more grateful than ever: "the very humble, very obedient, very faithful and very indebted subject and servitor." Thereafter, the complimentary closings remained the same; pledges to lay down the servitor's life for his master continued; and allusions to "the best master in the world" appeared frequently.[20]

Louis warmed to Richelieu's words and the success of his policy analyses. There is a world of difference between the royal letter of 1622 referring to the bishop of Luçon as being among those "who favor the prosperity of my affairs" and that of 1631 assuring the trusted servitor "that I hold to what I have promised you, right to the last breath of my life." Two years later, Louis wrote, "I will always be the best master who ever walked this earth."

The change was gradual, with some emotional high points. In 1626, when Richelieu feigned sickness and offered to resign if that would ease the political crisis, Louis fell all over himself trying to express his gratitude. He wanted his servitor's good health "more than you do," the ruler asserted, "provided you find it in the care and principal charge of my affairs." He noted his satisfaction that "everything, thanks to God, has succeeded since you have been here [in my council]." And he concluded, "I shall protect you against whomever it may be, and I will never abandon you. . . . Rest assured that I will never change and that whoever attacks you, you will have me as your second." In a society where dueling was still the highest form of self-protection and acting as "second" to one's dueling friend the greatest mark of devotion, there was no stronger way for Louis the Just, who expressed his feelings so awkwardly, to describe his relationship with Cardinal Richelieu.[21]

Did Louis XIII really mean what he said? Of course he did. Had he really done away with backbiting? No, there were always times when his darker side surfaced. So Richelieu was wise in following the practice common to early-seventeenth-century royal favorites and ministers, from Luynes and Lerma to Buckingham and Olivares. A series of pro-Richelieu fellow ministers, royal confessors, king's favorites, and other officials marched in review before the king from 1624 until the cardinal's death in 1642, all with Louis's full knowledge—first on occasion, and then more regularly, until by 1635 the king was surrounded by his own chief servitor's own servitors and surrogates.[22]

The system had its drawbacks, notably in the case of royal favorites. Richelieu knew he could never fill all of his master's emotional needs. Hence it was in his own interest to cultivate Louis's attachment to an innocuous young courtier whom the king liked. That courtier, however, once master of the king's heart, might try to poison his mind against the cardinal during a dark mood, just as Richelieu had done against La Vieuville. Richelieu would then have to wage a campaign against this former friend. It was not easy; as in other matters, he won his point only by playing on the king's political conscience. Even then, Louis had to see with his own eyes that his loved one was violating the vow he had made after Luynes's death never to let a favorite interfere with statecraft.[23]

The royal page-turned-favorite François de Barradat foolishly tested that rule in 1625–26, despite several reminders from the king that he was not to dabble in politics. The young nobleman must have been dizzy with his rapid rise at court to first gentleman of the chamber, captain of the royal château at St-Germain, and lieutenant general of Champagne. Richelieu, after writing several obsequious letters to Barradat, worked indirectly to undermine his favor. But Louis continued to indulge the favorite's whims, even after the young man spoke out on the controversial betrothal of the royal heir. When the king finally hinted that Barradat no longer had his favor, the obtuse favorite, instead of discreetly withdrawing, challenged his perceived rival, Souvré's son, to a duel. Furious at this affront to his personal will and his latest edict against dueling, the king banished Barradat with the exclamation, "You have no respect for the place where you are. If I did what I should, I would send you to the Bastille and you would see how the edict against dueling applied to you. Go!"[24]

Barradat's long-term successor, Claude de Rouvroy de Saint-Simon, was quite different. (See plate 7.) Personally unambitious and politically discreet, he was sent on secret royal missions involving Marie de' Medici and the dukes of Savoy and Mantua. He was also entrusted with royal messages for Richelieu. "My cousin," Louis wrote in 1634 to Richelieu, "as Saint-Simon is setting out to reach you, I have charged him to assure you of the continuation of my affection. I swear you to take care of yourself in these pressing circumstances, just as much for the love of yourself as for the love of me who loves you more than everything on earth. I will end this in praying to the good Lord with all my heart that He keep you in His holy care."[25]

And so Saint-Simon remained as favorite from 1626 until 1636, as first gentleman of the chamber, honorary councillor of state from 1629, governor of the town of Blaye from 1630, and duke and peer from 1635. In 1630, Louis had Saint-Simon and Richelieu fall on their knees to swear a pact ending a personal feud between them.[26] Only when the nobleman's loyalty to the king came into conflict with family bonds did the favor end. The disgrace bore all the marks of Louis's sense of justice. Saint-Simon's uncle had surrendered a town to the invading Spaniards. The favorite defended that conduct to the king, and warned his uncle to flee before a hanging in effigy could be followed by his actual execution. Louis abruptly banished his longtime friend.[27]

If royal favorites were a periodic worry for Richelieu, the royal council was his full-time concern. Louis XIII had previously been such a stickler for making formal decisions on major issues only after a council debate that the new chief minister could not simply rely on prior discussions with the king. Indeed, during the first years of their collaboration Richelieu deliberately used the forum of full-council discussion to test Louis's resolve on controversial policies. Naturally, he did his best to bring existing council members under his influence and to bring into the high offices of state persons who pledged their fidelity to him. The interaction between king and cardinal over the council's composition and functioning is fascinating to see.[28]

The council of 1624 was composed of holdovers from the days of Luynes, Schomberg and Condé, the Brûlarts, and La Vieuville. The only group of the reign not represented consisted of Henry IV's old servants, who (except for Sully) had all died by 1624, either in office or in exile. Aligre had been Louis's personal choice to become keeper of the seals shortly after Brûlart's disgrace, and then to succeed Brûlart as chancellor on his death late in 1624. The return of the warrior-nobleman Schomberg to the council in 1624 was also the king's doing. Indeed, Louis could hardly wait to welcome him back. Yet, despite Richelieu's urging, the ruler was not about to give Schomberg his old post as superintendent of finances in view of the fiasco of 1622. Louis simply wanted his old councillor's opinions on political and military matters, and so made him a minister without portfolio.

The king was hard pressed to find someone without Schomberg's administrative ineptitude or La Vieuville's irresponsibility to run the state's finances. Cautious and suspicious to a fault, Louis followed his recent pattern of dispersing authority in the justice and foreign affairs departments. He invited three "safe" civil servants to administer his finances jointly. Two accepted: Jean Bochart de Champigny and Michel de Marillac.[29]

Champigny was principled but ineffective. Louis pensioned him off within two years, then made him first president of the Parlement of Paris three years later, passing over more forceful candidates, including Richelieu's choice.[30] Marillac was a more complicated man. His father had been controller general, and his own long career was distinguished by religious zeal, dedication to state order, and a passion for neat governmental organization. He seemed to be the perfect surrogate for Louis XIII. The king may also have leaned toward him as a harmless way of pleasing Marie de' Medici, who was a Marillac family friend, and because his brother, Louis, was close to Richelieu. Unwittingly, then, Louis brought into his council someone whose dévot principles and rigid attachment to internal reform contributed greatly to new tensions within the government. Michel de Marillac clashed with Schomberg and Richelieu in council debates; and Louis de Marillac, who had been a faithful court informant during Richelieu's years in the political wilderness, was soon conspiring behind the scenes against the cardinal's power.[31]

Three council members in 1624 stood above the rest in rank and prestige: Louis XIII, Marie de' Medici, and Cardinal Richelieu. The king presided, or, if he was absent, Chancellor d'Aligre. Next to Louis sat his mother, because of her blood and length of service. Richelieu's position was less clear. He was not allowed to assume La Vieuville's old title of *principal ministre*; the hesitant king dropped that term altogether until 1629, when form finally caught up with the reality of Richelieu's powerful role and he began to be referred to in official documents as the principal minister. All Richelieu could obtain in 1624 was the title of *premier ministre* or *premier des ministres d'Etat*, which meant simply that he, in association with the other cardinal in the council, La Rochefoucauld, was the "first of the ministers" in ranking. La Rochefoucauld had had that title since 1622, and was called the *chef du conseil*; but in point of fact, he was the weakest of all the council members.

Beneath these formal arrangements, the triangular relationship of monarch, mother, and minister was rife with tension. While Marie's influence was not great enough to label the governing body a triumvirate,[32] she was pushy enough to make decisions both in and out of the council very, very difficult. She became jealous of her former protégé, listened to the backbiting criticism of dévots like Marillac and Cardinal Bérulle, and eventually spoke out in council against the cleric who had once dictated her speeches. She pushed and pushed until, in 1629 and 1630, she finally demanded that her son dismiss Richelieu. This placed Louis in precisely the position he sought to avoid: to choose between minister and mother.

Louis did his best to keep his mother content and contained. He made her regent for northern France during his absence at the siege of La Rochelle in 1627–28, and again during his campaign in Savoy in 1629. When they were separated, he was a faithful correspondent on government and personal matters. From Susa, he wrote of being "right to the last breath of my life your very humble and obedient son." But, except when she insisted on Gaston's marrying in 1626, Louis refused to follow his mother's political recommendations when these differed from his own inclination.

In the face of Marie's growing jealousy of the bond between her protégé and her son, Louis praised the cardinal's services: "My Cousin the Cardinal of Richelieu has so worthily served me on this occasion that I cannot say just how much I am satisfied with his care and diligence. They give me hope that the rest of my undertaking will go the same way; and that God, if it pleases Him, will continue to favor my designs."[33]

In the winter of 1629–30, Louis mustered his strongest argument, saying that "when he had been not at all inclined toward [Richelieu] she got him to employ him; and now that he loved him and was very worthily served, she wanted to have him ruined." Marie countered in vain "that he could employ him if he wished, but for her part she would never engage his services." Louis insisted on getting the three principals together in a meeting that left all of them in tears. An observer recalled that "the king threw so much passion into this reconciliation that it was achieved the next day."[34] Against her better judgment, Marie agreed to retain Richelieu and his relatives as leading members of her personal household. And so tensions continued.

Ultimately, Louis resolved such tensions as these by striking back. Irritated beyond measure by government problems involving human failures, he lashed out against the immediate wrongdoer and made sweeping cabinet changes that, not trusting his own judgment, he had previously hesitated to undertake. Let us take the examples of his two biggest cabinet shake-ups, one in 1626 over Gaston's marriage, the other following the Day of Dupes in 1630.[35]

The crisis of 1626 broke over cowardly behavior by the very person Louis had handpicked to head law enforcement, Chancellor Aligre. The ruler became set on marrying off his brother Gaston, only to discover that his chancellor refused to defend the council's decision to arrest the leading opponent of the marriage, Gaston's governor. Louis was doubly outraged, for after Aligre told Gaston he had nothing to do with the arrest, he then denied uttering such a disclaimer. The king called Aligre a liar, and gave the chancellor's seals to Marillac in the hope that he would be more vigorous in pursuing royal justice. Marillac's transfer from the finance department in turn freed Louis to find someone new to tackle problems that had been piling up under the controller general's well-intentioned but disastrous reliance on shaky loans.

The monarch was aiming high. He turned down both Richelieu's and Schomberg's candidates initially, hoping to bring back his father's financial wizard, Sully. Eventually he agreed to appoint as superintendent of finances Antoine Coiffier de Ruzé, marquis of Effiat, who had learned his trade under La Vieuville and was now recommended by Richelieu. The experiment worked well. Effiat brought the financial office from the brink of bankruptcy to moderate solvency, then combined this ministerial service with a second career as one of Louis's most trusted marshals. His death in 1632 was much regretted by a monarch who had come to depend on his efficiency.[36]

The major conciliar changes of 1626 were accompanied by a final weeding out of royal servitors left over from the coup d'état of 1617. All these men had unwisely exploited their easy access to their sovereign, badgering him too freely about his brother's marriage. As a result, the once-promising ministers Déageant and Modène lost their last positions at court. Luynes's brother was replaced as governor of the Bastille by the sibling of an emerging advisor to Richelieu, Father Joseph. And a minor governmental threesome, Sauveterre, Marsillac, and Tronçon, were disgraced. The fall of Tronçon and two other personal secretaries of the king allowed Louis to appoint the loyal personal scribe of his most important years, Michel Lucas.[37]

How did Louis XIII and Richelieu collaborate on this critical conciliar alteration? In a report to his absent chief minister, the king wrote, with astonishing vigor:

> It has been a long time since I told you that it was necessary to strengthen my council. It was you who have always hesitated, out of fear of the changes, but it is no longer the time to mull over what persons may say. It is enough that it is I who will this. . . . I want those who are in my council to get along with you.[38]

There was a similar pattern to Louis's purging of Richelieu's greatest tormentors from the council in 1630. Once again, as in the governmental crises of 1617 and 1626, the king held back. But when Marie tried to wring Richelieu's dismissal from a deathly ill Louis in September 1630, and then insisted on it after his recuperation on 11 November, she was duping herself about the outcome. While she and her friends were prematurely celebrating the cardinal's fall and the elevation of her creature Marillac as principal minister, her son withdrew on this Day of Dupes to Versailles, called Richelieu to his side, and cashiered Marillac.

Was this act unpremeditated? Far from it. Louis let his mother know that for over a year he had been certain of Marillac's treason; only his respect for her feelings had kept him from arresting her protégé, until new misdeeds finally compelled him to act.[39] That filial respect also delayed Marie's own fate. But since she spurned her son's face-to-face pleas after the Day of Dupes to be reconciled to Richelieu, Louis finally resigned himself to exiling her from the council to Compiègne.

There was a final act to this active/passive mother-and-son drama. In July 1631, the queen mother fled from her lightly guarded château to rally support near the eastern border. But when Louis instinctively sent guards to head her off, Marie was forced to chose between a humiliating surrender and an ignominious border crossing. Marie chose the latter. Mother and son corresponded until her death in 1642, but she was never allowed to set foot again on French soil.

Louis filled the void created by the Day of Dupes with key appointments, which served two purposes: they strengthened Richelieu's position by packing the government with his supporters; and they brought greater conciliar unity behind the policies Louis wanted. Charles de l'Aubespine, marquis of Châteauneuf, succeeded Marillac as keeper of the seals, and Nicolas Le Jay succeeded the deceased Champigny as first president of the Parlement of Paris. Soon after, Châteauneuf's friend and Richelieu's agent as an army intendant in Italy, Abel Servien, became secretary for war.

Some additional reshuffling between 1632 and 1635 brought Louis XIII's government fully in line with his emotional needs and political aims. Effiat's death in 1632 resulted in the reversion of the superintendency of finances to the king's prior scheme of administration under two longtime civil servants; only this time, both men were closely aligned with Richelieu. The more important of the two was Claude Bullion, who had survived every political regime from Ancre on. Holding a tight rein on financial expenditures during a period of alarmingly expanding war costs, he drew a revealing eulogy from the king on his sudden death of apoplexy in 1640: "The more I think," Louis wrote to Richelieu, "the more I miss him for his firmness. . . . I do not think that we can find one similar to him." Louis went on to express reservations to Richelieu about Bullion's surviving colleague, Claude Le Bouthillier, who had been a faithful family friend of both Marie and Richelieu but was under Bullion's shadow and more loyal than efficient: "I believe it is necessary for you to tell Monsieur Le Bouthillier that he should be a little firmer and stricter than he is; otherwise he will grant everything that we ask and there will be no money for the second half of the year." [40]

In 1633, Louis cashiered Châteauneuf for deserting Richelieu when the cardinal was hovering between life and death. The new keeper of the seals, Pierre Séguier, was a knowledgeable robe noble, and totally subservient to king and cardinal. When Aligre died in 1635, he automatically became chancellor. Meanwhile, Richelieu's creatures took full hold of the state secretaryships dealing with diplomacy and war.

Claude Le Bouthillier was secretary of state for foreign affairs from 1629 until his transfer to the finance office. He was succeeded by his son Léon, marquis of Chavigny, known affectionately by Louis and Richelieu as *le Jeune*. Not only did Chavigny follow Richelieu's wishes in the foreign affairs office, but he also played a crucial role in the king's emotional life. The king occasionally grumbled about le Jeune's administrative failings, but he knew Chavigny to be totally loyal, and hence Louis followed Richelieu's suggestion of entrusting the young man with watching his untrustworthy brother Gaston's every change in mood. Louis also knew that Chavigny was one of the persons Richelieu used as informant and manager of his moods. It did not bother the monarch; one suspects he even welcomed that brake on his *mauvaises humeurs*. Richelieu wrote to Chavigny, "You cannot know how better to serve the king nor oblige me than in doing everything you can to dispel His Majesty's frequent melancholy, and to free him from his anxieties."[41]

Early in 1636, the secretariat for war also changed hands. Servien was dismissed because of embarrassing quarrels with his fellow ministers and Louis's suspicion that he had not made adequate military preparations for the Spanish war.[42] His successor was Richelieu's man, François Sublet de Noyers. Sublet was sanctimonious but efficient in his duties. Until Richelieu's death in 1642 he maintained favor by doing his patron's bidding, informing his sovereign of every military detail, and joining Chavigny as manager of the king's moods.[43]

By 1636 Louis had completed his quest for a mode of governance that suited his personality and worked effectively. He had a council that was harmonious and efficient. He worked well with a trusted chief minister. He no longer had to contend with his mother. His system was, above all, a flexible one. If the occasion demanded, Louis could work in a formal council session or a gathering of a few councillors, apart from Richelieu (but still in contact through messages and intermediaries) or closeted with the cardinal.

To be sure, the system did not make Louis XIII look powerful, surrounded as he was by his powerful minister's own creatures and

plied by that servitor's magisterial position papers. Yet this paradoxical mode of governance should not puzzle us as it did Richelieu's nineteenth-century editor, who was amazed that the cardinal
"was obliged, more often than one believes, to give in to the
prince's will; . . . Louis XIII, even with his impatient obstinacy
and moody timidity, still managed to deflect the despotism under
which people believed him to have been perpetually oppressed."[44]
Nor do the facts limit us to the more recent conclusion that "in
critical circumstances Louis XIII did not hesitate to give proof of
personal initiative and to precede Richelieu in the adoption of energetic solutions."[45] For the partnership of king and collaborator
was not a ministerial tyranny interrupted by royal intervention, but
a continual interacting based on similar influences, mutual respect,
very different ways of thinking and even different guiding principles, and not a little anxiety on both sides to please the other.[46]

When Louis XIII insisted on going in person to the war theater
in 1635 without Richelieu, the two men experienced all the emotions of that complex partnership. Richelieu objected, then gave in
gracefully, and kept himself informed by fellow ministers of his
master's mood. Louis wrote a note of anger, then begged his minister to burn it, and finally, in the words of Bouthillier to Richelieu,
"reverted to his first thought that you did not approve his journey
and wanted to wear him down to cancel it." It was all very familiar
to the cardinal: "There was the change in visage, the burning heat
throughout [the king's] person triggered by the agitation of his
emotions." Yet in the midst of this turmoil, Louis was there to comfort Richelieu on his sister's death.[47]

When calm, Louis could report to Richelieu about his latest falling out with a favorite, ask what to write to his exiled mother, or
simply run random thoughts together: "My bad mood has gone
away; I recommend that you be merry, knowing well that melancholy is harmful to you. I will hold to what I promised you right to
the death." And in between bouts of grave illness, Louis could express concern for his servitor's own health: "Having ordered you
by my last [letter] to leave at the earliest chance to come to me, not
being able to suffer your staying any longer in danger of the plague,
I will add this word to tell you that you [must] not stop anywhere,
being greatly impatient to see you at my side."[48]

With similar devotion, Richelieu could write: "Sire, these three
lines are meant to tell Your Majesty that the honor of his conversa-

tion yesterday allowed me to sleep until 7 o'clock without waking up. This proves that emotional contentment is the best medicine there can be for rather delicate bodies such as those of the best master on earth and the most faithful, most passionate, and most obedient creature who ever was." [49]

9

ORDERING PRIORITIES

The five years of Louis XIII's rule that began with Richelieu's appointment and culminated in the fall of La Rochelle were a confusing but pivotal period in French history. Between 1624 and 1628, the king settled on basic policies that made possible fundamental political change during the rest of the reign. Five elements were involved in this process. Only one is universally known, though the oft-told story of a second ingredient is commonly linked to it. Two other factors have been glossed over. A fifth is unknown.

The most spectacular ingredient was Richelieu's promise to Louis on entering his service in 1624 that he would help him achieve certain broad aims. Unfortunately, the exact nature of what the cardinal promised has to be reconstructed from afterthoughts in his famous *Testament politique*. The striking similiarity between this "prediction" and historians' narration of the second ingredient—the actual course of events that followed—has led to a seemingly obvious conclusion: that Richelieu was firmly in control of events, setting and realizing a three-part agenda for destroying the Huguenot state within the state, imposing royal authority on great and ordinary subjects alike, and reducing the rival power of the Habsburg states.[1]

That the situation was less Cartesian than Richelieu's reconstruction has been known for some time by the best scholars.[2] Rather than there being a precisely ordered 1-2-3 chronological agenda, there was a great deal of moving back and forth. If left to speak for themselves, the events resemble political cartoons of the times that depicted king and cardinal on stormy seas in a fragile ship of state, buffeted by unpredictable waves of internal subversion, Huguenot revolt, and foreign crisis.

The model of a rational leader (Richelieu) controlling events is further undermined by our knowledge of the third and fourth elements in the political process, that is, what other subjects were saying and doing about the issues. Court debate and pamphleteering were extraordinarily heated, divisive, and confusing during and after the meteoric career of La Vieuville. One wonders, then, how even the extraordinarily gifted Richelieu could have found his way through the maze to the program he later said he offered to Louis. Along with the clarity of Richelieu's vision, his originality becomes somewhat suspect when we recall the actions associated with his predecessor. When La Vieuville was in favor, Louis XIII had made an alliance with the Calvinist Dutch, granting them financial aid for their war against Spain; negotiations were under way for the marriage of Louis XIII's youngest sister, Henrietta Maria, with the new king of Anglican England, Charles I; and a clandestine French expeditionary force was in the Alps, poised to fight the Habsburgs over the Val Tellina passes leading from Italy to the Dutch and German war theaters. To be sure, royal relations with the Huguenots were in a quiescent phase, with no sign of Louis's coming last wars; and La Vieuville's disgrace left the future of internal reform, particularly fiscal and economic, an open question.

The fifth factor shaping the future was Louis XIII himself. Whether Richelieu was resorting to flattery or not, a passage from his reconstructed vow of 1624 indicates the crucial role of this mysterious monarch. The passage is normally omitted when historians mention Richelieu's famous vow; yet it merits our attention:

> I dared to promise you, without rashness I believe, that you would find a cure for all the disorders of the state, and that your prudence, your vigor, and God's blessing would in short order give your realm a new look.

Louis was presented with a babel of voices in 1624 and 1625 urging him to return France to the "Golden Age" prior to the Wars of Religion. The trouble was that each voice and tract suggested a different route.[3] The words *reform, reformation, restoration,* and *renovation* were on everyone's lips. Louis himself took his cue from a speech suggested by Richelieu immediately after La Vieuville's disgrace, telling his council: "We shall see what I will do for the reformation of my state." [4] But what did reform mean, and how much attention could be devoted to it?

In his speech, Louis hinted that he could be generous to his subjects and get along well with the grandees of his realm. This conception of reform entailed the enhancement of private welfare and privilege; it was in sharp contrast to a different notion of reform enunciated in some post–La Vieuville tracts, which argued that "France was a body in need of a strict regimen for an indefinite period, during which it would be free to recuperate and regain its natural forces." Here was a reform agenda which assumed that the monarch could and should stay out of war if he wanted to succeed, and that success would be measured by disciplining subjects, not catering to their interests.

The most severe reform ideas appeared in a pamphlet that took its cue from the opportunity to clean up La Vieuville's corruption and its inspiration from Louis XIII's preeminent quality as "the Just." The tract, entitled *France in Convalescence to the King*, started with a "chamber of reformation" to prosecute the fallen finance minister's band of embezzlers, called for the abolition of venality of office and recovery of alienated royal lands and fees, and added cure-alls for "a thousand disorders in the state."

If we look at what Richelieu said and wrote during this period (as opposed to what he later recalled about his vow of 1624), it is clear that he leaned toward the benign version of reform as currently debated. His memos to the king from 1624 to 1629 were crammed with idealistic notions of how to make French society young, vibrant, and prosperous, among them tax cuts, domainal resumption, state commercial enterprises, and the abolition of venality. [5] In a revealing aside to his friend, Father Joseph, the cardinal-minister placed such reform in a general 1-2-3 list of priorities that differed in one important respect from his vow of 1624 as recalled much later. In his *Testament politique*, he equated reform with controlling subjects; to his friend he linked reform with their welfare:

> Three things entered my mind: first, to ruin the Huguenots and render the king absolute in his state; second, to abase the House of Austria [both Spanish and Imperial branches]; and third, to discharge the French people of heavy subsidies and tailles, enabling the king to repossess his *domaines* which are capable by themselves of sustaining him handsomely. [6]

As if Louis XIII did not have enough to think about with regard to reform, he was also deluged with dévot and bon Français arguments on the proper relationship between the state and religion. Within the Catholic dévot camp, there was an escalation of pamphlet rhetoric, from the *True or Friendly Word of Messieurs the Princes* in 1624, which echoed the regency's old policy of keeping the peace with Spain, to the stridently pro-Habsburg *Mysteria politica* and ultramontanist *Admonitio ad regem* of the following year. The latter unabashedly called on Louis XIII to be true to his celebrated virtue of justice by repudiating his anti-Habsburg alliances, following the sciptural "prohibition" of alliances with Protestant states, and fighting heresy abroad and at home.

The bon Français "patriotic" position was more complex. Little was said about the Huguenot state within the state, because no shared view existed. Some bons Français, like Constable Lesdiguières (who died in 1626) and Marshal La Force, were new Catholics who retained their old ties. Even Catholic bons Français hostile to Huguenot military autonomy were divided over whether the monarchy ought also to attack the Huguenots' right to exist as a religious body. Hence, bon Français writers focused on foreign policy. Recruited mainly by Cardinal Richelieu, they tried to convince the public that state interests dictated containing, not aiding, Habsburg power and that such a policy did not conflict with Catholic belief. Tracts like the *Discourse of the Princes and States of Christendom* argued that the Spanish king and Holy Roman Emperor were aiming at nothing less than universal monarchy. Consequently, the French state should support its traditional Protestant and Catholic allies in fighting the Habsburg "plagues and evils." The very title of another tract was a catalogue of Habsburg territorial aggression: *On the Progress and Conquests of the King of Spain and the House of Austria in Germany, Switzerland, the Grisons, Italy and the Frontiers of France Since the Death of Henry the Great.*

These secular bon Français arguments were obviously not enough for a religious age. Hence, the *Parallel of St. Louis and Louis XIII* played on the king's saintly character and anti-Huguenot record to reassure subjects that he would not undermine Catholicism in fighting Catholic rulers. Reflecting the confusion of religious and secular issues was the quasi–bon Français *Catholique d'estat* (National Catholic). Its scathing criticism of the *Admonitio* for equating Habsburg aims with international Catholicism was penned by a team that included a Protestant pastor and two devout Catholics, Fathers Bérulle and Joseph.

Plate 1. A suspicious, observant Louis XIII soon after ascending the throne as a minor king. By Frans Pourbus, the Younger, the Flemish-Mantuan portraitist patronized by Marie de' Medici. (Los Angeles County Museum of Art. Gift of Mr. and Mrs. William May Garland.)

Plate 2. Louis XIII around twenty-one years, prior to appointing Richelieu to his council. Painted by Peter Paul Rubens, when he was at the French court composing the Marie de' Medici cycle at the Luxembourg and an Emperor Constantine tapestry cycle for Louis XIII. (The Norton Simon Foundation, Pasadena.)

Plate 3. One of the most accurate portraits of Anne of Austria as a young queen of France, around her mid twenties. This Peter Paul Rubens portrait and the one reproduced here as plate 2 found their way into the art gallery of Anne's Spanish relations in Brussels in the 1640s. (The Norton Simon Foundation, Pasadena.)

Plate 4. A prematurely aged Louis XIII, whose sadness and fatigue have been perfectly captured by the brilliant portraitist and royal painter, Philippe de Champaigne. (The Prado, Madrid. GIRAUDON/Art Resource, N.Y.)

Plate 5. A penetrating portrait of Louis's most famous minister, Cardinal Richelieu, by Philippe de Champaigne. (University of Paris. GIRAUDON/Art Resource, N.Y.)

Plate 6. Charles d'Albert de Luynes, falconer to the teenage king, who helped Louis topple his mother and became his minister-favorite. By Moncornet. (Estampes collection of the Bibliothèque Nationale, Paris.)

CLAUDE DUC DE S.ˢSIMON Pair et grand Lou-
vetier de France, premier Ecuyer de la petite Ecurie du Roy, Gouver.ˢ
de Blaye, fait Ch'ʳ des Ordres le 14. may 1633.

1634. par Vouet

Plate 7. Claude de Rouvroy, duke of Saint-Simon, long-time personal friend and favorite of Louis XIII. By the king's painter, Simon Vouet. (Estampes collection, Bibliothèque Nationale, Paris.)

Plate 8. Louis XIII accepting the surrender of La Rochelle's Protestant rebels, with "Justice" and "Clemency" on their knees before the king, followed by "Repentence" and the bedraggled civic leaders, and the ordinary townswomen and babes in arms filing out from the town in the background. (Estampes collection, Bibliothèque Nationale, Paris.)

Plate 9. Cartoon commemorating Louis XIII's entrance into defeated La Rochelle, with a panoramic view of the siege of the city, complete with royal army pike squares and the famous royal dike. (Estampes collection, Bibliothèque Nationale, Paris.)

Plate 10. One of twelve triumphal arches erected for Louis XIII's *entrée* to Paris following his capture of La Rochelle. The king is depicted as Hercules in his chariot, crowned with laurel leaves and beneath a rainbow representing God's forgiveness of wicked humanity after the biblical Flood. Scenes below link the flourishing of flocks and crops with the royal horseman bearing an olive branch and a blindfolded justice holding the scales of justice. To make the point absolutely clear, a male and female demonic twosome burn in hell to Louis's left, and a rainbow arcs into a cluster of flowers on his right! (Estampes collection, Bibliothèque Nationale, Paris.)

Plate 11. Medallion of 1618, after the royal coup d'état against the king's mother and her favorite, Concini. "Justice" on a cloud holds the balance scales and sword to show that Louis XIII, "called the Just, applies himself solely to maintain and defend his Kingdom, whose troubles he has ended to his people's happiness." (Estampes collection, Bibliothèque Nationale, Paris.)

Plate 12. Medallion of 1631, after Louis's Mantuan campaign across the Alps against Savoy and the Habsburgs. The king, riding on horseback with his scepter, between the mountains, demonstrates that "no obstacle can prevent his courage from taking him wherever he wishes to go to impose the force of his arms." (Estampes collection, Bibliothèque Nationale, Paris.)

Plate 13. Medallion of 1635, justifying Louis XIII's declaration of war against Spain. An arrow is shot through the flames of the sky into the clouds, symbolizing "the king's just anger and resolve to give the Spaniards no quarter, for forcing him to declare war and punish their criminal assault against the Elector of Trier." (Estampes collection, Bibliothèque Nationale, Paris.)

Mᶫᴸᴱ DE LA FAYETTE,

FILLE D'HONNEUR DE LA REINE ANNE D'AUTRICHE.

Morte en 1665.

Plate 14. Louise de La Fayette, the gentle ascetic friend of Louis XIII, who sacrificed their happiness for a religious retreat. By Gatine. (Estampes collection, Bibliothèque Nationale, Paris.)

Plate 15. The frontispiece of Guez de Balzac's *The Prince* (1631), featuring an unflattering portrait of Louis XIII amid four of his greatest military scenes. (Estampes collection, Bibliothèque Nationale, Paris.)

Plate 16. The evening portion of a cycle depicting Louis XIII's daily occupations. Louis awaits a theater performance at court, in company with his brother Gaston, his wife Anne, and their oldest child, the future Louis XIV. (Estampes collection, Bibliothèque Nationale, Paris.)

Louis XIII was well aware of the issues being debated and of the arguments being advanced in literature and discussion, because there were advocates for all positions in his council. But basically his policies after 1624 resulted from the interplay of his personality and belief system on the one hand and, on the other, the immediate issues as they rushed in on him and were sorted out by his chief advisor.

Louis XIII already had a clear general notion of the things he stood for and against. He also had a habit of striking out impetuously against what he perceived to be the most immediate evil, and on behalf of the most pressing good. This combination explains in large part the consistency of policies he developed in the areas of reform, religious division, and foreign affairs between 1624 and 1627—and also much of the inconsistency in the ranking of his policy objectives. Where Richelieu was most influential was in getting his king to stick to a policy objective they had agreed on, or, if he thought another royal objective more attainable, in nudging his monarch to shift his priorities. But this précis is very abstract. Let us look over the king's shoulder as he worked in his own complicated way to choose his priorities.

In the winter of 1624–25, Louis was dissuaded from turning his prosecution of La Vieuville's financial coterie into the major act of criminal and financial vengeance he wanted. Richelieu reasoned that this type of royal reformism would scare away the state's creditors, whose loans were crucial to maintaining a full treasury.[7] Windfall fines from Louis's short-lived "chamber of justice" plus hard bargaining by Effiat with tax farmers and other state creditors allowed Louis to face other challenges in 1625. The Huguenot brothers Rohan and Soubise had drawn Louis's ire by refortifying the Protestant south from Montauban to Castres and using captured royal ships to seize the islands of Oléron and Ré, near La Rochelle. The Habsburgs frustrated Louis by holding on to the Val Tellina passes (so crucial for the transportation of Spanish troops from Italy to the Imperialist war zone in Germany and the Spanish-Dutch war theater) despite France's military alliance with Venice and Savoy in 1623. (See Appendix, maps 3 and 4.)

In the case of the Habsburg challenge, Louis was well coached by Richelieu not to be diverted from the Val Tellina to other potential battlegrounds. The king politely but firmly told the Dutch that they would have to be satisfied with his financial aid for their war against Spain. That was enough to stop Spanish forces from overrunning the Dutch Republic, and the 1625 entry of the Lutheran king of Denmark in the Thirty Years' War temporarily held back the advance of the Habsburg emperor's forces through Germany.

The minister did not need to get his master in the right mood to fight for the Val Tellina. In April 1624, before Richelieu's accession to power, Louis had repudiated the French ambassador to Rome for endorsing a papal plan to allow Spanish use of the Val Tellina passes. The envoy's approval, the king angrily informed his council, "had been given without his order, was directly contrary to his intentions, and he could not approve it."[8] Early in 1625, Louis upbraided the papal nuncio for telling him he was disrespectful of His Holiness; and French troops seized former Grisons fortresses from their papal and Habsburg garrisons.[9] All that prevented a "state of war" between France and Catholic Spain, Austria, Genoa, and the Pope himself was the fiction that the French expeditionary forces were fighting for France's allies—the Grisons, Venice, and Savoy. And Louis was indignant enough to cross that line if provoked.

When Pope Urban VIII hastily sent his own nephew, Cardinal Barberini, on a peace mission to France, Louis surprised the envoy with his bellicosity: "I have been careful until now to avoid anything that could provoke an open war between the two crowns; [but] if the king of Spain takes up arms against me, I will be the last to lay them down."[10] Barberini got nowhere when he suddenly changed his tactics and suggested, in a private royal audience, a compromise designed to play on the king's religious sensibilities. Why not grant the Val Tellina Catholics religious autonomy while retaining their vassal status under the Protestant Grisons in other areas? the legate asked. Louis quickly saw the trap. He had come a long way toward political maturity from the moment in 1620 when he had blindly linked French interests to the cause of international Catholicism. Sensing that the limited autonomy for Val Telliners would provide an excuse for Habsburg military protection of their faith, he retorted "that interests of state must not be mixed in any way with religious ones, and that he would never agree to anything that could alter the sovereignty of the Grisons, his allies, over the Val Telliners."[11]

Richelieu made sure that his sovereign took full responsibility for his bellicose response. A series of carefully balanced ministerial memos and letters stressed the need for military preparedness and asked Louis whether he wanted peace or war in Italy.[12] Then Richelieu had Louis summon the leading clerics, grandees, and judges to his council for a public debate.

Louis was already irritated with the legate for abruptly leaving for Rome without awaiting conciliar confirmation of his impromptu decision. And at the council meeting, propeace dévots like Marillac could not counter arguments tailor-made to the king's beliefs. Cardinal La Valette, son of Epernon and a new creature of Richelieu, quoted the papal theologians' admission that "religion prescribed obedience [by the Val Telliners] to legitimate sovereigns [the Grisons]." Richelieu concentrated on a secular argument designed to stir the royal blood: if Louis "cowardly" abandoned his allies, his reputation would be lost, and "his power, his wealth, and his arms . . . equally scorned." Louis's friend Bassompierre recalled from his negotiations in Spain that the Spaniards "had no other object in view than to make themselves masters of the Val Tellina." And Schomberg accused the papal legate of being pro-Spanish. Marie de' Medici turned on Schomberg for that remark, but to no avail. Without taking a vote in a council that had been badly divided on the issue, Louis, in full public glare, confirmed his stand against a truce.[13]

What made Louis XIII take on the Huguenots at home while committing himself to foreign allies over the Val Tellina? In brief, Richelieu may have convinced him it was a safe venture. The cardinal had fine-tuned La Vieuville's alliance with the Dutch and negotiations with the English, thereby isolating the French Protestants. The Dutch were pledged to send twenty ships against Soubise's forces on the western seaboard. And the May 1625 marriage of Louis's youngest sister, Henrietta Maria, to King Charles I of England was aimed at keeping the Anglican ruler from allying with either the French Protestants or Catholic Spain.

Richelieu's insistence on guarantees for Catholic worship in England and the Netherlands was the shrewdest aspect of his diplomatic maneuvering. Whereas La Vieuville had bothered Louis's conscience by ignoring religious considerations altogether, his successor got the minimum possible: Catholic worship in the English queen's quarters and at the French embassy in The Hague. Even the French dévots were mollified by Richelieu's ability to salvage something for the Catholic cause, and by the fact that one of their leaders, Bérulle, had been a key negotiator of the English marriage agreement. Yet the scrupulous Louis XIII might still have held back from once again waging all-out war on his own subjects had not Soubise, in panic, launched a preemptive strike on the approaching Dutch ships. Angered by that sneak attack when the parties concerned were officially at peace, the king sent his would-be favorite, Toiras (whom Richelieu did not like), and his boyhood companion Montmorency down to the Rochelais area. Soubise's forces quickly abandoned the islands of Ré and Oléron.[14]

The military pursuit of both the Huguenots and the Habsburgs was abruptly halted after only one season. Ideology was not the prime cause for these truces. Dévot propaganda opposed accommodation with heresy at home; and it complicated rather than dictated the terms of the Italian settlement. Nor was the domestic crisis known as the Chalais conspiracy the instigator, for it broke after the Huguenot truce, and well after treaty arrangements over the Val Tellina were well advanced. The real reason was the lack of money to wage war on two fronts. War costs from the miniwars of 1625–26 had already caused annual state expenses to spiral to forty million livres a year, twenty-five million more than was taken in. The deficit of fifty million was a staggering five times that of 1624. When both campaigns sputtered, Louis reluctantly gave in to Richelieu's pleas to negotiate with his heretic subjects, and the two of them gambled on French negotiators in Spain securing by diplomacy what French and allied arms had failed to win in the Alps.[15]

Louis almost scuttled Schomberg's delicate talks with the Huguenots. Richelieu wrote to his fellow minister to hide all news of rebel foot-dragging from the king: "It seems this expedient is necessary so that His Majesty will not grow sour on giving peace to his subjects on account of their continued disobedience." When a Huguenot peace team asked Louis to add to his title "the Just" that of "Father of his People," he relented. "You have conducted yourselves badly and insolently against me," he answered, "but I pardon you and grant you peace."[16]

The Treaty of La Rochelle, signed in February 1625, was really a truce. Dévots thought it a sellout, calling Richelieu the Cardinal of La Rochelle. Louis assumed he could keep his new fort to intimidate that port city; the Rochelais assumed it would be dismantled. Charles I and Buckingham had helped persuade their fellow Protestants in France to sign the treaty; both parties assumed this made England a protector of the Huguenots.[17]

Meanwhile, France's chief negotiator in Spain, the count of Fargis, signed the draft of a foreign peace treaty that conceded more than Louis XIII deemed prudent: the Spanish terms gave the Catholic Val Telliners religious autonomy from the pro-French Grisons. Was Fargis getting what he thought to be the best possible agreement for France, or did his concessions on the religious issue originate with the dévot lobby at the French court, where his wife was lady-in-waiting to Marie de' Medici and close to Bérulle? Historians have wondered, because Bérulle had been pressing the queen mother for peace at any price, saying "the Pope and all Italy expected it."[18] Whatever Fargis's motives may have been, Richelieu and Louis XIII insisted on unequivocal Grisons sovereignty over the Val Tellina passes. Louis XIII angrily sent Fargis's draft back twice to outflank Olivares, Philip IV, the Pope, and the dévots.[19]

The Treaty of Monzon, as ratified in the spring of 1625, was a French victory on paper: it called for Papal dismantling of the Val Tellina fortifications and endorsed Grisons overlordship. Dismantling was slow, however; French military rights were not mentioned; and, thanks to clauses giving the Val Telliners local religious and political rights, Grisons sovereignty was later interpreted as not including use of the passes. Louis XIII soon discovered that he had given up what he had refused to concede to the papal legate Barberini: Spanish troops were allowed passage by the Val Telliners through the Alps to the German and Dutch wars. Moreover, at the price of a brief era of goodwill with Spain (including an anti-Huguenot alliance which Spain did not honor), France had alienated its own Italian allies. Louis XIII learned his lesson. When the next opportunity for an Italian venture arose, over the Mantuan succession problem of 1629–30, he was uncompromisingly set on holding to his principles.[20]

Louis XIII's strategic retreat from costly military entanglements permitted the monarchy to concentrate for a few months on internal reforms. If we divide these reforms into general categories, it appears that Louis seriously tried out a number of options. There were Richelieu's early schemes for improving the economy; a grandiose governmental program to improve the general well-being of government and society; and finally Louis XIII's imposition of specific controls on subjects, ranging from special fiscal levies to harsh punishment of flagrant lawbreaking and plotting. On looking more closely at the evolution of reform, we can see that, in general, the king leaned toward the third option, despite occasional wavering over punishing friends and concern for the burdens of the average subject.

Richelieu's vision of a vibrant economy competing successfully with the world at large was in line with economic planning elsewhere in western Europe during the 1620s.[21] Yet he had to battle two insuperable obstacles: the conjuncture of an economy in recession, and the structural mentalité of a society perennially prejudiced against investing in business (as opposed to such socially acceptable institutions as venal offices).

In 1626, Louis XIII did away with the admiralty offices of the Atlantic and Mediterranean and created the much more encompassing office of grand master of navigation and commerce for his chief minister. The fleet created by the new grand master was soon to be used, with telling effect, against the Protestant port of La Rochelle; but it failed to drive Dutch, English, and other foreign commercial competition from French markets. Richelieu's dream of competing abroad through impressively titled trading companies and far-flung colonies also foundered on native indifference and stiff competition from the Barbary pirates in the Mediterranean, the Dutch in the north, the English in North America, and many rivals in Africa, Asia, and the Caribbean. He finally tried to assist French commerce, shipping, and industry with protectionist tariffs and subsidies, in line with Montchretien's *Treatise on Political Economy*, which had been dedicated to the king and queen mother in 1615—but these devices looked better on paper than in the real world.[22]

These economic schemes were part of a broader program that Marillac, Effiat, Schomberg, and Richelieu unveiled before a select body of thirteen high clerics, thirteen great nobles, and twenty-nine sovereign court judges who met as an Assembly of Notables from December 1626 to February 1627. Marillac, as past finance minister and current head of justice, spoke of tightening fiscal and juridical procedures. Effiat outlined the budget. Schomberg talked of military needs. Richelieu held out the hope of guaranteeing low taxation and a full war chest by buying out the private possessors of royal domain lands and fees and implementing tax-producing schemes that would stimulate the economy.

Yet nothing they said opened up notables' purses. Marillac did his best in an opening address that was a fusion of dévot ideals and praise for the king's virtues of piety, justice, wisdom, resolve, compassion, and hatred of vice and dishonesty. His prayer that the vice and misery of the three estates would vanish while the sovereign transformed the century begun at his birth (conveniently in 1601) into an "age of peace and prosperity," was no more effective than his colleagues' facts and figures. The assembly disbanded after approving many things in principle, but without providing support—not even the twenty million livres in seed money requested to launch the domain redemption scheme.[23]

To be sure, many royal proposals to the notables—dealing with administrative organization, budget procedures, and the well-being of the respective estates—found their way into individual government decrees and *règlements* between 1627 and 1630. In addition, both the reform spirit and many specific suggestions from the Estates General of 1614 and the Assemblies of Notables of 1617 and 1626 were worked into the Code Michau of January 1629, one of the most comprehensive legal ordinances of the early modern French monarchy. But this code was, in itself, only a statement of principles, just as were the individual royal decrees and *règlements* of the same era.[24]

The test was whether these wishes could be followed. Those in the Code Michau could not. French courts of law refused to enforce the code, since social prejudices ran counter to many of its articles. The king, within a year, disgraced its main author and leading advocate, Michel de Marillac. Other reform blueprints also amounted to nothing more than government streamlining: they looked good on paper, they may have made things more efficient in practice, but it is doubtful that they were of major import.

The most effective reforms were those that Louis backed: his latest antidueling decree; his prohibition of town and château fortifications in the interior of the realm, and his treason law amendments in the spirit of the swift justice he exercised following the Chalais conspiracy. Similarly, the most effective administrative achievement was tough ad hoc management by Superintendent of Finances Effiat, stressing low-interest loans coupled with timely royal gouging of the wealthy clergy and judges. When the return to war with the Huguenots in 1627 threw the budget completely out of control and made even Richelieu turn his back on comprehensive reform, these disciplinary devices of Louis the Just became the foundation for state building in the 1630s.

A few examples of this pragmatic subordination of the three estates to state needs will have to suffice. Sumptuary legislation may have failed to prevent wealthy commoners from dressing like nobles, but a host of forced loans and new venal offices reduced the income of the existing Third Estate judges and tax officials. On the eve of renewed fighting against the Huguenots in June 1627, Louis held a lit de justice at the Parlement of Paris to impose some of these expedients, defending them without his normal stutter. His long letter to

Procurer General Molé in November, written in his own hand, shows how strongly he felt:

> Here I am [at the siege of La Rochelle], in a rain that never lets up, barely recovered from a life-threatening illness, dealing with everything in person . . . to uproot the troubles and upheavals which have oppressed and afflicted my kingdom for more than sixty years. [But] where everyone ought to be contributing their most secret and cherished means to help such a praiseworthy and useful cause for the benefit of the entire state, [the judges] block assistance and scare off those who could provide it.[25]

Louis was equally sanctimonious with the higher clergy of the First Estate. In 1621 and 1625 he had compelled the reluctant Assembly of the Clergy to give special subsidies for his wars against the Huguenots. In 1628 they balked at his demand for the unusual sum of three million livres to help finance the siege of La Rochelle. In the midst of the showdown, Louis scrawled a note to Richelieu: "My cousin, I am sending you my reply to the deputies of the clergy, so that you can see whether you judge it appropriate as written." Obviously, Richelieu found it appropriate, even though he conveniently omitted the king's action from his memoirs.

The long reply is vintage Louis XIII, berating the clerics for the "shame" of being the only group denying support for the joint church-state project. He snidely noted that the money he requested "would be better employed than for the feasts they engaged in every day" and that the "free gift" must be drawn from the wealth of the higher clergy "and not on the poor curés."[26]

The Second Estate was in for an equally rude shock. At the Assembly of Notables, the king's friends Marshals La Force and Bassompierre complained that although the noble order had saved Henry IV's throne when the other orders had "deserted" him, now they found themselves pushed unceremoniously out of judicial and financial offices and even the king's council. Louis XIII replied cautiously that he intended to "favor his nobility with all the advantages he could." In the next few months he responded with a mixture of token concessions and severe demands. On the benign side, he tried (in vain) to make nobles engage in ignoble commerce by legalizing it, and he gave them a monopoly of household offices and top military and ecclesiastical posts. On the disciplinary side, he slashed their pensions, added yet another edict against dueling (superseding those of 1623 and 1624), set up a noble commission to authorize the demolition of château and town fortifications in the interior of the realm, and made it a capital offense to attack state policies and their authors (i.e., Richelieu) in printed tracts. Richelieu's hand can be seen in both the benign and the harsh sides of these reforms; Louis hand is especially evident in the latter.

The most spectacular example of Louis XIII's reforming action involving the nobility during this period was the execution of Bouteville for dueling. François de Montmorency, count of Bouteville, was a member of a distinguished provincial family and had the best connections at court. He embodied the noblest qualities of the fearless warrior in Louis's battles with the Huguenots. Unfortunately, he was also, at age twenty-seven, the champion dueler of France. Richelieu exaggerated only slightly in saying that Bouteville had his hand in every duel in France between 1624 and 1627. Some sort of showdown with Louis XIII was inevitable.

Just before Richelieu's rise to power Louis had tried to enforce an earlier revision of antidueling laws. But Bouteville had fled, and dueling tapered off. It reemerged in 1626. The count was in the thick of the fight, having returned to France just as the old law he had transgressed expired and the new—and more enforceable—edict of February 1626 was being unveiled. Combining the king's determination and his leading minister's ingenuity, the edict of 1626 addressed the pronoble parlementary judges' objection to executing every transgressor of previous laws. Duelers were put on notice that if they dueled or challenged anyone to a duel one on one, they would be stripped of their public posts; if they dueled with seconds—("Three Musketeers"–style) or killed an opponent, they would die. Furthermore, common knowledge alone—rather than virtually unobtainable witnesses, could send a nobleman to the executioner's block.[27]

No one paid any attention. Louis himself seemed ambivalent, for he let his disgraced favorite Barradat off with only banishment from court. Bouteville's case, however, was different from all the rest: he was forever getting involved in elaborate, blood-shedding duels over his honor, even when he tried to run away from them! Just before implementation of the new edict, he engaged in a duel of three against three that ended the lives of two opponents, including yet another boyhood companion of King Louis. At the beginning of 1627 Bouteville was drawn into yet another duel after his opponent, La Frette, called him a coward for refusing his challenge. A Bouteville second was killed, and the ace dueler promptly fled with his cousin Chapelles to the Spanish Netherlands to escape the new edict's penalties.

Louis XIII unwillingly led Bouteville at long last to his doom by giving the honor-ridden young man a partial pardon that looked like a slight: he would not be prosecuted if he returned to French soil but stayed away from court. Stung by this affront, Bouteville decided to evade no longer the baron of Beuvron, the would-be revenger of his last dueling victim, who had come unsuccessfully all the way to Brussels to challenge him. They fought a multiple duel, in the most public place in Paris Bouteville could think of to uphold his honor against his noble opponent and his royal master—the fashionable Place Royale.

Observers reported the king as being "so offended" that he sent Bassompierre after the fleeing Bouteville and Chapelles with Swiss guards, asked the parlementary prosecutors if the duo could be taken dead or alive, and "expressed great joy" at the news of their capture (while Richelieu and Marillac merely shrugged their shoulders and went on with their work). The instigator of the duel, Beuvron, escaped to England.[28]

As the trial proceeded, Louis managed to keep his emotions in check. When Bouteville's wife, three months pregnant, fell on her knees after mass, the king avoided her, commenting: "The woman brings me pity, but I wish to and must maintain my authority." The condemned man's uncle by marriage, Condé, got nowhere with the typical male noble arguments: "He has failed by error of the custom of your kingdom, which makes honor consist of undertaking perilous actions. . . . The universal quest for glory, not a personal design to disobey you, drew him into this disobedience."[29]

It is possible that Louis might have been swayed had Richelieu not constantly argued that a test case be made of Bouteville's flagrant defiance of the law. But, as we have seen in our discussion of the royal-ministerial partnership, the minister also made counterarguments for clemency.[30] Richelieu later wrote that he had never been more shaken than by this conflict of values, and by appeals that came from his own family.[31]

After the Parlement had sentenced Chapelles and Bouteville to decapitation, and their opponents to hanging in effigy, Louis armed himself as best he could against the shrieks of Condé's wife and the fainting of Mme de Bouteville. He cited his edicts, conscience, oath, and the blood of his nobility, "for which he had to answer to God." To Charlotte de Montmorency-Condé's cries for mercy he answered: "Their loss moves me as much as you, but my conscience forbids me to pardon them." According to the royal historiographer Bernard, Louis also exclaimed: "It is necessary for a little blood to be shed in this instance to stop the stream that flows daily."[32] Louis XIII insisted that the execution be public, nervously ordered the guards to seize anyone who so much as called for "grace," and had the surrounding streets blocked off with chains and carts.

Bouteville and Chapelles died bravely and repentant for their crimes, dignifying a scene that must have sickened the entire court. Louis himself had to be bled a week later, and immediately fell dangerously ill.[33] Was it worth it? Bernard contended that dueling was lessened, and history has accepted his verdict. In truth, the death on 22 June 1627 of a young nobleman who had killed twenty-two opponents was an exceptional act of state. In contrast to Henry IV and Marie de' Medici, who had condoned the socially acceptable crime of private dueling, Louis XIII simply said that state order was incompatible with flagrant lawless behavior in the name of noble honor.

During the rest of his reign Louis chose carefully where to draw the line. The axe fell on a beloved captain of the king's guards, but spared Protestant and Catholic officers in 1627–28, including Richelieu's cousin, who tried to settle the last of the religious wars by ritual duels. In 1636 Richelieu wrote to Louis that dueling had reappeared, to which the king replied: "It is something that must be remedied."[34] If there was true justice with regard to dueling, it came on an obscure day in 1629 when Louvigny, the feckless betrayer of the most tragic figure of a still greater cause célèbre, the marquis of Chalais, died in a duel.

While the stakes were high in the Bouteville case, those of the Chalais conspiracy a year earlier were higher. Bouteville was an individual defending noble autonomy against the principle of monarchical order; the Chalais conspirators numbered several noblemen and one noblewoman, whose treasonous thoughts were legitimated by their association with the royal heir, Gaston.

How could the king punish a brother who had to be honored and protected as the next ruler? How, indeed, could he mete out appropriate punishment to Gaston's treasonous followers? Complicating both issues was the question of how the king, in protecting his own authority, could throw the mantle of royal sovereignty over his minister, who, if an advisor, was also simply a subject. If it was treason for Gaston's followers to whisper about transferring the crown from Louis XIII to his brother, was it also treason for them to contemplate getting rid of Richelieu? At issue, ultimately, was whether French political society was a hierarchy of overlapping authorities or an entity with one sovereign authority.

These fundamental questions surfaced with Gaston's coming of age in 1626. At eighteen he was old enough to be married, ambitious enough to want a say in government affairs, and irresponsible enough not to be trusted in either endeavor. This bon vivant was the Prince Charming of the court, the darling of his mother, and the opposite of his serious twenty-four-year-old brother. When Marie de' Medici decided that it would be good to marry her wayward son to the wealthy heiress of a reliable grandee family, a compliant Louis XIII saw the logic, and a nervous Richelieu went along with the plans. Immediately, all the major relatives in line for the succession tried to convince Gaston to remain single. Here was an excuse to strike back at Louis XIII's tightening of state controls, his scandalous treaty with the Huguenots, and his personal advisor on these matters.

The initial ringleader was Gaston's governor, Marshal Ornano, whose irresponsible acts Louis had forgiven more than once. After the king in exasperation banished Ornano, Richelieu persuaded him to give the courtier one more chance on the grounds that only he could tame the prince. Instead Ornano turned Gaston against marrying, and, more damaging, he urged him to demand a share in power with the monarch. The chief minister was carefully collecting evidence, which he relayed to his monarch at Fontainebleau from the discreet distance of his nearby residence in Limours. Suddenly, the impatient king decided to act without the proofs Richelieu and Schomberg deemed necessary for a conviction.

On 4 May 1626 the marshal was arrested at the palace of Fontainebleau for "treason," following a guitar recital by the composed king during which royal guards blocked the escape routes. To an uncomprehending Gaston, Louis declared: "I love you, my brother, but I assure you that the marshal is an evil man and that he wishes to ruin you." The heir retorted that if he found out who had misinformed the king, he would kill them himself, in such a way that his lackeys could eat their hearts.[35]

The plot thickened. Gaston and his friends talked of killing Richelieu at Limours. Louis promptly gave his chief minister a special armed guard for life. Then the king heard that his half brother César was saying the crown would look good on Gaston's head and boasting that they would never see the king again except in a picture. On 13 June, Louis entrapped his half brothers César and Alexandre de Ven-

dôme at Blois, where all three had stopped en route to César's guber-
natorial seat in Brittany. There was much royal cunning and sangfroid
as Louis assured Alexandre in ambiguous language that if César and
he joined the royal tour they would be safe (if they were innocent).
But Louis spent a sleepless night before arresting the prince who had
conspired against him during their youth and another prince who
had been his childhood favorite.[36]

The agony was not finished. When the royal party reached Brittany, Louis's childhood playmate was arrested. The popular marquis
of Chalais was a scion of the Talleyrand-Périgords of ancient lineage,
former member of Gaston's household, and master of the king's wardrobe. He had been caught playing the double game of courting Richelieu while feeling so guilty of betraying his friends and the darling of
his eyes, Marie de Chevreuse, that he became hopelessly entangled
in their latest plotting.

From the sensational trial of the accused courtiers before a handpicked commission composed of ministers and judges from the Parlement of Brittany, rumors have come down to us of unspeakable
crimes. A fearful Richelieu and suspicious Louis XIII were convinced
that the conspirators really intended to kill the cardinal, declare the
king's marriage invalid and his throne vacant, and have his successor,
King Gaston I, marry Anne of Austria.[37]

What was the conspirators' retribution? Ornano's lips were sealed
by death in prison, brought on by kidney and bladder ailments. César
and Alexandre de Vendôme were too close to the throne to be dis-
patched: César was released in 1630, a repentant rebel and broken
man; Alexandre died in jail in 1629. Mme de Chevreuse, close companion of the queen, wife of a duke and peer, and relation of the
Rohans, was exiled to her estates—although instead of retiring from
court, she fled the country to a new conspiratorial base in Lorraine.
The royal cousin Condé made his peace, and Louis, on Richelieu's
pleading but against his better judgment, brought him back to court—
where he remained loyal to the king and a creature of the cardinal.
The other royal cousin, Soissons, was guilty enough to flee across the
Alps rather than accept Louis's offer to watch over Paris during the
king's later absence with the army.

Chalais paid the supreme penalty. Like Bouteville, he was visible
and vulnerable. Not only was he privy to friends' treasonous ideas,
but witnesses also alleged that, for seventeen consecutive days, he
had contemplated killing his king, and plotted to assassinate Richelieu and free Ornano. Richelieu later admitted that the testimony of

the state's chief witness, Louvigny, was a tissue of lies; the man had turned on Chalais because he, in a very human act of mercy, had stopped a duel between his best friends—Louvigny and Bouteville. The other key evidence came from the marquis's jailors, who heard his incoherent ramblings from a prison cell.

On 19 August 1626, Chalais died at Nantes, his head severed by over thirty clumsy blows from an amateur executioner's sword—after Gaston had spirited away the official hangman. Louis XIII struck from the sentence its most grisly clauses: the placing of the head at the entrance to a bridge and the severed quarters of the body on gallows along the main avenues of Nantes. Yet he refused to read the condemned man's petitions, saying: "That man is malicious by nature." On the day of the execution, Louis arose at the crack of dawn and then rode madly in an unusually exhausting day of hunting.[38]

Two weeks earlier, Louis XIII meted out a quite different punishment on his brother. Gaston had slowly been reduced from a cocky heir to a weakling who betrayed his fellow conspirators and bartered his submission to the institutions of matrimony and monarchy.[39] On 5 August, dressed in an old suit, he was hastily married by Cardinal Richelieu to the duke of Guise's stepdaughter. Thrown into the bargain was the huge duchy of Orléans, located harmlessly away from France's frontiers. Tragically, the new duke's wife, Marie de Bourbon-Montpensier, died ten months later after giving birth to a girl. Louis grieved with Gaston d'Orléans, and then returned to his habit of urging the younger man to make something of his life, writing "I think of you as another me."[40] Gaston, in turn, gave Louis XIII two more precious years of fraternal peace.

Behind this forced bonding of the two brothers was the king's conviction that all personal feelings, including his own, had to be sacrificed to royal family harmony, for without that harmony there could be no state order. The childless Louis had certainly risked humiliation in dictating a family marriage that might have given Gaston a son. Yet he had calmly said, before the wedding, "The repose of the state requires it." Understandably, the king had been particularly angry at Ornano for selfishly "poisoning" relations between the royal brothers. This got him thinking about his break with his mother in 1617—and to avoid guilt feelings he now laid the blame for that estrangement on Luynes. Louis was so tormented by the current crisis and past guilt over family unity that he banished some friends who had helped him turn the tables on Marie in 1617. What triggered this royal reaction? The conspirators had tactlessly suggested that Louis resist Marie's marriage plans for Gaston, just as he had her favor of Concini.[41]

One remaining family member caused the king as much anguish as all the other emotional upsets of the Chalais conspiracy combined. The person was Queen Anne; the torment stemmed from her alleged treason. We will never know the truth: only Louis and Richelieu saw the full evidence, and the latter's memoirs and his *Testament politique* are far from unbiased sources.[42] King Louis believed that Anne and Marie de Chevreuse knew of plotting to remove him from the throne. He arrived at the horrifying inference that his wife had actually entertained the notion of marrying his successor, King Gaston. Shaken by the thought of such a betrayal, Louis called Anne into his council on 10 September, and exclaimed: "You wished my death, and to marry my brother." Anne is supposed to have shot back "that she would have gained too little from the exchange to wish to blacken herself by such a crime for so paltry stakes." Chevreuse's attributed remark was even more stinging: "The king is an idiot and incapable of governing."

It is likely that Anne's guilt was no greater than overhearing gossip about her changing husbands; she could scarcely have avoided learning what those around her heard and said. Anne had also taken risks that showed courage. To protect her status as a childless queen (and incidentally avoid humiliation for her husband), she showed the king documents designed to sabotage the Gaston marriage plan, and she tried to talk Gaston out of marrying. She also showed poor judgment in snapping back at her husband's accusation with a tart, if honest, comment. Here was a man beside himself who had sacrificed his own feelings for family and state necessity. He was described in those harrowing days as anxious, angry, and silent at meals except for "suddenly striking his plate with a spoon or fork."[43]

It was not easy for Louis XIII to forgive Anne of Austria, under these circumstances, for the sake of state order. He could recall her lack of good sense in 1622 that had resulted in a miscarriage. He could remember her allowing the English royal favorite, Buckingham, into her quarters in 1623. He could picture the more recent scene of 1625, when Buckingham, while escorting Henrietta Maria from Paris to the English Channel, had caught an unsuspecting Queen Anne alone in an Amiens garden for a moment. Nothing happened, for she shrieked and her entourage had come running. Nor did anything happen when Buckingham slipped away from the English party to go back to Anne's residence, burst into her bedroom, and, on his knees, revealed his passion before an astonished queen and her court; the queen immediately ordered him out of her room. At Louis's deathbed, seventeen years after the Chalais affair, Anne begged him to believe that she had not contemplated a betrayal in 1626. Louis reputedly replied with his stoical wit and sad skepticism: "In the state where I am, I must pardon, but I am not obliged to believe."

Oddly enough, Louis did manage to continue "normal" relations with Anne in 1626 after accusing her of treasonous thoughts. Equally odd was their ability to have conjugal relations all through the Chalais affair itself, as Héroard's diary reveals. But oddest of all is that Anne became pregnant after the crisis ended—or thought she did. That "event" coincided with the pregnancy of Gaston's wife, perhaps an indication that Anne put herself in a psychological state not to be left barren. Perhaps, too, Louis in 1626 felt he was in a position of power over his wife, which relaxed him sexually. If there was a pregnancy, there was also a quick miscarriage. Another crisis would be needed before Louis and Anne produced the heir that made Gaston's penchant for attracting, aiding, and betraying plots against the king anachronistic.[44]

The outcome of the Chalais conspiracy, and of Bouteville's run-in with the law, put French society on notice that law and order were a top priority for Louis XIII. The subsequent royal siege of La Rochelle, from September 1627 to October 1628, made the perennial question of what to do about Huguenot dissent a top consideration as well. As with state reform, choice of a policy was not entirely premeditated. Tapié puts the case well: "While the traditional theory credits Richelieu with the intention of destroying the Huguenot party as a state within the state, . . . perhaps his attitude was uncertain or inconsistent and was in fact far more subject to events than responsible for them. Why indeed not?"[45]

By chance, Louis XIII stumbled onto a solution to the Huguenot question that had previously been a fantasy of the cardinal-minister, an unacceptable compromise to the dévots, and a practical impossibility. The king was maneuvered into attacking La Rochelle; and in bringing the Rochelais to their knees, he precipitated a collapse of Protestant power within the state that no other military victory could have accomplished. Furthermore, by concentrating on the specific crime of the Rochelais—political disobedience—Louis short-circuited the wishes of Marillac, Bérulle, and other dévot friends of Marie de' Medici for the more sweeping goal of outlawing Protestant worship.

How did a cardinal's fantasy to crush the Protestant "party" and a ruler's morality of protecting heretical worship while proscribing heretical revolt converge on La Rochelle? The king certainly had no love for the town's militants. In agreeing to halt the previous war, Louis had said he wanted to confer peace on the other Huguenot areas, "but as for the Rochelais who had rebelled so often and who had taken matters to such extremes, he intended to treat them differently." [46] He might, however, have lived peacefully with the Rochelais after the Treaty of La Rochelle, despite their continuing complaints over what they considered to be royal infractions. He had certainly put up with similar Huguenot haggling between 1617 and 1620, and again between 1622 and 1625. Nor was Richelieu that clear-sighted or single-minded on the broader question of the dangers posed by the Huguenot state within the state; he had blown hot and cold for years, shifting his mood as circumstances dictated.

The catalyst for the siege of the Protestant port town was a decision by Louis's brother-in-law, Charles I of England, and Buckingham, now Lord High Admiral of the scrappy English navy, to dabble in French waters. Anglo-French relations had steadily deteriorated after the marriage of Henrietta Maria to Charles in 1625. Louis and Richelieu were spoiling for a fight with England—Richelieu because he had built a fleet to rival the island state's seapower, Louis out of bad blood with Buckingham for brazenly courting Queen Anne. More fundamentally, the king and his minister bristled at Buckingham's offer to return to France as a mediator over disagreements on the implementation of the Treaty of La Rochelle. When the French king let the English favorite know that he would never again be welcome on French soil, Buckingham swore that if he could not come back as a friend, he would return as an enemy. [47]

In July 1627, Buckingham's amphibious operation landed eight thousand troops on the island of Ré, adjacent to La Rochelle. Louis got wind of his plans in advance and headed for the coast barely a week after Bouteville's execution. How important was his presence in this campaign? The fact is that while Richelieu was the brains behind the military strategy, and the grandee commanders and Gaston provided social luster, everything came to a halt for three months when the king fell ill at the outset of his trip. Was it a recurrence of the pulmonary problems he had contracted in the campaigns of the early 1620s, or part of his ongoing intestinal disorders? We do not know, but in any case July, August, and September were lost. Richelieu dared not second-guess his sovereign or upstage the soldier-grandees, and Gaston was barely able to function.

By September, Louis was strong enough to read his mail. Schomberg wrote to Richelieu: "I showed your letter to the king, who was very pleased to see the reasons for fortifying the hopes of what he wishes. He continues to do well and did not go hunting today."[48] Louis gave the go-ahead to strengthen the defense works around La Rochelle, whereupon the jittery Rochelais initiated the civil aspect of this religious war by firing on the siege workers. On reaching camp before La Rochelle in mid October, Louis backed Richelieu's plan to attack the English at Ré before they could join forces with the Rochelais; Keeper of the Seals Marillac and his brother, now a marshal, were ignored, along with the rest of the timid council majority. To give his military stand a moral backing, Louis added that he would never negotiate with the English on French soil regarding French subjects.[49]

Louis handpicked the soldiers for the dangerous mission to relieve Toiras's beleaguered forces on the island of Ré, self-deprecatingly telling rejects that someone must stay behind with him! With compass and maps in hand, the king waited for the best wind. The "descent on Ré" of 30 October caught the English off guard. Within a week, Buckingham's forces sailed for England, with the French in hot pursuit. Louis saw the Scripture passage for the day as blessing this "just" action; in his version, St. Michael had defended the French state against the bad angel of the English, "who, without injury or grievance, . . . in violation of the sanctity and faith of their alliances and ours, had come to make this unjust war on behalf of [our] rebelling subjects."[50]

The Rochelais' turn was next. It was Richelieu's idea to starve them into submission rather than attempt a bloody assault; however, it was Louis's decision—and one of the best of his life—to side with this advisor, make him his generalissimo, and give the siege an aura of justice. Not only did the king avoid the likelihood of a military stalemate, as at Montauban, but he also avoided a massacre, as had occurred at Nègrepelisse. To have blundered into either situation in as important a place as La Rochelle would have damaged royal prestige enormously, along with the king's moral authority over Protestant and Catholic subjects alike.

The winter period during the seemingly interminable siege was shaky. Right after death carried away his physician-friend Dr. Héroard in February 1628, Louis returned to Paris and his mother's side. Richelieu feared that leaving the siege might cause the king to go sour on the risky operation, and on the minister who had advised him to undertake it. But Louis was so broken up when he said good-bye that he could only utter his appreciation of the cardinal's service to an aide, after the two men had parted.[51] As spring returned, so did Louis, to the cheers of his troops.

The seaward side of the port was now sealed off by a dike designed by the king's architect, Métezeau, and a Paris master mason, Jean Tiriot, whom Louis called in to simulate the great dikes of antiquity that his historiographer Bernard had described to him.[52] The dike, plus French ships and batteries, twice held back English ships laden with supplies for the starving Rochelais, in May and September. On the landward side, Louis employed the severe side of his justice to starve the townspeople and garrison into surrender: anyone trying to escape, forage, or spy was warned back, fired at, hanged. When Rohan's mother requested an exit visa, the monarch replied that "he would not authorize any, either for her or for any woman from La Rochelle, and that they would all leave together when the siege was ended."[53]

When the twenty-seven thousand Rochelais had shrunk in number to eight thousand scarecrows, they gave in to an unconditional surrender. Even then, Louis suspiciously wondered whether the delegation of penitent, kneeling petitioners was really sincere! (See plate 8.) The city lost its independence, its chief places of worship to the Catholics, and its fortifications—which the authority-conscious king had razed despite Richelieu's plea to spare them in case they be needed again someday.[54] Yet Protestant worship was tolerated—a concession that surprised the Rochelais, and stunned the Catholic dévots. On the side of clemency there was a full pardon, except for the mayor and a few other unrepentant souls who were subjected simply to banishment from the town.

Even the royal triumphal entry was a scene of reconciliation. On 1 November 1628, Louis entered without pomp on horseback, preceded by his cardinal-minister and followed by his beloved guards. The townspeople weakly cried, "Mercy," Louis replied, "Grace," and they intoned, "Long live the king who has given us mercy." Ten thousand loaves of bread were distributed gratis, plus three thousand chariots of supplies at nominal army prices. Some survivors of the siege so gorged themselves that they died of overeating.[55] Louis reported the event with simplicity to his brother (who had left the front, frustrated at being under the king's shadow): "I have taken possession of that town, whose fortifications I find very fine and the misery greater than one could imagine."[56] (See plate 9.)

The siege had cost a staggering forty million livres and thousands of lives—the price paid for the beginning of the end of the Huguenot state within the state. Louis the Just was now "the Victorious" in the medallions, odes, and triumphal arches of the day. (See plate 10.) He had an army of thirty-five thousand and the option of either crushing the last Huguenot resistance in the southern mountains immediately or addressing a new Habsburg challenge across the Alps. As it turned out, Louis XIII would be able to take on the Habsburgs and the Huguenots, as well as the dévots—almost simultaneously!

10

ALAIS, MANTUA, AND THE DAY OF DUPES

Three months after subduing La Rochelle, Louis XIII embarked on one of the most daring exploits of his life. In the dead of winter, against the objections of his family and the dévots, he led thirty-five thousand foot soldiers and three thousand cavalry across the snow-driven Alps to fight Savoy, Spain, and the German emperor on behalf of the new duke of Mantua. He then reentered southern France and took the last fortified towns of the French Protestants. This whirlwind campaign of 1629 destroyed the Huguenot state within the state, and opened the first of France's "gates" beyond its borders. (See Appendix, map 3.)

There was a storm of protest. Dévots were aghast at the end product of the Wars of Religon, for the royally imposed "Grace of Alais" permitted the continuation of Protestant worship in local Huguenot communities, even as it dictated the dismantling of all remaining Protestant fortifications. The dévots were more horrified still that their Catholic king and his cardinal-minister had made rivalry with Catholic states a top priority. Tensions became unbearable in 1630, the year of the *grand orage*, or "great storm." Louis mounted a second rescue mission for Mantua, fell deathly ill, and then fended off a personal assault on his mode of governance, led by the queen mother, that became known as the Day of Dupes.

The Day of Dupes! The very words suggest a fundamental turning point in Louis XIII's reign, and in French and European history. For on 11 November 1630, a beleaguered king chose definitively between his mother and his chief minister; between the dévot program and a bon Français one; and between external peace and sweeping internal reform on the one hand and unceasing foreign war with the Habsburgs on the other.

What new perspective can we give to this famous dénouement of the Grace of Alais and the Mantuan War? Louis's court understood the main features of the personal drama between Marie and Richelieu. Modern scholarship has added its understanding of the underlying conflict between two plausible policies.[1] Yet this historical whodunit still has some mystery. We know little of the person in the middle who made the ultimate decisions on 11 November. It is time to find out where Louis XIII stood on the issues of 1629–30.[2]

Was the king caught between equally unflattering alternatives of caving in to his mother or following his chief minister's will? Historians think so, but that is an assumption. Did he have doubts about the policies he was pursuing during the preceding two years? Louis's recent biographer, echoing the greatest historians of the period, represents the scholarly consensus: "For his part, the king clearly leaned towards the solutions advocated by Richelieu, but his extraordinarily scrupulous conscience was not yet irrevocably committed, and we can say that right up to 11 November 1630 there was a constant conflict between the two policies."[3] To the contrary, Louis's policy stands were remarkably consistent from the moment he decided to take on the latest challenge by the Habsburgs, in tandem with a knockout blow against the Huguenots.

The king was fortunate that the Mantuan succession crisis did not break until his siege of La Rochelle was well under way. As it was, by the time the siege ended Louis had his hands full. The new Mantuan ruler was a subject of the French king, the duke of Nevers; his succession was disputed by the duke of Savoy, king of Spain, and Holy Roman Emperor. Spanish forces were already closing in on the key Mantuan town of Casale. The strategy devised by Louis and Richelieu was to take the royal army close enough to Savoy to intimidate the Mantuan duke's enemies into lifting the siege of Casale, after which they could besiege the southern Huguenots' remaining fortified towns. Part of the plan was for king and cardinal to lead the way, as they had at La Rochelle.

At a fierce council debate sometime in December 1628,[4] the personality and policy conflicts that would characterize the next two years were already evident. Marie de' Medici's position stemmed more from personal pique than from political convictions. She was a disruptive force, nonetheless. Marie was dead set against aid to the new duke of Mantua because of his role in princely revolts during her regency. She had also turned sour on Richelieu during the La Rochelle affair, believing, as the cardinal put it, "that I had total control over the king's mind and disregarded her [opinions]." The queen mother's plea that the exhausted army concentrate on crushing the Huguenots once for all, and that the king avoid a rupture with his sister Elisabeth's husband in Spain, was echoed in more statesmanlike fashion by Cardinal Bérulle and Keeper of the Seals Marillac. Outside the council chamber, Queen Anne and Queen Mother Marie did their best to dissuade King Louis from undertaking the hazardous winter expedition himself.

Louis wavered only on the question of whether he should lead his armies. After considering the compromise of going only as far as Savoy and letting Gaston take over the rest of the trek to Casale, he quickly reverted to the plan of going all the way himself, if an invasion was necessary. One can make what one wishes of contemporary belief that Richelieu's arguments were crucial to Louis's decision to support the duke of Mantua, and that the cardinal and his creatures played on the king's pride to get him to take Gaston's place. The fact is that Louis adopted a campaign consistent with his past actions, including accompanying his soldiers as had been his policy throughout his personal rule, with the exception of the miniwars of 1625.[5]

If there was a king who could be faulted here, it was not Louis XIII but his Spanish rival. Philip IV had allowed Olivares and his council to get him involved in a costly Mantuan venture and to transfer to the Italian theater the greatest general of the day, Ambrosio Spinola, who was on the threshold of winning the war against the Dutch. The king of Spain came to regret his decision more than any other authorization of his long reign; and he never made it to the war zone, despite his envy of Louis playing the soldier king. Spinola was witness to the difference between the rival styles of ruling. Stopping off at the siege of La Rochelle on his way from the Netherlands to Madrid to debate the Mantuan question, the Spanish statesman had formed a favorable impression of the French king as they talked at Louis's headquarters and examined the royal siege works. Spinola complimented Louis on leading his soldiers, regretted that Philip did not do the same, and returned to Spain to sing the praises of the royal resolve in France.[6]

This was the French monarch's first chance to fight on foreign soil, and he had the moral resolve to consider his fight a just one. By mid January 1629, the king was on his way south. From Grenoble he wrote to his brother, "I am going to seize the passages [in Savoy] necessary to reach Italy if they are refused me [by the Savoyards]." He went on to declare that if the Spanish ambassador in Paris said that peace was made in Spain, "I can assure you that it is not here; and nothing will halt my trip"; he added "Don't go to Lyon, because of the foul air there."[7]

At 3:00 A.M. on 5 March, the soldier-king half rode and half walked through snowdrifts to Richelieu's advance post, on receiving word that the duke of Savoy had blocked the Susa pass with barricades twenty feet high and twelve feet thick. A story by Saint-Simon's son has it that Louis overruled Richelieu's hesitations about storming the barricades. Whatever the truth, Louis led the assault with eight thousand crack troops, a scant hundred paces behind his suicide squad, the *enfants perdus*.

The taking of the Susa pass was celebrated in French verse as a greater feat than Louis's capture of La Rochelle. Cartoons justified the attack with lavish displays of the royal sword, balance scales, and hand of justice. In Philip IV's chapel, the imperial ambassador supposedly said that God had been on the French king's side. And Louis XIII's portrait was soon displayed prominently throughout Madrid.[8] The Spanish besiegers pulled back from Casale, and Savoy yielded French passage plus the temporary garrisoning of Susa as a guarantee of good faith. Louis placed his friend Toiras over French forces in Casale, and Marshal Créquy over the troops in Susa.

On the surface it was a total French victory, including a defensive alliance against Spain with Savoy, Venice, Mantua, and the Pope, who had grown fearful of Habsburg expansionism in Italy. In reality, the Spanish withdrawal was temporary, and there was bad blood between the French and Savoyard allies. Louis gave his word not to annex Savoy, but he taunted Duke Charles Emmanuel for his prediction that the French would find his forces tougher than the English had. The king was more pleasant to the duke's daugher-in-law, Louis's sister, Christine of Savoy, now six months pregnant; they embraced and he offered her captured Spanish flags, whereupon she responded, "You are the happiest prince in the world."[9]

Without awaiting full Spanish and Savoyard compliance, Louis took ten thousand soldiers from Susa to southeastern France. Soon Richelieu followed with an equal number. Together they planned a final anti-Huguenot campaign that would avoid the errors of the past. Instead of the early-1620s strategy of moving from siege to siege, someone suggested that the king make an object lesson of the most defiant of the southeastern Huguenot towns, and then cut off their supply lines to Castres and Montauban in the southwest.

Only the people of Privas held out, saying they would rather die in a fiery siege than by the noose of a vengeful king. They got their wish. Louis termed the Huguenot commander Saint-André's refusal to surrender unconditionally "insolence," and he informed Marie, "I am resolved to give them no quarter, and have them all hanged." When Saint-André reconsidered, it was too late. "I do not want to receive them on that condition, because they are the best men Monsieur de Rohan has," Louis wrote his mother. "By hanging them as I intend, and Saint-André first, it will be like cutting off Monsieur de Rohan's right arm to take these men from him."

Exemplary justice went awry when a powder keg exploded and the town was allowed to burn to the ground. The king later built a "bridge of reconciliation," called *le Pont Louis Treize* on today's postcards; but the visitor who crosses that stone monument three and a half centuries after the event will be greeted by latter-day Privadois Protestants exclaiming, "There is no reconciliation with Louis XIII!" In Louis's day, the "event" was memorialized with a cartoon showing a somber-faced king, looking older than his twenty-seven years, setting the torch to the citadel of Privas. But let us hear the king's own words, as penned to his mother: "At the surrender yesterday of the fort of Toulon, there was a little disorder because those inside took fear on seeing two companies of guards enter; several threw themselves over the walls, falling into the hands of the scum of the army who killed them, which distresses me, as Monsieur de Luxembourg will inform you."[10]

After Privas, the dominoes fell in place as town after town in the southeast surrendered on the king's approach. Louis's grumbling at being deprived since Susa of his free time to hunt was mitigated by the pleasure of entering Huguenot towns to the applause of his defeated but pardoned subjects, and by Catholic processions and rededication services in the communities' main temples. Louis the Victorious could write home: "All this land trembles, and they are beside themselves."[11]

The final settlement with Huguenot France was termed a royal "grace" bestowed on contrite subjects, not a treaty between two equal parties. Dated 28 June 1629, this Grace of Alais (today's Alès) may well have been Louis XIII's greatest achievement. Its language implied that France was no longer a hierarchy of special authorities, but a single state with one sovereign authority. In practical terms, it ended seven decades of religious wars on conditions that secured the Huguenots' unswerving loyalty to the monarchy. The privilege of worshiping publicly in the towns where they already had that legal right was in keeping with Richelieu's statement to the Montauban Protestants that they were fully subjects of the king—and it had a cardinal's corollary hope that someday they would become Catholics. Yet Louis XIII had consistently held this tolerationist position from the beginning of his personal rule; its genesis owed nothing to the cardinal. On his death-bed, Louis would once more ask—but not demand—that his Protestant marshals convert to the "true" faith.

The situation was similar with military and political clauses. After Alais, Louis took the Paris road and Richelieu crossed the southwestern ranges to supervise the demolition of the Huguenots' last defense works. It was a goal they had in common, going back in the king's case at least a decade. The proviso that Huguenot town privileges were to be retained or restored—except for the "insolent" Privadois and Rochelais (the latter now being assigned a royal intendant)—also reflected royal and ministerial politics alike. Richelieu wanted to prevent the rebirth of Huguenot autonomy at either end of the Protestants' homeland; Louis wished to forgive the repentant and punish the unjust.

Needless to say, the delicately balanced royal grace left the Catholic dévots unsatisfied. Until his death late in 1629, Bérulle continued to see Protestant victories by France's allies abroad and Protestant coexistence with Catholicism at home as religiously intolerable. Marillac harped on the secular aspects of both evils until his disgrace at the Day of Dupes.

The Grace of Alais, in all its parts, was the work of two men. Who is to say which was more important, the daring courage and moral principles of the master, or the political and military genius of the servitor? The one was incomplete without the other. Louis modestly told his court: "One must render the Cardinal the honor he deserves; all of the happy successes within and outside the realm have come by his counsels and his courageous judgments." Richelieu wrote with equal force: "All [Your Majesty's] subjects vie in their desire to render the obedience that is due him, not only as their king but as the most just, pious, and courageous of all those whom God has given to France up to the present." [12]

Other subjects combined grudging respect for the "great cardinal" with acknowledgment of Louis as the Just and Victorious. The grateful Huguenot leader Rohan, given an honorable exile and an opportunity to lead French forces in Italy during the next decade, said that his sovereign had come, seen, and conquered. Contemporary historians wrote that while Julius Caesar had coined that triple phrase, Louis XIII could expand on it and say, "I came, I saw, I conquered, I forgave." In the pictorial and literary depictions of Louis the Victorious after La Rochelle, Susa, and Alais, the king was praised for balancing punitive justice with clemency, valor with piety. Had the king died then, his achievements would have been considered exceptional.[13]

Even if Louis XIII had known how to enjoy success, there was no time to savor his foreign and domestic triumphs of 1629. Family and foreign problems encroached on every side as the year of the *grand orage* approached. Worse still, these problems were connected. First for the bad family news. Marie had not been satisfied with being made regent for northern France during the La Rochelle operation and the dual campaign of 1629. On Richelieu's return to court from the Protestant south, Louis summoned all his nerve to force the queen mother not to break with the cardinal in jealousy over the close royal-ministerial relationship.[14] Louis hoped that this triangular rapprochement would hold. He continued to keep Marie informed of every policy decision in 1630, even consulting with her as much as possible when they were separated; but he did not hesitate to go his own way, respectfully, when they disagreed. The question was merely when she would explode with resentment against that "ingrate," Cardinal Richelieu, whom she saw as the mastermind behind every unpalatable royal decision.[15]

Might Louis's frustrated mother find encouragement from her other son, who had triggered the Chalais conspiracy? The widowed heir, at twenty-one, combined a larger dose of his brother's restlessness and lack of self-confidence with a massive injection of their father's pleasure-loving irresponsibility. These traits were reinforced by the humiliation of being Louis's stand-in at La Rochelle in 1627 and the rejection of his wish in 1628 to fight the Huguenots elsewhere. How noble of Louis to ask Gaston to return to La Rochelle after the prince had fled that humiliation, and then veto an alternate post with the vague promise, "I will always have great satisfaction in employing you on the occasions that will be worthy of you."[16] Where would Gaston turn now?

Frustrated by Louis's decision to head the 1629 campaign after having momentarily been promised that role himself, Gaston had refused to join the army as its second-in-command.[17] Instead, this family Prince Charming used his uncanny knack for seeking revenge

In the most bizarre way imaginable: he decided to marry the daughter of Louis's ally, the duke of Nevers-Mantua. His plan was opposed by the queen mother out of hatred for Nevers, and it embarrassed the king, who was now caught between snubbing a foreign ally and alienating his mother. Louis finally threw in his lot with Marie, hoping that all would turn out well. This was no mere dalliance for Gaston, however; he had broken a horse's leg galloping to his lady love's side. With Louis away on campaign, and Marie acting as regent in Paris, Gaston got it into his head to spirit his sweetheart away to the Spanish Netherlands. Unable to consult Louis, the regent locked the lady in the king's apartments at Vincennes.

What a predicament for that punctilious royal judge! Luckily, the duke summoned his daughter to Mantua. Gaston, however, refused to give in to the subterfuges of brother, mother, and prospective father-in-law. He sulked off to his appanage at Orléans, then fled to Lorraine rather than face the wrath of his royal brother on Louis's return to Paris in September 1629.[18]

As this escapade unfolded, Louis experienced one mood swing after another. He had been conciliatory far longer than was necessary, then he let anger get in the way of wisdom, and finally he subordinated everything to reason of state. On the day Louis stormed Susa, he took pen in hand to express the hope that his brother would understand a Mantuan father's wish to see his daughter. In return, Louis magnanimously left it to Gaston's discretion to "spend some time on your estates, even though one of my greatest satisfactions would be to see you at my side."[19] Four months later, in July, Louis could no longer contain himself. He had Marillac relay, via Gaston's messenger, exactly what he felt: "I object to the little respect you show the queen our mother. I object to the little care you give to keeping the word you have so often and so solemnly given. . . . I object to the disorderliness and debaucheries of your life."[20]

Gaston's flight to foreign Lorraine required patient diplomacy, though, not moralizing monologues. The duchy lay between the Spanish territories of Franche Comté and the Netherlands, and close to the German theater of war. Louis lured his heir back to France in January 1630 with new titles and a pension, then waited anxiously until his prodigal younger brother finally came to see him in April. Less diplomatically, Marie chided Gaston for seeing her before paying his respects to their sovereign.

What had this prolonged drama over Gaston's love life, which had plagued Louis XIII from February 1629 to April 1630, done to royal

family and state affairs? Gaston was now in a relatively benign mood—
and well he might be: he was basking in the notoriety of his flight to
Lorraine, a tumultuous welcome on his return to court, and his role
as darling of the capital. Similarly, Marie's personal triumph in preventing Gaston's marriage helped keep her in line; it may have been
the key to her agreement with Louis in the fall of 1629 to get along
with Richelieu.

Unfortunately, the marriage fiasco had also led Gaston and Marie
to an understanding that spelled future danger for Louis. To be sure,
Marie never fully trusted her weak-willed son, and the pampered
Gaston never got over his bitterness at her veto of his planned second
marriage.[21] Yet at least they could focus individual frustrations on a
common scapegoat, Cardinal Richelieu. At the outset of Gaston's romance, Richelieu had inadvertently led the court to assume from his
coy reaction that he favored the marriage. Then, when Marie opposed
the union, Richelieu openly sided with her. Marie doubted his sin-
cerity, while Gaston felt betrayed by him.

Rumors had it that a vengeful Gaston d'Orléans and the wrathful
queen mother forged a powerful if uneven pact, "she to ruin the cardinal in the eyes of the king, and [Gaston] never to marry Princess
Marie [de Nevers]." A richly embroidered version held that the agreement was placed in a tiny gold box, which hung from the neck of a
prominent courtier, the duke of Bellegarde. The truth of the Marie-
Gaston relationship was more complicated than this romantic tale,
however. Gaston wrote awkwardly to Marie in May 1630 requesting
"the continuation of your good offices in order to keep those of the
king my lord, which is the most treasured thing in the world I possess." Marie, in turn, scolded Gaston for not visiting her. It would
take an extraordinary situation indeed to give them a chance of translating words on paper into action.[22]

Their chance finally came in the wake of new foreign policy developments. As 1630 began, Louis XIII opted to cross the Alps for the
second time in two years. The policy issue was the same as that which
had angered his mother and divided his council a year before: should
the king fight to uphold the duke of Mantua's rights? This time, however, the situation was more dangerous. The duke of Mantua had not
sworn fidelity to his overlord, the emperor, and the king of Spain had
not ratified the Susa-Casale agreement of the previous spring. Meanwhile, Spanish forces under Spinola seized the opportunity to besiege
Toiras's token French garrison at Casale; Emperor Ferdinand sent
some of his best soldiers from the German war to occupy the Val Tel-

lina and threaten the town of Mantua; and the duke of Savoy, once again, denied passage to French reinforcements. These actions constituted, in effect, a triple alliance against France, covered by the technicalities of vassal and treaty relations. (See Appendix, map 4.)

In fighting back, the French monarch covered himself morally, militarily, and politically. After the council session that decided on an expedition to relieve Casale, Louis exclaimed: "Since the Spaniards want war, we will ram it down their throats." This was all the ethical justification the king of France needed to resist aggression that, in the words of a great modern historian of Spain, "lent credence to Richelieu's claim that the Habsburgs would stop at nothing to achieve universal dominion."[23] (See plate 12.)

Militarily as well as ethically, Louis was better off than his foreign rivals. The duke of Savoy was old, dispirited, and about to be succeeded by an untried son, Louis's brother-in-law Victor Amadeus. Spain was busy enough fighting the Dutch. In Germany, despite Imperialist–Catholic League victories that had forced the king of Denmark out of the Thirty Years' War in 1629, Emperor Ferdinand II's northern army was vulnerable to attack by a new enemy, Lutheran Sweden. Ferdinand had also provoked a storm of protest by both Catholic and Protestant German princes against his 1629 Edict of Restitution, which called for Habsburg control of a massive restoration to the Catholic church of property illegally appropriated by Protestant states in the Holy Roman Empire over the previous seventy-five years. Not surprisingly, in Madrid and Vienna alike the decision makers argued over priorities and strategy. Hence, the muster of reinforcements was slow for the Italian venture. King Philip of Spain surveyed the situation gloomily and said, "God is angry with me and my kingdom for our sins."[24]

Still, Louis had his own military dilemma. Until Gaston returned to court from Lorraine, the king could not leave his realm. He made Richelieu commander-in-chief of his expeditionary force, giving him authority to do everything except make peace until they could formulate policy together. In a typical exchange, written in February 1630, Louis scribbled comments on a ministerial letter packed with information, then concluded: "There you have my feelings on the memoirs you sent me. However, I leave it up to your judgment and experience; and give you full power, without holding to the above, to do everything you see on the spot to be most appropriate for the welfare of my service, the assistance of my allies, and my reputation."[25]

The self-sacrificing ruler made equally interesting political moves.

When Gaston finally sought reconciliation with Louis in April, the king named his brother lieutenant general for northern France and commander of the forces guarding against an Imperialist invasion from the Rhineland, thereby co-opting him for Louis's war policy. Indeed, when the brothers met the prince firmly backed the initial conquests of the Italian expedition in Savoy.[26]

After leaving Gaston, Louis marched south to Lyon, where he left his mother and wife, and then continued on to join Richelieu in Savoy. That residence gave Anne little outlet for the resentment she harbored against Richelieu from the Chalais dénouement; but at least in Lyon she had friends to share her grief at yet another aborted pregnancy. More significantly, Marie was allowed to idle away her time holding court with such Richelieu-hating friends as the princess of Conti, the duke of Bellegarde, and the Guises and to play ruler with a skeleton council headed by Michel de Marillac. Louis gambled that his mother would be co-opted, like Gaston, for the nearby Italian campaign. The gamble worked—to a point. Although Marie disliked having the king in personal danger, during the early stages of the Italian war she opposed Marillac on the war itself. As late as May she was painting the Habsburgs as the villains and arguing that France should retain the gains it had made against all three enemy states. Her script could easily have been written by Louis: "There could be many drawbacks in sustaining a war in Italy in the present state of internal affairs [unrest and rebellion], but there are certainly greater ones in making a shameful peace that . . . surely would bring us more troublesome wars than those we may get into right now."[27]

In assigning roles for the Italian undertaking of 1630, Louis XIII overlooked one vital aspect of royal statecraft—his personal reputation. Wags said that he had given over every power except that of healing scrofula! Did such criticism bother Louis? He had become so used to sacrificing his own being to higher causes that the above acts made perfect sense to him once Richelieu explained them. A more crucial question was whether Louis could stand up under the constant strain of war and the criticism of his family, court, and country that surfaced as the Italian campaign took its toll of tax reserves, soldiers' lives, and the king's own deteriorating health.

During the first weeks, when Louis was grappling with decision making at a considerable distance from his commander-in-chief, there was cause to wonder. Bullion wrote Richelieu in March: "You know the temperament of the king, who doesn't want to undertake anything the moment one must look facts straight in the face, and uses the excuse of your absence. With good reason of course; for the weight would be too much for him, unless you took most of it off his shoulders."[28]

Yet when the first key decision had to be made, the king acted swiftly. Richelieu wrote in March that Charles Emmanuel of Savoy had refused passage through his domains; Louis gave the signal to take Pinerolo (Pignerol). Here was a fateful example of the moralistic monarch using the justice of one ally's cause and another ally's perfidy to justify a conquest of the greatest military significance. A few more victories like this and France could become as imperialistic as its Habsburg rivals. Marshal La Force's son proved clairvoyant in saying of Pinerolo: "It is the most important place we can take in Italy, because it gives us free entry and the relief capacity of transporting our food and arms from France via Dauphiné—which cannot be be done through Susa since it is still in the mountains."[29]

After the fact, Richelieu laid before Louis the hazards of keeping this splendid place: it might goad Spain and the emperor as well as Savoy into a full-scale war of monumental cost for France. "If the king is set for war," the cardinal wrote on 13 April, "it will be necessary to forget all thought of repose, economy, and reforms [*règlements*] within the kingdom." Of course, Richelieu was clever enough to hedge his bets in case Louis opted for a dévot solution, for he added: "If one wishes to make peace, it can be done not only without shame, but with glory." By the same token, this shrewd psychologist-advisor came ever so close to telling Louis exactly what he wanted him to do: "To say whether Pignerol should be returned or not I excuse myself from saying, being at a distance as I am. Still, I will say that if it is kept and put in the state [of readiness] that it is capable of, the king will have made the greatest conquest possible and will be in a position to become the arbiter and master of Italy."[30]

Louis had, in fact, made up his mind before this memo reached him. He was galloping toward the war in a state of euphoria. His doctor could hardly get him to remember to eat, as he traveled with the greatest young nobles of the sword—past Lyon, Grenoble, and into Savoy.[31] He was manic, and his mania was for war, not diplomacy or peace. The Savoyards, Spaniards, and Imperialists obliged. Louis found himself forced into occupying all of Savoy proper and advancing his troops into Savoyard Piedmont in order to contain the pesky Duke Charles Emmanuel. Yet despite these easy triumphs, his relief force of twenty thousand soldiers moved slowly toward Toiras's tiny band of three thousand men who were holding off eighteen thousand Spanish besiegers. Equally disheartening was the news in July that Mantua had fallen to twenty-five thousand Imperialists.

The summer heat and the plague worried Richelieu and Marie more than their master. Louis was determined to remain in Savoy and, if possible, to go with his relief forces to Casale. He complained almost with pleasure about his headaches, toothaches, swollen cheeks, and stomach disorders brought on by chronically erratic eating habits. Although a fearsome regimen of frequent baths, enemas, purgatives, and bleedings crept into his weekly routine, this was the price he was willing to pay to keep up his soldiers' morale. In June, when the queen and queen mother pestered the king to visit them, he and Richelieu returned to Lyon for five days, but only to confront Marillac on the war issue and keep Marie in line. They also brought along Schomberg and Effiat for a special council meeting.

The keeper of the seals had been insinuating for weeks that Richelieu was leading Louis to his death and his kingdom to massive revolts against war taxes, without a dauphin to ensure an orderly succession. Marillac's solutions? Peace through French withdrawal from Savoy and Italy, tax relief for the poor, rigorous prosecution of tax rebels, curbing of the parlements' powers in retaliation for their complicity in popular uprisings, and an all-out campaign to compel Huguenots to convert. At the June meeting, he focused on the danger of letting the king return to the war zone. Marie and Anne joined in with their personal pleas, one inside the council chamber and the other in its shadows. Richelieu, though wanting Louis at the front to halt the rash of army desertions, protested that "as far as the king's person was involved, [Richelieu] had said that [his health] should not be hazarded."

Marillac clinched the matter with a malaprop allusion to the king not making it back to the front and looking cowardly. This may have been the moment when Louis lost all respect for the justice minister's pusillanimous thoughts. Furious at the remark, he transferred the dévot advocate from Marie's side to Grenoble. The monarch who had cast aspersions on Ferdinand II and Philip IV for not leading their armies against him also had an irrefutable argument for his returning to Savoy: "There was no other way to retain the [battle weary] soldiers, who were already disbanding at the mere rumor of being sent to Italy."[32] This was no time to think of himself: one-third of his army had disappeared!

Louis never made it to Italy. In Savoy, his health worsened suddenly. Bleedings were no help. He was fortunate not to die, as did
Charles Emmanuel that month, and Spinola in September. Even after
the hostess of his residence was carried off by what appeared to be
the plague, the king made light of the threat to his own life. But soon
he could stand the strain no longer. Recently he had written with joy
to his mother and brother of Montmorency's battle victory; now fatigue caused him to despair over bad news. Complaining that his entourage would be the cause of his death if they kept him in the war
zone any longer, he said good-bye to Richelieu and his marshals and
returned to Lyon.[33]

The four-week separation of master and servitor from 25 July to 23
August was an anxious time on both sides, even though the king
knew well enough what he wanted to do in foreign affairs. On departing Savoy, he left instructions to defend Casale with all possible
means; and from Lyon he wrote to Richelieu saying that he intended
to keep Pinerolo. Military and diplomatic developments moved so
quickly, however, that it was impossible to act at such a distance from
his chief minister. The two men had talked with and authorized a
young Italian papal agent named Giulio Mazarini to find a way to end
the Italian war. But Louis was in no mood to accept the compromise
arrived at by this man (who, as Jules Mazarin, would become chief
minister of France): namely, that the Habsburgs would recognize the
new duke of Mantua if France would return Pinerolo to Savoy.

At the scene of the fighting, Richelieu was less rigid than Louis.
Fearful that Casale would fall before being relieved or a settlement
was reached, he wrote one of his most pessimistic memos: if the king
did not return Pinerolo to Savoy, he might well lose Casale as well as
the city of Mantua, and ultimately all his Piedmontese gains. The cardinal instructed Bouthillier to speak to the king and queen together
and get the king's answer, one way or another, after a council meeting, with the words "the above is my will."[34]

As if the Italian scene was not confusing enough, Louis and Richelieu ventured into central European politics. The cardinal's friend
Father Joseph had joined the career diplomat Brûlart de Léon at the
Diet of the Holy Roman Empire in Regensburg. The two Frenchmen
helped the anti-Habsburg German princes, jealous of growing Imperialist power, to pressure Ferdinand II into dismissing his leading
general, Wallenstein. But when the same diplomats tried to get the
emperor to recognize his nominal vassal as duke of Mantua and end

the Italian war, Ferdinand tied this action to French approval of a pro-Habsburg central European settlement.

The French king and his minister were playing a dangerous game that could bring either retreat from Italy or indefinite military involvement there and war with the Habsburgs in Germany as well. It was an awkward time for Louis. The only new royal decision was to renew the Dutch subsidies against Spain. A similar plan to subsidize King Gustavus Adolphus, who had just brought Sweden into the German war on behalf of the anti-Habsburg princes, was in doubt, for the "Lion of the North" held out for a full military alliance with France. Louis certainly did not want to make the wrong impetuous decision on the German or Italian question. Richelieu must rejoin him.

Richelieu was torn between the desire to stay and supervise the uncertain Italian operation and fears that his master might succumb to the views of Marie de' Medici's entourage if left alone in Lyon. Louis's letters, though, show nothing but affection, concern for the cardinal's health, and support. From the day they had separated, the large, childlike royal hand brought encouraging words: "As soon as I read your letter at 8 P.M. I gave orders according to your suggestions. . . . Be assured always of my friendship"; "I need [your presence] for several matters and can't do without it"; "Come as soon as you possibly can. Having given the necessary orders, there isn't anything that can keep you over there"; and, finally. "I cannot bear having you any longer in danger of the plague." [35]

Did Louis's actions follow his words? We have a curious report by the Venetian ambassador, Contarini, written three days before Richelieu reached Lyon. Its beginning sentences suggest royal ambivalence: "The king is abandoning the [Italian] undertaking at the most decisive moment, without respect for his pledged word. . . . He is revealing the greatest inconstancy in all his actions. . . . He is beginning to talk of returning to Paris, not finding things here according to his tastes." Yet at the very time that Contarini wrote, Louis was ordering provisions for his court and troops from northern France for Casale! [36] Was the Italian in the dark, or simply fretful about a pro-Venetian outcome? His report changes as it progresses—Louis becomes resolute, Richelieu the nervous wreck:

> [The king] is writing to the cardinal that he has no intention of returning Pignerol. The cardinal himself no longer knows what course to take. He lets it be known and regrets being involved in this war. . . . He seeks a way out, but an honorable one. . . . From day to day he moves

closer to the opinions of the queen mother, being resolved not to be opposed to her.[37]

Richelieu's own difficult relations with his former patron, Marie, were enough to make him worry. When they met again, she exploded. Fortunately, Louis had resisted efforts by his mother's friends to turn him against his minister. "They have tried in vain," the ruler told Bullion; "they will never divide me from the cardinal, whose merits and services eclipse all the others, without exception."[38] Royal character, plus the calming company of the best male favorite of his life, Saint-Simon, helped Louis here.

On Richelieu's arrival, Louis closeted himself with his mother and minister to smooth things over. Soon after, Marie took the king to task for following his minister down a path to an Italian quagmire: "So that's the good advice you are getting!" The king held his ground: "The cardinal is not God, . . . but even if he were an angel, he could not have made provision for everything with any greater foresight and prudence than he has; and I have to say that he is the greatest servitor France has ever had."[39]

With Richelieu at his side, Louis set in motion new peace moves for Italy. The day after their reunion, Richelieu instructed Father Joseph and Brûlart de Léon to conclude a "nonlimited" peace with the emperor on Italian affairs; and, in Italy, Schomberg was sent a blank treaty to be negotiated on the spot.[40] At the same time, however, a regional truce, arranged by the papal agent Mazarini, was set to expire in mid October. The tension was mounting at Lyon.

Richelieu's letter to Father Joseph contained an enigmatic statement that peace "will come much more easily by you than by us, since we have to deal with three heads which are such that when two wish one thing, the third doesn't want it." Within this triangle, where did the king stand? If anything, he was more determined to hold on to French gains in Italy than was his minister, and far more than Marie must have been at this point.[41]

Louis was in ecstasy when French relief forces took Avigliana (Veillane), upstream from Casale. Writing to his brother on 2 September, the king claimed that he wanted "only public peace by securing my allies from the oppression that menaces them." In reality, he meant to keep Avigliana permanently for France, for he boasted of making it "one of the best [i.e., most defensible] places in Italy." The new duke of Savoy, Victor Amadeus, might be Louis's brother-in-law,

but he was taking "the same evil path" as his father; and the Habsburgs were making "unjust propositions." The king of France concluded to his heir: "I have omitted nothing on my part that could lead
to a sure, honorable, and lasting peace; [God] will, in the end, punish
those who wish to give the appearance of desiring it and in reality
seek only to prolong war."[42]

Suddenly, everything was thrown into confusion. On 22 September, Louis XIII came down with chills and fever, which his doctors
associated in general terms with the plague, and more clinically with
dysentery. The physicians administered the first of many bleedings!
By the twenty-fifth the king asked his confessor to let him know when
all hope was gone, so he could prepare his soul for death. Two days
later, on his twenty-ninth birthday, he made a general confession. His
mother listened to him say that he had always tried to please her; he
asked forgiveness for any past wrongdoing. His wife sobbed when
Louis requested forgiveness for any trouble he had caused Anne during their marriage.

On 30 September, Louis XIII received the last sacrament; he then
whispered to the throng of courtiers at his bedside, via his confessor,
Father Suffren: "Finding myself here on my deathbed, I ask you to
pardon every instance in which I have offended you; and I will not
die in peace if I know you do not forgive me. I ask you to say the same
thing to all my subjects on my behalf."

Unexpectedly, those who had rarely been moved by this serious
Louis the Just were in tears. "It is for us, Sire, to beg your forgiveness," they cried out. "You have never offended us. Forgive us, Sire!"
Then Louis called his wife to his side. Suffren's account tells the story
more eloquently than any historian's words: "They embraced each
other tenderly and spoke from the heart rather than their lips, and
by tears rather than by voice." The monarch then transmitted last-
minute instructions to Richelieu, his childhood friend Montmorency,
and other intimates. And he was bled—for the seventh time of the
illness.[43]

Late in the day, an abscess broke in his intestines and discharged
the pussy matter that had nearly caused his death. Within two days
Louis moved to happier quarters. Irritated that the possibility of a
relapse prevented his joining the French forces in Italy, he had to
escape the boredom of Lyon. On 18 October, less than three weeks
after the climax of his illness, the monarch left for the capital.

Now he could deal with the political twists and turns that had occurred while no one knew whether they would have to answer to King Louis or King Gaston. At the top of the king's list was an impossible peace that his plenipotentiaries had signed at Regensburg on 14 October. Panicked at the thought of war continuing while the throne was in question, they had signed, albeit with reservations, an Italian peace that called for French withdrawal from Casale and restricted French dealings with anti-Habsburg states in northern and central Europe.

Louis left others to debate the Treaty of Regensburg at a council meeting on the twenty-sixth at Roanne, while he resumed the road to Paris. It seems highly unlikely, however, that he left no instructions with Richelieu to defend "his [i.e., Richelieu's] policy before the queen mother and Marillac." [44] We have access to the truth: "As soon as the king had news of this bad treaty from Germany," Richelieu informed Schomberg in Italy, "he told himself that you [Schomberg] would absolutely not accept it, and that there was no way on earth that he would stop the rescue of Casale." [45] That royal reaction, on 21 October, lies behind a royal letter of the twenty-second to Brûlart de Léon, calling for major amendments before the general treaty could be ratified. It also helps explain why Marie—despite her joy, shared with Anne, at the initial word of peace—sided with Richelieu against Marillac when the council backed the king's letter on the twenty-sixth. [46] That same day, Mazarini galloped between Schomberg's relief force and the Spaniards at the gates of Casale with a new truce. Now nothing was settled! [47]

The stage was set for the Day of Dupes drama, in which Louis XIII was no helpless bit player between stars. To be sure, during his recovery at Lyon, Marie and Anne had browbeaten him into an apparent concession to consider his minister's status when the international situation and his health permitted. Clearly, the deathly ill son could not say no unequivocally to his mother's face! Yet the situation here is strikingly similar to the mother and son's showdown in 1617 over Barbin, and his words of entrapment to Alexandre of Vendôme in 1626. In each instance, the listener read into the king's words something he was never prepared to yield. [48] The proof is that as soon as Louis saw Richelieu at Roanne, he warned him to be on his guard; and, although too ashamed to say what he had muttered to Marie in a moment of weakness, Louis ordered his servitor to court his mother all the way back to Paris. [49]

On reaching the Paris basin, Louis got reassurances of Condé's goodwill for Richelieu, and tried to keep Gaston from allying with Marie. "You can rest assured that whenever my brother speaks of you," he wrote Richelieu on 28 October, after the brothers' first reunion in six months, "I will support you always as one should."[50] Two weeks later, when everyone was back in the capital, Louis called his brother and minister together and swore Gaston to an oath of loyalty to Richelieu. Later that day, however, Gaston let Marie know that he might still shift his allegiance. The date was 9 November 1630.[51]

The tenth began well for Louis. At a council meeting, a consensus was reached on the wording of the Treaty of Regensburg, and it was agreed to follow Mazarini's plan, which would clear all foreign troops out of the duke of Mantua's territories. The council voted to keep Susa and Pinerolo, pending a general settlement; their new commander would be Louis de Marillac. Was Richelieu placating Marie? Or was Louis XIII trying to undercut her hostility to his advisor at the price of ignoring his own bad feelings about the Marillacs? In any case, the personal diplomacy did not work.

On leaving the council chambers, Marie relieved Richelieu of all his posts in her household. Gaston, for his part, refused to come to the cardinal's rescue despite his repeated, frantic pleas in the ensuing hours. Then, on the king's orders, Richelieu prepared to visit the queen mother for the courtesy formality of relinquishing the offices of grand almoner, household superintendent, and head of her personal council.

The unrehearsed scene of 11 November was brief and emotional. The place was the queen mother's new Palais du Luxembourg, next to Louis's temporary residence at the Hôtel des Ambassadeurs and Richelieu's at the Little Luxembourg (pending vaulting repairs at the Louvre). Louis had come to bid his mother adieu before going to his beloved Versailles. She demanded that he choose between her and his advisor. He asked her to be patient. Richelieu, slipping in to take his permanent leave of Marie, begged forgiveness on bended knee. She called him an ingrate, Louis said nothing, and the cardinal withdrew. Louis XIII went to his makeshift quarters, then on to Versailles.[52]

Courtiers assumed that the king's mother had carried the day; for hours on end, people came to congratulate her. She made plans for a new ministry headed by Michel de Marillac—as if Louis XIII would ever have agreed to a list of councillors dictated to him! How did he respond from his town house and hunting lodge? Saint-Simon helped him calm down, but the favorite's tale of persuading a bewildered monarch to call Richelieu to his side instead of dismissing him does not ring true. Nor is there any supporting evidence for a similar story centered on Richelieu's creature Cardinal La Valette. The king was his own man, just as he had been during family showdowns in 1617, 1620, and 1626.[53] An unembellished diary tells the real story of the Day of Dupes: "[after the Luxembourg scene,] each person believed the cardinal ruined. The king ordered [Richelieu] to follow him to Versailles; and His Majesty, with a visage revealing indignation, also ordered M. the Keeper of the Seals to follow."[54]

If anyone was bewildered, it was Richelieu—despite proofs of royal affection and support right down to the Day of Dupes. The intense minister-psychologist was on the verge of fleeing from a political life that had made him envied, hated, and subject to abuse at every moment by the jealous patron Marie. In the end he obeyed his master's command, buoyed by the encouraging words of Schomberg's son, Father Joseph's brother, and Bouthillier. Richelieu went to Louis's retreat. They talked for four hours. A skeleton council, composed of Bouthillier, Bullion, and La Ville-aux-Clercs, was assembled to carry out orders.

The results? Before dawn, orders went to Marshal Schomberg in Italy to arrest Louis de Marillac, on suspicion of wanting Richelieu murdered. Next morning, La Ville-aux-Clercs took the seals from Michel de Marillac, whom Louis had lodged overnight at a country house just outside Versailles to "await [the king's] will"; Louis's bodyguards then took him prisoner. La Ville-aux-Clercs also gave Marie the king's message that he had acted against a person whose treason had offended him for over a year. When she prepared to go to Versailles on 13 November, Louis had their confessor relay a precise message: if she were coming "to speak about the keeper of the seals, she could spare herself the trouble." She did not go. The key prosecutorial posts of keeper of the seals and first president of the Paris Parlement were assigned to sure men: Châteauneuf, who had been with Louis and Richelieu in Savoy, and Le Jay, who had rebelled against Marie and Concini and then allied with Richelieu.[55]

The nineteenth-century editor of Richelieu's letters, not knowing what to think about the French ruler on the Day of Dupes, wrote: "If Louis XIII's weakness bothers us, his common sense reassures us." The excellent twentieth-century analyst of Louis's psyche has equally ambivalent words: "When [Louis] reaffirmed his loyalty to Richelieu on the Day of Dupes he did so by escaping from his mother and sneaking off to Versailles. He managed never to see her again."[56] But Louis XIII's withdrawal to Versailles was not Louis XVI's flight to Varennes. And his curt refusal to see Marie about a nonnegotiable issue was an intelligent act. After persistent attempts to make his mother accept Richelieu in three-sided summit meetings and one-on-one exchanges, he had finally found a way to stop her in her tracks. There would be plenty of occasions for mother-son confrontations, face-to-face, during the next months, as the governmental "revolution" behind this second coup d'état of Louis XIII's personal rule unfolded.

11

GOVERNMENTAL REVOLUTION

As stunning as the coup d'état of 11 November 1630 was to Louis XIII's France, it was not an isolated event, but part of a broader historical process. The policies that had evolved during the first thirteen years of Louis XIII's personal rule continued during his last thirteen. What the Day of Dupes did alter was the degree and scope of political change. The king of France disciplined his family and court more than before; he whittled away more extensively at the autonomy and privileges of groups within the society of orders; and he pursued more foreign policy initiatives along previous anti-Habsburg lines. This acceleration of the pre-1630 pace amounted to a governmental revolution, the outlines of which were clear by the time France began a twenty-five year war with Spain in 1635.[1]

The quickened pace of political change had no single overriding cause. An economic conjuncture of deep subsistence crisis, made worse by the acute lack of coinage to pay taxes, certainly intensified the conflict between sovereign and subjects over the same resources. Equally important were the basic social structure and popular mentalité of the realm, which assumed subjects' privileges to be inalienable rights, thus forcing monarchical demands to be couched in terms just as strong. Yet human beings and their actions were more powerful in this drama than was the backdrop of conjuncture, structure, and mentalité. Center stage was held by the French people, who objected to war and taxes and controls, and their king, who was intent on doing what he thought was right for them, acting on the advice of an improvising minister. The drama did not follow a prepared script, nor did it have a preordained final act.

First on Louis XIII's mind was what to do with his most recalcitrant subjects: Marie de' Medici, Gaston d'Orléans, and Anne of Austria. He still wanted his mother to get along with his advisor; he wanted his only brother to make something of his life; and he wanted to be a good husband and produce an heir. He also did not want to see the three of them act as a unit. This was a formidable family agenda, even with the psychological advantages derived from the coup d'état of November.

During the first weeks after the Day of Dupes, the king tried personal diplomacy. In summit meetings involving Marie, their mutual confessor, Suffren, Richelieu, and sometimes Gaston and Anne, Louis persuaded his mother to resume attendance at council meetings. Marie remained sullenly silent in council, however, refusing to look at the cardinal. Rumors reached the king that the remnants of the dévot party were still influencing her.

Meanwhile, Louis persuaded Gaston, in Richelieu's presence, to "love, assist, and protect M. le cardinal de Richelieu on all occasions, in accordance with the wishes of the king." Louis also made it clear to Queen Anne that he was unhappy with the moral support she had given her mother-in-law on the Day of Dupes. And he kept his eyes on Marie's friend and Anne's lady-in-waiting, Mme du Fargis, who had urged the queen to oppose Richelieu.[2]

Louis was very open in his battles. When Marie first came to see him at St-Germain on 19 November, he told her that he would "honor and serve her always as he should, but that he [was] obliged to maintain the cardinal to the death."[3] Two days later, he launched into an impromptu speech to delegates from the high tribunals of Paris, who had come to confer over the renewal of the paulette. He made his points with breathtaking directness: "He had done all he could to prevent the violence of the queen, his mother, and he would always bear all sorts of respect toward her. But because M. le cardinal had served him so well and faithfully both inside and outside the kingdom, he was resolved to employ his services more than ever; and to protect him before all and against all."[4]

Marie assumed that Richelieu had dictated this speech. In truth, the cardinal was not privy to it, and he later bewailed the king's undiplomatic words on his behalf to Bullion. The cardinal desperately wanted to be reconciled with the queen mother. Her coldness had left him "so plunged in gloom," Bullion wrote, "that he is no longer recognizable." He could scarcely think of anything else, even his master's assurance of being morally as well as politically committed to him. Louis told Richelieu that he would have been disgraced had he been guilty of wrongdoing against the queen mother; but instead, the minister's behavior had been exemplary. Hence the king could stand up to his mother in good conscience.[5]

Good conscience did not necessarily permit retribution if Marie, Gaston, and Anne failed to cooperate, however. One wonders how Louis managed to embrace the strategies he employed as family bonding came loose at the end of the year of the "great storm." Richelieu undoubtedly put it into his mind to purge some of the bad influences at court, but the king had to make the decision to act. He did so in two successive purges of the royal family household staffs. The first was preventive: to remove "evil" associates of his family. The second was aimed directly at his family and their friends.

As 1630 came to a close, a reluctant monarch, who looked older than his twenty-nine years, exiled his wife's lady-in-waiting and some of her Spanish servants. The ambassador of Spain found his access to the queen mother's quarters controlled, with a rebuke from the king that Philip IV would never have permitted for a day what Louis had put up with for years. Caught in this web of intrigue was someone Louis surely did not want to see go: his *premier valet de chambre* Henri Beringhen, son of a beloved Huguenot servant of his childhood, who had made the mistake of falling in love with Mme du Fargis.

The second purge was prompted by Gaston's electrifying announcement, on 30 January 1631, that Richelieu's slashing of his entourage's pensions freed him from his oath of loyalty. The duke of Orléans did not know that his own brother had pared down the chief minister's generous budget suggestions, not the other way around. In turn, Louis suspected the worst: the jewels given to his fleeing brother by their mother as a parting gift would surely pay for a rebel army. Gaston's timing was uncanny. Paris winesellers were rioting against a new royal tariff; and the law courts were furious with Effiat for suspending the paulette until they paid much higher renewal fees.

Louis galloped from Versailles to tell Richelieu, "Don't be afraid of anything; I will be your second against everyone, without excepting my brother. My honor is involved; any harm done to you I will treat as done to myself and I will know how to get revenge for you."[6] An extensive housecleaning followed, beginning with the queen mother's closest friends. Louis jailed Marie's physician, severed his own relations with their joint confessor, Suffren, and sent the princess of Conti into an exile which may have caused her sudden death by apoplexy. Marie retained the dévot Suffren; but Louis's new confessor was Father Maignon, cousin to the new secretary for war, Servien! Louis also sacrificed his constant companion, the free-spirited Marshal Bassompierre, who had defiantly corresponded with his fellow marshal Louis de Marillac, now under indictment for treason. The sad monarch told his friend that he was not a criminal but that he had to enter the Bastille to avoid being corrupted.

Louis's most stunning retaliatory act was against his defiant mother, who had resumed her boycott of his council to spite Richelieu. The king's normally uncritical biographer, Batiffol, compares Louis's reaction to this behavior with preparations for an execution.[7] In reality, it was a long-delayed and much-deserved second exile. Louis, Marie, and Anne went to Compiègne, on the opposite side of Paris from Gaston's Orléans. After days of trying to get his mother to sign a capitulation, Louis called a council meeting on 23 February. At the debate's end, he forced Richelieu to speak. Warily, the minister laid out four solutions, ranging from his own retirement to Marie's temporary exile. Louis chose the latter, had the château of Compiègne surrounded by fifteen hundred soldiers, informed his wife, and then left with Anne for Paris.

Louis XIII's handling of this family quarrel of 1631 was successful with only two family members. He brought Condé into a position of prominence as a counter to Gaston, and he placated Anne by naming as Mme du Fargis's successor his old bête noire, Marie de Chevreuse. Since Anne's mischievous friend had been living in Lorraine, her recall was timely, for that anti-French duchy was a likely future haven for Gaston. In addition, Louis pressured his wife into being reconciled with Richelieu. Shortly after, Anne's doctors announced that she was expecting. But alas, whatever had happened in her bed, with Louis taking charge of a penitent wife, no heir (and perhaps no pregnancy) came of it. Another dramatic marital conjuncture would be necessary for the incompatible couple to produce the future Sun King.[8]

By contrast, Marie de' Medici's ultimate fate was a horrifying one that neither she nor her conscience-ridden son anticipated. She spurned an honorable exile at Condé's former residence in Moulins, then embarked on the flight of July 1631 that took her unexpectedly to the Spanish Netherlands.[9] Until the day he died, Louis regretted this second exile—just as he had her first one at Blois. It amounted to a life sentence, for the unrepentant mother's repeated pleas to return could not be honored. Her activities on Habsburg soil were closely watched. Marie finally moved to London, then to Holland, and thence to Cologne, where she died in obscurity a few months before Louis.

Gaston preceded his mother to the frontier by four months, after panicking at the approach of Louis XIII with an army toward Orléans. He entered Spanish Franche Comté, then moved to Lorraine, where he secretly married the local duke's sister in 1632. What had started as a family quarrel was now linked to the anti-French policies of Lorraine, Spain, and the Holy Roman Emperor.

This development was far more dangerous than anything Louis had faced in the 1620s, even surpassing the *grand orage* of 1630. Marie and Gaston tried to rally to their side the entire society of orders, through legal appeals to the law courts and published letters of protest to their monarch. The heir's public pronouncements took the dévot view of the miseries of war straight to the king and his people:

> Less than a third of your subjects in the countryside eat regular bread; another third has not only been reduced to begging but languishes in such lamentable need that some die of hunger while others subsist like beasts on acorns, grass, and similar objects. I have seen these miseries with my own eyes since leaving Paris. . . . God grant that the outcry from these wretches' hearts . . . will not provoke [Heaven's] ire and will cause it to fall only on the head of the Cardinal, the sole cause of their misery.

Marie de' Medici's most famous pamphleteer, Mathieu de Morgues, made an equally eloquent appeal in his *Most Humble, True, and Important Remonstrance to the King*. Morgues cried out against royal suppression of parlementary remonstrances, provincial privileges, popular petitions, and the needs of poverty-stricken peasants. Surely Louis the Just would exercise his traditional virtues of clemency and justice rather than give free rein to his chief minister's ambition, avarice, and violence.

In invoking Louis XIII's famous justice on behalf of their cause, the royal family complemented the rhetorical tradition of the French judiciary. As recently as the siege of La Rochelle, Mathieu Molé had justified resistance by the Parlement of Paris to the forced registration of onerous new tax laws, in very similar terms:

> Kings command whatever they please, but it is not necessary for the execution of their commands to create a new order, new officials, and new laws; instead they should follow the traditional ones and assign to each

what belongs to him according to the functions of his office. Then everyone in general, and each person in particular, will render due obedience, and the prince's just orders will be most readily followed.[10]

The opposition's arguments also distinguished between a good, but misled, king and his evil minister. We can attribute that distinction to two main factors: early modern veneration of the divinely anointed priest-king who miraculously healed the diseased, and a conviction on the part of Marie, Gaston, and many lesser subjects that Cardinal Richelieu was in total control of royal policy. Not surprisingly, the queen mother and heir both filed suits with the Parlement of Paris, alleging that the cardinal's "tyranny" over the king and country made him a criminal of lèse-majesté.

That argument not only played on the unpopularity of the chief minister, but it also did further damage to the ruler's reputation. Batiffol exaggerates only slightly in saying that this "validated the legend of Louis XIII as the cringing tool of an autocratic minister, who had at his mercy a master capable only of being jealous and hating him." This propaganda led a decade later to the cruel epitaph:

> Here lies the King, our good master;
> For twenty years the valet of a pastor![11]

In the end, the heir's sword proved less mighty than his pen. At the beginning of 1632 Gaston moved to the Spanish Netherlands, then invaded France with a makeshift army of five thousand cavalry and infantry to "free" Louis XIII from his chief minister. On 1 September, the forces of the duke of Orléans and his distinguished supporter, Henri de Montmorency, were destroyed at Castelnaudary by Marshal Schomberg's seasoned royal troops. The dead included a rebel half brother of the king, the count of Moret. Louis pardoned his heir, who did not participate in the battle, and their official peace treaty upheld the myth that Gaston had been misled by evil advisors in charge of a "Spanish" army.

That settlement left Montmorency, with seventeen wounds more dead than alive, as a scapegoat. The king's soldiers had hoped that the quintessential gentilhomme of the day would somehow escape, and they captured him with the greatest reluctance. He paid the supreme price for gallantly supporting a princely friend and defending provincial liberties. Montmorency was governor of the sprawling southern province of Languedoc, whose Protestant fortifications had so recently been razed. He had hoped to rally his huge local network of clients, from nobles and clergy to judges and members of the provincial estates. Unfortunately, though, the province had just settled a three-year conflict with the monarchy over Effiat's plan to change the *pays d'états* into a *pays d'élections*, with taxes to be administered by royal élus, not the local estates assembly. Having agreed on a more moderate financial contribution, most provincials chose not to join Montmorency.

The duke of Montmorency was tried not by the Parlement of Paris, sitting as the Court of Peers, but by the Parlement of Toulouse acting on commission for the monarchy. Richelieu tearfully supported the parlementary verdict of guilty, even though Montmorency had offered him asylum when Louis was near death in 1630. Louis was even closer to his boyhood companion and valiant victor of the Huguenot and Italian wars. Steeling himself against Queen Anne's impassioned plea and the universal grief of the royal court at Toulouse, not to mention cries in the streets of "Grace! Grace! Mercy! Mercy!" the monarch remained outwardly unmoved.

To the captain of the king's guards who presented the marshal's baton and ribbon of honor while begging on his knees for clemency, Louis replied: "No! There will be no grace; he must die. One should not be upset to see a man die who has so fully merited it. One should only be disturbed that he has fallen by his error into such a great misfortune." Yet in executing another boyhood playmate, Louis revealed his inner torment. To Gaston's appeal for mercy, Louis responded that "the state's welfare required that Montmorency pay for his mistake." Then the king turned from his brother's messenger to hide his tears.

What a heavy price to pay for being Louis the Just. When Marshal Châtillon pointed out "the grief etched on the faces of the entire court," the monarch looked up from his chess game and said, "I would not be king if I had the feelings of private persons." If the Montmorency family's version of what happened is true, Louis had added reason to be troubled. The fallen man's brother-in-law, Condé, later spread the story that Richelieu had manipulated Louis XIII by specious reason of state arguments, and that the Most Christian King of France, on his deathbed, admitted hiding for eleven years his remorse over denying clemency to the First Christian Baron of France.[12]

Louis could not help feeling sympathy for the thirty-seven-year-old descendant of four constables and six marshals, who had distinguished himself as admiral of the fleet, marshal of France, knight of the king's orders, and governor of Languedoc. By contrast, there is no evidence that the king ever felt remorse over his treatment of the Marillac brothers.

The venerable elder Marillac, Michel, spent his last two years in exile at Châteaudun translating the Book of Job, engaging in correspondence that was monitored by Bouthillier, and admonishing his relatives not to speak ill of his alleged persecutors. He died in August 1632, firm in the conviction that he had always acted in the interests of God and king. A year later, his saintly niece cofounded with St. Vincent de Paul the Sisters of Charity to care for the poor. Meanwhile, Michel's younger brother was subjected to an extended trial for treason that bypassed the sympathetic regular courts and ended in a 13–10 vote for the death penalty. The entire undertaking has the stench of a judicial murder, for the judges were handpicked, concluded their work at Richelieu's residence of Ruel, and found the man guilty of nothing more than embezzlement of army funds. Marshal Marillac was executed at the Place de Grève on 10 May 1632, protesting his innocence.[13]

Somehow, Louis de Marillac had brought out the worst in the king's character and governmental revolution. The monarch has been described as having "pursued his soldier's doom with singleminded intensity, . . . with fastidious relish."[14] Why was Louis so harshly unrelenting over hearsay that Marillac had considered killing his advisor if he, Louis, had died at Lyon? As in the Chalais case, the ruler was determined to stand by his trusted servitor. In addition, the general situation in 1631–32 looked perilous. Richelieu feared a linkage between the flights of Gaston and Marie de' Medici, anti-French activity in Brussels, Lorraine, and Vienna, and the internal opposition just then beginning to form around Montmorency.[15]

The way Louis XIII handled the situation also conformed to his own way of dealing with disagreeable family-related problems. It was in character to repress dissatisfaction over his marshal's less than brave leadership at La Rochelle and in Italy; to appoint Marie's creature to the Mantuan command on the eve of the Day of Dupes as a means of keeping her under control; and then to act on political instinct in the heat of the 11 November crisis to get rid of someone he had considered incompetent, dangerous, and evil. Even so, Louis de Marillac's death sentence was a blot on the reign comparable to the massacre at Nègrepelisse in 1622.

Had Louis XIII's justice leaned more frequently in this arbitrary direction, his governmental revolution would have lost one of its most powerful supports. For his repressive acts needed the moral justification that their author was scrupulously fair, both in punishing and in forgiving his subjects. As it was, Hay du Chastelet's *Observations on the Life and Condemnation of Marshal Marillac* presented only the flimsiest defense for this particular case of royal justice. That royal pamphleteer snidely asked: "How should we judge a Catholic speaking of his king, reputed to be the most just, pious, and Catholic ruler ever to hold the scepter, who recommends serving him with the proviso, 'after God'?"[16]

Louis XIII's sense of justice was not the only royal virtue put to the test in the early 1630s by opposition at the top of his society. He needed all his celebrated valor and prudence to prevent discontented grandees from linking up with revolts among the lower social orders. Without prudent management, the royal-parlementary quarrel over the paulette would have ended not in compromise in 1631, but in his alienated venal officials giving serious consideration to the legal appeals of Gaston and Marie, and perhaps even condoning regional fiscal rebellion.[17] Louis's valor was also at stake, as subjects took their appeals across the border to the king's external foes. Montmorency's death was cause enough for Gaston d'Orléans to flee from France yet again, and sign a treaty of alliance with the King of Spain. Little did anyone foresee that Louis the Just and Victorious would blunt escalating internal opposition, and use its connection with foreign states to justify territorial aggression abroad as well.

Some of the stiffest opposition came from the Parlement of Paris. The judges in the capital rejected Effiat's 1630 offer to renew the paulette for judicial and financial officials, in return for a fee amounting to 25 percent of the value of their offices. The parlementarians delayed registration of new fiscal expedients. They remonstrated against the procedures of Marillac's trial. They went so far as to amend a royal edict that declared all servitors of the renegade heir guilty of high treason in order to exclude his domestic servants. And they opposed the special Arsenal Chamber established to try Gaston's clients.

Louis XIII fought back with every weapon at his disposal. He countered Gaston's and Marie's appeals to the Parlement by declaring that an attack on Richelieu was an attack on his own person: he would not merit the name Just, he said, unless he protected his servitors.[18] When the parlementary judges amended his edict against Gaston's supporters, Louis had them file into the Louvre, where he tore apart their amendment "as a scrap of paper that threatened his authority and could ignite a conflagration." The ringleaders were temporarily exiled. To their colleagues' protest that the entire court was obedient, the king shot back that if he wanted to learn about obedience he would look to his companies of guards.[19]

The relationship between king and cardinal was far from smooth on parlementary matters like this. At times Louis waved his minister's *billet* at the Parlement to show that they agreed on demanding obedience. Sometimes Richelieu used the king's anger to maneuver the parlementary leaders into concessions. And occasionally Richelieu told his master that it would be prudent to compromise, provided the judges were repentent.[20]

Louis prudently reduced the high courts' paulette fees in August 1631, while retaining them for the lesser courts. He was also conscious of the roles of each governmental echelon, telling the parlementarians that he could overrule them if they exceeded their authority, just as they could rule on appeals from lower courts. But in January 1632, Louis XIII staggered the Parlement (as well as Richelieu and the stridently antiparlementarian Keeper of the Seals Châteauneuf) with an impromptu tirade on his exclusive right to political authority. Louis had summoned a parlementary delegation to Metz, where he was monitoring Gaston's movements. First President Le Jay maladroitly compared the king to the autocratic Louis XI, which touched off the response, "I am not prepared to answer you, but I want you to know that you are the only [subjects] who have tried to encroach on royal authority." There followed the sternest judicial lesson of the reign: "You are established solely to judge between *maître* Pierre and *maître* Jean, and I will return you to your proper role; and if you persist in your actions, I will cut your nails to the quick."[21]

Louis took his revolution to the provinces as well as to Paris, with scant regard for the distances involved. During the 1620s the western and southern Huguenot towns and nobles had felt his presence. Now it was the turn of the crescent of privileged provinces known as pays d'états, from Montmorency's Languedoc in the southwest to Burgundy in the east, with their regional cultures, dialects, and customs. Subjects could not help being impressed; their king's appearance reinforced local support, intimidated the disloyal, and undermined provincial autonomy.

Burgundy was a prime target, because of elite and popular tax resistance going back to 1630. On Louis's way to Savoy that year, Michel de Marillac had forced Dijon's city fathers to kneel while a benevolent king promised not to introduce a rumored wine tax. But Marillac and Effiat had also brought the royal tax regime of élus to the province. So Burgundians, like Languedocians, directed their anger at the transformation of their pays d'états into a pays d'élections. Then Gaston passed through on his flight from France in 1631, and Marie's old friend, Governor Bellegarde, tried to rally the discontented to Gaston's side. Louis XIII descended on the province, curbed the municipal privileges of Dijon, and abolished the élus in return for a financial contribution. The Parlement of Dijon obligingly registered a royal decree against Gaston's followers, including Bellegarde. The fleeing governor was replaced by Condé.

Farther south, in Provence, similar opposition had gathered against the new élus. The governor of this pays d'états was another friend of the queen mother, the duke of Guise. Neither he nor the parlement and town council of Aix had done much to stop a tax revolt in 1630. Youths roamed the streets shouting, "Long Live the King! Down with élus and thieves!" An effigy of Superintendent of Finance Effiat was burned, and a royal intendant for justice and finance fled. Although Provence was too far away from Gaston's line of flight in 1631 to require the king's presence, Louis condemned the continuing Provençal unrest in his letters and conversations. Condé marched in with five thousand soldiers, the élus were withdrawn for a fee, and Aix's municipal autonomy was circumscribed. Guise had the sense to accept the verdict of the Day of Dupes and go into voluntary exile. He was replaced by the leader of Louis's 1617 coup d'état, Marshal Vitry.

In Languedoc, the royally imposed Edict of Béziers of 1632 was milder than the settlements in its sister provinces, because the struggle over the élus had ended before Montmorency's rebellion began. As Schomberg fought Governor Montmorency in the western part of the province, Louis XIII was enjoying a triumphal march past welcoming throngs of Huguenot townspeople in the east. From Lyon he made royal entries to Nîmes, Lunel, Montpellier, Narbonne, Carcassonne, Castelnaudary, and finally Toulouse. Today's tourist can find only one local trace of Louis's retributive justice: the mountain-top town of Les Baux resisted, and so we see the ruins of the walls and château, standing incongruously with charming medieval craft shops. Louis met the estates of the province at Béziers, and told the gathering that he was rewarding their loyalty by suppressing onerous new taxes. Schomberg became the new governor, and was succeeded by his son on his death at the end of 1632.

Other disloyal governors were summarily replaced by grandees loyal to the king and their patron, Richelieu. In Picardy, Chevreuse succeeded Elbeuf. Richelieu's brother-in-law, La Meilleraye, became lieutenant general of Brittany. The sea-conscious cardinal assumed the governorship of Brittany. Marie lost Anjou to Cardinal La Valette, while the latter's fiery father, Epernon, retained Guienne. Louis's untrustworthy cousin Soissons was now assisted in Dauphiné by Marshal Créquy.[22]

What did these changes at mid reign signify? Everywhere, Louis XIII clamped down on opposition within the society of orders by controlling, weakening, and infiltrating rather than destroying corporate bodies. Disloyal provincial governors were replaced by persons of the same high social status. The pays d'états and their assemblies fended off the élus. Executive justice encroached on the functions of the courts of law, but the paulette and right to remonstrate continued. Trouble-shooting royal agents commissioned as intendants of justice, finance, and police (like the one at La Rochelle in 1628) and other commissioners—known, because of their servicing of the military's material needs, as intendants of the army—assumed many functions of the venal officials. Yet more than one intendant was run out of town by a hostile community. Royal revenues increased significantly, from 43 million livres in 1630 to 57.5 million in 1632. But, as Richard Bonney points out, nearly half of that income came from the sale of offices and related fees, and a fifth from windfalls like Montmorency's confiscated wealth, the creation of special indirect taxes, loans, and other extraordinary means. Ordinary revenues were a mere 8.4 million.[23]

In what sense, then, was this truly a governmental revolution? The changes were less radical than the streamlining envisaged by the 1629 Code Michau and its inspirer, Michel de Marillac. The political system that came to be may also have been less healthy than the prior "representative government" of Renaissance France, which Russell Major has extolled.[24] Yet in terms of what was practical and attainable, the changes were revolutionary enough to scandalize subjects, both great and humble. In a society where hierarchy, ranks, and orders were eternal structural truths, to have undermined traditional institutions was radical surgery.

Indeed, the shock to popular structures and mentalité was so great that its success required, at its center, a Louis the Just. Only a priest-king, and one who was a stickler for justice, whether retributive or benevolent, could have validated the changes of the early 1630s. Michel de Marillac, who wished to run roughshod over all privilege, would have failed miserably in any attempt to effect such change. Richelieu's sense of when to compromise, while crucial to success, was offset by his unpopularity, which undermined the moral buttressing he sought to give his master's political changes. Other key councillors, from Effiat and Servien to Bullion and Bouthillier, were primarily technocrats, albeit important ones.[25]

In assessing the magnitude of political change during this time, we must also weigh the role of foreign policy. This was a two-way process. Costly foreign policy lay behind many of the fiscal, military, even judicial controls on subjects associated with the internal governmental revolution. The power derived from these royal controls inside the kingdom in turn allowed Louis to be more aggressive outside the kingdom than in the past. Even when he was simply reacting to the possibility that border provinces and surrounding states would cooperate against him, this power provided a great moral thrust to what was billed as a just policy of protecting the French state and its allies.

Richelieu had written more than one position paper on the opportunity to open "gates" into the Rhineland and Low Countries. Now the opportunity to complement the gates already opened to Italy came in the guise of defending German "liberties" and punishing Gaston's foreign allies. In mid 1631, the Franco-Habsburg Treaty of Cherasco guaranteed the Mantuan succession without restricting Louis XIII's freedom in northern Europe. Subsequent secret French agreements with the thoroughly intimidated Duke Victor Amadeus of Savoy allowed France to keep the gate of Pinerolo leading to Italy.

Louis XIII was well briefed to make decisions on the German and Dutch wars. (See Appendix, map 4.) As usual, there were copious memoranda, often based on data gathered by Richelieu's agents headed by Father Joseph. These memoranda were thoroughly discussed both in council debates and private talks between the king and his advisor. While the papal nuncio and Father Joseph still raised the moral issues that had bothered the dévots, policy-making was less acrimonious now. It was generally agreed that, at the very least, Habsburg soldiers must be kept out of the lands just east of France. Yet by sending his most trusted marshals to Picardy and Champagne, the monarch readied himself for a variety of possibilities.

Louis readily concurred with Richelieu that the flow of French subsidies to the Dutch must be maintained. He also had much enthusiasm for the January 1631 Treaty of Barwälde, which subsidized Sweden's fight for German princely liberties against Habsburg Imperial power, while guaranteeing Catholic worship in the war zone. And Louis began to court German princes who were unhappy with their emperor's power; a secret agreement with Duke Maximilian of Bavaria in May 1631 was aimed at detaching the German Catholic League from the Imperialists.

This warrior-king did not, however, leave the implementation of foreign policy to his marshals, ministers, ambassadors, and allies. Louis's body might be failing, his periods of exhaustion longer, but his energies were nonetheless amazing. After pursuing his fleeing brother through Burgundy in March 1631, he returned to Paris, then in September headed east after his mother's escape from Compiègne. Scoffing at reports that he would soon die, and proudly proclaiming to the Paris law courts his support for his chief minister and his intention to end his family's harassment, Louis crossed Champagne to the enclaves of Metz, Toul, and Verdun outside France proper.

These three bishoprics, surrounded by a patchwork of petty lands under French or Imperial suzerainty, were of prime importance. Although occupied by France for almost a century, their bishops were customarily drawn from the hostile house of Lorraine, and their overlord was the Holy Roman Emperor. Louis XIII was therefore staking a bold claim by showing up in Metz and Verdun and turning them into major fortified places. In addition, the French king sent La Force's army of Champagne into Spanish Luxembourg in pursuit of Gaston's mercenary troops. On the way, La Force occupied Sedan, capital of the French vassal duchy of Bouillon, which had allowed military passage to Gaston and the Imperialists.

More ominously, the king took his own troops into Moyenvic, which bordered Lorraine and had been occupied by Imperial troops. Louis completed his eastern campaign of 1631 by punishing Charles IV of Lorraine. That vassal of the French king had dared to give asylum to the royal heir and provide soldiers for the emperor's German war. His chastisement took the form of the Treaty of Vic, which gave France a foothold in Lorraine and the right of passage.

How long could Louis XIII limit his foreign policy to objectives that looked reasonably defensive and morally upright? Gustavus Adolphus put him to the test in the autumn of 1631 by defeating everything in the path of the thirty-five-thousand-strong Swedish army. The Swedes smashed Tilly's army at Breitenfeld, occupied Catholic principalities west of the Rhine, clashed with France's Catholic ally Bavaria, and interfered with Catholic worship and property. Then the Lion of the North tried to lure the Most Christian King into an open war with the emperor: the Swedes would withdraw from the Rhineland to concentrate on the Imperialist heartland, leaving Louis free to fill the power vacuum by occupying the mass of semi-independent Alsatian lands between Lorraine and the Rhine, which were nominally under the emperor's authority.

At a crucial council meeting on 6 January 1632, only Father Joseph spoke out against alienating Catholic Germany and provoking open war with the emperor through this expansionist opportunity. Louis XIII postponed a decision. The next day, Richelieu changed his mind, and his king chose to continue the current policy of indirect involvement in the contest between the Habsburgs and their German and Swedish opponents.[26]

Louis still wanted to have it both ways: to subsidize the Swedes while building a pro-French third party in western Germany. He lost Bavaria to the Imperialist side, but gained protective custody over several Rhineland principalities, notably the archbishopric of Trier. In February 1632, flushed with hope, the king wrote to Richelieu: "I rejoice in the good news that you send me about Germany, and I hope that with the help of the good Lord and your counsels the Spaniards will cause us no harm." The following month Richelieu disabused his master of this illusion, writing: "The face of things is changing. . . . Spain, the emperor, and Lorraine have united against France."[27]

So 1632 was to be another year of madcap travels for the French monarch. In May, he was at Calais on the English channel, replacing local governors sympathetic to Gaston and Marie, who were just across the border in the Spanish Netherlands. From there Louis and Richelieu headed for Lorraine, where he relished making Duke Charles apologize for once again supporting Gaston. The Treaty of Liverdun in June authorized French garrisoning of towns in Lorraine on the route from France to Verdun. As luck would have it, Gustavus Adolphus withdrew from the Rhine to pursue the reinstated Imperial general Wallenstein. Louis sent an army to prevent Spain from taking over the Rhineland ministates vacated by the Swedes, then returned to Paris. From August to October, however, he traversed southern France in response to his brother's invasion and Montmorency's revolt. It was a strange year, ending in Richelieu's grave illness on his way back to Paris with Queen Anne, and the cashiering of Châteauneuf for allowing military plans to reach Lorraine through his temptress friend, Marie de Chevreuse. Was there never to be any rest?[28]

Like it or not, Louis was being drawn from indirect into direct war with the Habsburgs. The death of Gustavus Adolphus at the battle of Lützen in November 1632 removed the unreliable but strongest anti-Imperialist leader in Germany, and coincided with Gaston's third flight to Lorraine, and eventually to the Spanish Netherlands. Louis's fears grew when he learned that, during his previous stay in Lorraine, Gaston had married Duke Charles's sister, Marguerite. An indignant monarch had the Parlement of Paris nullify his heir's marriage on the grounds that he had not approved it. It worked! The bewildered Gaston quarreled with his mother, left his wife in Brussels, and was welcomed back to France by his brother late in 1634. Louis was less indulgent with his brother's new in-laws. He marched into Lorraine's capital of Nancy in September 1634 as the Parlement of Paris awarded the entire duchy to its suzerain, the king of France. Meanwhile, several towns and seigniories in Alsace placed themselves under French protection.

Could Louis XIII continue to nibble away at the frontier in the name of self-protection and still avoid an open break with the Habsburgs? Theoretically yes, even after a combined Imperialist-Spanish victory at Nordlingen in September 1634 over the armies of Protestant Sweden and Germany (with the Spanish troops conveniently using the Val Tellina passes to enter the war theater). Neither Richelieu nor Olivares wanted war. Neither Spain nor France, and certainly not the war-torn Holy Roman Empire, could afford a Habsburg-Bourbon war, either economically or fiscally. Yet neither Bourbon nor Habsburg leadership wanted the other side to be in a superior position in Europe.[29]

Unless France intervened, Nordlingen spelled the end of the German war—to the advantage of the emperor. Hence Richelieu, with great reluctance but keen understanding, worked toward two new alliances that would prevent Habsburg hegemony at the price of bringing on the war that had been avoided in 1631. In February 1635, a Franco-Dutch defensive and offensive alliance promised French military assistance against Spain. In April, the Treaty of Compiègne promised France's military entry in the German war as an ally of Sweden, (although it quibbled over whether Louis XIII would be technically at war with the emperor at the same time and insisted on Catholic worship where the Swedes had suppressed it). The treaty came none too soon to prolong the Thirty Years' War, for Emperor Ferdinand had already negotiated the Peace of Prague with most of the princes of Germany by compromising on religion and princely "liberties."

While Richelieu held back from finalizing the Dutch and Swedish agreements, Louis kept pressing him onward, as he had in 1633 and 1634.[30] The king, convinced he was in the right, was psychologically set for war. All Richelieu could do was choose which Habsburg power his Bourbon king would cross swords with first. He did not want it to be the emperor, for that would antagonize too many potential German allies.[31] In the end he got his wish, for Louis disliked the Spaniards more than the Imperialists, and Spain made the first flagrantly belligerent move. In March 1635, Spanish troops seized the person and land of France's German ally, the archbishop of Trier.

A lesser affront to another French ally, the duke of Mantua, had caused the almost insoluble Mantuan war of 1629–31. Undaunted, the French royal council voted unanimously on 1 April 1635 that the Most Christian King could not accept Philip IV's seizure of the archbishop of Trier. On 19 May, a French herald in Brussels solemnly announced Louis XIII's declaration of war on Spain. (See plate 13.) The king was already at the border of the Spanish Netherlands, poised for action. Technically, he remained at peace with the Holy Roman Emperor of the German Nation, a legal fiction that ended the next year. In Italy, he was allied with Savoy, Parma, Modena, and Mantua; and Louis's former rebel foe, the inveterate Huguenot soldier Rohan, was poised to recapture the Val Tellina in the service of France's old ally Venice.

Louis the Just was now committed to an all-out war. Less than six months before, he had gone to Parlement promising relief from the miseries of rebellion, war, plague, and recession. Wartime taxes were to be revoked and the taille reduced by one-fourth. There were to be curbs on tax exemptions and luxury purchases by the well-to-do. Special *grands jours* tribunals would combat noble lawlessness in the provinces. And the crown would provide new support for commerce and shipbuilding. Despite these promises, the coming of the Bourbon-Habsburg conflict in 1635 signaled not the modification but the acceleration of Louis XIII's governmental revolution. Louis was a very old thirty-three with only eight years to live. His war would outlast him, and so would the end product of his political changes. That bequest can be summed up in two words: it was a warfare state.

PART IV

The Legacy of Louis XIII
1635–43

12

WARFARE KING, STATE, AND SOCIETY

Louis XIII's declaration of war on Philip IV of Spain in 1635, which was followed a year later by hostilities with Emperor Ferdinand, placed enormous strains on his person, his state, and French society. We can only guess at all the effects wartime living had on the king's deteriorating constitution, yet it surely hastened his death. He fretted constantly about how to raise money, men, and supplies for his troops; and he exposed himself to the grim conditions his soldiers endured, from the moment the first shots were fired until just before his death eight years later, as a prematurely aged forty-one-year-old.

The stresses that Louis's foreign involvement placed on his state and society are more easily pinpointed. While his soldiers were not unprepared for warfare, the administrative and financial resources necessary to expand his forces from under one hundred thousand to around a quarter million men in arms were simply not available in 1635. Wartime pressures therefore greatly accelerated the governmental revolution of the previous years, with the emergence of a warfare state that was geared to fight year in and year out.

The amount of money transferred from subjects to the state reached dizzy heights. Treasury receipts, considered high at 57 million livres in 1632, had risen to 72 million in 1633, 120 million in 1634, and—at least on paper—208 million in 1635. Thereafter income remained stable at an annual level of around 100 million livres. If we focus on the army alone, figures are still more dramatic: military expenditure had averaged under 16 million during the 1620s, stayed around 20 million in the early 1630s, then soared to 33 million in 1635 and past 38 million by 1640.[1] The accompanying administrative adjustments were naturally just as striking: all but four of the major provincial estate assemblies disappeared; former ad hoc commissioners in some parts of the state became regular features throughout the realm as intendants of justice, finance, and police; and relations between soldiers and society came to be regulated by army intendants.

An even more telling measure of the ongoing governmental revolution is seen in its impact on French society. The number, intensity, and duration of protests at every level of the society of orders defy imagination. Louis XIII found a quarter of his realm thrown out of control during revolts by the southwestern Croquants in 1636–37, his authority challenged by the poor and powerful of wealthy Normandy in 1639, and the justice of his wartime demands questioned repeatedly by articulate princes, prelates, and parlementarians, as well as by less eloquent—but equally concerned—provincial nobles, urban paupers, and peasant communities.

Let us follow the tortuous path of this warrior-king, as he set out for his state's borders and strained the resources of his society. At Louis XIII's disposal in 1635 were his regular bodyguards, musketeers, cavalry; native infantry units of Picardy, Piedmont, Champagne, and Navarre; Swiss mercenaries; and fresh reinforcements who had been pressed into service during the civil and foreign campaigns of the 1620s and early 1630s. Now he added still more companies, making a total of one hundred regiments of foot soldiers and six full armies.

French soldiers fought Spaniards in the Low Countries and held Lorraine and Alsace against possible attacks by Austrian, Bavarian, and Spanish troops. In Burgundy they were poised for battle with Spain and the emperor in Spanish Franche Comté. In the Alps they blocked the Spaniards' troop route through the Val Tellina. A Pyrenees front was added after 1640, to take advantage of massive revolts by Philip IV's Portuguese and Catalan subjects.

Yet the war did not begin well for Louis. A northeastern offensive failed. The Grisons defected—taking with them the Val Tellina passes—to the Habsburg side. And the young duke of Savoy died, leaving Louis XIII's sister Christine to battle as regent for her infant son against pro-Spanish in-laws. To further complicate matters,

Pope Urban VIII shifted from his pre-war concern over Habsburg expansionism to exerting moral pressure on both the Bourbons and the Habsburgs to sheathe their swords.

The nadir of Louis XIII's wartime fortunes came in 1636, when Spanish troops invaded France from the east, marched through Picardy, and laid siege to Corbie. Parisians fled in terror at the sight of enemy scouts on the horizon. A flustered chief minister counseled the king to take the "reason of state" precaution of withdrawing his royal person from the danger zone as well. Louis did exactly the opposite in a foolhardy, instinctive, and, as it turned out, entirely correct move. The year before, he had defied his minister in going to the Lorraine front. Now he directed both minister and marshals to join him in hurling back the invaders. The crisis ended suddenly: Louis halted Parisian grumbling against his alter ego with a stirring defense of the cardinal, hanged two of his commanders in effigy for surrendering their border posts, and rescued Corbie.[2]

From then on Louis XIII was either with his troops, preparing himself for a campaign, or telling his marshals he would soon be in their midst. During the terrible "year of Corbie," Louis had personally ordered his ministers to use every means to keep a discouraged Condé at the siege of Dôle in Franche Comté, even if it meant exaggerating French fortunes elsewhere or intimating that the royal chief was on his way with a relief force. The year 1637 began with the king preparing to dash off to quell Norman disorders on the panicky suggestion of Bullion, then staying put thanks to Séguier's more optimistic assessment. Then Louis spread a rumor that he would go to Provence to settle differences between Governor Vitry and the army chiefs, even though he admitted having "no desire" to take the Lyon road.[3]

In 1638–39 the warrior-king traveled from the Spanish Netherlands border and the siege of St-Omer—where he busied himself fortifying places that France would eventually retain at the Peace of the Pyrenees in 1659—south to Sedan to keep an eye on the count of Soissons, who was in nearby exile. Then, to press his own sister Christine of Savoy into a closer alliance and shield her from Spanish influences, Louis galloped all the way to Lyon and Grenoble, before retiring to Fontainebleau and St-Germain. The trip had taken a great deal of royal energy, including the nerve-wracking experience of threatening to arrest his own sister—but it had been worth it, for his troops were now in Turin.

On and on the warrior-ruler pressed. In 1640 and 1641, the demands of the warfare state slackened sufficiently to take him only on short forays—to Amiens and, more boldly, to face his invading cousin Soissons at Sedan. But in 1642 he undertook an exhausting journey that equaled his prime-of-life Huguenot campaigns of the 1620s. Louis had decided to accept an offer by the rebel Catalans to make him "count of Barcelona." He galloped south to Lyon, Nîmes, Avignon, and Arles, then, leaving a gravely ill Richelieu behind, sped westward to Montpellier, Narbonne, and the siege of Perpignan. He was rewarded with the permanent seizure of Roussillon from Spain. (See Appendix, map 4.)

While Louis was overseeing French victories from Flanders to the Pyrenees, other successes came to his marshals and foreign allies. The Habsburgs held on to the Val Tellina, but French troops occupied Breisach on the east bank of the Rhine river, following the death of Louis's German ally, Bernard of Saxe-Weimar. The Breisach bridgehead was a splendid acquisition: it covered recent French conquests in Alsace, cut the Spanish supply lines between Italy and the north, and acted as a gate for future French troop deployment with the Swedes against the emperor. The Dutch, meanwhile, were recapturing Breda and defeating Spain at sea. Best of all, court and country agitation inside Spain thwarted Olivares's plans for a Spanish version of the warfare state: in 1643, Philip IV dismissed his beleaguered minister.

As the war dragged on, dragging down his body in the process, Louis kept a clear view of his objectives. He sought peace, but on the condition of keeping the gains of the 1620s and 1630s, those points beyond the borders of his father's state. He was prepared to fight on to retain the gates outside France at Pinerolo and Roussillon, not to mention protecting his capital city by pushing the frontier eastward into Alsace and northward into the Spanish Netherlands. This point warrants emphasis, for historians have seen Louis XIII's aggressive foreign policy as Richelieu's doing alone.

Louis's letters of the late 1630s bristled with emotional involvement as they narrated in copious detail the war's advance.[4] He suggested commanders and command positions, and the shifting of companies and regiments. He admitted the agony of sleepless nights when, in 1636, he thought Cardinal La Valette would be defeated before military relief forces could reach him. In 1638, he wrote with sarcasm to Richelieu that Olivares was "always well disposed toward peace," and in the same phrase "that the Swedes now have some advantage, and so I believe we will have peace, for which I pray to God with all my heart." That same year, while impatiently awaiting the birth of his first child at Anne's side, he confided to his chief minister that he was bored with female company and wanted to get back to his soldiers.

In 1639, the soldier-king entertained the possibility of a truce, but with the utmost suspicion. As he read over Richelieu's draft treaty, Louis struck out every phrase that could be construed as restoring France's wartime acquisitions to their previous possessors. These acquisitions had been gifts from God, were crucial to French security, and if lost would only have to be reconquered in a later campaign. That same year, Louis took up his pen in praise of the Protestant Dutch victory over the Catholic Spaniards at Fort de la Croix: "I pray to God that [the defeat] will cause [the Spaniards'] hearts to leap to their throats."

Courtiers did not read their monarch's letters, so they failed to grasp the meaning of his pious hopes for peace or his mood swings as the fortunes of war ebbed and flowed. All they knew was that the king's latest Jesuit confessor, Father Caussin, was troubling his conscience. Was it over the prolongation of war with fellow Catholics? In reality, Caussin found the king vulnerable not on his foreign war as such, but on the misery it caused his subjects, as well as the difficulties for domestic and international harmony caused by his falling out with Queen Mother Marie and his bad relations with Queen Anne. Furthermore, Father Caussin triggered not so much fear of God as royal anger when he said that the king would be called to account by the Deity after death. King Louis let Secretary of State Chavigny know that the pressure exerted on his conscience in the confessional threw him "into a rage [*extrème colère*] against the said father, regarding the entreaties he had so inappropriately [*hors de propos*] made."

Cardinal Richelieu did not have to work hard on King Louis's indignation against the royal confessor's charges (although the fearful minister left nothing to chance, as usual). When Caussin alluded to the king's responsibility before God for Swedish atrocities in Germany, and called the Franco-Swedish alignment as evil as an alliance with the Moslem Turks, Louis the Just shot back: "I would be glad to see the Turks in Madrid to force Spain into peace; and then I could join [the Spaniards] to make war on [the Turks]." Louis promptly dismissed Father Caussin and placed France under the protection of the Virgin in the hope that Mary would intercede with God and bring France peace—with, of course, territorial acquisitions.[5]

Clarity of royal purpose did not, however, mean self-confidence on military or political strategy. In fact, Louis depended on Richelieu more than ever as his life ebbed and his goutish pains, head aches, stomach disorders, and failing lungs took their toll. Typical was a royal note from the château of Monceau on 13 October 1640, following a briefing by Marshal La Mothe-Houdancourt, whom Louis found "very well informed." The king saw the flaw in the marshal's plea to maneuver in Italy for good winter quarters, for this would free the enemy to advance elsewhere. Yet in expressing his personal reservations to Richelieu, Louis concluded lamely: "All of these are simply thoughts that came to me, about which I tell you all [word illegible] to follow up the good ones and disregard the bad ones. I leave it all to your good judgment."[6]

One could cite many other letters in which the master deferred to the servitor: on where he should visit, even on what to reply to his mother if she wrote a congratulatory note on the birth of his child. Most pathetic of all was Louis's admission that his reply to a letter from Secretary for War Sublet de Noyers did not make much sense because he was beside himself over a lover's quarrel with his latest male favorite, Cinq Mars. Yet underneath this self-deprecation and self-destructive emotional outpouring, there was a royal judgment that could not be ignored. This fact was understood perfectly by Richelieu, by the marshals, by the superintendents of finance, and by the secretaries of state, including Chavigny, who watched the king's every mood on behalf of his patron, Richelieu. When, for example, King Louis feared that an attack on Arras in the Spanish Netherlands was too risky to undertake, Richelieu backed away from an engagement.[7]

The cardinal's death in December 1642 changed some things that he had persuaded a reluctant monarch to agree to, but not major matters, and, above all, not the war. Louis released a few political prisoners who had been particularly close to him, such as Bassompierre and Vitry, whose incarceration he had authorized with misgivings on Richelieu's advice. But in the post-Richelieu royal council, the most influential voice was that of a protégé of Richelieu, whom Louis had earlier employed to try to avoid the war of 1635 and more recently had entrusted with the task of shoring up the Franco-Savoyard alliance against the Habsburgs: Jules Mazarin.

Louis XIII had found in the former papal agent Giulio Mazarini a new minister who could speak of peace but act in the interests of an ongoing war, and a cardinal of the Catholic church who could deflect the arguments of the dévots and father Caussin. In short, Cardinal Mazarin could work very well with Louis the Just. In the ministerial infighting of the last months of the reign, Mazarin grew in political favor with Louis, while the rigidly sanctimonious Sublet de Noyers was unceremoniously replaced with the quietly efficient intendant of the army in Italy, Michel Le Tellier. As the king's end approached, his physical suffering and bad moods complicated the conduct of war and search for peace; but there is no evidence that on his deathbed in May 1643 he saw his conflict against the Habsburg rulers as anything but a just war.[8]

Nor is there a shred of evidence that Louis XIII had misgivings about the warfare state that his foreign conflict had spawned. Just as this soldier-king proudly published his personal war reports in the royal *Gazette*, so too did he approve the administrative adjustments his ministers deemed necessary to make to attain his military objectives. Without accountability, his army's size, morale, and effectiveness would plummet. Somehow close tabs must be kept on his irregularly paid and none-too-reliable soldiers, not to mention their officers, who chafed at controls from above and padded figures during official musters in order to inflate their own income. Louis assumed, too, that mechanisms would be found to tap civilian wealth more fully for the war effort. When Bullion and Bouthillier told a doubting king that funds on paper were already allocated, he insisted that they find ready cash elsewhere.

When the taille, the basic tax levied on land, reached such high levels that it triggered peasant revolts, the finance ministers turned to indirect levies on wine and meat. These assessments inspired a host of urban revolts by angry wage earners, shopowners, and innkeepers. Wealthier individuals from the world of money lending, and the judges and tax agents they aspired to join as colleagues, also contributed. The financiers, eager to move from their lucrative but ignoble world, bought blocs of royally created venal offices of justice and finance, thereby gaining entry to the nobility of the robe. Existing robe officials, scandalized by the entry of these parvenus and the prospect of sharing fees, were further outraged by blatantly direct attacks on their wealth, the most obvious one being an arbitrary increase in the value of existing offices, which naturally increased the officeholders' annual paulette fees.[9]

Since all these mechanisms still left the treasury short, Louis's finance ministers borrowed, and at interest rates double the 10 percent allowed by Effiat shortly before. In many cases, through an agreement called a *traité* over a loan contract, or *partie*, moneylenders called *traitants* and *partisans* were awarded the right to reimburse themselves simply by collecting taxes or selling new state offices. One tax after another was privatized until, shortly after Louis XIII's death, even the taille was franchised. As crude as the mechanism of tax farming was, and as costly to the state, it produced instant cash.

Paradoxically, this privatizing of taxation also entailed the expansion of the state's fiscal administration at the local level. Wherever there was a partisan or traitant, there were sure to be royal fusiliers armed with fusils to help his reimbursement projects. And wherever there were taxes to be collected, either by traitants or by élus and trésoriers, there were bound to be royal *commissaires* to oversee local tax assessment, collection, and litigation. These special commissioners were becoming known as intendants. One immediately thinks of the infamous royal hatchet man Isaac Laffemas, dubbed "the cardinal's hangman." Though he was extraordinarily brutal in the way he carried out special tasks for his ruler, the shift in the basic functions of his commissions from the mid 1620s to a decade later was typical of what was happening to commissions and commissaires throughout France.

Earlier in the reign, when Louis the Just was concentrating on justice against grandee plots and ministerial insubordination, Laffemas had fitted in as a dutiful special judge. In 1624 he had been part of the king's personal attack on La Vieuville's financial associates through the chambre de justice. In 1631–32 we find him sitting in the special Chambre de l'Arsenal and acting as intendant in Champagne against Gaston's treasonous associates. But in 1633, as Louis turned his attention more and more to external matters and means of financing them, Laffemas's commission as intendant over justice at Châlons was combined with duties as army intendant for the militarily crucial Metz-Toul-Verdun triangle.

Chancellor Séguier later recalled that the intendants, as a regular part of government, were "established by the late king in 1635." That was too precise a dating for an ongoing process. Yet war needs after that date swelled the numbers of intendants in the northeastern war zone and in other regions where wartime fiscal impositions met local opposition. Laffemas typified the results as commissioner in Amiens, the Ile de France, Limoges, and elsewhere. The cocky intendant caught his proverbially skeptical monarch's attention in boasting to Louis that as a local intendant he would bring in enough tax money to pay for two years of fighting.[10]

Commissaires-turned-intendants elbowed their way into functions that until then had been almost the private preserve of huge sections of the society of orders. Under the direction of Sublet de Voyers (a former intendant himself), army commissioners placed increasing civilian control over army commanders, even though the latter were nobles of the sword and race, whereas the intendants' status did not surpass the robe nobility. Adjudication of soldiers' clashes with civilian subjects and punishment of spies and traitors, as well as the direction of supplies, munitions on land, and needs of the navy at sea, all came within the sphere of the army intendants.[11]

The better known intendants of justice, finance, and police helped governors maintain order against provincial tax rebellions. They made judicial decisions that bypassed regional law courts. They nudged aside provincial estate delegates and royal élus and trésoriers when the existing tax systems in both pays d'états and pays d'élections buckled under the weight of wartime demands. Intendants even joined royal fusiliers to protect the traitants. By the time Louis XIII died, there was one commissioner for every *généralité* under the trésoriers' care, and one per pays d'états. The last full year of Louis's life also marked the official transfer of the administration of the taille from the élus and trésoriers to the intendants. It is ironic that the élus—whom Marillac and Effiat had wanted to introduce to the pays d'états before the Day of Dupes but who then were withdrawn in return for financial concessions by those outlying provinces—were virtually bypassed everywhere by a much more powerful royal agent during the decade and a half following Effiat's death in 1632.[12]

Here was a major step toward the intendant-dominated local administration of France's ancien régime (leaving aside the setback of Louis XIV's minority, when the revolt of the parlementary Fronde in 1648 temporarily swept aside Louis XIII's tax farms, taxes, and intendancies). What stand did the king himself take on this crucial trial-and-error process? Probably he had no firm views other than backing whatever ministerial experiments brought money to his war chest.[13] The creation of new élections by the bureaucratically inclined ministers of finance and justice, Effiat and Marillac, had caused more trouble than they were worth. The troubleshooting commissaire was a natural stopgap replacement. It needed little imagination for the new ministers of the 1630s—Servien, Bullion, Séguier, and Sublet de Noyers, all of whom had once been commissaires—to adapt the old royal vehicle to the warfare state's needs. Nor did it take genius for the pragmatic Cardinal Richelieu to support an administrative change that could be made simply by altering the wording in a royal commission. Together, these servitors of Louis XIII hit on exactly the means the king was seeking to keep his foreign war going.[14]

As Louis XIII's stopgap measures became standard features of his state, they undermined the autonomy of the various estates, orders, and institutional arms of the society of orders. The three estates of the realm continued to exist as legally distinct groups holding their same relative places in terms of social status and political rank. But the power each group wielded was eroded by the warfare state's incursions on their time-honored privileges. We can see in miniature what was happening by glancing at the assemblies of estates in those provinces that had weathered the storm of élection creations.[15]

Languedoc represents the privileged province par excellence, even after the defeat of its Huguenot towns and Montmorency's patronage system. Its assemblies of estates continued to meet year in and year out to pare down extortionate royal fiscal demands. Nevertheless, the estates had to reckon with the levies the royal governor, intendants, and troops actually laid on the Languedocian populace beyond what their assembly authorized.[16]

In Brittany, Richelieu acted as governor in 1634 to "restore the estates to their ancient liberty." His demands for money via his cousin were so great, however, that three years later his local agent and relative, La Meilleraye, said he had collected as much as he could without employing "extreme violence." In Burgundy, the estate assemblies were controlled by Condé as governor and his client Machault as intendant. And in Provence, following the debacle of the Cascaveoux revolt, the estates were replaced in 1639 by an assembly of urban representatives.

Then there was wealthy Normandy, where élus overlapped with the estates. In 1634, the estates' vote of four hundred thousand livres for the taille was arbitrarily raised by the crown to two million, without consultation. The provincial governor did not convoke the estates during the first three years of the full-scale Bourbon-Habsburg war. When they met for the next—and last—time during

Louis XIII's reign, in 1638, the frustrated delegates refused to go through the formality of approving the three million livres plus military and administrative expenses that they knew would be collected regardless of their wishes. The assembly of estates withered away, lamenting that its only power now was to complain of its impotence, in remonstrances to the king.

Separately as well as collectively, the estates of the realm suffered. Take the First Estate clergy, for example, whose autonomy vis-à-vis the secular state protected their national assembly's vote of a nominal *don gratuit*. As pious as was this royal descendant of St. Louis, the king insisted that the Catholic church share his state's defense expenses. Already uncomfortable with Louis's angry demands for aid against rebel Huguenots during the 1620s, the clergy were aghast when "the Most Christian King" requested money for his wars with Catholic Lorraine, Bavaria, Spain, and Austria. By 1641 the clerics' contributions had soared to 5.5 million livres, double the amount given for the siege of La Rochelle.

Clerical immunity from the principle of outright taxation hung by the single thread of the unenforced royal Declaration of St-Germain in 1639. This decree asserted the French monarchy's right to assume control of the inalienable property, or mortmain, of the French clergy in case of dire national need. When individual clerics protested against that principle, Louis angrily banished the offenders from the Assembly of the Clergy—yet it is doubtful he could have raised his righteous indignation to the institutional level. Indeed, he sanctioned the publication of Pierre de Marca's temperate concordance of the sacerdotal and state spheres of authority, which drew back from attacking mortmain in principle.[17]

The Second Estate, by its very nature as a warrior nobility, was a much more natural supporter of its soldier-king's foreign ventures. An overwhelmingly noble officer corps led Louis XIII's six armies into the Bourbon-Habsburg war of 1635–59; and a traditional royal-noble arrangement, the *arrière-ban*, was what Louis fell back on during the Spanish invasion of 1636. That time-honored principle of noble volunteerism called for—and got—the gentilshommes of the Paris basin to go to the front. Some families were represented by their entire male youth; some brought virtually their entire community into battle. Here was the continuation of the noble family loyalties to the monarchy displayed by the duke of La Rochefoucald, who had come with fifteen hundred Poitevin gentilshommes to the siege of La Rochelle, exclaiming: "Sire, there is not a single one of these who is not my relative." Many of the great nobility and princes of the blood also helped maintain internal order against tax revolts as provincial governors and their lieutenants.

Yet all was not harmony in the ranks of an estate that carried out what remained of feudal obligations to its royal liege lord almost instinctively. Though proud to pay the "blood tax" of dying in their king's armies, provincial nobles drew the line when Louis's wartime agents tried to circumvent their tax exemptions. In Dauphiné, where the taille had been levied on the commoners themselves rather than on their land, intendant Jacques Talon convoked the local nobility to rubber-stamp the monarchy's 1633–34 decision to assess commoner property, including that held by noble families. Their objections were ignored; and when the king's ministers discussed how Talon's successor should proceed during the late 1630s, the privilege-conscious Sublet de Noyers lost out to the fiscally rapacious Bullion. Where the taille remained personal, and hence no ministerial maneuvering could break the nobles' exempt status, the monarchy resorted in 1639 to levying special *subsistances* for the army's upkeep. Rampaging soldiers carried out royal decrees to take food, forage, beasts, and free billeting on noble lands.[18]

Under these circumstances, it is not surprising that many noble representatives at the Breton estates meeting in 1637 hailed Brittany and its traditions, not the French state, as their *patrie*. Norman gentilshommes did likewise during the massive popular tax revolt of their province in 1639. Others went even further. During the popular tax revolt of the Croquants in 1636–37, the baron of Montesquiou, whose castle dominated the Dordogne River, led the entire commune of St-Cyprien in its tax revolt. Condemned by the intendant Foullé to have his home razed and his head removed, he somehow escaped, and later received a council pardon.

Yet the fear of social disorder was enough to draw other disgruntled nobles to the side of royal order. The Croquants of Astarac, "believing as they had that [the local nobles] favored their sedition," reacted with "great astonishment" in 1640 when fifty Gascon gentilshommes joined intendant Foullé's cavalry and *fantassins* to crush the rebels.[19]

At the top of the noble ranks, too, there continued a measure of the earlier grandee ambivalence toward Louis XIII's treatment of their kind, and occasionally an echo of the rash of conspiracies that had marked the early part of the reign. But the number and intensity of these protest acts were far less than in previous years. The two provincial governors who fell from power after 1635, Epernon and Vitry, did so because of feuds with their peers, not acts against the state. Epernon's son, the duke of La Valette, was condemned to death in absentia by a special court for negligence as a military commander. His crime? In the king's own words to the judges, he was being punished "not for cowardice or ignorance of the duties pertaining to his rank. But he did not want to take [the Spanish town of] Fuenterrabia."[20]

Outright acts of treason were tragicomic nonevents. In 1636, when Parisians and princes turned their wrath on Richelieu for the siege of Corbie, Gaston failed to give the awaited signal to his noble comrades to slay the king's alter ego. Without the heir's sanction, his fellow conspirators dared not strike a blow. In 1641, the royal cousin Soissons and the quasi-independent duke of Bouillon fled to the Habsburg side, only to have the count of Soissons meet an inglorious death as part of a madcap, Spanish-financed invasion. Whether killed by a French agent or by accidentally blowing his brains out as he lifted his visor with a pistol (as one version holds), this was a dreary dénouement to princely revolt.

The last conspiracy of the reign was important enough to merit comment here as well as in our later discussion of the aging king's personal life. Cinq Mars, last royal favorite and son of Marshal Effiat, thought he could oust Richelieu and outwit Louis XIII. The plan was for Spanish troops to support a courtly coup d'état that would proclaim Gaston lieutenant general of the realm and give the heir control of enough French territory to sign a Franco-Spanish peace treaty. Was this a serious protest against the warfare state or just a personal fantasy? Whatever the case, Louis turned against his favorite, and swift executive trials managed by Richelieu and Chancellor Séguier soon ended the lives of Cinq Mars and his companion de Thou.[21]

The only post-1635 military rebellion by the nobility against Louis XIII's warfare state came after his death, in the shape of the princely Fronde of 1649–53. Although the immediate havoc this event caused suggests that Louis's innovations were so fragile they could not outlive their founder, the noble Frondeurs' ignominious collapse in fact proves the opposite. A much more formidable challenge to Louis XIII's wartime changes, however—without which the nobles would never have attempted their own Fronde—was the parlementary Fronde of 1648.

After Louis's death, the Parlement and other high courts of Paris momentarily forced Louis's widow and her minister Mazarin to do away with the late king's wartime taxes, extralegal justice, and intendants. Were those innovations then fundamentally flawed? Not exactly. The Fronde of 1648 was triggered not by the widespread unpopularity of Louis XIII's warfare state, but by Anne's acceleration of its innovations as regent during their son's minority. Public belief held that a regent could not innovate the way an adult monarch could—and indeed, after Louis XIV reached his majority in 1651, his father's innovations were gradually restored.[22]

Yet if Louis XIII did not cause the parlementary Fronde, he certainly pushed his venal officials at the head of the Third Estate to the breaking point. Richelieu fully understood the value of compromise with the parlements, financial high courts, and lesser tribunals and bureaus; but Louis XIII assumed that the justness of his cause would prove daunting to them. That stand did cause confusion among his permanent judicial and financial officials, the guardians of royal law and order. They were alienated enough, however, to interpret justice finally on behalf of the king's subjects; they thus blocked fiscal measures with procedural delays and, by example, incited others to resist.

Louis's employment of a lit de justice in December 1635 was a spectacular example of the tension between royal and parlementary notions of what was just. During his thirty-three-year reign, that kingly ritual of entering the Parlement to recover his powers as chief justiciar of the realm was employed a record number of times—twenty, according to the lit de justice's historian, Sarah Hanley.[23] At the 1635 ceremony, he compelled the highest tribunal of his realm to register no less than forty-two fiscal edicts for his war, many of them creating venal offices.

The Paris jurists were spared the fate of the high provincial judge who died soon after being told by Louis: "On your knees, little man, before your master!" Even so, they felt themselves verbally abused and their loyalty impugned as their moralizing king made more and more demands after 1635. "The money I request is not for frivolities or foolish extravagance," he exclaimed. "It is not I who speak to you but my State and its needs. Those who question my wishes harm me more than the Spaniards do."[24]

Verbal attacks were combined with the exiling and jailing of individual parlementarians who opposed other fiscal changes. In 1638, a number of judges went to the Bastille for protesting the reduction of interest payments on state-backed bonds. The following year, Louis exiled key parlementary judges and jailed a *maître des requêtes*, after the Parlement joined the maîtres (normally its rivals, as council members and intendants) against a royal enactment creating twenty-four offices of maîtres. Ultimately peace was restored by a 50 percent reduction in the number of offices.

Finally, in 1641, Louis XIII unveiled a royal edict that reviewed the Parlement's interference in state affairs since 1610 and forbade its cognizance of matters "that might concern the State, and its administration and government." This broad but ambiguous prohibition, imposed at a lit de justice, was as far as a Louis the Just could go in the direction of authoritarian rule. It seemingly eliminated parlementary-royal conflict, but left intact practices that allowed the courts to continue battling on behalf of subjects; namely, venality and the paulette were untouched; the royal custom of registering all new laws at the appropriate law courts was tacitly acknowledged; and the validity of parlementary remonstrances against laws, pending a royal response, was explicitly recognized.[25]

The rest of the Third Estate lacked the venal officials' defenses, yet they too expressed their feelings about Louis XIII's warfare state. We can call these tax protests by peasant communities and urban craftspeople a variety of things, ranging from blind furies to popular revolts, but whatever our twentieth-century labels, they were an integral part of the seventeenth-century tension between Louis XIII's statist concept of justice and justice as conceived by the society of orders.[26]

The invasion by "foreign" traitants, fusiliers, and intendants of communities already bedeviled with hail, flood, heat, and high prices triggered a local brand of primitive justice. If Louis the Just could be an amalgam of virtues and impulses, and gentilshommes and judges were confused in loyalties, why should those rooted to the soil or shops of the realm by any less complex in their political rhetoric? The *Request of the Communes in Arms of Périgord to the King* began: "Sire! The very glorious name of Just which Your Majesty has acquired. . . ," and it concluded with a request for justice and liberty—code words signaling the rebels' intention to punish tax-gouging *gabeleurs*, restore old usages, and inaugurate the mythical golden age. And just how suppliant was a grievance-laced "submission and supplication" by the syndics and deputies of the *châtellenies* of Saintes in Angoumois, even in "confessing themselves to being very criminal and obligated to His Majesty . . . [and imploring] his clemency and kindness"?[27]

The justice sought by the southwestern Croquants in 1636–37 and the Norman Nu-Pieds of 1639 was a major shock to Louis XIII's state. (See Appendix, map 5.) Despite their derisive nickname (from the crunch they felt from taxes), the Croquants' uprisings covered between one-fourth and one-third of France. They met in bands, with sticks, pikes, and occasionally firearms, but always in dead earnest. From the Loire to the Garonne, they opposed the warfare state's attempt to turn their undertaxed region into a high-tax area like north-central France. Louis XIII alternated between concern for his "poor people" and anger at their lawlessness. Eventually, however, the Croquants submitted to timely concessions and armed repression.[28]

The Nu-Pieds revolt was begun by barefoot salt panners in the shadow of Mont-St-Michel and spread rapidly through other parts of Normandy that, although rich and privileged, were unhappy because of the recent economic depression and heavy taxation. As the village church bells tolled, peasants, artisans, and poor noble *hobereaux* formed a motley army of some twenty thousand half-disciplined men. The rebels called for an end to all taxes imposed since Henry IV's time and requested sympathy from as far away as Paris. Ultimately even the provincial capital of Rouen—where Joan of Arc had been martyred two centuries earlier for making a patriotic cause too popular—erupted in carefully targeted violence against the hated collectors of new sales taxes. A clockmaker led the way as vigilantes sacked tax offices and murdered fiscal agents within the quaint monastic chuch of Saint Ouen; then the sanctuary was purified so that religious services could resume as if all were normal![29]

In vain, the Parlement of Rouen tried to end this ritual of violence and purification. Louis XIII chose to intervene with his own brand of justice. A royal army filled out with foreign mercenaries destroyed the peasant host, and Chancellor Séguier hastened to Rouen to initiate yet another contemporary ritual act. As the minister of justice brought the full weight of royal authority and ideology to bear on the local scene, even the customary bid for clemency by the local archbishop, on his knees in penitence for the local flock, was prohibited. Séguier lectured country-bumpkin nobles on their complicity with peasant rebels and meted out verbal sentences. There were a few ritual hangings, some local tribunals were temporarily replaced by royal commissions, and the Parlement of Rouen, which had resented the creation of a rival fiscal court, now suffered the added humiliation of being suspended from its functions. The judges found that they had not done enough for order, despite their having confronted howling rebel crowds at the risk of their lives.[30]

Tapié ends his account of the crisis by saying that "everything depended on Louis XIII."[31] He refers however, not so much to the Norman revolt as to the fate of the foreign war that brought it on. In truth, Louis was responsible for the war, its continuation, the resulting warfare state, and his government's heavy-handed suppression of revolts against wartime innovations. Eventually the parlements of Normandy and Paris won royal absolution for their sin of allowing a provincial revolt: their penance consisted of approving the fiscal devices that Bullion and Bouthillier had conjured up, Richelieu knew to be inflammatory, and Louis XIII considered necessary.

And so it remained right to the end of Louis's reign. Defying economic adversity and human misery, royal government was the only major growth area of the times. Regular taxation had doubled since 1610, and the sevenfold leap in the number of subjects on state payroll between 1516 and 1665 included a major surge under Louis XIII.[32] Perhaps only a Louis "the Just" could have effected, justified, and maintained that statist expansion.

13

KING AND CULTURE

Modest and unassuming as he was in his tastes, Louis XIII had no interest in bequeathing to the world a Louis Treize style of art, interior design, literature, or music. Of course, he could not avoid being a patron of the arts; but he did it as a duty, allowing his mother, brother, and chief minister to play the role of enthusiastic Maecenas.[1] His close friend Bassompierre despaired of the lack of royal cultural leadership, telling the assembled notables in 1627 that the king's "inclination is in no way directed toward building, and France's finances will certainly not be exhausted by his sumptuous edifices—unless one wishes to reproach him for the miserable château of Versailles, which a mere gentilhomme would not want to boast of erecting."[2]

Yet there was a strong connection between this diffident royal patron and the culture of his times, albeit less than in the political realm. In politics, his personal judgmentalism translated into policies that changed France. In cultural matters, the impact of his personality was more complicated and subtle. His personal tastes, notably in court and church music, merely added a few Louis XIII compositions and performances to the total without shaping it. His dislike of pomp certainly hindered the flourishing of the arts. Yet his somber, pious, self-denying attitude toward life was not that far removed from the motivations of many of the artistic, religious, and literary giants among his subjects.

256

In part, this was simply because Louis was a mirror of the age: a pious supporter of the Catholic reform movement; a quasi-Jansenist in his emphasis on individual contrition; a royal version of Corneille's stage figures, sacrificing desire to duty. Yet the mere fact that Louis was king meant that his attitudes influenced cultural trends as well.[3] We can safely say that his personal morals reinforced the religious trends of the time. And we can cautiously suggest that in artistic and literary matters, his dislike of flamboyance, focus on piety, and penchant for discipline affected emphasis, content, and perhaps style.[4]

The Baroque church skyline of Louis XIII's Paris and provincial towns had its temporal origins in Henry IV's reign; it was to culminate in Louis's widow building a chapel for her favorite religious and political retreat at Val de Grâce. In between, the raising of domed ceilings and multistoried façades went hand in hand with the French clergy's acceptance of the decrees of the Council of Trent in 1615, the publication of the Savoyard St. François de Sales's *Treatise on God's Love* in 1616, and the serious-minded Louis XIII's coup d'état in 1617.[5]

Nowhere was Louis's influence on church architecture more evident than in the first Paris church built in the Jesuit style. The inspiration for adapting the design of the Jesuits' mother church of Il Gesu in Rome to French tastes goes to a priest-architect, Etienne Martellange. Louis donated land near the Place Royale in 1619—when his mother was in exile and the future Cardinal Richelieu in oblivion. The church was named after the monarch's patron saint and founder of his family, Louis IX, and the cornerstone was laid by the king himself in 1627. His cardinal minister celebrated its first mass in 1641. And Louis willed that his heart should be interred in the Eglise St. Louis, now known as St. Paul and St. Louis.

The church of St. Louis toned down Italian Baroque emotionality with classical restraint, a characteristic of Louis XIII architecture in general. It had a single nave without aisles, supported by heavy pillars and rounded arches that led the worshiper's eye soberly to the focus of the Catholic Reformation, the altar. The Baroque dome overhead heightened the drama by sending light from heaven to illuminate the celebration of mass at the point where nave and transept intersected. The outside façade of two modestly adorned stories topped by a narrow top story that curved inward to a gentle peak was similar to the new exterior of the Gothic church of St. Gervais, which Salomon de Brosse had added in 1617.

It may be straining the evidence to suggest that Louis XIII had any effect on the architectural side of the Catholic Reformation other than through his patronage of the Jesuit style. But the saintliness of this priest-king certainly had something to do with the mission of the generation of saints and the numerous religious orders that sprang into existence and erected one church, chapel, school, and hospital after another during his reign. In 1619, St. Jeanne de Chantal established the Visitation order in Paris as a sanctuary for spiritually inclined women, whom she then sent into the streets of Paris to care for the sick in body and frail of spirit. In the provinces and the capital, the Italian Oratory movement to train priests professionally found a champion in Cardinal Bérulle, an intensely religious man noted for his 1623 book *Grandeurs of Jesus* and for his Oratory schools that combined classical learning and Christian charity. And there was the beautiful but ascetic Mme Acarie, inspired by Bérulle, Sales, and the Marillacs, who introduced St. Teresa's Spanish asceticism to France in the form of the Carmelites. Between 1604 and 1630 that order alone founded forty-six houses.

By the latter date, lay and clerical organizations were strong throughout the realm, including the Madeleine and Orphan hospices organized by women for women, and described for us in Kathryn Norberg's study of rich and poor in Grenoble.[6] In Lyon, Philip Hoffman's research on the local religious community has detected a dozen new churches and chapels erected between 1627 and 1643.[7] Louis XIII approved of all this work, turning against only those elements of the Catholic reform movement that questioned his own religiosity in foreign policy endeavors.

The king was in fact an unusually unworldly man in royal robes. It was to the Visitadine convent that Louis's friend Louise de La Fayette retired after their hopelessly chaste love affair of the 1630s; and the sad king visited the holy adolescent for weeks afterward at the convent grill. Closer to the end of his life, he contemplated abdicating when his son was a few years older, and retiring with four monks to Versailles to think of God. On his deathbed the monarch called in the incarnation of the age's social conscience, St. Vincent de Paul, for a briefing on his projected good works; then the pious monarch sighed, "Ah, Monsieur Vincent! If I get better I want all the bishops to spend three years with you."[8]

Both Louis's sacrificial and judgmental sides drew him to that quintessential saint of peasant stock. Indeed, the king himself could just as easily have uttered St. Vincent's remark, "Let us love God, but at the expense of our arms, our sweat, and our appearance."[9] At the very time the saintly subject was beginning his career by turning Carnival into Lent in the Lyonnais area in 1617, the saintly monarch was launching his personal reign by curbing vices.

St. Vincent's judgmental side reflected only mildly the Catholic reform's puritanism of which the contemporary Company of the Holy Sacrament was the harshest exponent; Louis XIII was somewhere in the middle. St. Vincent cared for galley slaves, abandoned children, street women, and incurables. He also established, under Queen Anne's patronage, the Salpêtrière, "where [all the poor] will be taken care of, instructed, and put to work." [10]

The work of the Compagnie du Saint Sacrement, founded in 1627, can be summed up in the words of its founder, the duke of Ventadour:

> Receive the unfortunate, plague-stricken, convicts, peasants afflicted with gallstones or who lack seed; rescue the innocent from the provost's archers, and the debtors from usurers' knavery; reform the dress of the Marseille women who exhibit their breasts; run freethinking bookstores into the ground; purify the St-Germain fair and [Parlement] gallery; attack gambling and dueling; educate teachers for elementary schools; drive out Jews, Protestants, and the Illuminati. [11]

A historian of these well-intentioned charitable activities by Louis XIII's clerics and laypersons has wisely noted that "the time, effort, and money expended by elites upon such strange endeavors as the rehabilitation of prostitutes and the detection of fornicators makes no sense unless the Counter Reformation is taken into account." [12] It makes all the more sense if we note who the counterreformers' king was. In the 1630s, Louis the Just took up his pen to instruct Chancellor Séguier: "You will give me an unspeakable pleasure by seeing to the punishment of swearing and blasphemy that are current, not just in Paris but throughout France—not to mention thefts, murders, and duels." The royal font of moral justice added that he would be Séguier's "second," to prove that his "conscience was not to be found wanting before God." After Louis's death, the pamphleteer-historian Jean Danès added the eulogy, "He reformed abuses, regulated all the orders of the realm, policed the towns, eliminated embezzlement, repressed violence, drove out dissoluteness, punished blasphemy." [13]

Louis XIII was no theologian, but he became interested when religious arguments affected royal policy and authority. When choosing high clerics who would be a credit to religion, he kept in mind his personal preferences and political considerations, just as other monarchs did. He relied heavily on Richelieu's recommendations for vacant benefices, placed cardinals and archbishops in charge of armies and navies, and had great affection for a man who exemplified the fusion of military and religious careers, Cardinal La Valette.[14]

On 10 February 1638, Louis XIII made the most symbolic religious-royal act of his reign when he placed "our person, our estate, our crown, and our subjects" under the special protection of the Virgin in thanksgiving for successes during the intervening two years of war. What Louis called "success" was a strange confusion of the sacerdotal and the secular: he thanked God for using him as his special instrument to strike down the rebels' "pride" and restore God's holy altars throughout the realm; and he pleaded with the Virgin to understand that he fervently wanted peace against "the onslaught of foreign enemies and the scourge of war."[15]

That famous vow was linked in the public mind with two of Louis XIII's most pressing agendas. Drafted late in 1637, it was designed—consciously or unconsciously—to cloak with a religious mantle Louis's increasingly aggressive war against fellow Catholic monarchs. By pure chance, a second agenda became involved. Shortly after the draft was written, a dauphin was conceived, and the baby arrived seven months after the official vow. In September 1638, the proud royal father could blend the religious and royal worlds innocuously in exclaiming: "This is a miraculous show of the grace of the Lord God; for it is surely right to say this of such a beautiful child after my twenty-two years of marriage and my wife's four unhappy miscarriages."[16]

The king's less innocuous linking of his vow to the Virgin with the war brought him face to face with a theological development within French Catholicism that he did not like: the rise of Jansenism, a Puritan-like movement that had originated in the Spanish Netherlands. Like the earlier dévots and then Father Caussin, the French Jansenists placed the international mission of the Catholic church before state interests; but they also linked the dévot condemnation of Louis's alliances with Protestant states against Catholic rulers to their own uniquely demanding theology. While Richelieu, the Jesuits, and many other Catholics thought an individual Christian could obtain God's grace through "attrition" (recognition of wrongdoing and fear of hell), the influential Jean du Vergier de Hauranne, abbé de Saint-Cyran, was now advancing the view that a religious penitent must be in a state of extreme "contrition" before receiving absolution, communion, and divine grace. Pushed to its logical conclusion, that combination could put Louis XIII in a bad light before both God and the world. Could the Most Christian King receive God's grace unless he performed the extremely contrite act of ending his war with fellow Catholic rulers?

That Louis XIII and the Jansenists should so confront each other was doubly ironic. The king's morose, suspicious, judgmental outlook was not that far removed from Saint-Cyran's theology, which David Ogg describes as "beginning with the Fall and ending with the Flood," or his philosophy of "perdition for the unfortunate many and ascetic gloom for the fortunate few."[17] Equally ironic was Saint-Cyran's grounding in the social, religious, and royal mainstream of the day. Raised in a robe family and educated by the Jesuits, he had vigorously argued in the mid 1620s on behalf of royal foreign policies against the pro-dévot pamphlet, *Admonition*. Even when a sudden religious experience turned him into a contritionist advocate at the religious community of Port Royal in Paris, he seemed protected by close friendships with Cardinal Bérulle, St. Vincent de Paul, and a powerful theologian of the Spanish Netherlands, Cornelius Jansen (whose greatest work, *Augustinus*, would appear posthumously in 1640).

Jansenism was rooted in the theology of one of the great early fathers of Christianity, St. Augustine. But already in the late 1630s, French Catholics with an authoritarian and hierarchical outlook were suspiciously viewing Jansenist tenets as being subversive of religious, royal, and social authority. Louis XIII was particularly disturbed, detecting in Jansenist tracts a serious personal as well as ideological threat. In 1635, Jansen caused a sensation with his *Mars Gallicus*, a pamphlet against the Franco-Swedish alliance. By 1637 the tract had reached the French public, as *The French "Mars," or France's War*. Royalist replies invoked the king's pious nature in reassuring Catholic subjects that his alliance with heretics would not harm their religion. These replies included plausible sounding titles like *How the Piety of the French Differs from That of the Spaniards Within a Profession of the Same Religion* and *Gallican Vindications*—the latter winning for its author a place in the royally supported Académie française.[18]

French Jansenists outdid Jansen. In 1638, an Oratorian priest named Séguenot published a work called *Virginity* in which he proclaimed that confession without contrition was fruitless. Richelieu was able to trace the argument of this book back to Saint-Cyran's theology and focus the royal wrath on the French Jansenist leader. Worse still for the abbé, he was one of a handful of French theologians consulted by Louis XIII on another matter who refused to use theology

in the cause of reason of state. Louis wanted the theologians to declare Gaston d'Orléans's second marriage with the foreign Lorraine
princess unsacramental because the king had not authorized it. Saint-
Cyran obstinately pushed in the opposite direction by attacking not
only the royal argument but also the very principle of invoking religion in the cause of statecraft. Worst of all was when the abbé dragged
the king's solemn vow to the Virgin of 1638 into the issue, declaring it
a scandalous manipulation of religion: "There is nothing more capable
of offending God than causing religion and piety to serve politics." [19]

Louis the Just had the offending cleric imprisoned before the end
of 1638. In arriving at that decision, he balanced his chief minister's
wish for severity and the intercession of scrupulously apolitical defenders like St. Vincent de Paul, who could see some good in Saint-
Cyran's religion. It is impossible to tell exactly what the king thought
as he weighed the pros and cons. On the one hand, the punishment
he meted out fitted the crime, according to Louis's scale of justice. He
had banished Caussin for assailing his conscience in the confessional;
was it not just to imprison a man who had been even sharper on the
attack? Moreover, Louis could not have taken kindly to someone who
accused him—of all persons—of misusing religion.[20] On the other
hand, Louis did free Saint-Cyran after Richelieu's death, which suggests second thoughts. Before he could think out the next step, however, both the royal judge and the forgiven subject also joined their
ultimate Judge.

A king of France was expected to pay closer attention to the cultural affairs of the royal court than to the life of the church. Louis XIII
obliged by nudging forward the renovation of the medieval fortress-
palace of the Louvre, started some work on a palace east of Paris at
Vincennes, and fussed over a few formal gardens and interior redeco-
rating at St-Germain and Fontainebleau. Yet this set of credits scarcely
compared with the imposing Luxembourg residence on the southern edge of the capital that his mother commissioned. Designed by
Brosse, this palace boasted a theatrical cycle of paintings by Peter
Paul Rubens eulogizing Marie's political life (now in the Louvre Museum). North of the Louvre, Richelieu employed the king's castoff architect Jacques Le Mercier in creating the Palais Cardinal, which
boasted an enclosed grand residence with two courtyards and extensive garden right in the center of the capital. Louis did not mind. He
even proffered his own design sketches, which were hung in the architect's chamber.[21]

The king must not have been so solicitous of his brother's architectural fantasies, which matched Gaston's hopes of one day succeeding to the throne. One wonders what would have happened to French art and architecture had the heir's two wishes been realized. At the family château in Blois, Gaston had François Mansart add to Francis I's ornate mannerist creation an Orléans wing with an orderly columned ground floor, two pilastered upper stories, and a high pitched mansard roof. If the project had been completed, this study in symmetry would have resulted in grandeur fit for a Louis XIV: Gaston wanted to turn the new wing into an entire palace, with side halls to house his dazzling art collection and a rear rotunda leading to terraced gardens.

But Gaston never succeeded Louis XIII; and the king left his own restrained imprint on secular architecture.[22] Brosse helped his monarch by toning down Marie de' Medici's plan for her Luxembourg residence. In her desire to have something for herself far grander than the antiquated and dingy Louvre, the king's mother had in mind the elaborately designed Pitti Palace of her native Florence. Starting in 1615, the queen mother's architect built the main *corps de logis* in such a way that it camouflaged the intended effect of elaborate wings and courtyard. In a brilliant, decisive alteration, Brosse made the main rectangular block blend with the four pavilions at its corners to give the façade a solid, elongated appearance. The wings were kept low, and the peaks of the pavilion roofs were cut off at the top so as not to break with the central part. First-, second-, and third-story windows were placed symmetrically behind ballustrades to form a continuous line that zigzagged from pavilion to main building and on to the other pavilion.

Louis XIII deserves some credit for the development of a palace style in line with Brosse's aesthetically pleasing Luxembourg. For it was the king alone who commissioned, approved, and checked construction progress on Philibbert Le Roy's plans for his first Versailles getaway in 1623–24, and its successor in 1631–34.[23] Louis chose for his country retreat a gentle rise overlooking his favorite hunting forest and used his household budget (not state funds at large). The result was a modest Brosse-like two-story main building with two-story pavilions at the sides, topped by slanted roofs cut off at the apex. The pleasing horizontal lines, red brick, golden stone, and blue slate roofs recall Henry IV's Place Royale in Paris, which Louis XIII and his entourage made a center of courtly festivity and genteel living. An equestrian statue of Louis, donated by Richelieu, was placed in the square in 1639.

It is little wonder that the term *Louis Treize style* has come to be used in reference to the design of the Place Royale, the Palais du Luxembourg, and the Versailles lodge, along with the building materials used in their construction.[24] Here was something sufficiently simple, aesthetically pleasing, and rooted in existing noble-château architecture to suit Louis XIII's emotional needs. Despite the shocked reaction of seventeenth-century courtiers to his Versailles retreat (which the famous son of Louis XIII's favorite, Saint-Simon, called a "petit château de cartes"), the building and its style represented the reign faithfully. A detailed description of its interior was drawn up in 1630; and we even find an allusion in a touristic guidebook of 1639, *Le voyage de France*: "It's worth visiting Versailles during your stay in Paris."[25] Louis XIV honored his father by enclosing this curious royal hideaway rather than razing it and beginning anew.

For the principal royal residence, the Louvre, Louis XIII must have realized that something more elegant and regal was required than his normal tastes allowed. Certainly his mother had often enough pointed out the inadequacy of a medieval building with dark corridors and cramped rooms. From 1624 to 1627, then, Louis pushed forward the plans of the palace's sixteenth-century royal architects, who had replaced part of the medieval turreted Louvre fortress that guarded the Seine River with what is now the southwest corner of the modern Louvre's much larger square court.

Louis XIII had the rising architect Le Mercier turn his talents from town-house building to the challenge of continuing the western wing of the new corner palace toward the north, away from the river. This was all done in conformity to the mannerist tension between classical harmony and rich modern decor and was accomplished so faithfully that today's tourist cannot tell where the original architect Lescot's corner stops and Le Mercier's extension begins. But in addition, Le Mercier's clock pavilion in the middle of the western wing gave the newest part of the Louvre a pleasing effect. His modest flattened dome, above the clock and the fourth story of the pavilion, harmonized with the short attic and the two full stories below, while blending with the west wing's continuation to its northern end. Today, as we stand within the square court, we can reflect on the difference between the gentle curves in the Lescot–Le Mercier wing and the severely linear north and east wings created in Louis XIV's image.

In the realm of painting, Rubens did not impress the French with his overly theatrical style. The Spanish Netherlander's historical tableaux for Marie reveal a dutiful heir looking up adoringly at his mother as his father hands over authority, and a boy king holding on for dear life in a storm-tossed boat. These representations were not entirely convincing either as history or as psychology. Rubens's individual portraits of a maturing Louis and Anne are truer to the character. (See plates 2, 3.)

A more faithful and aesthetically pleasing artistry from Louis's early years was a series of portraits by Frans Pourbus, now scattered from Florence to Los Angeles. A Flemish painter with an unerring Baroque eye for human character, Pourbus painted nobles and commoners naturally, and immortalized the playful visage of Louis's father. When he turned to the boy king, the artist caught the exact mixture of suspicion, seriousness, and uncertainty revealed in Louis's pursed lips and guarded look. (See plate 1.)

As Louis reached adulthood, he drew on the talents of two remarkably different painters. One, Simon Vouet, a son of one of Henry IV's artists, has been largely forgotten today. After practicing late-Renaissance and early-Baroque techniques for fourteen years in Rome, Vouet returned to France and in 1627 was appointed *premier peintre* to the king. From his studio at the Louvre he brought vivid primary colors, illusion, and grand themes to the interiors of what seemed to be every church, palace, and hôtel of the Paris basin. Yet the overall effect was subdued, at times flat, and even insipid when his subject was a stiff and uncomfortable monarch lavishly bedecked for a portrait session.

In Vouet's *Vow of Louis XIII* the king, weighed down by his dress and cloak, gazes upward at a contorted Christ on the cross—who, dramatically illuminated, is the obvious center of the scene. Not flattering, but appealing to the ruler, one can be sure! A less dramatic painting of Louis XIII offering St. Louis a model of the Eglise St. Louis is a product of Vouet's studio—perhaps the collaborative work of the generation of young painters apprenticed to that leading artist. Louis IX beckons downward beside the church's façade as a slightly pleased and almost handsome Louis XIII, with open arms and thronged by onlookers, half returns the saint's gesture.[26]

The other major court and church painter of the mature Louis XIII's years was Philippe de Champaigne. Born the year after his future king in the Spanish Netherlands, he worked with Rubens on the Luxembourg interior, then became a premier peintre to Louis in 1628. Champaigne worked with Vouet to portray the great events of

Louis XIII's personal reign on the walls of Fontainebleau and St-Germain. But whereas Vouet could not get beyond externals, Champaigne captured the religious and royal ethos of the reign.

Stunning examples of Champaigne's mastery can be seen in his triple portrait of Richelieu in the pose of an unusually austere Catholic cardinal; his simple renderings of Angélique Arnauld and her nuns of Port Royal, in their white robes with red crosses; and his astonishingly candid studies of Louis XIII. (See plate 4.) The artist's *Louis XIII Crowned by Victory*, although celebrating the surrender of the rebels of La Rochelle, depicts almost emotionlessly a dignified, dutiful, and none-too-dominating soldier-king standing motionless with one hand on his cane and the other on his hip. A slightly more animated winged angel hovers at his side with a laurel wreath in her hand and the port of La Rochelle behind her. The deeply religious Champaigne's sure brush strokes, which so unerringly described the asceticism of his monarch, were echoed by yet another exemplar of the king's selfless qualities, Mother Angélique, when she wrote to the princess of Guémené in 1625: "We act criminally if the slightest superfluous outlay makes us thieves in God's eyes [by depriving] our poor brothers." [27]

An amazing variety of artistic creativity survived and even flourished under this ruler's asceticism. Vouet's protégé, Nicolas Poussin, contributed a strong classical influence from Rome, where he resided after 1624 except for his brief tenure in 1640–42 as premier peintre to the king. There was Eustache Le Sueur, who fled from the temptations of popular commissions to pursue sublime religious art. To the three Le Nain brothers we owe a sympathetic look into the lives of Louis XIII's humblest subjects, breaking bread and sipping wine in the manner of a lay mass. Similarly, the sculptor-medalist Jean Varin evokes sympathy for a prematurely aged king. One famous bust is more penetrating than any camera lens: sorrowful royal eyes are underscored by deep lines; a neatly trimmed, faintly elongated moustache fails to hide a slightly open mouth that suggests resignation; and the famous longer shock of curly hair falls awkwardly over the left shoulder.

A visit to Nancy's ducal museum brings us face to face with one reason for that royal sadness. There reside Jacques Callot's series of engravings "The Miseries of War," which record in minute detail the suffering that Louis XIII's wars brought to the land of the dukes of Lorraine. Callot even etches a scarecrow of a king on the throne dispensing military justice, with the commentary:

The sight of this Leader, ever so shrewd,
Who punishes the wicked and rewards the good,
Should inspire in his soldiers an honorable mood.
For only their virtue brings every good news,
And in all their vice there is no excuse,
Nothing but shame and an ultimate noose.[28]

The Louis XIII passed on to us by his painters and sculptors betrays a dislike of self-glorification and pomp that signaled an essentially unexuberant court life within his buildings and grounds. Even the gardens he enjoyed as a boy did not blossom when he grew up. He employed Jean Le Nôtre, the second-generation member of a distinguished family of landscape architects, but to undertake only modest projects like the terracing of the Tuileries Gardens west of the Louvre. Meanwhile, the Boyceau-Menours held the posts of controllor and intendant general of the king's gardens, authored a *Treatise on Gardening According to Reason and Art* (1638), and designed the original gardens and park at Versailles.

Louis XIII's own gardening interests tended toward gathering vegetables for cooking, in which he excelled—but only at informal picnics where he did not have to perform. We have snapshots of a carefree king mixing with ladies in plumed hats and bright dresses, serving his guests, and eating in their company.[29] Louis enjoyed that break from a palace routine which dictated that everyone stand while the king ate in solitary splendor.[30]

When necessary, Louis held joyous Te Deums and other religious celebrations, but he preferred to worship quietly, simply, and at least once a day. Apart from his ceremonial entry to the capital with his bride in 1615 and his triumphal return from vanquished La Rochelle in 1628, his entrées at Paris and in provincial centers were played down. Music was one of the few things capable of soothing his frayed nerves during emotional crises; he supported many musical events, and some lavishly.[31]

One fixed item on the annual agenda was the flurry of court entertainment during Carnival (perhaps Louis could rationalize that it would be followed by Lent). (See plate 16.) A central feature was the *ballet de cour*, a loosely coordinated mixture of acting, dancing, poetry, music, and sheer spectacle. It ranged from the spectacular display of floats, fireworks, and equestrian games in celebration of Louis's betrothal, at the Place Royale in 1612, to the indoor ballet *Tancrède* in 1619. In *Tancrède*, the king modestly led a band of adventurers, while musicians and dancers floated down to the stage on clouds. In 1627, just before the siege of La Rochelle, Louis allowed himself and his courtiers the luxury of twelve ballets.

The 1635 *ballet de la Merlaison,* performed at the expropriated Chantilly estate of the recently executed duke of Montmorency, was a very special event. It was one of those occasions when Louis took control of everything, from plot and stage scenery to the composition of the music itself. He felt completely at ease here, for he was simply reenacting his regular hunting expeditions against blackbirds. But did he play himself? Alas, he billed himself as a merchant of hunting snares and a farmer. One wonders how he thought this would impress the young Marie de Hautefort, chaste object of his current erotic fantasies!

In 1641, Louis XIII's absorption with his foreign war drew him to take top billing at a martial ballet. In the opening scene announcing the "prosperity of France's arms," disorder was attacked by an eagle from the sky and two lions from their caves. This prepared the way for the "Gallic Hercules." Nine successive ballet scenes were needed to celebrate past royal sieges, from Casale to Arras. In the finale, the curtain raised to reveal King Louis and Queen Anne seated in royal splendor.

Louis XIII 's musical talents extended from the lowly hunting horn to the lute, and perhaps the spinet as well. His compositions ranged from ballets to love songs to liturgical settings. He also created an outstanding twenty-four-piece string ensemble. Louis's music was in harmony with the musicologist Marin Mersenne's not entirely complimentary view of contemporary French composers in general. Mersenne's *Harmonie universelle* of 1636 has Italians portraying "the passions and moods of the soul and the spirit . . . while our Frenchmen are happy simply to caress the ear with a never-ending sweetness in their singing, which drains the life of it." [32]

During the 1630s, Louis's musicians could be heard up to three times a week, performing the latest royal compositions for his newest female favorites. In 1635, as the war clouds gathered overhead, the monarch forgot his cares by treating the court and papal representatives to his own evensong arrangement. The round of musical and other entertainment he indulged in after his firstborn arrived was recalled by his niece years later. Yet this was the ruler who wrote shyly to his chief advisor, "I am thrilled that my music pleases you." [33] On his deathbed, Louis ordered his lute brought in; and as his musicians sang the psalms of David to his airs, the dying king joined in with the bass part.[34]

In the realm of letters, king Louis reigned over a French creative outburst that dazzled his most erudite subjects.[35] What place was there for a ruler who could scarcely rise above the mechanical trade of building and running his own printing press? The king paled by comparison with his intellectually alert advisor, who patronized writers, established the *Académie française*, wrote plays, and played royal censor. Little wonder that historians dismiss Louis's intellectual role by quoting Tallemant des Réaux on the king's slashing of literary pensions after Richelieu's death.[36]

Louis XIII's main literary influence lay in his support of a few enterprises he liked, and in the intrusion of his judgmental spirit into those he did not. There was also a striking parallel between the disciplinary tone he gave to political society and trends in the world of letters. While Louis did not cause these trends to happen any more than writers dictated his politics, the parallelism suggests an undocumentable mutual influence.

The king supported and wrote for Théophraste Renaudot's *Gazette*, founded in 1621 as France's first regular newsletter. In its pages Louis reported on war, publicized royal entertainments, diverted blame from his errant brother to Gaston's followers, and methodically kept Queen Anne's name out of the public eye.[37] As he closed in on Lorraine, he wrote up the campaign and gave himself modest billing as captain of his guards. His enemies were cast more prominently as bad persons: "I think it would be a good thing to print in the Gazette the news [of the Spanish governor of Perpignan being caught reconnoitering on French soil]," he wrote to Richelieu. "It will show everyone that they are the aggressors against us."[38]

The right thinking that Louis expected in political writings and practice paralleled contemporary disciplining of the French language. The court poet François Malherbe praised young Louis for his authoritarian nature and, before dying in 1628, led his own authoritarian crusade to purge French of "disgusting" Gascon compounds. Malherbe also championed classical Alexandrine twelve-line tragic verse. Meanwhile, Louis began to take on literary libertines. Théophile de Viau, whose sensual verse preached a pantheist love of nature, was tried for heresy in 1623; he escaped burning at the stake only to take asylum with a family fighting for another lost cause—the dueling, rebelling Montmorencys.

Even Guez de Balzac, whose faultless letters became a model of acceptable French prose, had difficulty finding royal favor because he was befriended by libertines and patronized by the politically defiant Epernon. In 1631, Balzac tried to court king and cardinal with a political treatise, *The Prince*. But its argument that Louis XIII was without sin and therefore, politically, could do anything caught the eye of the censor, the ire of the Sorbonne theologians, and the disapproval of the modest monarch.[39] (See plate 15.)

During Louis's early personal reign, the center of literary and social refinement was the Parisian salons, weekly gatherings of writers and nobles hosted by prominent ladies. While the king was busy purging the palace of bawdiness left over from his father's reign and mother's regency, at nearby salons writers polished their prose and nobles became *honnêtes hommes et dames*.

Catherine de Rambouillet opened her famous "blue chamber" to the public in 1617.[40] At the end of a series of richly decorated rooms (which included eight Flemish tapestries donated by the king), Voiture read his poetry, and installments of Honoré d'Urfée's *L'astrée*, in which the shepherdess Astrée is politely courted without passion by her shepherd admirer, became the "breviary of the ladies and gallants of the court."[41] At the Rambouillets' hôtel in town, violence-prone nobles psychoanalyzed Astréan love. At the Rambouillets' country château, hunting parties turned into pastoral picnics. And with the support of the king, academies were opened by the Oratorians to teach gentlemanly courtesy and athletic grace. The climax came in 1632 with Nicolas Faret's publication of *The "Honnête Homme," or the Art of Pleasing at Court*.

Louis XIII loved the theater. His love was well served by Pierre Corneille, whose plays took the literary development of the reign to its highest achievement. French theater had already progressed from Alexandre Hardy's elaborate, fast moving melodramas of the 1620s to Jean Mairet's classically ordered plays of the mid 1630s. Drawing on the three Aristotelian unities of time, place, and action, Corneille focused dramatically on inner character and ennobling themes. Classical rules and baroque emotionalism were a perfect setting for the most spectacular and controversial Corneillian play, *The Cid*. To introduce a French theater audience to that Spanish hero right after the beginning of the war with Spain was tempting royal fate. Worse yet, in Corneille's play the king of the dueling Cid refrains from punishing that suitor for killing the father of his would be love over a matter of honor. How could Corneille expect a real-life Louis the Just to tolerate a conflict between noble honor and royal justice in which a make-believe monarch left it to the woman caught in the middle to decide between revenge and marriage?

The play's first performance in 1636 profoundly affected Louis XIII's nobility. Condé's young son—who was destined both to win a great French victory against Spain five days after Louis's death and to lead the Frondeur army against his successor—was reduced to tears. Louis reacted through the Académie française, which Richelieu had transformed from a private gathering of litterateurs into a literary watchdog a year before. At the academy's inaugural ceremonies, Louis XIII had charged it with regulating the French language just as he did society through royal règlements. In keeping with that royal admonition, the academicians censured the dénouement of *The Cid*, while admitting "the powerful effect and delicacy of several of its sentences."[42] The later plays of a chastened Corneille focused more clearly on the subordination of private violence to state order.

Whereas the Corneillian spirit of subordinating passions to duty reminds us of Louis XIII's own lifelong odyssey,[43] there was another struggle in the world of ideas that was beyond the king's comprehension: the early modern scientific revolution. In France, the conflict between new science and old authority was less confrontational than Galileo's run-in with the papal Inquisition, which pitted the Italian astronomer-physicist's reliance on human reason and observation against biblical revelation and Aristotelian science. Indeed, the mathematician-philosopher René Descartes began his own quest for truth as a means to combat France's libertines and skeptics—prompted by none other than that staunch traditionalist Cardinal Bérulle. Later, Descartes's own disciple and organizer of France's leading intellectual circle, Mersenne, attacked the skeptics as well, in his *Impiety of Deists, Atheists, and Libertines of This Age* (1624).[44]

Descartes chose to defend traditional beliefs with the skeptics' own weapons, but from his haven in the Dutch Republic, not his native France. Yet even then, he suppressed his *Treatise on the World* in 1633 because it agreed with notions Galileo had just been censured for holding as the truth. In 1637, the originator of Cartesianism finally published his most famous work, the *Discourse on Method*, in Leyden—in French, and anonymously.

Proclaiming a sure deductive method of inquiry that would make the human race "masters and possessors of nature," the discourse unwittingly undercut all intellectual authority by relying on reason alone—even to prove the existence of God. To be sure, Descartes in this work, as well as in his comprehensive *Meditations* of 1641, explicitly ruled out the questioning of political and social authority. But Cartesian philosophy eventually joined other elements of the scientific revolution in creating the eighteenth-century Enlightenment. The Enlightenment, in turn, assaulted the divine-right monarchy and society of orders that Descartes had respected, and that had vied for primacy in Louis XIII's world.

14

THE INTIMATE LOUIS

Anecdotal history has dismissed the aging Louis XIII as a fawning lover of brainless young men and a hopeless prude with women, unlikely the father of his own son. This biographer has even heard the spurious story that Mazarin sired the future Louis XIV whispered to him in the Bibliothèque nationale (though Mazarin was out of France both before and during the gestation period). Some writers have gone out of their way to give the paternity award to Buckingham, who died a decade earlier! To get to the truth, we must examine Louis's intimate life in its totality.

As Louis passed from early adulthood to premature middle age, his relationships took on a set pattern. He continued to be obsessively drawn to both men and women, but now it was to younger not older persons. Luynes was followed by Barradat, Saint-Simon, and Cinq Mars. Mme de Luynes (now Mme de Chevreuse) was succeeded by Marie de Hautefort and Louise de La Fayette. Each of these young male and female flames conformed to one of two opposite types. The Louis the Just who was torn between punishing and pardoning subjects also alternated between petulantly demanding and gentle, understanding friends. To complicate matters, the king's relationships often overlapped—and they always paralleled his ritual of dutiful lovemaking with his estranged wife. The most dramatic sequence of these entanglements led directly to the conception of Louis's heir and successor which, to be sure, was no accident, though it has routinely been depicted that way.

The pattern of Louis's relationships with women began with Mme de Chevreuse, an early exemplar of the attractive, pleasure-loving, willful, and quarrelsome favorite-type that led Louis XIII time and again to distraction, love spats, and unhappiness. He never quite got her out of his life; long after his brief adolescent infatuation, the woman he sarcastically called "the Messiah" haunted him because of her close friendship with Queen Anne and her involvement in schemes running counter to King Louis's politics: the Chalais conspiracy, Châteauneuf's falling out with king and cardinal, and Lorraine's hostility to France. Together with Queen Mother Marie de' Medici and Queen Anne of Austria, the duchess Marie de Chevreuse just about turned Louis XIII into a misogynist.

But not quite. In the spring of 1630, the fourteen-year-old Marie de Hautefort caught his eye. She was a pink-cheeked, spirited innocent with blue eyes and golden hair in the queen mother's household. He was in need of distraction. The monarch fell in love instantly. Louis politely begged his mother's permission to visit the girl. He donned colorful clothes and forgot all about hunting. Yet he dared not touch her; there is even a story that one day he used a pair of silver tongs to snatch a gossipy note she and the queen had tauntingly hid in her stirring bosom. In spite of this reserve, he became insanely jealous at the attention other men paid her.[1] No wonder that Tallemant des Réaux concluded that Louis XIII had nothing of the lover in him but jealousy.[2]

The obsession, seemingly broken in 1635 with Louis's sudden interest in Louise de La Fayette, resumed two years later, only to be terminated by Louis at the end of the decade. And as the relationship progressed, simple infatuation was darkened by lovers' quarrels. Louis had discovered someone well endowed to feed on his suspicious, judgmental nature. To make matters worse, the king had the bad sense to make the object of his desires lady-in-waiting to the queen. Anne and Hautefort found mutual comfort in giggling at the royal suitor's prudishness and smirking at his petty jealousy. This state of affairs continued right through the queen's first full-term pregnancy. To read Louis's letters to Richelieu about *la créature* is an eye opener: here was a powerful monarch helplessly baring his soul down to the last detail.

Let us eavesdrop as the stormy entente neared its end. A convenient date is 27 November 1638. We find Louis fuming to Richelieu that "the creature is always in a foul mood," while gloating that an imminent victory over the Habsburgs might hasten peace. By January

1639, the monarch was less pessimistic and more self-deprecating about his personal affairs: "I didn't want to let you know about the reconciliation between Madame Dotefort and me until we could chat together in private, for the first day went by with great coldness on her part and much submissiveness on mine." Louis went on to confide about a second reconciliation, arranged by a certain Chemerault who was sworn to guarantee it!

When Louis was not making eyebrow-raising pacts like this, he was trying to impress the "creature" with his magnanimity. "I am thinking tonight of offering Madame Dotefort a pension of 1,200 ecus," he wrote, "to make her understand that I don't harbor any resentment, and to show her that I will always repay her bad deeds with good ones." Alas, to no avail. A week later Louis complained to his minister, "The creature is in a bad mood. One doesn't know how to act with her since she finds fault with whatever one does to try to please her." The bewildered ruler wrote that he was set on escaping to the all-male haven of Versailles for "rest"; he still had a headache despite a "remedy," but if he felt better he would go deer hunting "to make me forget."

Could Louis enlist the help of others? He certainly tried. He asked his advisor to pass on a love note—if he deemed it apropos. Richelieu was made witness to promises of good behavior by Hautefort. Her own relatives were told to remind her of these vows, as if they could make her behave when the royal plaintiff had failed. As an afterthought, the king asked his advisor to prevent the young lady from confiding his intimate talk to the queen's ears. Finally this sequence ended in March 1639 with Louis limply complaining: "Every single day I see the bad will she bears against me. It drives me to despair, since I love her so much." Late that year, he managed to banish her definitively.[3]

Unhappily, the woman for whom Louis left Hautefort in 1635 was the only female friend who fitted the opposite model, that of sweetness; and tragically, even this idyll with Louise de La Fayette was transitory. Some historians have wistfully speculated on how the king's declining years might have turned out had their friendship blossomed. The suggestion is implausible, given Louis's and Louise's shared virtues of piety and justice, and their common fetish for self-denial.[4]

La Fayette, the daughter of poor country nobility, had entered Queen Anne's service as a twelve-year-old. At seventeen Louise, with her blue eyes, pretty face, and purity of trust, captured the heart of a

monarch twice her age. (See plate 14.) She brought out the king's
warmer and affectionate qualities, deeply suppressed by the persona
of Louis the Just. Her code name in the Louis-Richelieu correspondence, *la fille* or "the maiden," spells out the difference between La
Fayette and Hautefort. She liked to ride with the king, and she listened with rapt attention to his stories about the royal hunt. He felt
so comfortable with this innocent maiden that he even confided his
occasional doubts about the progress of his war with the Habsburgs.
Undoubtedly he let slip remarks about his chief minister's imperiousness, and perhaps misgivings about some foreign policy moves.

No one doubted that Louis and Louise's daily companionship was
platonic, just as no one could help noticing that it was extraordinarily deep and intense. Court poetry made fun of her and angered
him. More seriously, their constant companionship between 1635
and 1637—whenever he was home from military campaigns—made
Queen Anne jealous; she was wounded by the king's attention to this
stripling, even though she had been disdainful of his normal aloof-
ness. Worst of all, Louise's quiet pleas to the king to change his personal and public life alarmed Cardinal Richelieu. By the time the paci-
fist Father Caussin became confessor to the king in March 1637,
Louise was urging her royal master not only to live as a proper husband with his wife, but also to seek a rapprochement with his mother
in the Spanish Netherlands, and perhaps even to make peace with
the Spanish and Austrian Habsburgs.

Richelieu did his best, first to make this saintly lady his client, then
to get rid of her in the most convenient way: he suggested she join a
religious order. The unworldly young woman had for some time been
thinking along those lines herself. Yet as soon as Richelieu entered
the contest for her soul, she had second thoughts, sensing the hidden
motives of his recommendation. Louise's doubts about leaving her
king were reinforced by Father Caussin's pleas that the liaison was
pure, and conducive to international and domestic tranquility.[5]

King Louis was no idle observer of this drama over his personal
happiness. Indeed, his Corneillian inner struggle over giving up the
light of his life was far more emotional than his tight-lipped decisions
in 1617 and 1631 to exile his mother. Bravely he told Father Caussin,
"It is true that she is very dear to me; but if God calls her to religion,
I will in no way hold her back."[6] His mind raced to alternatives he
had already whispered to Louise. One was to give up everything—
his marriage, throne, and love—and retire to a monastery. Just as

impetuously, he was drawn to the opposite fantasy of carrying off his beloved to the all-male haven of Versailles.

The memoirs of Mme de Motteville, faithful aide to the queen and perceptive observer of the king, do full justice to Louis's moral and political dilemma. She wrote, in unadorned candor: "The virtue of the most perfect persons is not always consistently strong. . . . This great prince, who had earned the name the Just for being faithful to God all his life, was not during these particular circumstances." Then Motteville added a simple psychological truth that prepares us for the ending of this real-life tragedy. La Fayette's expression of pure love for her king, she wrote, "ought to have brought happiness into his life," but "that prince was in no way destined to be happy."[7]

When Louise recoiled in horror from sinning at Versailles with her monarch, he hung his head in shame for "falling away from his accustomed modesty." Louis gave in to royal and religious duty: he kept his throne and let his loved one go. On 9 May 1637, she took her leave in the queen's chambers. As Anne looked on, Louis broke down in tears, and Louise stoically rode off in her carriage to join the Sisters of the Visitation.[8]

La Fayette had yet to play her greatest role in the life of her king and his kingdom, aided by Louis's inability to put her completely out of his mind. During the summer and autumn of 1637, he would snatch an hour here and there from the cares of war and government and slip away to the Visitadine convent. The nuns kept a discreet distance, but we know something of the couple's conversations from Father Caussin's correspondence with Sister Louise. To hear him, she was an agent of God, working on the monarch "for the peace of Christendom, the relief of his people in the direst of straits, the union of the royal house [meaning reconciliation with Marie and Gaston], and to lead him to a saintly and cordial affection for the queen in the constant hope that God would give his blessing on their marriage."[9]

On 5 December, five days before Louis dismissed Caussin for troubling his conscience, he saw Louise for the last time. He lingered at the grille until a rainstorm prevented the completion of his journey from Versailles to the monks of St-Maur. After trying to wait out the rain rather than take temporary quarters at the Louvre, where his wife was staying, the king of France finally gave in to the urgings of his male companions and slept in Anne's bed. Exactly nine months later, the future Louis XIV was born.

It is possible that the conception took place a few days earlier, when Louis and Anne had had one of their routine late-night visits. The king and his physicians temporarily traced the pregnancy back to the earlier date. But the crucial question is not when Anne conceived, much less whether Louis was the father, but how it could have happened after a barren twenty-two years and how, unlike Anne's previous four or five pregnancies, it could have gone full term.

La Fayette's urgings to Louis to make a baby clearly played a role, for she was the one he was most likely to listen to. The timing of the Louis-Louise breakup was also crucial. For a king who always craved intimate company and had recently ended a ten-year relationship with his male *favori* Saint-Simon, the loss was devastating. Louis was left with precious few ways to fill the void. He had sworn to honor Louise by never taking another female favorite, and he had divulged that vow to his court.

Richelieu drew attention to the royal dilemma by reminding the tortured king that he could not do without some sort of special friend. His master wrote back, on 4 June 1637:

> If I must love someone I would rather try to get back with Hotefort than with any other girl at court. However, it is not my intention to get involved with anyone, as I have just told you, and also because I have promised this to La Faiette (to whom I have never gone back on my word nor she to me). I will persist right to the death in this design not to get involved with anyone, and I will try to live the best I can on earth in order at the end to win Paradise, which is the sole goal one should have in this world.

On the rebound, Louis did pay attention to Hautefort. But the experience was so unsatisfactory that he was now vulnerable to his last and least desirable resort. He hinted as much in the same letter to Richelieu. "You should know," he stiffly wrote, "that since I have been here [at Fontainebleau], I haven't spoken to any woman or girl except the queen."[10]

One last development was necessary for the marital union to bear fruit: the king's discovery of a four-year correspondence by the queen with her friends and family in the Spanish world. As in the case of Anne's previous pregnancies, Louis suddenly found himself in a position of moral superiority over his wife, and she was in a most awkward situation. Just as with couples who believe they cannot conceive and then do so after adopting a child, Louis and Anne were prepared psychologically by this extraneous event.

In itself, Anne's letter writing was not a crime. Every royal family in early modern Europe had mixed blood; it was natural for a French queen to be in touch socially with her brother on the throne of Spain and with the Cardinal Infante. France and Spain, though, had been at war, first covertly and then openly, the entire time of her correspondence. Secret letters under these circumstances looked suspicious. Could Queen Anne have passed military secrets or committed disloyal acts in her letters from Paris to Madrid and Brussels? Richelieu and a highly suspicious Louis XIII certainly wanted to know. Today we can find out for ourselves by looking at the cardinal's transcribed copies of the letters.[11]

The letters written to Anne told her far more about enemy plans than hers said about the French. Indeed, she was privy to nothing confidential, so she could have betrayed nothing had she wanted. All she wanted was an outlet for her frustrations as a neglected queen, and she had found it in the privacy of her letters to Philip IV of Spain, the Cardinal Infante in the Spanish Netherlands, and her exiled friends, Mesdames de Chevreuse and du Fargis. Her favorite phrase was "Dios save la mortification que es par mi." Anne's writing preserved her sanity, damped her seething discontent, and reinforced her religious inclination to accept God's will for her personal future.

True, the queen of France committed to paper some shocking anti-French sentiments: she actually hoped that her relatives and in-laws on the Spanish and English thrones would join forces against France. Yet before war actually was declared in 1635 between her husband and her brother, Anne had been in anguish to see the situation "irrevocably moving toward a rupture," and she had blamed the Spanish ambassador's insolence with Richelieu for contributing to the war's outbreak.[12] And what of an earlier remark to the French negotiator with Spain that she hoped the emperor would win the German war? It stemmed purely from Catholic zeal, and political naïveté. Her strongest feeling on foreign policy was a recurring personal fear: that a diplomatic shift could unwittingly end her elaborate courier network via the English and Spanish ambassadorial staff. She almost went out of her mind at the rumor of closer Anglo-French relations: "I will be deprived of news from the Infante, news from him being not a little satisfaction."[13]

Anne curtly dismissed her exiled friends' pleas to reconcile Louis XIII with the exiled Marie de' Medici. She had neither rapport nor influence with her husband's advisor, she added for good measure. Mme du Fargis asked if she could do something to help Gaston. She replied: "I will tell you flatly that I am very angry with him." She negated rumors in Brussels that Louis was close to cashiering Richelieu or had told him "that his violent acts and usurpation of power will place his realm in peril." Fargis even had a successor picked out, the ex-minister La Vieuville, self-exiled in Brussels. To hear Fargis, he was "the salt of the earth, faithful to France, unwavering servitor of the queen and Monsieur [Gaston], and capable of the heavy burden of the ministry." How Anne must have smiled at being asked to pressure her husband to replace Richelieu with the cardinal's predecessor, whom Louis had arrested in the first place for usurping royal power.

To put to rest the question of Anne's "treason by mail," let us turn to Fargis's letter of 1 December 1636. This dispatch urged the queen to squelch antiwar caballing at court once for all and excoriated the princes Gaston and Soissons for their latest harebrained flight from France. Fargis also gave the childless queen advice on which Louis, Anne, and Richelieu could all agree: "For God's sake, for the sake of ending these quarrels, make a son. You will be the best princess in the world and the happiest. For surely everything else is not worth much by comparison."[14]

These last lines led France's queen not to treason, but, through fear, to a great service to the monarchy. Feeling vulnerable because of Spanish rumors that Louis might end their marriage (though he never had any such thought), she desperately wanted a pregnancy to ensure her position, though at the same time she contemplated giving up and joining her relatives in Brussels. Louis, however, brought those uncertainties to an end with his investigation. Launched after the suspicious monarch ferreted out vital links in Anne's network—which Richelieu had suspected for some time—the inquiry did not take long.[15] The king's chief advisor, the chancellor, and others gathered the evidence and interrogated everyone from Anne to her friends at the convent of Val-de-Grâce. And on 17 August 1637, Anne and Louis undercut their last psychical resistance to pregnancy by penning two mémoires.

One of these documents, drafted in the king's hand, was entitled "Memoir of Things I Wish of the Queen." In the other one, Anne thanked Richelieu for interceding against a worse fate than the one laid down and agreed to suspend her undercover letter writing as well as to have all future correspondence monitored. She admitted remorse for hoping that Anglo-French amity would not occur and for similar "bad conduct." Louis in turn forgave Anne for knowing about Fargis's wish of 1631–32 that the king's death would lead to a marriage between King Gaston and Queen Anne (knowledge that Anne had earler denied).[16]

These were potent words indeed! In Anne's bottom lines, she promised "never to fall back into similar transgressions [*fautes*] and to live with the King our most honored seigneur and husband as a person who wishes to have no interest other than that of his person and his State." Below, in Louis XIII's hand, was written:

> After having seen the frank confession which the Queen our dear wife has made concerning what has displeased us for some time in her conduct, and in view of the assurance she has given us to conduct herself in future according to her duty toward us and our State, we declare to her that we will completely overlook everything that has happened. We wish to put the matter completely behind us [*n'en voulons jamais avoir souvenir*]. We wish to live with her as a good King and a good husband should. I sign this with the countersignature of the Secretary of State.[17]

This formalized peace was the king's way of obliquely dealing with his anguish. It mirrored his many pacts with Marie de Hautefort, his agreements with male favorites, his bizarre swearing of Richelieu and Saint-Simon to an accord on their knees, even his vows to the Virgin Mary and the virgin La Fayette. But there was one cardinal difference: the pact between husband and wife on 17 August 1637 placed the king in a position of moral superiority and his wife in one of deference, which allowed him to play the role of Louis the Just in his wife's bed while suppressing his real feelings. He could judge and forgive; she could accept the royal pardon in gratitude. The triple event of 5 December—Louis's last visit with Louise de La Fayette, the fortuitous rainstorm, and the queen's conception—followed naturally.[18]

One could expect only so much of Louis XIII, however. The period of waiting for the expected dauphin was awkward in the extreme. Louis returned from the war three times during the summer of 1638 to see Anne: dutifully at first, perhaps even hoping to escape boredom (as he had admitted to Richelieu about earlier visits with his wife),[19] and finally with the expectation of seeing his firstborn. Alas, August 1638 passed; the physicians' "count" of the pregnancy proved to be a month off. The king grumbled that the queen's superb health meant that she was "not so close to childbirth as we were told."

Hautefort was plaguing him too. He changed his mind from one hour to the next over whether to put up with that "Hotefort female" or be done with her once and for all, Chavigny wrote Richelieu.

Louis's father would have gotten his girlfriend pregnant while waiting for his queen to give birth to an heir. Louis's son would later sit in one carriage with his wife, his current flame, and his former mistress. Louis himself could only lament to his chief advisor and confidant, misogynistically: "I have found the female sex here to have as little sense and as much impertinence in their questions as they usually do. It wearies me that the queen hasn't yet given birth so that I can go back to [the army in] Picardy if you judge it apropos, or elsewhere—if only I could be done with these women, no matter where!" He also wrote, near the end: "It wearies me that the queen has [not] given birth in order to free me from this place." As if her sole function in giving birth was to gratify his other wishes![20]

In Louis XIII's beloved St-Germain, Anne of Austria finally gave birth on 5 September 1638 to a baby boy. Louis went repeatedly to see his son that day. Chavigny wrote to the ambassador to Rome: "The king's joy cannot be expressed in words, nor that of the entire court."[21] In point of fact, the king was recovering from a fever he had caught while hunting shortly before the birth.

His subjects knew no restraint in welcoming the baby dubbed "the God-given" or *Dieudonné*. Lamps were lit in windows, fireworks launched into the skies, plays performed and poems read, and there were services of thanksgiving. Louis was in better health to celebrate the birth of a second boy, Philippe de France, on 21 September, 1640.[22] Few have doubted the paternity of that offspring, who gave a double assurance that Louis's line would continue.

He was not much of a father, however, partly due to his wish to control the mother. While Anne was expecting Louis had selected as governess someone she detested. "If there were no other reason," Louis told Bullion, "this reason alone would confirm [me in my] decision."[23] Though Louis saw his boys often enough, when he frightened the heir with his absurd nightbonnet he leaped to the conclusion that the queen had turned the baby against him, and he contemplated taking the children away from her. As Louis approached death, he also tried to keep Anne from having full powers as regent for Louis XIV's minority, bequeathing to her a council whose votes were to be binding. On her husband's demise she promptly had the will broken, lavished affection on their firstborn son, and brought him up politically as well.

Yet Louis XIII had a strong impact on his successor. The son inherited the father's secretiveness, his knack for making an arrest without warning or outward emotion, and a touch of cruelty. Louis XIV also owed to his father's example some of his own sense of the responsibility of kingship. Mazarin's later influence as a surrogate father to Louis XIV is also connected to the biological father. After Richelieu's death, Louis XIII found more solace in Mazarin's company than with anyone else, and he named him the heir's godfather. There is a touch of truth in the humorous story concerning the formal christening on 21 April 1643 concerning the common traits of the dying father and his four-year-old-son. When asked by his father what his name was, the lad is supposed to have said, "Louis XIV," to which Louis XIII responded, "Not yet, not yet, my son; but you may be soon, by the grace of God."

Other sides to Louis XIII's character reappeared strongly in his younger son, for Philippe was bisexual, with a powerful inclination toward ineffectual relations with men. Was this sheer coincidence, or was it heredity? Can it be traced back to early childhood experiences? There may well have been enough time for Philippe to be affected by his father's ways of relating. More directly, however, Anne set out to ensure a different court scene from her husband's; she reinforced stereotypic masculinity in Louis XIV and reared Philippe not to be the threat Gaston was to Louis XIII.[24]

Philippe was two when his father's last personal liaison with a male favorite came to an ignominious end. Courtiers were far more uncomfortable with the disagreeableness of a Cinq Mars in 1639–42, and a Barradat in 1624–26 than with that of their female counterpart, Marie de Hautefort. Society could tolerate a king being a fool in love with a woman, but people were ambivalent about a king being a weakling before another man. This reaction likely had everything to do with current concepts of knightly valor and little to do with attitudes about homosexuality. Early modern people were used to males frolicking together under many circumstances—as Louis and Gaston, and the child Louis and Henry IV, did when they occasionally slept or rested together. Furthermore, church disapproval of sex except for procreation was not as pronounced for divinely anointed royalty as for lesser mortals.[25]

In 1624, Louis XIII had been smitten by François de Barradat. This attention quickly went to the head of the handsome youth. He put on airs, thought only of himself, and kept the king on edge. People muttered that the king was out of control in this relationship; even Richelieu was careful to write groveling letters to the high-flying *favori*. It was left for the near-contemporary Tallemant des Réaux to refer to the sexual side of this liaison with highly suggestive, but unprovable, turns of phrase. He wrote that Louis "loved Barradas violently; one accused him of committing a hundred indecencies [*ordures*] with him"; and he alluded to homosexuality now crossing the Alps from Italy, just as the decrees of the Council of Trent had.[26]

Three weeks after Louis abruptly banished Barradat in 1626 for dabbling in politics, he became attracted to another teenage noble page in the royal stable. Claude de Saint-Simon was as perfect a male counterpart to Louise de La Fayette as the court could provide. His fierce loyalty and devotion made up for short stature, homeliness, and barracks language (which never offended the prudish but smitten king). (See plate 7.) Saint-Simon was constantly at his master's side when Louis fell ill on his way to La Rochelle in 1627. During the ruler's near fatal illness of 1630, the *favori* scarcely moved from his bedside. This was not a relationship to make tongues wag.[27]

Saint-Simon's skill in hunting and handling horses appealed to Louis. Legend credits the younger man with winning the king's affections because of his ability to play the hunting horn without salivating. He also taught his master how to change horses without dismounting: a fresh horse was brought alongside the king's tired beast head to tail, allowing him to put one foot in the new animal's stirrup and swing his body across its back.

Louis XIII invented a lover's language by which they could communicate their feelings to each other alone.[28] Physical love is less certain. Saint-Simon actually tried to get his monarch to become involved sexually with Marie de Hautefort, after being a party to an unseemly love triangle involving all three. Louis knew his *favori*'s motives were altruistic and forgave the indiscretion on condition he never repeat it.

Eventually even the selfless Saint-Simon had to find a better outlet for his emotions. By 1634 he could be found slipping away from the king's quarters to be with one of his "wenches." Louis could no more tolerate this behavior than he could stand the thought of Marie de Hautefort getting married.[29] Their once idyllic relationship deteriorated into lover's quarrels. During the year of Corbie, Louis instructed Richelieu to let Saint-Simon go to the battle zone "to get rid of his *mauvaises humeurs.*" The phrase became a common entry to the royal-ministerial correspondence. Saint-Simon would probably have remained in favor, though, had he not crossed the king in shielding his uncle from royal punishment for surrendering to the Spaniards and suffered banishment as a consequence. On Louis XIII's death, Saint-Simon thought of hurling himself into the vault after the royal coffin. The favorite's son, Louis de Saint-Simon, famous for his memoirs on the court of Louis XIV, praised Louis XIII above both his successor and his predecessor and visited the late king's grave every year.[30]

The king's last male liaison made Barradat look like a budding Saint-Simon. Richelieu had taken a liking to the brave and dashing but spoiled son of his deceased colleague and creature, Marshal Effiat. When the open conflict with Spain erupted in 1635, the fifteen-year-old Henri d'Effiat, marquis of Cinq Mars, was made commander of one of Louis's new companies of bodyguards. Two years later he was entrusted with orders to Father Caussin to become the king's confessor. In 1639, the youth fought in his monarch's presence at the northeastern front; by the year's end, Louis told Marie de Hautefort that his affections now belonged to Cinq Mars. The king was thirty-eight, his *favori* nineteen.

We need not accept at face value Montglat's recollection that Richelieu had, through his agents in the king's household staff, manipulated Louis XIII into liking Cinq Mars. This is simply an example of that courtier's generalization that the king was "very susceptible to impressions from others, letting himself be so ruled by the cardinal that he loved and hated according to [Richelieu's] wishes."[31] The fact is that Cinq Mars gained friends easily: he captivated Richelieu as well as Louis XIII.

Louis succumbed to the lure that had swept him off his feet before. Cinq Mars had the handsome beauty of Luynes and Barradat, the youth of Barradat and Saint-Simon. The king was utterly blind to his friend's self-centeredness, ostentatiousness and promiscuity—characteristics Louis had spent a lifetime trying to eradicate from court and country. The spell that Monsieur le Grand cast on the king was stronger than Marie de Hautefort's had been.

Louis XIII's passion for Cinq Mars utterly astounded courtiers, who a short time before had seen their ruler mesmerized by Marie de Hautefort's charms and attracted to other young ladies in the queen's household. Gaston's servitor Goulas wrote that the king "loved M. le Grand *ardemment*," a phrase that indicates extraordinary fervor, while leaving unsaid what form the fervor took. Tallemant, in turn, said that Louis "l'aimait esperdument"—that he loved the youth to distraction. The same raconteur tells a story of a lovers' tryst that, although no contemporary mentions it, is at least authentic in conveying the ardor which Goulas mentions. The story is that one day someone interrupted a surprised Monsieur le Grand rubbing himself from head to toe with jasmine oil, and a moment later the king appeared at the door. Tallemant (and he alone) also informs us of a rendezvous to which Cinq Mars came "adorned like a wife," while his royal master—"fort négligé"—"started kissing his hands almost before this minion got [in bed with him]." The only sure ring of authenticity in the tale is the choppy, impatient way the king spoke ("couche-toy, couche-toy"); and Tallemant's suggestion that the suspicious king noticed his friend's reserve, occasioned by the playboy's desire to be with a female love.[32]

Louis XIII's letters to Richelieu recorded every "dirty look" by the favorite, every admission of the king being "beside myself." "This sloth, this procrastination and neglect of what he says he will do," Louis wrote late in 1640, "is more common than ever." The poor king scarcely knew what to tell his confidant:

I think [Cinq Mars] will put in writing to M. de Noyers something about his promptitude. I beg you not to put any faith whatseover in his words until you have heard me [tell my side] in his presence and before Gordes, who has witnessed everything. I haven't slept a wink all night out of rage, and am really upset. I can't put up any longer with his haughtiness, because it's gotten too much out of hand.

The upsets left the king an emotional wreck. The letter to Richelieu quoted above was written at 9:00 A.M. The next one was penned at 9:00 P.M. the same day. Louis said that he had received his *favori* most graciously during the day, and that he had immensely enjoyed the day's hunt, which had bagged a wolf and four foxes. But as 1640 gave way to 1641, the ruler began accusing Cinq Mars not only of being "haughty" but also of the "stubbornness" Louis himself had been charged with as a child.[33]

Quarrels and complaints alone could not break the spell. Indeed, as 1641 gave way in turn to 1642, the king gave Cinq Mars license to criticize Richelieu, just as he had allowed himself the weakness of deprecating Luynes behind his back and had listened to Louise de La Fayette's oblique criticisms of Richelieu's politics. The *favori* began to think that he might supplant the powerful cardinal as a result of his hold over the king's heart. Did Louis listen? There are conflicting reports. The most damaging evidence was a royal confession to Chancellor Séguier—which came embarrassingly long after the fact, when Cinq Mars was under arrest for treason. Louis nervously admitted of possibly complaining to Cinq Mars about Richelieu when in a bad mood, and thereby encouraging his minion to continue criticizing the minister. The king defended himself awkwardly by adding: "But when he went so far as to suggest that it was time to be quit of my said cousin [the cardinal] and to offer to do the deed himself, I was filled with horror and revulsion at his wicked thoughts."[34]

We can give the king some benefit of the doubt here, for he had told the swaggering Cinq Mars on several occasions that if it ever came to choosing between favorite and minister, he would automatically cashier the former. That promise was in keeping with Louis's vow after Luynes's passing never to let a favorite interfere with politics. There was also the precedent of his breaking with Marie de' Medici after the Day of Dupes. Yet we are left to ponder why he failed to act against Cinq Mars the moment his favorite hinted at Richelieu's assassination.[35] Why, indeed, did Louis wait until the swelled young head turned in frustration to plotting a coup d'état, which involved a secret promise of Spanish military aid and aimed at ousting Richelieu and authorizing Gaston to negotiate a Franco-Spanish peace?

We must also ask why the ruler refused to take any preemptive action against this threat until he had irrefutable proof he could not ignore. During April, May, and early June 1642, rumors abounded as Louis and Cinq Mars joined the royal army's siege of Perpignan in Spain while a mortally ill Richelieu stayed behind in Narbonne. Toward the end of May, Richelieu urged Louis through his fellow ministers to stop the rumor mongering; at the very least the king could declare to the world "that he is most satisfied with the cardinal's services, that if someone is against him [Richelieu], he holds them to be against his own person; and if someone has evil intentions on [Richelieu's] life, he will [defend the cardinal as] his second." But neither Richelieu at a distance or his messenger Chavigny, nor Sublet at the king's side, could get Louis to make that symbolic gesture, let alone banish Cinq Mars's right-hand man, de Thou.[36]

And so the rumors continued. As Louis's own health took a turn for the worse and he alternated between arguing with his minion and complaining himself about his minister's peremptoriness, the king's entourage began to ask whether he would abandon the campaign and his minister altogether and head for Paris, as he had in the midst of the long-drawn-out siege of La Rochelle. Sublet de Noyers reported to Richelieu that he thought the cardinal's supporters could hold the line, but "if Cinq Mars has room to maneuver and agitate he will destroy in a week all that we have built up in an hour's discussion [with the king]."[37]

Louis XIII tried to reassure his advisor: "Contrary to all the false rumors that are being spread, I love you more than ever; we have been together far too long for us ever to be separated." These words failed to reassure Richelieu, however, and they have left historians at odds. Chevallier labels Louis's inaction nauseating, and Burckhardt calls his words scarcely reassuring; but Avenel, in contrast, speaks of the king's surge of confidence and affection for his chief minister.[38] Treasure does not suggest that Louis had anything to feel guilty about. Finally Vaunois, in examining what Treasure passes over, concludes awkwardly: "It is possible that [Louis] amused himself with Cinq Mars's mocking of Richelieu and that he had recounted to his confidant certain of his 'displeasures' as he had formerly to Mlle de La Fayette. But it is not plausible [*vraisemblable*] that these momentary lapses led to complicity with Cinq Mars."[39] My own opinion is that Louis had no intention either of ending the campaign in Spain or of dismissing his advisor, and that his infatuation with Cinq Mars, plus the lack of concrete evidence of an organized plot, dulled any suspicions he may have had about his minion's true aims.

On 10 June, the king's health finally forced him to take leave of the torrential rains and his troops surrounding Perpignan. He kept the siege going in his absence, though Sublet thought the monarch was afraid Richelieu would criticize his personal withdrawal.[40] Two days later the bigger question of the conspiracy was resolved, when Chavigny reached Louis with a copy of the treaty between the conspirators and Spain, which Richelieu had just obtained.[41] A curious transcription of the affair combines a newsletter telling of the king's response and his subsequent letter to Richelieu. The pamphlet reads: "After great inner torment on [the twelfth], His Majesty let himself be persuaded by reasons of state not to abandon M. le Cardinal in the slightest, as being extremely necessary to him, but on the contrary to get rid of M. le Grand and the others in his party." The king's undated letter is more direct: "My Cousin, go to some place which the doctors will prescribe for your health, and take care wherever it may be of my State, as of my children, and of all my family. I love you more than anyone else in the world."[42]

Louis's "inner torment" over having to arrest Cinq Mars and de Thou showed in his wondering aloud to Chavigny and Sublet de Noyers whether his favorite's name on the incriminating document was an error. Knowing the bitter truth, he acted immediately, but according to Sublet he remained in a daze for days on end. The secretary thought that only Mazarin's presence could restore the monarch's emotional health.[43] When Louis saw Richelieu again, at Tarascon on

28 June, he cried bitterly; he was sheepish and anxious about receiving a ministerial lecture for being played the fool by his favorite over the fortunes of his state.

The awkwardness reappeared one last time after king and cardinal were both safely back at the capital, and it lasted from 27 October to 30 November 1642, just ten days before Richelieu's death. The servitor, still uncertain about his master's feelings, tried to force Louis to make humiliating promises that would have stripped the monarch of personal as well as political autonomy. Louis dragged his feet, telling Chavigny that "he wished to satisfy [the cardinal], but that he also wanted to keep his own honor intact." Finally the king agreed to one important concession: he dismissed four of his beloved guards, (including the captain of musketeers, M. Tréville of *Three Musketeers* fame), whom his advisor believed were too close to the king's fallen favorite.[44]

Meanwhile, on 12 August the fallen royal favorite's personal fate had been played out to its bitter end on the scaffold at Lyon. Louis was not there; he had left Séguier and Richelieu to supervise the hand-picked tribunal's work while he rejoined his wife and sons in the Paris region.[45] At the hour of Cinq Mars's execution, the king looked up from his chess match and said: "Monsieur le Grand will very soon be passing his time badly." Gaston's servitor Goulas bitterly attributed Louis's words to "the extreme hardness of his heart." A contrary explanation, however, centered on Louis the Just's virtues, was offered by the continuer of Bernard's royal biography. According to this view, Louis stayed away from the trial so that he "would be touched less by compassion for his *favori*." The royal historiographer added: "But his steadfastness had already fortified him to a considerable degree against giving in to the tenderness of such feelings; the consideration of his State was dearer to him than his very own feelings."[46]

Each reader will have to decide whether Louis the Just was cold and indifferent or whether he was masking other emotions when he received the simultaneous news on 15 September 1642 of the fall of Perpignan and Cinq Mars's execution. As Sublet de Noyers reported to Richelieu, the king was overjoyed with the news of Perpignan's fall and unemotional regarding his last favorite's fate: "His Majesty did not appear to me to be at all afflicted when I told him of the deaths of M. le Grand and M. de Thou. He only showed impatience to know if they died in a Christian spirit."[47] The king had reason to be impatient. Rejecting a posture of Christian humility, the former favorite refused to have his eyes blindfolded before the descent of the executioner's axe. By that act, Cinq Mars broke with the protocol that alone would have made Louis XIII comfortable with the dénouement of this drama.

An amalgam of many external influences and inner urges, with a loving but at times cruel father and cold mother, a brother who lent his name and arms to rebel subjects, a wife who was herself caught in an impossible position and failed to attract his love, quarrelsome male and female favorites, and a minister who became famous at the king's expense, Louis XIII was nonetheless a major force in the molding of early modern France. It is sad that he could not have better enjoyed his role, that he could not escape boredom except through demeaning relationships or mechanical occupations, both of which undermined his stature in the eyes of subjects. Yet the irrefutable fact remains that this very human, imperfect person made his reign the Age of Louis XIII. A different, more self-assured, more appealing monarch would have allowed us to draw a more pleasant portrait of the age. But the age would have been very different from the way it was.

Conclusion:
Louis XIII Beyond the Grave

Louis XIII fell ill for the last time in February 1643 while staying at his boyhood residence in St-Germain. He kept rallying, attended his council, and walked in his gardens. But in April he retired to his chambers, with their view of the basilica at St-Denis, where shortly he would join France's past kings and queens.

He made all the arrangements for the transition to his widow's regency. Saint-Simon was recalled, and he wept at his master's bedside as he listened to instructions about the funeral. La Vrillière, considered Louis's most trustworthy secretary of state, drew up his will and broke down reading it. The king's deportment was above reproach, except in exclaiming to his chief physician: "I would have lived much longer if it had not been for you." That witticism bothered those who wrote about their monarch's last days, for early modern people expected death to be exemplary, especially in the case of their earthly lord. Being a model of royal virtues, Louis obliged by apologizing to Dr. Bouvard. He begged his wife to forgive him for the grief he had caused her; she had a cot placed in an adjoining cabinet and kept vigil day and night till the end. He blessed his children, after which the oldest said he would jump in the moat if the king died. To his sobbing entourage he regretted not having achieved international peace and expressed his hope that his death would leave subjects in tranquillity and rest.[1]

A lifetime of bad eating habits, disregard for physical health, and constant manipulation of bodily functions by his doctors finally broke down the king's strong constitution. His intestines were inflamed and ulcerated, making digestion virtually impossible; tuberculosis had spread to his lungs, accompanied by a habitual cough. Either of these major ailments, or the accumulation of minor problems, may have killed him, not to mention psychological weaknesses that made him prone to disease or his doctors' remedies of enemas and bleedings, which continued right to his death.

Death came on 14 May 1643, the thirty-third anniversary of his father's death. Following his instructions for inexpensive ceremonies, the body was embalmed, placed in a lead casket covered with plain velvet adorned by a cross of white satin and gold-embroidered coats of arms, and the remains drawn by six horses in a day-long solemn cortège to the last resting place at St-Denis. Along the route, windows were lit with candles and lanterns.

Did the "universal grief," which historians say was the last such expression of general sorrow at a French monarch's passing, represent pure form, or something more? The Venetian ambassador gives us an ambiguous answer: "The people, by the loss of the departed king, are plunged into great sadness. His Majesty was always well liked, whether due to the natural instinct of the nation or the merit of his particular qualities."[2] Perhaps we can get behind that tantalizing ambiguity to uncover contemporary assessments of those royal qualities. It is certainly worth trying, for although contemporaries do not always say what they believe, their insight is informed by the beliefs, assumptions, and problems held by the subject of their assessments. It would be a pity to let that informed opinion pass into Louis XIII's grave and rely solely on later judgments.[3]

The truism of Louis XIII's time was that he embodied to perfection the virtues of a ruler. Some of that praise can be discounted because of the convention mentioned by Richelieu's biographer Vialart: it was not right to divulge a king's secrets, only his virtue.[4] Yet a few persons got around that obstacle by alluding to the complexity inherent in being virtuous; they said wryly that Louis the Just had all the virtues except likability. Behind that comment lay two different assessments.

To those who approved of Louis the Just's statebuilding, it was enough for him to be "good" by placing the severity of his justice before his personal empathy for subjects. Hence the pamphlet histories that emphasize Louis's having been born under the sign of Libra, his vanquishing of the tyrant Concini, his meting out of the death penalty to archduelers and chronic rebels, his pacification of La Rochelle, his journeys over Susa Pass and into Lorraine and Roussillon against perfidious allies and treaty-breaking adversaries. A compendium of Hay du Chastelet's pamphlets from the reign summed up the favorable portrayal in 1639: "a magnanimous and just king . . . practicing so purely all the virtues he cultivated, freely exposing his person for the defense of the Church and his allies, and holding the balance scales firmly to reward the good and punish the bad."[5]

To be sure, the royal historiographer Charles Bernard managed only awkwardly to work the king's massacre at Nègrepelisse and his sack of Privas into the theme of justice. More adroitly, the Oratorian preacher at the Louvre, Abra de Raconis, said in a typical funeral panegyric that Louis XIII "had used the severity of justice [only] when he had to, in order to maintain his authority, and halt the course of lawlessness in his state."[6]

Those individuals who did not like the authoritarian bent of Louis's virtues were circumspect until he entered his grave. Goulas touched on this phenomenon when he wrote: "The rising sun [is] adored, and the setting sun left without worship or offerings."[7] It was left for the master of character sketches La Rochefoucauld, who was thirty when Louis XIII died, to confide to his memoirs: "He was severe, mistrustful, hating the world."[8] Back in 1637, Mathieu de Morgues had prefaced his collection of anti-Richelieu pamphlets by appealing to the king's justice rather than attacking the king himself:

> For crying too loudly against [Richelieu] for having stripped Your
> Majesty of the glory of your undertakings (royal family concord, peace,
> the heart and wealth of your subjects, the strong places of your State
> which are the pieces of your crown) . . . I could ask pardon and remon-
> strate that you should imitate the clemency of that incomparable Henri le
> Grand . . . but I believe it more appropriate to call on the quality of
> Louis the Just.[9]

It was only in private correspondence with fellow clerics that the king's former confessor, Father Caussin, felt free to criticize the king for the faults that Morgues attributed to Richelieu. He did so by suggesting that the king had "political sins" (*péchés de roi*) as well as "personal" ones (*péchés d'homme*). Among the former he listed "church troubles, oppression of the people, division within the royal family, injustice exercised in the general affairs of the state."[10]

Drawing on contemporary attitudes toward Louis XIII's justice and other virtues, I have argued that his punitive side was crucial to the hallmarks of the reign, from his seizure of power in 1617 to his declaration of war in 1635. Without the judgmentalism that underlay

Louis's acts of state, these might never have been tolerated by the age. And although I recoil in horror at what to us are sadistic words and acts, I have been obliged to test my feelings against what Louis's contemporaries and he himself thought and felt. Subjects hailed the death of Concini, and saw justice in the execution of Montmorency (while hoping Louis would pardon him). Louis XIII, I have argued, had personal feelings about these and other acts of his justice, but he thought that he would not be acting as befitted a king if he expressed them; hence he came to be viewed as unfeeling and—after his death—sadistic. By contrast, his ebullient father, after Henry III's assassination of the Guise brothers, got away with the bloodcurdling remark that it was a pity he did not also kill Marguerite de Valois and Catherine de' Medici—the later Henry IV's own wife and mother-in-law.[11]

Contemporary judgments of Louis XIII's qualities shaded into evaluations of his responsibility for the acts that emanated from his justice. Scipion Dupleix's *History of Louis the Just* argued that "the king's virtue" had restored the French state. Unfortunately, though, this quasi-official history divided the reign into three eras, each associated with a "powerful minister": first Concini, then Luynes, and finally Richelieu. Having admitted that, Dupleix could not get his readers to believe that "the king's projects [had] been secretly drafted between His Majesty and [Richelieu, their] deliberations leading to mature decisions, undertakings directed with prudence, and executed with vigor." Critics of Richelieu had a more simplistic two-period division of the reign. Morgues dutifully gave Louis XIII most of the credit for crushing the Huguenots and pursuing the Mantuan succession venture through his "presence, vigilance, and good conduct"; policies falling after the Day of Dupes, however, were blamed on Richelieu's "crafty placing of bad impressions in the king's mind."[12]

Vialart's analysis of royal governance was more realistic than either Dupleix's or Morgues's, placing Louis XIII midway between "eminent" kings and incompetent ones "incapable of ruling by themselves or by the advice of others." For Vialart, Louis XIII exemplified an intermediate typology of rulers who lacked the capacity to judge everything on their own but were "quite capable of evaluating the judgments of their councillors, and of governing in that way."[13]

We have here the embryo of Louis XIII's decision-making process as presented in the course of this biography. In my view, the king did much more than merely react to advice; rather, his mode of governance encompassed a complicated two-way involvement of two men's personalities and ideas. Louis XIII's mode of governance, I have argued, involved the king's keen judgment, which Richelieu then fully exploited; the minister translated his ruler's firm political beliefs into sophisticated policy, while Louis struggled—with Richelieu's help—to trust his own judgment. In stressing this last factor, I have taken into account the doubts expressed by Vialart's contemporaries about Louis's diffidence. The king's household servitor Antoine wrote in his diary of Louis's last days, "He had much imagination, memory, and judgment; and yet he distrusted himself, preferring other persons' instincts to his own." [14] And the archbishop of Toulouse wrote in his memoirs:

> France had a most pious king, who feared God and was the enemy of all vice. He was extremely generous, had a perfect knowledge about his Estates, a comprehensive grasp of the affairs of war and of his realm. Heaven smiled on him, bestowing abundant blessings on all his undertakings, giving him marvelous success; so that he would have been the most accomplished of all Princes had he only had a little more confidence in himself, and good opinion of his affairs. [15]

The most intimate judge of Louis XIII's role—Louis himself—took to his grave the secret of how he had reconciled his acute understanding and his diffidence. How could a twentieth-century biographer get beyond the grave to the thoughts, acts, and feelings of a human being who has been aptly described as "coldly groping through life and doing his duty. . . . Perhaps his greatest failing was his stammering and his inarticulateness"? [16] Fortunately, contemporaries recorded enough of Louis XIII's words and the context of his acts to allow me to use the techniques of reconstruction outlined in the introduction of this study. I was able thereby to get around the conspiracy of silence that followed Louis's death.

Louis XIII's successor was curious enough to commission a study of his life, and he heard stories about the late king's hunting prowess and hounding of Huguenots; but Anne had deliberately suppressed all mention of her late husband's mode of governance from her son's political education. [17] The verdict of Louis XIV and his age was that Richelieu had ruled France and its king. Even the sobriquet Louis the Just was forgotten. [18] What remained in the collective memory about Louis XIII was the knowledge that during his personal reign the Huguenot state within the state had been destroyed, violent political crime curbed, the fiscal and administrative power of the state enormously expanded, and the power of the Habsburgs so challenged that, by the time of the peace settlements of Westphalia in 1648 and the Pyrenees in 1659, Bourbon France had gates opening on the outside world in the Rhineland, the Alps, and the Pyrenees.

I have sought to present plausible evidence that links all of these achievements with Louis's person. My conclusion is that (1) Louis XIII was a constant factor during the course of his reign; (2) he had his own view of the world, expressed in the title "Louis the Just"; (3) this worldview powerfully molded his age, just as he himself had been formed in part by outside influences while growing up; and (4) Louis also had specific notions that led to tenacious policies—most notably his aversion to the Spaniards, his dislike of dueling, his insistent toleration of Huguenot worship while putting down what he considered to be unprovoked revolt by Huguenot towns and grandees, and his implacable opposition to the independence of fortified towns and to great nobles flouting his laws. And he expressed all of these notions well before Richelieu's ministry of 1624–42. The attack on Huguenot power and town walls began in 1620, the assault on insubordinate grandees in 1617. In foreign affairs, after almost assisting the emperor at the outset of the Thirty Years' War, Louis developed an anti-Habsburg position that was well in place by the beginning of 1624.

Above all, I believe that this less-than-great person at the top of society—Louis XIII, alias Louis the Just—stamped his times not just as the reign of Louis XIII but as the Age of Louis the Just. He did it with powerful support and genius from Cardinal Richelieu. Yet one cannot imagine Richelieu without Louis XIII. May I express the historically heretical position that it is possible to think for a moment of Louis XIII without Richelieu?

Louis, after all, presided over more political executions than any other ruler in French history. His sense of justice and duty, which accommodated incredible batterings from his family, nevertheless doggedly overcame his mother and brother and somehow helped him to sire an heir with his wife. Although he discovered one childhood friend after another turning against him, he managed (and I think *not* easily) to turn on them in reply. He rallied his army at Corbie instead of withdrawing as Richelieu advised; he made his way over Susa Pass in impossible conditions to meet Richelieu, and waded with his soldiers across the waters of the Atlantic to Rié, cheating both death and the English. Scion of St. Louis, he blended with the Catholic revival begun before his reign and willed his heart to the Jesuit Church of St. Louis. Louis also had his nasty side, his backbiting, his bad moods that left Richelieu painfully uncertain of his support—and in the Cinq Mars affair wondering whether Louis had been willing to consider having him assassinated. The last-mentioned traits are not edifying aspects of Louis's ruling, just as the massacres at Nègrepelisse and Privas are horrifying blots on his character. Yet they, along with the more pleasantly recalled deeds of the king, are peculiarly Louis Treize acts—not the doing of Gaston or Marie or Luynes or Richelieu. And there is consistency, for Louis always stayed with Richelieu and with the same policies once they had been laid down.

When Louis XIII died and the funeral eulogies began, clerics fumbled for words. They settled on a passage from Isaiah. This verse sums up what they saw in their late king and, in keeping with the troubles of his life—both self-inflicted and imposed from without—announces unwittingly Louis's rendezvous with history.

> The just perish,
> and no one takes it to heart;
> men of good faith are swept away, but no one cares,
> the righteous are carried away before the onset of evil,
> but they enter into peace;
> they have run a straight course
> and rest in their last beds.[19]

Still, the last word remains with portraits chiseled in stone after his successes had become clear in the late 1630s. Inscribed on equestrian statues of Louis XIII in the Place Royale and the main square of Reims were dedications to Ludovico Justo the Pious, Clement, Victorious, and Ever August Most Christian King of France and Navarre.[20] We are still searching to know what the words mean.

Appendix

Map 1. Louis XIII's France

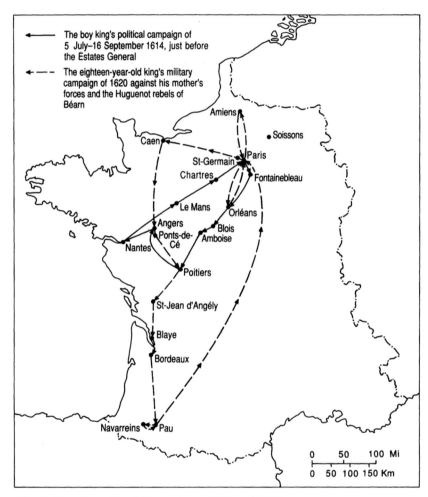

Map 2. Two Early Royal Campaigns, 1614 and 1620

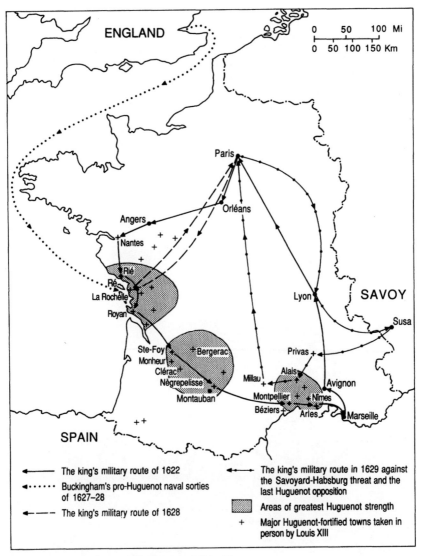

ENGLAND

0   50   100 Mi
0 50 100 150 Km

Paris

Orléans

Angers

Nantes

Ré

Ré
La Rochelle

Royan

SAVOY

Lyon

Susa

Ste-Foy   Bergerac
Monheur
Clérac
Nègrepelisse
Montauban

Privas

Millau   Alais
Montpellier   Nîmes
Béziers   Arles

Avignon

Marseille

SPAIN

←	The king's military route of 1622	←	The king's military route in 1629 against the Savoyard-Habsburg threat and the last Huguenot opposition
◄····	Buckingham's pro-Huguenot naval sorties of 1627–28		Areas of greatest Huguenot strength
←–	The king's military route of 1628	+	Major Huguenot-fortified towns taken in person by Louis XIII

Map 3. The Huguenot Challenge, 1621–29

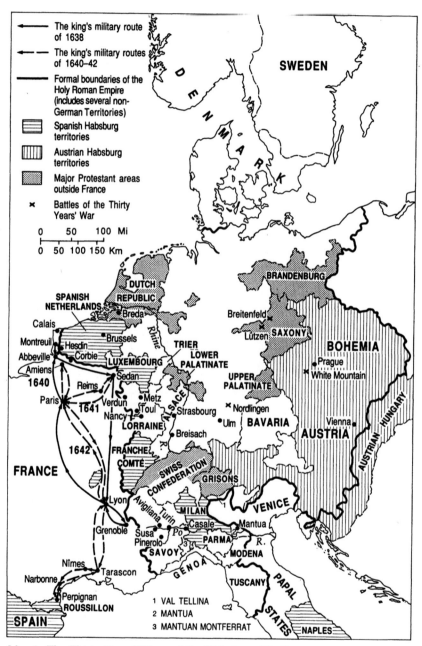

Map 4. The Thirty Years' War and the Habsburg Challenge, 1618–43

The king's military route of 1638

The king's military routes of 1640–42

Formal boundaries of the Holy Roman Empire (includes several non-German Territories)

Spanish Habsburg territories

Austrian Habsburg territories

Major Protestant areas outside France

× Battles of the Thirty Years' War

0   50   100 Mi
0   50 100 150 Km

SWEDEN

DENMARK

BRANDENBURG

DUTCH REPUBLIC

SPANISH NETHERLANDS

Breda

Calais
Montreuil   Hesdin   • Brussels
Abbeville   • Corbie
Amiens
1640   Reims
Paris   1641   Verdun   • Metz
                      • Toul
Nancy
              LORRAINE
1642   FRANCHE-
             COMTÉ

FRANCE

Rhine

TRIER
LOWER PALATINATE

Breitenfeld
× Lützen   SAXONY

LUXEMBOURG
Sedan

UPPER PALATINATE

ALSACE
Strasbourg

× Nördlingen
• Ulm   BAVARIA

Breisach

SWISS CONFEDERATION   GRISONS

BOHEMIA

• Prague
White Mountain ×

Vienna
AUSTRIA

AUSTRIAN HUNGARY

Lyon
Avigliana   Turin
Grenoble   Susa   • Po
           Pinerolo
           SAVOY

MILAN
Casale
PARMA

VENICE

Mantua

R.

MODENA

Nîmes
Narbonne   Tarascon

GENOA

TUSCANY

PAPAL STATES

Perpignan
ROUSSILLON

SPAIN

1 VAL TELLINA
2 MANTUA
3 MANTUAN MONTFERRAT

NAPLES

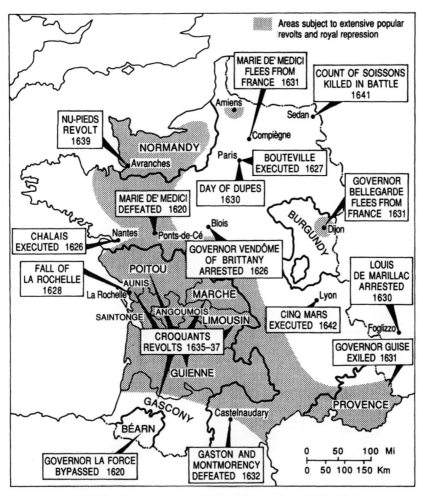

Map 5. Popular/Elite Opposition and Royal Repression, 1617–43

Areas subject to extensive popular revolts and royal repression

MARIE DE' MEDICI FLEES FROM FRANCE 1631

COUNT OF SOISSONS KILLED IN BATTLE 1641

NU-PIEDS REVOLT 1639

Amiens

Sedan

Compiègne

NORMANDY

Avranches

Paris

BOUTEVILLE EXECUTED 1627

GOVERNOR BELLEGARDE FLEES FROM FRANCE 1631

DAY OF DUPES 1630

MARIE DE' MEDICI DEFEATED 1620

Blois

BURGUNDY

Dijon

CHALAIS EXECUTED 1626

Nantes

Ponts-de-Cé

GOVERNOR VENDÔME OF BRITTANY ARRESTED 1626

LOUIS DE MARILLAC ARRESTED 1630

FALL OF LA ROCHELLE 1628

POITOU

AUNIS

La Rochelle

MARCHE

Lyon

SAINTONGE

ANGOUMOIS

LIMOUSIN

CINQ MARS EXECUTED 1642

Foglizzo

CROQUANTS REVOLTS 1635–37

GOVERNOR GUISE EXILED 1631

GUIENNE

GASCONY

PROVENCE

BÉARN

Castelnaudary

0   50   100 Mi

0 50 100 150 Km

GOVERNOR LA FORCE BYPASSED 1620

GASTON AND MONTMORENCY DEFEATED 1632

Notes

Introduction: Interpreting Louis XIII

1. Armand Baschet, *Le roi chez la reine ou histoire secrète du mariage de Louis XIII et d'Anne d'Autriche* (Paris, 1866), p. 2.

2. The biography is Pierre Chevallier's *Louis XIII: Roi cornélien* (Paris, 1979). For other studies, see the bibliography under "Biographical References to Louis XIII."

3. See the bibliography under "Louis XIII's Letters."

4. The best examples of the Louis-Richelieu correspondence are in Archives du Ministère des Affaires Etrangères (AAE), Mémoires et Documents, France (hereafter cited as France mss.), 244, 2164.

5. Bibliothèque Nationale (BN) manuscrits français (hereafter cited as mss. fr.), 4022–27; Jean [or Jehan] Héroard, *Journal sur l'enfance et la jeunesse de Louis XIII (1601–1628)*, ed. Eudore Soulié and Edouard de Barthélemy, 2 vols. (Paris, 1868).

6. Armand-Jean du Plessis, Cardinal de Richelieu, *Mémoires*, critical Société de l'Histoire de France ed. (SHF), ed. H. de Beaucaire et al., 10 vols. (Paris, 1907–31), for the period preceding 1630, and the conventional Michaud and Poujoulat ed. (MP), 2d ser., vols. 7–9 (Paris, 1836–39), for the prior years; Richelieu, *Lettres, instructions et papiers d'état*, Documents inédits ser., ed. Denis-Louis-Martial Avenel, 8 vols. (Paris, 1853–77); Richelieu, *Les papiers: Correspondance et papiers d'état. Section politique intérieure*, ed. Pierre Grillon, 5 vols. (Paris, 1975–82).

7. Elizabeth Marvick, *Louis XIII: The Making of a King* (New Haven, Conn., 1986), preface; idem, "The Character of Louis XIII: The Role of his Physician," *Journal of Interdisciplinary History* 4 (1974); see also Madeleine Foisil, "Le Journal d'Héroard, médecin de Louis XIII," *Etudes sur l'Hérault* 5

307

(1984). We will know much more on this subject and the young Louis XIII when Foisil's eagerly awaited scholarly edition of Héroard appears.

8. Even the Foreign Affairs archives have been shaped by Richelieu, including the years prior to his entry to Louis's council in 1624, by the fact that many of its holdings come from the cardinal-minister's papers.

9. Other biographies have focused on very different periods of their subjects' lives, including one of England's Henry VIII by Lacy Baldwin Smith that looks at the crotchety old man letting his guard down. Biographers of Louis XIV have detected signs of a mid-life crisis, only to hesitate to put their "hunches" in print because of a lack of conventional proof!

10. These sources are listed in the bibliography under "Contemporary Image-Making on Louis XIII."

11. The late William F. Church was especially eager to know how I would deal with that collaboration, probably knowing that I would not give Richelieu the top billing that minister received in Church's magisterial work, *Richelieu and Reason of State* (Princeton, N.J., 1972). J. Russell Major's excellent study on *Representative Government in Early Modern France* (New Haven, Conn., 1980), 450–52, exemplifies the magnetic influence of Richelieu, even on a historian hostile to him. After a fine character sketch of the teenage king Louis XIII and the suggestion that his personality lay behind the policy of "restoring order" to pre-Richelieu France, Major adds: "The evil genius of Richelieu had not yet directed his attention away from domestic reform."

12. Alexandre Dumas fils, *Les grands hommes en robe de chambre: Henri IV, Louis XIII et Richelieu* (Paris, 1877), 2:313. See also his *Three Musketeers*, Everyman ed. (London, 1911), e.g. 19: "Louis XIV absorbed all the lesser stars of his court in his own vast radiance; but his father, a sun *pluribus impar* [a play on Louis XIV's famous motto, *nec pluribus impar*, implying that the son was without equal and the father unequal to many], left his personal splendour to each of his favourites, his individual value to each of his courtiers." And, in describing the dénouement of the fictitious diamond studs affair, where Louis learns that his wife's suitor, Buckingham of England, has been assassinated (p. 633):

> The joy of the king was lively. He did not even give himself the trouble to dissemble, and displayed it with affection before the queen. Louis XIII, like every weak mind, was wanting in generosity.
> But the king soon became dull and indisposed; his brow was not one of those that long remained clear. He felt that in returning to camp he should re-enter slavery; nevertheless, he did return.
> The cardinal was for him the fascinating serpent, and himself the bird which flies from branch to branch without power to escape.

Here Dumas combines a number of Louis's well-documented flaws to create an overall effect that is simply fiction.

13. Gédéon Tallemant des Réaux, *Historiettes*, ed. Antoine Adam (Paris, 1960), 1:334–35.

14. Pierre Bayle, *Dictionnaire historique et critique*, 5th ed. (Amsterdam, 1734), 3:785–801, including n. T, p. 796, col. A (article on Louis XIII). On Bayle's views of favorites and ministers, see his articles on Timoleon, general of the Corinthians; Michel de l'Hôpital; Henry III; Concino Concini; Leonora Galligaï; and Ruffin, favorite of Emperor Theodosius. The copy I consulted is in the possession of the family of the great specialist on seventeenth-century French philosophy, Léon Brunschvig.

15. See Henri Griffet, *Histoire du règne de Louis XIII* (Paris, 1756), 3:615–16.

16. Marius Topin, *Louis XIII et Richelieu: Etude historique accompagnée des lettres inédites du roi au cardinal de Richelieu* (Paris, 1876).

17. Michel Carmona, *La France de Richelieu* (Paris, 1984), 378–79.

18. Orest Ranum, *Richelieu and the Councillors of Louis XIII: A Study of the Secretaries of State and Superintendants of Finance in the Ministry of Richelieu 1635–1642* (Oxford, 1963), 16.

19. Carmona, *La France de Richelieu*, 381, goes so far as to refer to co-decisions, in which the king alone had the "power to decide." Cf. Victor-L. Tapié, *France in the Age of Louis XIII and Richelieu*, trans. and ed. D. M. Lockie (New York, 1975); Georges Pagès, *Les institutions monarchiques en France sous Louis XIII et Louis XIV* (Paris, 1933); Geoffrey R. R. Treasure, *Cardinal Richelieu and the Development of Absolutism* (New York, 1972); Hubert Méthivier, *Le siècle de Louis XIII* (Paris, 1971).

20. See Carmona, *La France de Richelieu*, 382–83; Richelieu, *Papiers*, 1:50–51.

21. Louis Batiffol, *Le roi Louis XIII à vingt ans* (Paris, 1910); idem, *Au temps de Louis XIII* (Paris, 1903); idem, *Richelieu et le roi Louis XIII: Les véritables rapports du souverain et de son ministre* (Paris, 1934) (a later work more measured in its judgments and handling of sources); Charles Romain, *Louis XIII: Un grand roi méconnu, 1601–1643* (Paris, 1934); Louis Vaunois, *Vie de Louis XIII*, 2d ed. (Paris, 1961).

22. Chevallier, *Louis XIII*, 648. Interestingly following his conclusion Chevallier adds an appendix with the above-quoted passage from Griffet.

23. See, e.g., Georges Mongrédien, *Etude sur la vie de Nicolas Vauquelin* (Paris, 1921), 75–76.

24. On Ariès and Hunt, see Marvick, *Louis XIII*, xviii–xvix.

25. Paul Guillon, *La mort de Louis XIII: Etude d'histoire médicale* (Paris, 1897), 132; J.-M. Guardin, *La médecine à travers les siècles* (Paris, 1865), 314.

26. Marvick, *Louis XIII*, introduction and conclusion.

27. Ibid., epilogue, 220–24. In her earlier, preliminary article, "Childhood History and Decisions of State: The Case of Louis XIII," *Journal of Psychohistory* 2 (1974): 198, Marvick's role for Louis seems to parallel mine: "Moote's apparent view is that Louis was more likely than his minister to be the force behind the policies adopted. This is also mine." She adds, "for the moment I would . . . suggest that [Richelieu] 'learned' Louis very well."

28. Pierre Goubert's *Louis XIV and Twenty Million Frenchmen*, trans. Anne Carter (New York, 1975), and Robert Mandrou's *Louis XIV en son temps* (Paris, 1973) are brilliant examples of the Annaliste reduction of political leaders to a role very subordinate to structures, conjunctures, and collective mentalités. This is true also of what is perhaps the greatest of all histories written in the twentieth century, Fernand Braudel's two-volume masterpiece *The Mediterranean and the Mediterranean World in the Age of Philip II*, 2d ed., 2 vols., trans. Siân Reynolds (New York, 1972–73). A well-known anecdote relates that when Braudel first met his mentor, Lucien Febvre, and said he wanted to work on Philip II and the Mediterranean, Febvre replied that it was a good topic but that an even better one would be "The Mediterranean and Philip II." For the strengths and weaknesses of the Annales school, see my essay "The *Annales* Historians," *Queen's Quarterly* 85 (1978).

29. A superb summation of the Annales economic and social findings which touches on their connection with the growth of royal taxation and bureaucracy can be found in Fernand Braudel and Ernest Labrousse, gen. eds. *Histoire économique et sociale de la France* (Paris, 1977–83), vol. 1, esp. pt. 1, *L'état et la ville [1450–1660]*, ed. Pierre Chaunu and Richard Gascon.

30. Carlo Ginzburg, *The Cheese and the Worms: The Cosmos of a Sixteenth-Century Miller*, trans. John Tedeschi and Anne Tedeschi (Baltimore, 1980).

31. I refer here to Madeleine Foisil's banquet address, "La formation de Louis XIII," and her panel discussion with Elizabeth Marvick on "Seeking the Real Louis XIII," moderated by myself, at the thirteenth annual meeting of the Western Society for French History in 1985, at Edmonton, Canada.

32. An earlier version of the differences between Elizabeth Marvick and myself over the use of psychology can be found in our exchange in her "Childhood History," 191–98. In that critique, I questioned the importance of psychological findings about the young Louis XIII in shedding light on his statecraft. My position now is that any psychological insight is helpful, but that one has to be careful not to transfer back to the subject under investigation cultural, social, or intellectual norms (such as the concept of sadism) that either were not part of that age or must be proved to have been.

33. Robert Darnton, *The Great Cat Massacre and Other Episodes in French Cultural History* (New York, 1984).

34. Among works published right up to the time I completed this book, there are especially strong representations by Sharon Kettering, William Beik, and Richard Bonney of the importance of systems within which Louis XIII worked.

35. Braudel, *The Mediterranean*, vol. 2, especially the conclusion.

1. A Dauphin's World

1. The account by Héroard can be compared with that of Louis's midwife, Louise Bourgeois [or Boursier], *Récit véritable de la naissance de messei-*

gneurs et dames les enfans de France, in *Archives curieuses,* ed. M. L. Cimber and F. Danjou, 1st ser., vol. 14 (Paris, 1837).

2. On the changing political climate, see Roland Mousnier's superb study, *The Assassination of Henry IV: The Tyrannicide Problem and the Consolidation of the French Absolute Monarchy in the Early Seventeenth Century,* trans. Joan Spencer (London, 1973); David Buisseret, *Henry IV* (London, 1984); and Mark Greengrass, *France in the Age of Henri IV: The Struggle for Stability* (London, 1984).

3. There is a revisionist doctoral dissertation by Ronald S. Love, *"The Religion of Henri IV: Faith, Politics, and War, 1553–1593"* (1987); and an equally provocative analysis of Catholic assumptions by Michael Wolfe, "The Conversion of Henri IV and the Origins of Bourbon Absolutism," *Historical Reflections* 14 (1987). On Henry IV and the Huguenots, see also George A. Rothrock, *The Huguenots: A Biography of a Minority* (Chicago, 1979).

4. Héroard, *Journal,* 1:427.

5. Tallemant des Réaux, *Historiettes,* 1:60.

6. Compare my view of Louis's personality with that of Marvick in "Childhood History" and *Louis XIII,* chaps. 1–6, where she stresses external molding as opposed to the dauphin's intrinsic qualities.

7. Charles Bernard, *Histoire du roy Louis XIII, 1601–1643* (Paris, 1646), 1:5–7.

8. BN ms. fr. 4022, fol. 503.

9. On the uncritical side, see Lucy Crump, *Nursery Life 300 years Ago: The Story of a Dauphin of France, 1601–29* (London, 1929); and Ida A. Taylor, *The Making of a King: The Childhood of Louis XIII* (London, 1910). Louis Batiffol's somewhat idealized young Louis, in *Au temps de Louis XIII,* is useful because it quotes extensively from Héroard's manuscript journal. Philippe Ariès in *Centuries of Childhood: The Social History of Family Life,* trans. R. Baldick (London, 1962), sees Louis's childhood as typical of premodern extended families in which children were very quickly, if coldly, integrated into adult relationships. David Hunt's *Parents and Children in History: The Psychology of Family Life in Early Modern France* (New York, 1970) is harsher on Louis's entourage, but his criticism is muted by his assumption that the dauphin's nurturing was typical of the time. The most severe critic of Louis's entourage as being both nasty and untypical is Marvick, whose articles and book on Louis are summarized in *Proceedings of the Western Society for French History,* 13:50.

10. See Héroard, *Journal,* 1:177–82, 374; François Annibal d'Estrées, *Mémoires,* SHF ed., ed. P. Bonnefon (Paris, 1910); and François Duval de Fontenay-Mareuil, *Mémoires,* MP ed., 2d ser., vol. 5 (Paris, 1837), 27.

11. Compare Héroard's account, *Journal,* 1:83–96; and Marvick's interpretation, "Childhood History," 156–57, on this incident. Marvick's rendering of the published abridgment of Héroard is literal here, and somewhat freer in the wording and ordering of the sequence at other points in her analysis (e.g., in quoting a February 1604 altercation between mother, father, and dauphin, cf. Marvick, "Childhood History," 153, and Héroard, *Journal,* 1:63). Obvi-

ously, the differences between Marvick and myself in rendering some words and sequences contribute to our differing views of the young dauphin's personality and its external molding. For the first 3 1/4 years of Louis's life, however, we cannot be absolutely certain of Héroard's original wording and chronology of emotional scenes involving the heir's little world, since only a condensed version of the original manuscript remains, edited or written by Héroard's nephew, Simon Courtaud (BN ms. fr. nouvelles acquisitions 13008 [hereafter cited as nouv. acq.]). Thereafter we *can* see how much the original manuscript by Héroard himself (BN mss. fr. 4022–27) differs from the Courtaud condensation and the published Soulié/Barthélemy edition, in both sequence and wording, and ultimately meaning. This situation makes even more significant the future edition by Madeleine Foisil of the original journal, which Marvick, Foisil, and several other scholars have gone through but is too massive to quote or cite extensively in a short, one-volume biography of Louis XIII's entire life.

12. For a few examples of how the dauphin's entourage alternated between making him a spoiled brat, crushing his ego, and applying firm, caring discipline after the hat episode, see BN ms. fr. 4022, fols. 1r, 13r–14r, 16v–17r, 156r, 481r; and François de Malherbe, *Oeuvres*, Grands Ecrivains de la France ed., ed. M. L. Lalanne (Paris, 1862), 3:130–31, who notes regarding Louis's fit after losing at chess: "The queen heard about it, and had him whipped by M. de Souvray, and commanded [the latter] to raise him to be more gracious; she deemed this necessary because this prince, while being extremely generous, will not brook any failure to yield to him."

13. On mother, father, and heir, see Batiffol, *Au temps de Louis XIII*, 51n.1, quoting the Venetian ambassador; and Auguste-François Anis, *Etude historique et littéraire: David Rivault de Fleurance et les autres précepteurs de Louis XIII* (Paris, 1893), 69, quoting the papal nuncio. Marvick follows the tradition of playing down Marie's role. By contrast, Batiffol, especially in his biography of Marie, is unrelentingly hostile, perhaps because he wants to show only the good side of Louis.

14. For the above quotes, see Louis Batiffol, *La vie intime d'une reine de France au XVIIe siècle: Marie de Médicis (1600–1617)*, 2 vols. (Paris, 1906), 1:269–70, 272; BN ms. fr. 3818 (correspondence of Louis XIII and his family), fols. 6–7.

15. BN ms. fr. 4022, fols. 155v–56r; and Héroard, *Journal*, 1:157.

16. Buisseret, *Henry IV*, 108–10, judiciously summarizes Henry IV's relations with Marie around the time of the dauphin's birth, placing most of the blame on the husband for their last nine years of "mutual recrimination and misunderstandings."

17. Pierre de L'Estoile, *Mémoires-Journaux*, ed. G. Brunet et al. (Paris, 1875–96), 7:321.

18. Buisseret, *Henry IV*, 109.

19. *Mercure françois* (Paris, 1605–44), 1:102.

20. On the preceding episodes, see Héroard, *Journal*, 1:42, 45–46, 68–69,

73, 83, 87. Cf. Batiffol, *Au temps de Louis XIII*, 14–15nn., and idem, *Louis XIII à vingt ans.*

21. Compare the study by Louis's preceptor Nicolas Vauquelin des Yveteaux, *L'institution du prince* (1643), in *Oeuvres complètes*, ed. G. Mongrédien (Paris, 1921), 160, and Marvick's articles and her *Louis XIII*. Among Héroard's remedies, Marvick includes the cutting of the membrane under the infant dauphin's tongue, at the physician's "behest." That is a reasonable inference, but Héroard's journal simply records the surgeon doing it.

22. BN ms. fr. 4022, fols. 24r, 30v; Héroard, *Journal*, 1:45, 76, 80, 108–9, 119, 123, 135.

23. Thirteenth annual conference of the Western Society for French History, address and panel discussion by Foisil.

24. BN ms. fr. 3798 (Louis XIII's personal family correspondence), fols. 12, 32, 45. My interpretation of these letters and of Louis's relationship with Mme de Montglat differs from that of Marvick, who calls the governess "despised, abused, and abusing," and concludes that Louis never exhibited the slightest spark of tender feeling for her (Marvick, "The Childhood of Louis XIII," *Proceedings of the Western Society for French History* 13 [1986]: 50; idem, *Louis XIII*, chap. 4, incl. n. 33).

25. See Héroard, *Journal*, vol. 1, lxii–lxiii. For a very different view, see Marvick's "Character of Louis XIII," 369–71, where Louis's attachment to Héroard is described as unhealthy and ambivalent. That theme is further developed in her *Louis XIII*.

26. See, e.g., Guardin, *La médecine*, 313–15.

27. BN ms. fr. 4022, fols. 28v, 426r, 441–43. Two of Louis's sketches from the ages of five and six are reproduced in Marvick, "Childhood History," 155, 160.

28. Héroard, *Journal*. 1:149, 160–61, 171, 205, 260.

29. Ibid., 1:246, 270–72.

30. Héroard's *De l'institution du prince* is reprinted in the appendices to Héroard, *Journal*, vol. 2. Marvick's *Louis XIII* has a fresh perspective on that work.

31. Héroard, *Journal*, 1:312, 364.

32. Ibid., 1:386.

33. Fontenay-Mareuil, *Mémoires*, 76–77.

34. Malherbe, *Oeuvres*, 3:131.

35. BN ms. fr. 3798, fol. 44. Again, Marvick's interpretation of Louis's adaptation of royal virtues differs; see her *Louis XIII*, chap. 7.

36. Unfortunately, the only trace of the address by Madeleine Foisil at the thirteenth annual conference of the Western Society for French History and the subsequent panel discussion between Marvick and Foisil is a one-page abridgment of Marvick's formal response (see Introduction, n. 31, above). I have incorporated aspects of that extraordinary *colloque* in this chapter, and am indebted to both participants for their insights. For an excellently balanced analysis of the dauphin's world that lies between Marvick's and Foisil's

views, see Hester W. Chapman, "Louis XIII (1601–1643)," in *Privileged Persons: Four Seventeenth-Century Studies* (New York, 1966). It is interesting that Foisil shuns the unpleasant sides of the dauphin's world, whereas Marvick omits the supportive elements.

2. The Boy King

1. See Greengrass, *France in the Age of Henry IV*, 192–207.

2. See especially Jean Baptiste Matthieu, *Histoire de Louis XIII*, in Pierre Matthieu, *Histoire de Henri IV*, vol. 2 (Paris, 1631), 1–4; and Héroard, *Journal*, 2:4.

3. The official royal account, in *Mercure françois*, omits Brûlart's gesture. On political thought, see E. Thuau, *Raison d'état et pensée politique à l'époque de Richelieu* (Paris, 1966), 16–18.

4. Godefroy Hermant, "Histoire de Beauvais: Les débuts du règne de Louis XIII," in *Louis XIII et Richelieu: Lettres et pièces diplomatiques*, ed. Eugène Griselle (Paris, 1911), 73–74, is an excellent but little-known account. Cf. *Mercure françois*, 1:424; and L'Estoile, *Mémoires-Journaux*, vol. 10, incl. supplement.

5. For the *lit*, see Hermant, "Histoire de Beauvais"; and Griffet, *Histoire du règne de Louis XIII*, 1:14–17, which is based on extensive contemporary manuscripts.

6. On the constitutional implications of the *lit*, see especially Sarah Hanley, *The Lit de Justice of the Kings of France: Constitutional Ideology in Legend, Ritual, and Discourse* (Princeton, N.J., 1983), 243–53. Hanley's emphasis on ceremony and rhetoric, which makes her study so novel and exciting, leads her to read greater constitutional importance into the events of 14–15 May than the fast-paced but often unrehearsed acts by regent and judges seems to indicate. Mousnier, *Assassination of Henry IV*, 232–35, provides some details not in Hanley, while making the entire crisis look less scary than it was.

7. The funeral arrangements and ceremonies can be followed in the *Mercure françois*. For the shifting constitutional meaning of the royal succession from medieval to early modern forms, see Ralph E. Giesey, *The Royal Funeral Ceremony in Renaissance France* (Geneva, 1960); Ernst H. Kantorowicz, *The King's Two Bodies: A Study in Medieval Political Theory* (Princeton, N.J., 1957); and Richard A. Jackson, *Vive le Roi! A History of the French Coronation from Charles V to Charles X* (Chapel Hill, N.C., 1984).

8. Jackson places the *sacre* of Louis XIII at the center of the ceremony's historical evolution, depicting the coronation of 1610 as "a display of royal grandeur and dynastic succession."

9. For the *sacre*, see Matthieu, *Histoire de Louis XIII*, 10–20; *Mercure françois*, 1:530–42; and Hermant, "Histoire de Beauvais," 93.

10. See Marc Bloch, *The Royal Touch: Sacred Monarchy and Scrofula in England and France* (London, 1972), and my review of it in *Queen's Quarterly* 81 (1974).

11. A detailed, sympathetic study of Marie is contained in J. Michael Hay-

den, *France and the Estates General of 1614* (Cambridge, 1974). The regent's way of governing, in consultation with those she trusted, is treated fairly by the eighteenth-century scholar Griffet, who follows the contemporary evaluation of Estrées closely.

12. Mousnier's *Assassination of Henry IV* is as definitive a treatment as we will ever see of the aftermath. A relevant article is Harriet L. Lightman's "Queens and Minor Kings in French Constitutional Law," *Proceedings of the Western Society for French History* 9 (1981); see also her 1981 Bryn Mawr College doctoral dissertation of the same title.

13. On Marie, Louis, and the Huguenots, see L'Estoile, *Mémoires-Journaux*, 10:333–34; Héroard, *Journal*, 2:51, 117; Malherbe, *Oeuvres*, 3:466; Vaunois, *Vie de Louis XIII*, 140; François-Thommy Perrens, *L'église et l'état en France sous le règne de Henri IV et la régence de Marie de Médicis* (Paris, 1872), 2:90n.1. For the religious and other aspects of the young Louis XIII's apprenticeship as king, see Marvick, *Louis XIII*, chaps. 7–10.

14. On Louis's education see L'Estoile, *Mémoires-Journaux*, 10:316; Héroard, *Journal*, 2:71; Perrens, *L'église et l'état*, 2:90n.1; Vauquelin, *L'institution du prince*; and Anis, *David Rivault de Fleurance*.

15. On Marie's foreign policy, cf. Jean-Hippolyte Mariéjol, *Henri IV et Louis XIII (1598–1643)*, vol. 6, pt. 2 of *Histoire de France depuis les origines jusqu'à la Révolution*, ed. Ernest Lavisse (Paris, 1905), 153–54; J. Michael Hayden, "Continuity in the France of Henry IV and Louis XIII: French Foreign Policy, 1598–1615," *Journal of Modern History* 45 (1973); and idem, *Estates General*, 34–53.

16. On Louis's incipient bon Français orientation, see Héroard, *Journal*, 2:89; L'Estoile, *Mémoires-Journaux*, 10:4, 381. One has to be careful with evidence on the young king's views of Jesuits, Leaguers, and Huguenots, since most contemporary observers had strong biases: anti-Leaguer Catholics and Protestants said Louis did not like being surrounded by Jesuits, and the papal nuncio said that Louis considered Huguenots to be "bad servitors."

17. Malherbe, *Oeuvres*, 389–90.

18. *Mercure françois*, 3(1):317–27.

19. Ibid., 330–55.

20. In sorting out the complicated maneuvering, motivations, and responsibilities for royal policy I rely heavily on Hayden, *Estates General*. See also the balanced assessment by Richard Bonney, *The King's Debts: Finance and Politics in France, 1589–1661* (Oxford, 1981), 77. For varying contemporary assessments, see Fontenay-Mareuil, *Mémoires*; Matthieu, *Histoire de Louis XIII*; Malherbe, *Oeuvres*; the near-contemporary G. Girard, *Histoire de la vie du duc d'Epernon* (Paris, 1655); and Griffet, *Historie du règne de Louis XIII*.

21. See Héroard, *Journal*, 2:49; Chevallier, *Louis XIII*, 151.

22. Malherbe, *Oeuvres*, 3:398–400; Héroard, *Journal*, 2:134.

23. On Louis, see Malherbe, *Oeuvres*, 3:392, 399.

24. See Héroard, *Journal*, 2:133–34; Malherbe, *Oeuvres*, 3:389, 393–94, 417–18; Matthieu, *Histoire de Louis XIII*, 31–32; Girard, *La vie du duc d'Epernon*,

269. The pardoned nobleman resumed his old ways a year later and eventually died from a duel. Probably Louis heard of that just conclusion.

25. Héroard, *Journal*, 2:137; Chevallier, *Louis XIII*, 150. Louis's words on hearing of the treaty were: "Peace is made; I think it was the [official] prayers of forty hours that caused it."

26. See the verbatim report of Louis's historian Bernard, *Histoire du roy Louis XIII*, 1:33.

27. Malherbe, *Oeuvres*, 3:414.

28. Morgard was released from galley service in 1619, and this time wrote an almanac predicting only good things for Louis XIII! See Hayden, "The Uses of Political Pamphlets: The Example of the Estates General of 1614–15 in France," *Canadian Journal of History* 21 (1986); and idem, *Estates General*, 57 (text and nn. 6, 7). There is an excellent University of California, Berkeley, doctoral dissertation by Jeffrey Sawyer, "Printed Propaganda and Political Power in Early Seventeenth-Century France, 1614–1617" (1982), now being turned into a book.

29. Héroard, *Journal*, 2:153. For the trip, see the accounts by *Mercure françois*, Héroard, and Malherbe.

30. See Hayden, "Political Pamphlets," 148–49.

31. *Mercure françois*, 3(1):285–88; Malherbe, *Oeuvres*, 3:460.

32. C. Rossignol, *Louis XIII avant Richelieu* (Paris, 1869), 27–30, comments on the uncertainty of when and in what context the sobriquet was first used. Tallemant's explanation typically twists the facts, turning Louis's self-deprecating remark into an explanation that Richelieu gave the king his sobriquet to avoid having him called "the stammerer" (*Historiettes*, 1:334–35).

33. See Malherbe, *Oeuvres*, 3:464; *Mercure françois*, 3(1):361–63, 488–89.

34. BN Cabinet des Estampes, series Qb[1] "Histoire de France," 1614.

35. Chevallier, *Louis XIII*, 150–51, quotes the ambassador. For specific mother-son conflicts, see Héroard, *Journal*, 2:22, 53; L'Estoile, *Mémoires-Journaux*, 10:348; Fontenay-Mareuil, *Mémoires*, 74.

36. Louis's sharp tongue is given a prominent place in Marvick's *Louis XIII*. The story of Louis's preceptor Fleurance dying from an altercation (which is suspect from the start because it was told by the teacher's jealous predecessor, Vauquelin) goes as follows: One of Louis's pet dogs bit Fleurance on the leg; the tutor kicked the dog and caused it to whine; Louis in anger gave Fleurance several punches, "affecting the said sieur de Fleurance so much that he took to his bed, where fever overcame him, and he died of it soon after" (Vauquelin, *L'institution du prince*, 176–77).

37. Matthieu, *Histoire de Louis XIII*, 33; Héroard, *Journal*, 2:159.

38. See, inter alia, Malherbe, *Oeuvres*, 3:464.

3. King, Estates, and State

1. "Correspondance de Marie de Médicis et de Louis XIII [1614, 1617]," in *Revue rétrospective ou bibliothèque historique, contenant les mémoires et docu-*

ments pour servir à l'histoire, ed. M. J. Taschereau, 20 vols. (Paris 1833–38), 16:433–34.

2. The best treatment of the subject is Hayden, *Estates General.* See also George Rothrock's two excellent articles, "The French Crown and the Estates General of 1614," *French Historical Studies* 1 (1960), and "Officials and King's Men: A Note on the Possibilities of Royal Control in the Estates General," *French Historical Studies* 2 (1962); and Bonney, *King's Debts.*

3. Mousnier, *Assassination of Henry IV*, 280.

4. See Major's corrective to Mousnier's extreme view, in *Representative Government*, 406–7.

5. Roland Mousnier's monumental two-volume *Les institutions de la France sous la monarchie absolue, 1589–1789* (Paris, 1974–80) is by far the best introduction to the social basis of early modern French government; cf. my review in *American Historical Review* 86 (1981). The studies of sixteenth-century institutions by Roger Doucet (*Les institutions de la France au XVIe siècle,* 2 vols. [Paris, 1948]) and Gaston Zeller (*Les institutions de la France au XVIe siècle,* 2d ed. [Paris, 1987]) are still quite useful, however, as is Pierre Adolphe Chéruel's institutional dictionary with its emphasis on the seventeenth century (*Dictionnaire historique des institutions, moeurs et coutumes de la France,* 2 vols. [Paris, 1910]). One of my favorite works remains the often ignored and frequently maligned Vicomte Georges d'Avenel, *Richelieu et la monarchie absolue,* 4 vols. (Paris, 1895) (the author of which is often confused with the editor of Richelieu's correspondence, Denis-L.-M. Avenel).

6. The dukes and peers are the subject of Jean-Pierre Labatut's exhaustive study *Les ducs et pairs de France au XVIIe siècle* (Paris, 1972). On the governors, see Robert Harding, *The Anatomy of a Power Elite: The Provincial Governors of Early Modern France* (New Haven, Conn., 1978).

7. Compare Mousnier's classic *La vénalité des offices sous Henri IV et Louis XIII* (Rouen, 1945; 2d ed. Paris, 1971), which stresses the monarchy's success in manipulating the paulette renewals, and my *Revolt of the Judges: The Parlement of Paris and the Fronde, 1643–1652* (Princeton, N.J., 1971), where emphasis is on the dangers the monarchy encountered. James B. Collins, *Direct Taxation in Early Seventeenth-Century France* (Berkeley and Los Angeles, 1988), reassesses the effectiveness of both the political and the financial policies of the monarchy concerning the paulette.

8. Pierre Blet's excellent *Clergé de France et la monarchie: Etude sur les Assemblées générales du Clergé de 1615 à 1666,* vol. 1 (Rome, 1959), passes over the patronage aspects of the subject.

9. Hayden, *Estates General,* is definitive on the composition of all three estates.

10. Apart from the original controversy between Roland Mousnier, as advocate of the "society of orders" conception, and Boris Porchnev, as expounder of a class conflict interpretation, there is a gentle, yet firm modification of Mousnier's now accepted thesis in Hayden, *Estates General,* 86–88.

11. See Mousnier, *Assassination of Henry IV*, for an extreme version of this interpretation.

12. On the Gallican episode, see Robert Arnauld d'Andilly, *Journal, 1614–1620*, ed. Achille Halphen and Edmond Halphen (Paris, 1857), 23–29; Héroard, *Journal*, 2:172; Perrens, *L'église et l'état*, 2:287–88; and *Mercure françois*, 3(2):348. Blet's incomparable command of the sources is somewhat undermined by hesitation to believe that the clergy would become involved in an embarrassingly bitter shouting match; see *Clergé de France*, 1:74–75, incl. n. 141.

13. Arnauld d'Andilly, *Journal, 1614–1620*, 46, 51; and Berthold Zeller, *Louis XIII: Marie de Médicis, chef du conseil (1614–1616)* (Paris, 1898), 77–78, provide the political coloring that the official *Mercure françois*, 3(2):230, omits.

14. *Mercure françois*, 3(2):64.

15. Ibid., 211–22.

16. See ibid., 405–15, for the speech.

17. My view of Luçon's speech was formulated before reading Elizabeth Marvick's *The Young Richelieu: A Psychoanalytic Approach to Leadership* (Chicago, 1983), 213. I agree wholeheartedly with her conclusion that the future Cardinal Richelieu's speech in 1615 "painted a dazzling picture" of the king he hoped to make Louis XIII into, though my emphasis is on how the king fitted the picture into his own worldview rather than on Richelieu offering himself as a "surrogate for the king."

18. *Mercure françois*, 3(2):91, 95–101.

19. Quoted in Hayden, *Estates General*, 105.

20. *Mercure françois*, 3(2):191.

21. The first quotation is from Major, *Representative Government*, 409; the second, from Hayden, *Estates General*, 197.

22. *Mercure françois*, 3(2):425.

23. Mathieu Molé, *Mémoires* (really documents), SHF ed., ed. Aimé Champollion-Figeac (Paris, 1855–57), 1:20–21.

24. A first-rate history is Joseph H. Shennan's *Parlement of Paris* (London, 1968); see also my *Revolt of the Judges*, chap. 1.

25. Molé, *Mémoires*, 1:27. A slightly different version can be found in Griffet, *Histoire du règne de Louis XIII*, 1:102.

26. See Fontenay-Mareuil, *Mémoires*, 86; and Arnauld d'Andilly, *Journal, 1614–1620*, 73–74.

27. See Griffet, *Histoire du règne de Louis XIII*, 1:102–6; Molé, *Mémoires*, 1:27–52; and Arnauld d'Andilly, *Journal, 1614–1620*, 75–79. Cf. my *Revolt of the Judges*, 56–58. The manner in which the monarchy responded to the parlementary challenge of 1615 contradicts Richelieu's later claim that Marie and her entourage did not feel threatened. Perhaps the cardinal-minister's interpretation was based on his own views of the Parlement. In later years it was Louis XIII who bristled at parlementary acts, while Richelieu sought to placate him enough to work out a compromise.

28. See B. Zeller, *Marie de Médicis, chef du conseil*, 26–27.

4. *Royal Marriage and Coup d'Etat*

1. Matthieu, *Histoire de Louis XIII*, 36.
2. Quoted in Gabriel Hanotaux and duc de La Force, *Histoire du Cardinal de Richelieu* (Paris, 1893–1947), 2:105.
3. See Chevallier, *Louis XIII*, 150–51; Hanotaux and La Force, *Cardinal de Richelieu*, 2:105, both quoting the Venetian ambassador.
4. A good sketch of Luynes's early career can be found in Chevallier, *Louis XIII*, 153–59.
5. On this episode, see B. Zeller, *Marie de Médicis, chef du conseil*, 25–26, quoting the Florentine ambassador; Héroard, *Journal*, 2:164–67.
6. Malherbe, *Oeuvres*, 3:490.
7. Héroard, *Journal*, 2:176–77, 179.
8. Malherbe, *Oeuvres*, 3:501–2.
9. Fontenay-Mareuil, *Mémoires*, 84.
10. See Bernard, *Histoire du roy Louis XIII*, 1:55; Matthieu, *Histoire de Louis XIII*, 50.
11. Héroard, *Journal*, 2:183–84; BN ms. fr. 4025, fol. 213r–v (the fuller manuscript version of Héroard); Bernard, *Histoire du roy Louis XIII*, 1:58; and B. Zeller, *Marie de Médicis, chef du conseil*, 172–73.
12. On the marriage events, see BN ms. fr. 4025, fols. 222–24; Héroard, *Journal*, 2:185–86; "Ce qui s'est passé lors de la consommation du mariage du roi", in *Revue rétrospective*, 2:252; Tallemant des Réaux, *Historiettes*, 1:333. Cf. also the reconstructions by Armand Baschet, *Le roi chez la reine ou histoire secrète du mariage de Louis XIII et d'Anne d'Autriche* (Paris, 1866), 181–208 (based on excellent sources); Louis Vaunois, *Vie de Louis XIII*, 2d ed. (Paris, 1961), 192–98 (a more balanced account); Ruth Kleinman, *Anne of Austria: Queen of France* (Columbus, Ohio, 1985), 25–27 (which plays down the unusualness of the official consummation); and Chevallier, *Louis XIII*, 100–102 (which focuses more on Marie's intentions than on Anne and Louis's ordeal). Historians' second-hand reading of Héroard's account does not inspire the greatest of confidence. The physician's nineteenth-century editors were so embarrassed by his reference to Louis's *glande rouge* that they abbreviated it as *g... rouge*. Most scholars have followed that puritanical omission, while a few writers, assuming that Héroard recorded the popular term that he and the rest of the king's entourage had used in teasing Louis during his early childhood, have filled in the phrase as *guillery rouge*. Only Marvick has taken the trouble to read what Héroard actually wrote in his manuscript, and hence she gets the doctor's phrase right.
13. Héroard, *Journal*, 2:202. On the context of the arrest, see Arnauld d'Andilly, *Journal*, *1614–1620*; Matthieu, *Histoire de Louis XIII*; and Griffet, *Histoire du règne de Louis XIII*.
14. To understand this promising ministry, historians will have to get beyond two rival misconceptions: first, that anything associated with Concini

must have been bad or ineffectual, and second, that everything related to the future Richelieu must have been inspired. Barbin, in particular, needs reexamination, even though his handwriting is impossible. Marvick's *Young Richelieu* stops at the closure of the Estates General of 1614–15; her *Louis XIII* touches on the triumvirate's maneuvering.

15. Héroard, *Journal*, 2:194.

16. Matthieu, *Histoire de Louis XIII*, 60. Héroard, *Journal*, 2:196, has a crisper version: "That's how one has to treat the stubborn and bad" (after angrily hitting the disobedient dog hard) and "reward the good men just as much as dogs" (giving the same dog a biscuit when it obeyed his command). Louis had similarly settled a dispute between his foot valets and pages of the stable over who should escort him at his majority; he had his former governor give a dozen baton blows to the *valet de pied* that Louis considered to be "the most seditious," after the valets questioned his will three times. See Malherbe, *Oeuvres*, 3:455.

17. We await a first-rate study of Concini and Galigaï. Georges Mongrédien's *Léonora Galigaï: Un procès de sorcellerie sous Louis XIII* (Paris, 1968), although factually sound, is as weak in interpretation as studies of the couple by George Delamare (*Le maréchal d'Ancre* [Paris, 1961]), Fernand Hayem, (*Le maréchal d'Ancre et Léonora Galigaï* [Paris, 1910]), and Alfred Franklin (*La cour de France et l'assassinat du maréchal d'Ancre* [Paris, 1913]).

18. In his memoirs, Richelieu later allowed himself the liberty of saying of his early benefactor that he could not have had an intimate liaison with Marie because of a double hernia.

19. This was not an isolated incident. Another crowd had blocked Concini's departure from the capital; hostile justices then condemned the favorite's henchmen to death for beating up a shoemaker who had led the throng; and a howling mob stopped an attempt to cut the guilty down from the gallows.

20. François de Paul de Clermont, marquis de Montglat, *Mémoires*, MP ed., 3d ser., vol. 5 (Paris, 1938), 11.

21. On these incidents, see Malherbe, *Oeuvres*, 3:368, 373–74; and Héroard, *Journal*, 2:58. In trying to change court protocol, Concini was on the right track when he said that "the king had been treated as a joke, but he would have [Louis] treated as a monarch." Had he encouraged the king to speak for himself, the favorite might not have mortally offended his sovereign.

22. On one occasion, Louis was ordered to assure the colonels, captains, and district militia leaders of the capital that rumors of Concini disbanding their forces were false.

23. The most objective account is Estrées, *Mémoires*, 135–43; see also Bernard, *Histoire du roy Louis XIII*. Richelieu's views can be followed in his *Mémoires*.

24. Henri de Rohan, *Mémoires*, MP ed., 2d ser., vol. 5 (Paris, 1837), 510.

25. The papal nuncio was the reporter here, as cited by Vittorio Siri, *Mémoires secrets, tirés des archives des souverains en l'Europe contenant le règne de Louis XIII. Oeuvre traduit de l'italien* (Amsterdam, 1774–84), 12:20. Bernard, *Histoire du roy Louis XIII*, 1:76, is equally worth quoting: "It was greatly displeasing to [the king] that a male and female foreigner, whose background was so obscure, should cause his entire kingdom to go up in flames, thwarting his will, wresting from him the means to display his courage."

26. On these events, see Arnauld d'Andilly, *Journal, 1610–1614*, 221–22, 224; and Héroard, *Journal*, 2:202–4. Héroard's account rings true, but he was also clearly upset by a recent fight with Concini to keep his post as Louis's doctor.

27. On the plot, compare Guichard de Déageant, *Mémoires envoyez à M. le Cardinal de Richelieu* (Grenoble, 1668), and Jean de Caumont de Montpouillan, *Mémoires*, in Jacques Nompar de Caumont, duc de La Force, *Mémoires*, ed. marquis de La Grange, vol. 4 (Paris, 1843). Other leading accounts are those of Matthieu, *Histoire de Louis XIII*; Bernard, *Histoire du roy Louis XIII*; Montglat, *Mémoires*; Paul Phélypeaux de Pontchartrain, *Mémoires*, MP ed., 2d ser. vol. 5 (Paris, 1837); and a witness now assumed to be Luynes's brother, Honoré d'Albert de Cadenet, duc de Chaulnes, *Relation exacte de tout ce qui s'est passé à la mort du mareschal d'Ancre*, MP ed., 2d ser., vol. 5 (Paris, 1837). Marvick, *Louis XIII*, has the most penetrating scholarly reconstruction; see below, n. 29.

28. Cf. La Force, *Mémoires*, 4:32–33; Déageant, *Mémoires*, 44; and the excellent account by a newsletter writer, Nicolas Pasquier, in Etienne Pasquier, *Oeuvres*, vol. 2, cols. 1273–82. Mongrédien, *Léonora Galigaï*, 149n.1, concludes that Montpouillan appeared to exaggerate his role. Later on, Montpouillan proved to be an impetuous doer and, eventually, a reluctant rebel, while Déageant went on to become an excellent administrator fully capable both of taking responsibilty and of shifting with the political wind. The argument over which of these two men brought about Louis's acquiescence in Concini's likely assassination is without end.

29. I differ with Elizabeth Marvick's conclusion that Louis XIII directly ordered a murder: "By 1616 he seems to have conceived the plan of killing Ancre in order to seize power in fact"; and (in reply to my commentary) "in my view Louis did intend for Concini to be killed and he did communicate this intention to the murderers" (Marvick, "Childhood History," 173, 197). Marvick's *Louis XIII*, chap. 14, expands on that thesis, but with the qualification that "probably Louis tried, in giving orders for the murder, to avoid being explicit." Our difference in interpretations can be attributed to ambiguity in the sources themselves as well as to our divergent views of Louis's personality. A cryptic account handed down by Luynes's brother Chaulnes to the jurist d'Ormesson family exists, but it does not help to clarify the problem (Bibliothèque Municipale de Rouen [BMR], ms. Leber 5767 [2], fol. 5v). Here the first plan was to take the king to Amboise; when that was prevented,

"finally [Ancre's] death was decided on, [causing] the king anxiety . . . since more than twenty persons knew the plot for over four days, and still the marshal was not alerted." Chaulnes's longer account has Louis making long speeches on "the resolution I have taken to get rid of [*me defaire du*] Mareschal d'Ancre" (*La mort du mareschal d'Ancre*, 452). But Louis never made long speeches, and his language was always terse. Moreover, the author has the king refer to the brother of Chaulnes and Luynes as Luxembourg, whereas that brother was known as the seigneur de Brantes until his elevation to duke of Luxembourg in 1621. I believe some of Chaulnes's account to be accurate, since he was intimately involved in the coup d'état. But the long-winded speeches he attributes to Louis and others (including himself, referred to in the account as "sieur de Chaulnes" and not as de Cadenet as he was called then) look like embellishments at best and fabrications at worst.

30. See the memoirs of Fontenay-Mareuil, who was at the military front at the time, for a curious condemnation of Luynes and unnamed companions: "There was no kind of artifice they left unemployed to have the king approve what had been done. So it wasn't strange that at his age, and with his paucity of experience and knowledge, he let himself be persuaded by everything they told him, and totally forgot that he had not wanted to have [Concini] killed, believing as he did that it could not have been otherwise" (p. 118).

31. Molé, *Mémoires*, 1:145–46.

32. The medallions are depicted in the BN Cabinet des Estampes Qb[1] series for 1616–18.

33. See the BN Lb[36] series for these pamphlets.

34. See Bernard, *Histoire du roy Louis XIII*, 1:80–81.

5. Seeking an Effective Mode of Governance

1. Fontenay-Mareuil, *Mémoires*, 118.

2. See, e.g., Chevallier, *Louis XIII*, 245. Contrast the praise given to Louis XIII by the son of his later personal favorite, Louis de Rouvroy de Saint-Simon, in Saint-Simon, *Oeuvres complètes*, ed. René Dupuis et al. (Geneva, 1964), 1:404.

3. Tapié, *France*, 96, 126.

4. Fontenay-Mareuil, *Mémoires*, 118.

5. See Molé, *Mémoires*, 1:145–46; Fontenay-Mareuil, *Mémoires*, 118–19; BN ms. fr. 17487, "Mémoires de monsieur de Marillac contenant ce qui se passa en France depuis la mort du mareschal d'Ancre jusques au retour de la Reyne mère à la cour," fols. 8v–9r; Chaulnes, *La mort du mareschal d'Ancre*, 460; Batiffol, *Louis XIII à vingt ans*, 78–80.

6. An often-reproduced cartoon sequence is almost as graphic as the account in Pasquier, *Oeuvres*, vol. 2, cols. 1273–82. See Philippe Erlanger, *Louis XIII: Le stoïcien de la monarchie* (Paris, 1972).

7. Pontchartrain, *Mémoires*, 387. Cf. Chaulnes, *La mort du mareschal d'Ancre*, 458: "Many thanks, many thanks to you; at this hour I am king."

8. For a different viewpoint, see Marvick, *Louis XIII*, chap. 15.

9. Héroard, *Journal*, 2:213. Mongrédien, *Léonora Galigaï*, 175, 203, suggests that Louis XIII rued Galigaï's execution as an "unnecessary injustice," and he blames what he calls her "assassination" on Luynes's desire to acquire her personal fortune. It does not occur to Mongrédien that the king wanted justice to be meted out to Galigaï.

10. See Arnauld d'Andilly, *Journal, 1614–1620*, 212–14; and Matthieu, *Histoire de Louis XIII*, 87–88.

11. See Bernard, *Histoire du roy Louis XIII*, 1:82–83; and Chevallier, *Louis XIII*, 170.

12. On 16 May 1617, Marie wrote to Louis to honor his "promise" at their farewell to release Barbin (BN ms. Baluze 323, fol. 3r).

13. AAE France ms. 775, fols. 119r, 120–23, 258–59, summarizes some of the correspondence. For the decree against Barbin, see AAE France ms. 772, fols. 16–17.

14. Chaulnes, *La mort du mareschal d'Ancre*, 461.

15. Chevallier, *Louis XIII*, 175–77, 211–12, is a good corrective to Richelieu's memoirs, but Chevallier's focus on "Luynes and his friends" leaves the impression that they controlled the king's mind.

16. The best way to follow Luynes's career is to read the extensive pamphlet literature. Batiffol's *Louis XIII à vingt ans* uses these sources selectively to play down the role of the king's favorite and thereby rehabilitate the king. At the other extreme is Berthold Zeller's *Le connétable de Luynes. Montauban et la Valteline* (Paris, 1879), which praises the favorite as a strong minister in charge of Louis's government.

17. Compare Fontenay-Mareuil, *Mémoires*, 164, and Richelieu's memoirs. Hostile pamphlet opinion is exemplified by *La chronique des favoris*, where the Albert brothers "dispose absolutely of the ordinary and special perquisites of state," and the ghost of Henry IV tells Louis XIII to banish favorites and appoint a balance of faithful advisors inclined to "the conservation of his person and his state." Cf. *Advis au Roy sur le rétablissement de l'office de Connestable par un bon françois, serviteur du Roy, et amateur de son Estat et de son grandeur*. Both pamphlets are in BN series Lb³⁶, no. 1803B: *Recueil des pièces les plus curieuses qui ont esté faites pendant le règne du Connestable [de Luynes] jusqu'à présent* (1622).

18. Chevallier, *Louis XIII*, 173–208, has a judicious assessment but assumes Luynes's dominance. Only a thorough study of ministerial correspondence (e.g., between Brûlart and Puysieux, in AAE France ms. 774, fols. 37–38, 53–57, 111, 149, 192–93; BN ms. fr. 15617, fols. 114–15) will give us the full story. Yet the dynamics of royal decision making can be seen in a letter by Secretary of State Pontchartrain to the baron of Béthune, who was negotiating Marie's capitulation in 1619: "I showed your letter of 21 March to His Majesty. He read it himself in the presence of Monsr. de Luynes to whom His Majesty confides everything, as you know; and afterwards [the king] wanted to have it read again in his council, where His Majesty and Messrs. his ministers praised your prudent conduct and your dexterity. His Majesty

especially liked the part where you blamed M. d'Espernon for freeing the queen mother from Blois" (BN ms. Cinq Cents de Colbert 97, fol. 59).

19. See BN ms. fr. 4026, fol. 527r; cf. Schomberg to Luçon, 15 December 1621, AAE France ms. 774, fol. 206. Modène wrote to Luçon, 17 January 1622: "[The king] has taken full cognizance of his affairs and nothing is proposed, resolved, or expedited except in his presence and by his orders. He is a marvel of industry" (AAE France ms. 775, fol. 244r).

20. Fontenay-Mareuil, *Mémoires*, 120.

21. See Chevallier, *Louis XIII*, 177–86. The peace negotiations with Marie in 1619 reveal how difficult it was for Louis's servitors to deal with his stubbornness. The baron of Béthune took a quite different line in reporting back to the king than he did to Luynes. To Louis, he emphasized the difficulty of getting Marie to permit punishment of her servitor Epernon, whom Louis had singled out for punition. But to Luynes, Béthune reported that he would be satisfied with the formality of not negotiating in Epernon's presence and that if the latter insisted, he could "listen in" (BN ms. CCC 97, fols. 42–50). The original royal instructions, read at the council meeting of 5 March, with Brûlart, du Vair, Luynes, Jeannin, and Secretary of State Pontchartrain present, and signed by Pontchartrain and Louis, are in BN ms. CCC 97, fols. 1–5.

22. BN series Lb[36], no. 1410.

23. On Louis's vow and subsequent behavior, see Montglat, *Mémoires*, 14; François de Bassompierre, *Journal de ma vie*, SHF ed., ed. A. de La Cropte de Chantérac, 3:6–9; and AAE France ms. 775, fols. 101–5, 108–10 (Louis de Marillac to Richelieu, 3 July and 4 September 1622).

24. Even as Schomberg lost favor at court, the king's trust in that advisor's political judgment remained high. See Louis de Marillac's reports to Richelieu, AAE France ms. 775, fols. 106–12: on 20 August 1622: "Since Cardinal de Retz's death, war is declared between Puysieux and Schomberg. Puysieux has on his side Bassompierre, Joinville [later duke of Chevreuse], and other men of little stature. . . . The king has complete confidence in Schomberg and knows that he sees [Condé] only to dissuade him from his bad designs, and prevent an open rupture which would be bad in the present [Huguenot war] conditions"; on 4 September: "Schomberg has no favor but [retains his] credit; and although absent, the king sends for his advice and follows it"; and on 5 October: "The king does nothing without Schomberg and says his absence delays the siege."

25. For court intrigues as well as the king's views, see Arnauld d'Andilly's *Journal inédit*, ed. Eugéne Halphen and Jules Halphen (Paris, 1888–1909), for 1622–23; and Louis de Marillac's reports to Richelieu, AAE France ms. 775. As early as 15 July 1622, Marillac wrote that Condé had "completely lost the king's favor" since the monarch had become set on peace (fols. 105–6). See also Bonney, *King's Debts*, 106–8.

26. On the fall of the Brûlarts, see, inter alia, Puysieux's earlier correspondence in Hector de La Ferrière, "Marie de Médicis et Louis XIII, d'après des lettres inédites," *Revue des sociétés savantes des départements* 3d ser., 4 (1864):

134, 137; Fontenay-Mareuil, *Mémoires*, 172; Arnauld d'Andilly, *Journal inédit, 1623*, 11; *Journal inédit, 1624*, 6–9; and Chevallier, *Louis XIII*, 267, quoting Louis's verbatim report to the papal nuncio.

27. On La Vieuville's fall, see Arnauld d'Andilly, *Journal inédit, 1624*, 51–52; Bonney, *King's Debts*, 110–13; and *La remerciement de la Voix publique au roy*, BN series Lb³⁶, 2245.

28. The opinion of historians is not surprising, considering contemporary belief. A courtly correspondent of the French ambassador to Rome wrote on 4 May 1624: "There has occurred here a noteworthy change, for the queen mother has the same or greater power than you have ever witnessed; and Monsieur le Cardinal de Richelieu [has been] introduced by the king into the Council of Affairs with such high recommendations of his capacity, fidelity, and probity, that everyone looks on him already as the all-powerful" (BN ms. fr. 15620, fol. 3; published in Richelieu, *Lettres*, 2:4n.2).

29. The correspondence (originals and copies) is in many archival sources. The best account is Batiffol, *Louis XIII à vingt ans*, chap. 6.

30. See BN ms. fr. 17487, especially fols. 13–24, 30–33, 53–59; Griffet, *Histoire du règne de Louis XIII*, 1:242; and Batiffol, *Louis XIII à vingt ans*, 343–46.

31. See Siri, *Mémoires secrets*, 19:47–53; Gabriel de La Rochefoucauld, *Le cardinal François de La Rochefoucauld* (Paris, 1926), 159–60; and Fontenay-Mareuil, *Mémoires*, 136. Batiffol, *Louis XIII à vingt ans*, 351, which appears authoritative, includes in the council debate a minister who had died the previous year!

32. Regarding Louis's instructions for Luçon "to give [Marie] salutary advice, and to try to persuade her that the king was fully disposed to accord her the most just satisfaction," see Siri, *Mémoires secrets*, 19:163–64; and Avenel's note in Richelieu, *Lettres*, 1:580n.2. Louis's handwritten note, which accompanied the official royal letter drafted by Déageant to Luçon, reads: "I ask you, M. l'Evesque de Luçon, to believe that the enclosure is my will, and that you can do me no greater pleasure than to carry it out."

33. Siri, *Mémoires secrets*, 19:156; La Rochefoucauld, *Le cardinal de La Rochefoucauld*, 167.

34. On Louis's relations with Epernon, see AAE France ms. 772, fols. 9–10; Matthieu, *Histoire de Louis XIII*, 90; Bassompierre, *Journal de ma vie*, 2:134–37; Griffet, *Histoire du règne de Louis XIII*, 1:241–42; and Batiffol, *Louis XIII à vingt ans*, 350–52. Guillaume Girard, *La vie du duc d'Epernon*, 290–95, sees the rivalry between Luynes and the veteran court favorite Epernon as the cause of the latter's troubles.

35. BN ms. fr. 4026, fols. 144r–45v, 149r–50r. Curiously, all of these details were omitted by the editors of Héroard's diary.

36. See Matthieu, *Histoire de Louis XIII*, 108; and above, n. 21.

37. Ibid., 110–13.

38. Bassompierre, *Journal de ma vie*, 2:138–9.

39. For the confusing conciliar picture, see Siri, *Mémoires secrets*, 20:179;

Griffet, *Histoire du règne de Louis XIII*, 1:252–53, 260; Bassompierre, *Journal de ma vie*, 2:151–57; and Arnauld d'Andilly, *Journal inédit, 1620*, 18. On the king's role, see Bernard, *Histoire du roy Louis XIII*, 1:90–91, 157–59; and Griffet, *Histoire du règne de Louis XIII*, 1:260. Batiffol, *Louis XIII à vingt ans*, 184, quotes the official version of Louis's statement from a newsletter: "With so many dangers looming, we must take on the greatest and closest ones, which are in Normandy; my opinion is for me to go straight there and not wait in Paris to watch my kingdom preyed upon and my faithful servitors oppressed."

40. Arnauld d'Andilly, *Journal inédit, 1620*, 21–22; Matthieu, *Histoire de Louis XIII*, 130.

41. Bernard, *Histoire du roy Louis XIII*, 1:97–100, 110; Fontenay-Mareuil, *Mémoires*, 149–50; Griffet, *Histoire du règne de Louis XIII*, 1:264–65.

42. Cardinal Guido Bentivoglio, *Lettres sur diverses matières de politique et autres importans sujets*, ed. Veneroy and Minazio (Lyon, 1730), 187. See also Arnauld d'Andilly, *Journal inédit, 1620*, 34, 41–43; and Griffet, *Histoire du règne de Louis XIII*, 1:268–70.

43. Arnauld d'Andilly, *Journal inédit, 1622*, 12.

44. Quoted in Chevallier, *Louis XIII*, 270. Louis's suspicions could not have been laid to rest by Marie's transparent letter of condolence following Luynes's death, suggesting that "as your mother, [I] will never have any interests other than yours." She added, somewhat gratuitously, that Louis should show "that it is you who act in your state" and pay attention to the "good and salutary counsels of those who truly care for your well-being"(BN ms. Dupuy 92, fol. 204r).

45. See especially Arnauld d'Andilly, *Journal inédit, 1623* and *1624*; and Bonney, *King's Debts*, 110, incl. n. 2.

46. Chevallier, *Louis XIII*, 270, notes the limits of Marie's influence: "However, if the king and ministers received through the mediation of the queen mother the opinions and recommendations of M. de Luçon, the latter learned very quickly that they were not in the least adopted."

47. According to the papal nuncio, after the treaty Louis went around saying that he had bought peace at the price of promoting Luçon to the cardinalate (ibid., 222).

48. See Fontenay-Mareuil, *Mémoires*, 164; Chevallier, *Louis XIII*, 264–65, quoting the papal nuncio and the Venetian ambassador; and the raging pamphlet warfare, exemplified by the 1624 tracts *La Voix publique* and *La réponse à la Voix publique envoyée de la cour*, in the Lb³⁶ series. The pamphleteering of 1622–24 is a curious return to the pro-Concini message of 1617 in *Les larmes de la France, à ses enfans mutinez* of a king ruling with good favorites and the anti-Concini message of *Le roi hors de page, à la royne mère* against bad advisors ruining the king's legitimate power (Lb³⁶ [1617]). Here is constitutional thought based on issues endemic to the early modern European Age of Favorites and of rulers who were far from the "great person in history." There

is a good research topic here for someone combining the disciplines of history and political science.

49. See Fontenay-Mareuil, *Mémoires*, 175; Montglat, *Mémoires*, 15; and the Florentine ambassador's report, quoted in Chevallier, *Louis XIII*, 268. Louis was fighting off the propaganda of his entourage as well as his own fears. Louis de Marillac wrote to Richelieu after Luynes's death: "I am especially warning you that I have found the ministers to be afraid of you, and want to make the king apprehensive of your being a favorite and ambitious." Marillac added that he was working through one of the king's current personal favorites, Esplan, to counter that propaganda and incline Louis toward Richelieu (Marillac to Richelieu, 29 December 1621, AAE France ms. 775, fols. 88–90).

50. Louis's *lettres de cachet* against La Vieuville charged the latter with "changing resolutions made in our presence without our knowledge, negotiating with ambassadors in residence at our court against our orders, passing off to us as true various suggestions with the intent of giving umbrage to those on whom we could rely with confidence, and turning against us the hatred he aroused by abusive acts against individual persons" (BN mss. Dupuy 92, fols. 251–52; 581, fol. 132).

51. See Louis XIII, *Lettres à la main de Louis XIII*, ed. Eugène Griselle (Paris, 1914), vol. 1, passim.

6. Fighting for Just Causes

1. Aleksandra D. Lublinskaya, *French Absolutism: The Crucial Phase, 1620–1629*, trans. Brian Pearce (Cambridge, 1968), argues the case for continuity in royal policy regarding the Huguenots during the 1620s. Andrew Lossky agrees in his perceptive commentary following my article "Louis XIII, Richelieu, and 'two-headed monarchy,'" *Proceedings of the Western Society for French History* 10 (1982). Yet Louis XIII's role in that continuity is not addressed by the Lublinskaya/Lossky thesis. Nor does their thesis supplant Tapié's traditional view that Louis and his ministers neglected foreign affairs in pursuing the Huguenots (*La politique étrangère de la France et le début de la Guerre de trente ans* [1616–1621] [Paris, 1934], esp. 619–23). On interpretations of French foreign policy from 1617 through 1624, see below, n. 35.

2. Louis XIII, *Lettres*, 1:196–97, 20 April.

3. Mousnier, *Vénalité*, argues that the monarchy routinely used the threat of suspending the paulette to secure money and obedience from the officials. My *Revolt of the Judges*, chap. 2, stresses the counterproductiveness of that strategy.

4. Bonney, *King's Debts*, 98.

5. Arnauld d'Andilly, *Journal, 1614–1620*, 319–20.

6. For Louis's early decrees, see Molé, *Mémoires*, 1:148, 152–53.

7. Contrast Fontenay-Mareuil, *Mémoires*, 124, and Matthieu, *Histoire de Louis XIII*, 87–88.

8. Héroard, *Journal*, 2:94 (text and n. 1).

9. Batiffol, *Louis XIII à vingt ans*, 176–77, is the fullest account.

10. See Arnauld d'Andilly, *Journal, 1614–1620*, 212–14; and Matthieu, *Histoire de Louis XIII*, 87–88.

11. Louis XIII, *Lettres*, 1:116–17, 125; Batiffol, *Louis XIII à vingt ans*, 180.

12. Héroard, *Journal*, 2:256.

13. Louis XIII, *Lettres*, 1:312–14.

14. Batiffol, *Louis XIII à vingt ans*, chaps. 3 and 5, provides massive documentation on Louis's religion at this time, but is despairingly inattentive to the nuances.

15. According to Bernard, *Histoire du roy Louis XIII*, 1:149, the royal decree resulted from an appeal by representatives of the Assembly of the Clergy, which "greatly moved" Louis.

16. See ibid., 1:152, 157, 162–63; Fontenay-Mareuil, *Mémoires*, 154–55.

17. See BN ms. fr. 4026, fol. 250 (compressed in Héroard, *Journal*, 2:239).

18. Bernard, *Histoire du roy Louis XIII*, 1:149.

19. See ibid., 148; and Fontenay-Mareuil, *Mémoires*, 121.

20. See the journals of Arnauld d'Andilly; Bernard, *Histoire du roy Louis XIII*; *Mercure françois*; and Vaunois, *Vie de Louis XIII*.

21. On the above, see Matthieu, *Histoire de Louis XIII*, 132; Bassompierre, *Journal de ma vie*, 2:210–13; Louis XIII, *Lettres*, 1:70–72; and Richelieu, *Mémoires*.

22. See Bernard, *Histoire du roy Louis XIII*, 1:163–64; Matthieu, *Histoire de Louis XIII*, 133; Griffet, *Histoire du règne de Louis XIII*, 1:272; La Rochefoucauld, *Le cardinal de La Rochefoucauld*, 190; Arnauld d'Andilly, *Journal inédit, 1620*, 50–57.

23. Detailed information on Louis's treatment of the Protestant warrior nobility can be found in Matthieu, *Histoire de Louis XIII*, and Griffet, *Histoire du règne de Louis XIII*.

24. Louis XIII, *Lettres*, 1:98.

25. See, inter alia, Bernard, *Histoire du roy Louis XIII*, 1:235, 237; *Mercure françois*, vol. 7 (1621), 159.

26. See especially *Mercure françois*, vol. 7 (1621), 509–60, 620–21; and Bernard, *Histoire du roy Louis XIII*, 1:235–41, 258.

27. *Mercure françois*, vol. 7 (1621), 31, 636–37, 648–51; Arnauld d'Andilly, *Journal inédit, 1621*, 68–70; B. Zeller, *Le connétable de Luynes*, 68; Batiffol, *Louis XIII à vingt ans*, 265.

28. Bassompierre, *Journal de ma vie*, 2:364. A contemporary drawing of the siege of Montauban is contained in BN, Cabinet des Estampes, series Qb¹ ("cliché" 71C50641).

29. "I am so indignant about the death of the seigneur de Boisse," Louis wrote, "that I am resolved to punish the guilty and return Monheur to obedience" (*Lettres*, 1:147n.3).

30. Griffet, *Histoire du règne de Louis XIII*, 1:142.

31. Louis XIII, *Lettres*, 1:228; Bernard, *Histoire du roy Louis XIII*, 1:378–79. See Griffet, *Histoire du règne de Louis XIII*, 1:348–55, for a judicious evaluation of what happened.

32. See BN series Lb³⁶. A later pamphlet-history by N. Charpy, *Le juste prince ou le miroir des princes en la vie de Louis le Juste* (1638), conflated the campaigns of 1621 and 1622, arguing that "those who refused his bounty were unable to avoid his justice" while stressing that Louis "wished to vanquish his subjects and stop having them perish; he wanted his soldiers to be victorious, not cruel" (Lb³⁶ 3149, pp. 24–27).

33. See Arnauld d'Andilly, *Journal inédit*, 1622, 61–62, 74; Bassompierre, *Journal de ma vie*, 3:111–16, 149–50; and Héroard, *Journal*, 2:280 (text and n. 1).

34. I follow Lublinskaya, *French Absolutism*, 210–11, who is more positive than most historians on the Peace of Montpellier. Cf. Louis XIII's personal evaluation to Condé, as quoted in a letter by the duke of La Force to his wife (Héroard, *Journal*, 2:280n.1).

35. Victor Tapié, *France in the Age of Louis XIII and Richelieu*, 97–115, is typical of French historians in concluding that "forty years of ceaseless struggle from 1620 to 1659 were to be necessary to avert the dangers with which [France] was faced as a result of Spain's success." Gabriel Hanotaux's once famous but now dated history of Cardinal Richelieu is cast in even more preordained terms: "The House of Austria, saved by Luynes in 1621, forced upon France more than a century of bloody effort" (Hanotaux and La Force, *Cardinal de Richelieu*, 2:394). Chevallier has attained greater objectivity by paying attention to the contemporary dispatches of foreign ambassadors at Louis's court (e.g., *Louis XIII*, 195–96, 225). Foreign scholars have taken the lead in questioning traditional French assumptions about the "inevitable" Bourbon-Habsburg conflict. See especially John H. Elliott, *Richelieu and Olivares* (Cambridge, 1984)—written by a British specialist on Spain! The Russian scholar Lublinskaya in her *French Absolutism*, argues that from a strategic viewpoint Louis's government had to place the Huguenot issue before foreign affairs in the early 1620s. On her less convincing view that Luynes also tried to ensure Habsburg reconciliation to French interests before embarking on campaigns against the Huguenots, see Tapié, *France in the Age of Louis XIII and Richelieu*, 474–75n.24 (note by Lockie).

36. Contemporary bewilderment over the intricately connected foreign and domestic situation is reported by the papal nuncio, quoted in B. Zeller, *Le connétable de Luynes*, 12–13; and in greater detail by Tapié, *Politique étrangère*.

37. I agree with Tapié that in 1620–21 Louis XIII was "intervening more and more directly in the affairs of his realm, and having his opinion prevail in council decisions"; and I find B. Zeller's view of Luynes as the instigator of a stronger foreign policy unconvincing. I am bothered, however, by Tapié's conclusion that Louis's conduct "betrayed the defects and inexperience of his

age." I would stress as creative precisely those qualities of Louis XIII that Tapié criticizes in saying, "Louis XIII was neither a mere clerk nor a states man, but a *gentilhomme* full of courage and valor carried away by generous and short-sighted resolutions" (Tapié, *Politique étrangère*, 622). See also B. Zeller, *Le connétable de Luynes*, 175.

38. Tapié, *Politique étrangère*, 425.

39. See ibid., 426–31; Siri, *Mémoires secrets*, 20:195–99.

40. Tapié, *Politique étrangère*, documents the French government's blundering, while revealing that the German Protestants were as blind as the French. Conversely, we can follow the papal nuncio's consternation as Louis backed away from military support for the emperor; see Bentivoglio, *Lettres sur diverses matières*, 281–313.

41. On the terms *bon Français* and *dévot*, see above, p. 45.

42. My view on Louis XIII's moralizing parallels the argument of William F. Church's *Richelieu and Reason of State* on the overlap between reason of state and Christian morality. Yet I am uneasy with Church's tendency to take at face value the ethical rhetoric of Richelieu and his pamphleteers.

43. See Griffet, *Histoire du règne de Louis XIII*, 1:116–17, 125; Batiffol, *Louis XIII à vingt ans*, 155–56; Chaulnes, *La mort du mareschal d'Ancre*, 483–84.

44. See the journals of Héroard and Arnauld d'Andilly.

45. Carl. J. Burkhardt, *Richelieu and His Age*, trans. Bernard Hoy, Edwin Muir, and Willa Muir (London, 1962), 1:162–63, comes closest, without giving specific credit to Louis: "Even before Richelieu's assumption of office the foreign policy of France regarding the Valtelline had been unobtrusively returning to the anti-Spanish line which Henry IV had thought out so thoroughly and held to with almost foolhardy boldness."

46. See John H. Elliott, *The Count-Duke of Olivares: The Statesman in an Age of Decline* (New Haven, Conn., 1986), 62, 72, 83; and reconstructions by Lublinskaya (*French Absolutism*), Tapié (*France in the Age of Louis XIII and Richelieu*), and Chevallier (*Louis XIII*).

47. Similarly, in writing to his sister Elisabeth (now Queen Isabella of Spain) of his desire for Franco-Spanish amity, Louis sternly insisted on her husband keeping his word to implement the treaty. See Louis XIII, *Lettres*, 2:348–49; Batiffol, *Louis XIII à vingt ans*, 181–83.

48. See Chevallier, *Louis XIII*, 241–42.

49. Lublinskaya, *French Absolutism*, 260–70, has an excellent evaluation of La Vieuville's record on external affairs.

50. B. Zeller, *Le connétable de Luynes*, 86.

7. Growing Up in Public

1. The best guide to the king's correspondence during these years is Louis XIII, *Lettres*, vol. 1.

2. Ibid., 132.

3. Ibid., 152–53, 155, 165. Marvick, "Childhood History," 175, sees Louis's writing as being narcissistic.

4. See BN mss. fr. 4026, fol. 444; 4027, fol. 138; Héroard, *Journal*, 2:257; Pontchartrain, *Mémoires*, 396.

5. The expression is Héroard's, but Arnauld d'Andilly and Bernard have similar observations.

6. Héroard, *Journal*, 2:255.

7. BN ms. fr. 4026, fol. 251r.

8. Héroard, *Journal*, 2:245; Bassompierre, *Journal de ma vie*, 2:387 (text and n. 2, editor's comment). Marvick's compressing of Bassompierre's *elle* and *lui* focuses Louis's cruelty exclusively on the duke of Luynes ("Childhood History," 163). Bassompierre's editor attributes Louis's turning against Mme de Luynes to her habit of making fun in Anne's company of the king's prudery and inability to express thoughts of love.

9. Héroard, *Journal*, 2:218, 285.

10. Usually Louis's letters to his mother read like a proud and dutiful royal son reporting on the progress of his quest for authority. Occasionally he could relax and be charming, as when he said he would wear the scarf she had given him when he reviewed his troops (Louis XIII, *Lettres*, 1:60–61).

11. The assumption that Louis had no chance of personality maturation or even enjoyment during his adolescence was strongest in the nineteenth century, although it remains to this day. Chapman's sensitive sketch of Louis XIII in his *Privileged Persons* is a rare exception. Contrast the comment by Heroard's editors, *Journal*, 2:242n.1; and Guardin, *La médecine*, 315, who asserted that Louis experienced neither the perils and storms of adolescence nor the unbounded élan of youth: "[His] heart did not pound nor his inner being thrill."

12. See BN ms. fr. 3818, fols. 13, 40; and Martha W. Freer, *The Married Life of Anne of Austria*, 2d ed. (London, 1865), 1:8.

13. Chaulnes, *La mort du mareschal d'Ancre*, 484.

14. See Kleinman, *Anne of Austria*, 38–39. For a sketch of the teenage Anne by someone whose family was close to her then, see Françoise Bertaut de Motteville, *Mémoires pour servir à l'histoire d'Anne d'Autriche*, MP ed., 2d ser., vol. 10 (Paris, 1838), 14.

15. The fullest assemblage of sources on the consummation is Baschet, *Le roi chez la reine*, chaps. 13–14. Cf. Chevallier, *Louis XIII*; Vaunois, *Vie de Louis XIII*; and Batiffol, *Louis XIII à vingt ans*. Freer, *Married Life of Anne of Austria*, has interesting details. The editors of Héroard's manuscript (BN ms. fr. 4026, fol. 133v) missed nothing essential for this important day.

16. Curiously, Héroard's editors did miss virtually all of this information; see BN ms. fr. 4026, fols. 134–35, 139v.

17. Matthieu, *Histoire de Louis XIII*, 122–23. Louis's letters to his sisters reflect his concern. To Henrietta Maria, he wrote of being "grandement affligé." He was typically less emotional in writing to Anne's father, letting

Philip III know only that God had listened to his pleas and the prayers of his people (Louis XIII, *Lettres*, 1:47–8).

18. See especially Matthieu, *Histoire de Louis XIII*, 126–27; and Bernard, *Histoire du roy Louis XIII*, 1:160–61.

19. See BN ms. fr. 4027, fols. 26v–27r; Héroard, *Journal*, 2:270–71; Arnauld d'Andilly, *Journal inédit, 1622*, 17–21; and Bassompierre, *Journal de ma vie*, 15–16, 421–27 (app. 1). Bassompierre's account of the king's reaction is worth quoting: "The affair was hidden as well as it could be from the king while he was in Paris. . . . [Later] people let the king know how and in what circumstances the queen was injured, and they stirred him up so much against those two ladies that he sent [a messenger] to the queen . . . and he wrote to each one a letter letting them know they were to retire from the Louvre" (*Journal de ma vie*, 3:15–16). A lively chat with Joan Bowditch at the Society for French Historical Studies 1981 meeting has led me to think that the embryo might have been malformed, and the miscarriage nature's way of preventing a greater disaster. Cf. Kleinman, *Anne of Austria*, 56.

20. Héroard left marginal indications of the king's conjugal duty for 4, 8, 11, 16, and 18 March, 13 *and* 14 April, and 21 June 1624, for example. As for circumstances, he recorded the same event for several days in October 1624, following Richelieu's entry to power, and on 8 and 11 June 1626, during a crisis involving treason by the king's half brothers which left Louis a light and impatient sleeper, as well as a frequent communicator with his mother and his chief minister. See BN ms. fr. 4027 for those dates; and below, n. 32.

21. See Louis XIII, *Lettres*, vol. 1, and Bassompierre, *Journal de ma vie*, 3:421–27 (app. 1).

22. The dramatic change in Anne's situation is brought home by the fact that during the couple's separations during recent military campaigns, Louis had made her regent for northern France, to the anger of his mother. Just before the queen's miscarriage, the king forced the queen mother to apologize for giving orders in Anne's quarters. See Chevallier, *Louis XIII*, 260.

23. Ruth Kleinman's biography, *Anne of Austria*, shows just how trapped and powerless Anne was. It is strange that historians have passed over the degree of control Louis XIII exercised over his wife and her destiny. Perhaps it is part of the *roi fainéant* myth.

24. See Arnauld d'Andilly, *Journal inédit, 1623*, 30, and *1624*, 10–11.

25. Chapman, "Louis XIII," 34–35, brilliantly gets beyond scholars' speculation about Louis XIII's relationship with Luynes by noting the bisexual potential in all human beings and by focusing on the favorite's genuine care and compassion that elicited the young king's ardent, obsessive attachment to him. Vaunois, *Vie de Louis XIII*, 251–57, just as effectively overturns the supposed evidence in Héroard's published journal of a homosexual relationship (apart from the word *shameful*) by comparing its suggestively abridged phrases with the innocuous language of the original manuscript. I am not sure, however, that Vaunois's point that Louis was an individual of rare moral self-control rules out a physical union with Luynes, as he suggests.

26. My interpretation stops short of Marvick, "Childhood History," 163, which analyzes Louis's behavior toward Luynes in sadomasochistic terms: "Clearly Luynes represented tendencies repressed by Louis in himself: laziness, fear of battle, failure of discipline, genital gratification. Needless to say, the young king's indulgence of Luynes had a reverse side—sadistic gratification. The side in himself which he had repressed was rediscovered in the former falconer."

27. Louis also wrote to Condé, "I cannot bear the loss that has just come to me through the death of my Cousin, the Constable" (*Lettres*, 1:259).

28. On contemporary views, see Montglat, *Mémoires*, 14; and Fontenay-Mareuil, *Mémoires*, 164. Surprisingly, Batiffol (see *Louis XIII à vingt ans*, 566–72), is one of the most critical historians on this aspect of Louis XIII's life.

29. BN ms. fr. 4026, fols. 522v–27v; Héroard, *Journal*, 2:265. On Louis's quite different views about having given so much political favor to Luynes, see above, chap. 5.

30. See Arnauld d'Andilly, *Journal inédit, 1623*, 29–30; Montglat, *Mémoires*, 15; Batiffol, *Louis XIII à vingt ans*, 540–41; Chevallier, *Louis XIII*, 261; and Tallemant des Réaux, *Historiettes*, 2:234.

31. Rohan, *Mémoires*, 511, 544; Fontenay-Mareuil, *Mémoires*, 120.

32. See Héroard, *Journal*, 2:258, 276, and comments by the editors in 1:xxv; Marvick, "Childhood History," 160; and Batiffol, *Louis XIII à vingt ans*, 144n.3. Two days before Louis's safe-conduct episode, he was almost killed by a rebel cannonball, then made love to Anne that night (BN ms fr. 4026, fol. 451r).

33. Héroard, *Journal*, 2:281–2.

8. Partnership of King and Cardinal

A short paper on some of the themes of this chapter appeared as "Louis XIII, Cardinal Richelieu, and Two-headed Monarchy" in *Proceedings of the Western Society for French History* 10 (1982). I am especially appreciative of comments by Andrew Lossky and J. Michael Hayden.

1. See Georges Pagès, *Institutions monarchiques*, 40; Ranum, *Richelieu*, p. 16; and below, n. 16. For some astute comparisons of Louis and Richelieu, see Romain, *Louis XIII*, 92–95.

2. In seventeenth-century medical terms, "bad humors" meant an excess of the last four basic humors (phlegm, blood, bile, and melancholy); see Pagès, *Institutions monarchiques*, 26–27. For Louis's political views, see Batiffol, *Richelieu et Louis XIII*; Topin, *Louis XIII et Richelieu*, "Introduction"; and Romain, *Louis XIII*. On Richelieu's political ideas, see his *Lettres*, 2:83, and *Testament politique*, ed. Louis André (Paris, 1947). But note the words of caution about conventional scholarly views urged by Méthivier, *Le siècle de Louis XIII*, 52–58; and Tapié, *France in the Age of Louis XIII and Richelieu*, 134, 140. Elizabeth Marvick, in her paper "Richelieu and the Testament Politique: An Attempt at Attribution," presented at the Twenty-seventh Annual Meeting of

the Society for French Historical Studies at Bloomington, Indiana, in 1981, argues that parts of Richelieu's *Testament politique* were a private, collaborative enterprise of king and minister, designed to justify, glorify, and encourage royal acts.

3. On Richelieu's own physical and mental health problems, see Pagès, *Institutions monarchiques*, 37–38.

4. Ibid., 27; Richelieu, *Testament politique*, 266.

5. See Richelieu, *Lettres*, 3:183.

6. Richelieu, *Testament politique*, 266. On the Schomberg case, see Arnauld d'Andilly, *Journal inédit, 1626*, 27, 39–40; *Mercure françois*, 13:380–84; and Richelieu's "Mémoire que le roi a fait faire sur l'appel des enfants de M. de Schomberg," which eventually found its way into the cardinal's *Mémoires*, SFH ed., 6:299–304.

7. See Marvick, *Young Richelieu*.

8. There is still room for a fresh sociopolitical history of Richelieu, despite the many existing biographies. Here is a subject to tax the most brilliant twentieth-century scholar! The new edition of the cardinal's papers (including letters to him) is an immense help, as is Joseph Bergin, *Cardinal Richelieu: Power and the Pursuit of Wealth* (New Haven, Conn., 1985). See also Ranum, "Richelieu and the Great Nobility: Some Aspects of Early Modern Political Motives," *French Historical Studies* 3 (1963); and R. Herr, "Honor Versus Absolutism: Richelieu's Fight Against Duelling," *Journal of Modern History* 27 (1955).

9. Richelieu, *Papiers*, 1:368. In a typical letter, Louis wrote: "If I hadn't begun to take the waters today and didn't dare leave, I would have brought you my answer [to Richelieu's *billet*] myself. I will tell you, therefore, that you can convene the council tomorrow at 3 P.M. here [at St-Germain]; or at Ruel if your health, which you must place above all other considerations, does not permit you to come here" (AAE France ms. 244, fol. 49; Topin, *Louis XIII et Richelieu*, 186).

10. Richelieu, *Testament politique*, 268.

11. Marvick, "Childhood History," 163.

12. Cf. Andrew Lossky's commentary on my paper "Two-headed Monarchy," in *Proceedings of the Western Society for French History* 10 (1982).

13. AAE France ms. 244, fol. 6r.

14. In the summer of 1630, Richelieu sent Louis a memo dictating the precise, harsh words he should use in dressing down the duke of Guise for trying to turn the queen mother against his war in Italy. The memo began, "The king can say to M. de G, if it pleases him. . . ." Bouthillier wrote back to Richelieu: "The king is very indignant with M. de Guise's behavior; he will say even more than is suggested in your letter" (Richelieu, *Lettres*, 3:804 [text and n. 1]).

15. Louis wrote from St. Germain on 15 January 1636, at 8:00 A.M.: "I learned something which confirms the opinion I gave you yesterday [when briefed by Richelieu about a problem during their rendezvous]." On Louis's favorite subject, military details: "My Cousin, I saw the Marquis de La Force

and his instructions. It seems to me that he needs a little artillery equipment or at least some munitions of war, as per the memoir I have drawn up, which I have sent you. For if he finds the least obstacle such as barricades or road-blocks, without little firepieces he will not easily force them." From the many royal *billets* on finances and rebellion: "You will speak to the superintendents to have them give [money]. . . . You will have word of the sedition in Rouen, which I believe should be remedied, and such things not tolerated." When one of the king's musketeers killed a nobleman and the slain man's brother complained, Louis notified Richelieu "so that the [parlementary] Procuror General does his duty and sends an investigating team. . . . I intend justice to be done. We knew nothing here about the quarrel until after the accident occurred. If we had known, it would have been remedied promptly" (AAE France mss. 2164, fols. 18, 34; 244 fols. 63, 71).

16. Ranum, while noting the difficulty of finding the truth, leaves open the possibility of strong involvement by the king: "Louis took the *métier du roi* very seriously, and insisted on being informed of [the smallest details]. In the complex problems of government, where goals and policies were defined, Louis's role is more difficult to determine. Little is known about this aspect for either Louis or Richelieu, because their thoughts and actions, as indicated in their correspondence, do not clearly delineate their political personalities" (*Richelieu*, 16).

17. One must read the entire *avis* of the cardinal to judge what he rec-ommended—and even then the verdict is far from clear. As against the con-ventional historical wisdom that Richelieu stiffened the royal resolve (a view repeated in the servitor's *Testament politique*), consult the almost convoluted *avis* itself, in Richelieu, *Papiers*, 2:219–23; the copy in the cardinal's *Mémoires*, SHF ed,. 3:71–77, which Grillon has discovered to contain a foreign docu-ment placed within the *avis*; Batiffol, *Richelieu et Louis XIII*, 166–67, who wishes to show a firm monarch and hence interprets the document as show-ing Richelieu leaning toward a lesser penalty; and the moderately revisionist Chevallier, *Louis XIII*, 323–24, who follows Batiffol's reasoning and prose very closely.

18. See *Mercure françois*, 13:417–18, 420–24.

19. Richelieu, *Lettres*, 3:201.

20. Ibid., 2:32–34, 123, 214–15; Richelieu, *Papiers*, 1:206–7, 359–60.

21. AAE France ms. 244, fols. 12, 29; Topin, *Louis XIII et Richelieu*, 127; Richelieu, *Papiers*, 1:353–54.

22. See Ranum, *Richelieu*, 13, 181–84.

23. The personal aspects of Louis's relationships with his favorites after 1624 are discussed in chap. 14.

24. See Montglat, *Mémoires*, 16; Griffet, *Histoire du règne de Louis XIII*, 1:524–26; and also scattered references in the journals of Arnauld d'Andilly and in Richelieu's *Papiers* and *Mémoires*.

25. Dated 28 November 1634, at St-Germain (AAE France ms. 244, fol. 87). Cf. Louis to Richelieu, 22 November 1635: "Saint-Simon sends word that

Nancy is in great danger. . . . That prevented me from sleeping all night. It is very necessary to act promptly" (AAE France ms. 2164, fol. 31).

26. Arnauld d'Andilly, *Journal inédit, 1630–1632*, 72. The reporter called the ritual a "strange form."

27. The favorite chose the worst military crisis of the reign to test his master's friendship. Precipitous surrenders by border-garrison captains to the invading Spaniards "made the king so angry that he started proceedings against them with full rigor" (Fontenay-Mareuil, *Mémoires*, 256).

28. There is no way to document adequately the following sketch on conciliar government, based on printed and archival sources, monographs, and manuals of various offices (most easily accessible in the main reading room and *cabinet des manuscrits* reference shelves of the Bibliothèque nationale). But see Ranum, *Richelieu*; Batiffol, *Richelieu et Louis XIII*, esp. 1–21; and Mousnier, *Institutions de la France*, 2:132–52.

29. Mathieu Molé declined in order to avoid a conflict of interest with his role as procuror general in the Parlement of Paris, which he did not wish to relinquish (Bassompierre, *Journal de ma vie*, 3:193). Louis later made him parlementary first president.

30. After a long vacancy in that office, Richelieu gingerly brought the vacancy to the king's attention at council on 8 November 1629. Louis asked him to suggest someone, then rejected his choice, President Le Jay, saying that although that judge was "very clever and capable," he did not want to be "reproached" for appointing someone who had had three *abolitions*. The king concluded "that he did not see anyone filling more worthily that post than the *bonhomme* M. de Champigny." Marillac's gushing praise of this choice as "inspired by God" reflected his support but does not prove that his opinion determined Louis's choice. See Arnauld d'Andilly, *Journal inédit, 1628–1629*, 134–35; BN ms. fr. 14027, fol. 30; and Major, *Representative Government*, 518.

31. Louis de Marillac's letters to Richelieu, in the AAE France 770s volumes, constitute a mysterious and capital source on Richelieu's pre-1624 years. Nicolas Lefèvre has left us a fascinating contemporary eulogy of Michel de Marillac's life; see BN ms. fr. 14027, esp. fols. 1–30. Lefèvre said that as a councillor of state, Marillac had respected only the chancellor and superintendent of finances, not favorites and other "men of the court" like Concini and Luynes (fol. 80r).

32. For the conventional view of a triumvirate, see Chevallier, *Louis XIII*.

33. Richelieu, *Lettres*, 3:254n.1. The editor, Avenel, assuming that Richelieu routinely dictated Louis's letters, was puzzled by this one, prefacing it with the remark: "The king wrote a letter the same day [as Richelieu's own letter to Marie, stressing the Duke of Savoy's obstinacy], which we would surely have attributed to Cardinal Richelieu, if the name of this minister had not been noted with great praise. [The king's letter] made no mention of these difficulties, and he declared himself most satisfied with the Duke of Savoy." See also BN mss. fr. 3828, fol. 16; 3829, fols. 18, 74.

34. Bassompierre, *Journal de ma vie*, 3:69. Cf. Arnauld d'Andilly, *Journal inédit, 1628–1629*, 131–32; Griffet, *Histoire du règne de Louis XIII*, 1:681–83; Bernard, *Histoire du roy Louis XIII*, 2:236–37.

35. On these crises, see also below, chaps. 9, 10.

36. See also Bonney, *King's Debts*, 120–24; and Major, *Representative Government*, 499. For partisan contemporary views, see Richelieu's *Mémoires* and Lefèvre's life of Marillac, BN ms. 14027, fols. 30, 186. Marillac said that the best part of becoming keeper of the seals was escaping the "purgatory of finances."

37. See *Mercure françois*, 12:374; and Tronçon's self-defense to Louis, BN ms. Baluze 323, fol. 70.

38. Topin, *Louis XIII et Richelieu*, 133–34.

39. The message was delivered by Secretary of State La Ville-aux-Clercs immediately after Marillac's detention. See Arnauld d'Andilly, *Journal inédit, 1630–1632*, 124.

40. Ranum, *Richelieu*, 165.

41. Ibid., 80n.3.

42. Servien said that the king "was reduced to having to choose whom he wished to retain," Bullion or himself. Richard Bonney, *Political Change in France Under Richelieu and Mazarin, 1624–1661* (Oxford, 1981), 15n.3. On Servien's fall, see Ranum, *Richelieu*, 100 (text and n. 1), 161; A. Fauvelet du Toc, *Histoire des secrétaires d'estat*, (Paris, 1668), 275–76 (including an enigmatic letter by Richelieu); and Hermann Weber, "Vom verdeckten zum offenen Krieg: Kriegsgrunde und Kriegsziele Richelieus 1634–5," in *Der dreissigjährige Krieg*, ed. Konrad Repgen (Munich, 1988). I am indebted to Geoffrey Parker for this article in its original form as a paper at a conference at Munich in 1984 on the Thirty Years' War, and to Andrew Lossky for passing the paper on to me. The seventeenth-century community of scholars lives on today!

43. On the enigmatic Sublet, see Ranum, *Richelieu*, 100–19. The remaining two secretaryships remained in the hands of the Loménie-Brienne and the Phélypeaux-Pontchartrain families through this period. The family representatives were relegated as in the past to routine secretarial business, and disdained currying favor with Richelieu. Yet I suspect that they remained important, perhaps even crucial, to Louis XIII's need for persons who could combine efficiency, administrative knowledge, and total trustworthiness to carry out key royal orders (somewhat like Louis's longtime personal favorite Saint-Simon in military-diplomatic matters). Louis singled out Henri-Auguste de Loménie de La Ville-aux-Clercs to do his hatchet work with Michel de Marillac and Marie de' Medici after the Day of Dupes; and Louis Phélypeaux de La Vrillière to draw up and present his last will and testament. The near-contemporary sources on their role smack a bit too much of the view that Louis was Richelieu's dupe to be taken at face value. See ibid., 68–71, including the long quote on p. 70.

44. Richelieu, *Lettres*, 5:161–62 (part of a long *nota* by editor Avenel, pp. 155–62).

45. Chevallier, *Louis XIII*, 287.

46. Ranum comes closest to my interpretation here: "Louis XIII did not lose control of the situation, however, once Richelieu arose to dominate the councils. . . . [He held] Richelieu responsible for the actions of his favourites; and while combining assurances of affection with a long history of ministerial disgraces, Louis insisted on being informed of all decisions made in his name, and in having the last word" (*Richelieu*, 182). Roland Mousnier's introduction to the French edition of Ranum, *Les créatures de Richelieu*, trans. Simone Guenée (Paris, 1966), 13, suggests that both Louis and Richelieu put a higher premium on the loyalty of servitors than on their intellect. See also Méthivier, *Le siècle de Louis XIII*, 45–52; Chevallier, *Louis XIII*, 282–96; and Batiffol, *Richelieu et Louis XIII*, 22–99.

47. The conflict can be followed in AAE France ms. 2164, ending with fol. 29; Richelieu, *Lettres*, 5:155–62; and Topin, *Louis XIII et Richelieu*, 245–50.

48. AAE France ms. 2164, fols. 22, 29.

49. Richelieu, *Lettres*, 4:634.

9. Ordering Priorities

1. After noting past disorder and disrespect of Louis's authority at home and abroad, Richelieu recalled that "I promised him I would use all my faculties and all the authority he chose to give me in order to ruin the Huguenot party, cast down the pride of *les grands*, reduce all subjects to their dutiful place, and restore his name among foreign nations to its rightful position" (*Testament politique*, 95).

2. For a succinct critique, punctuated with contradictory policy statements by Richelieu, see Major, *Representative Government*, 494–95. The most balanced judgments are in Méthivier's little book, *Le siècle de Louis XIII*, and the English version of Tapié, *Louis XIII and Richelieu*, including footnotes and bibliographical commentary by D. M. Lockie. Lublinskaya, *French Absolutism*, accepts Richelieu's "grand design," while arguing for its continuity with past royal policy.

3. On pamphlet views see *Mercure françois*, vol. 10; Church, *Richelieu*; and Thuau, *Raison d'état*. Elliott, *Richelieu and Olivares*, is brilliant on contemporary ideas of "restoration" and "reform."

4. Richelieu, *Papiers*, 1:104.

5. See especially the unpublished royal *règlement* of 1625, in Richelieu, *Papiers*, 1:248–69; and Bonney, *King's Debts*, 130–32, 131n.1. Richelieu's idealistic view of the three estates called for topical royal councils with balanced representation from the clergy, nobles of race, and robe officials. The clergy were to implement the Tridentine reforms, and the old nobility were to be given top civil, military, and ecclesiastical posts. The abolition of venality and judicial fees, royal resumption of alienated lands and rights, and a shift from peasant-based land taxes to a 5 percent sales tax and a universal salt tax would relieve peasants and artisans.

6. N. Goulas, *Mémoires*, SFH ed., ed. Charles Constant (Paris, 1879), 1:18–19.

7. See Charles Vialart's near-contemporary account, *Histoire du ministère d'Armand Jean du Plessis Cardinal duc de Richelieu, sous le règne de Louys le Juste, XIII du nom* (n.p., 1650), 1:62–65, on Richelieu's discussion with Louis. Lublinskaya, *French Absolutism*, 267, notes Louis's consistent support of a "regime of economy" after 1617.

8. Secretary of State Herbault to Marquemont, in Antoine Aubery, *Mémoires pour l'histoire du Cardinal de Richelieu recueillis par le sieur Aubery*, 5 vols. (Cologne, 1667), 1:130. Cf. Griffet, *Histoire du règne de Louis XIII*, 1:416–17; Rohan, *Mémoires*, 544.

9. See Siri, *Mémoires secrets*, 31:2–7, 87–91.

10. Griffet, *Histoire du règne de Louis XIII*, 1:445–46.

11. See Vialart, *Histoire du ministère de Richelieu*, 1:184–85.

12. See Richelieu's "memoir for the king" in May, and a second memoir and letter in August 1625 (Richelieu, *Papiers*, 1:181–86, 206–7). Cf. Vialart, *Histoire du ministère de Richelieu*, 1:185, for the chronology.

13. The best accounts for this unusually well documented meeting are in Griffet, *Histoire du règne de Louis XIII*, and Vialart, *Histoire du ministère de Richelieu*. Cf. Arnauld d'Andilly, *Journal inédit, 1625*, 155–56. Richelieu, in his memoirs, gives himself all the credit for persuading Louis. Marillac's opposition over the previous weeks is noted in Bonney, *King's Debts*, 124.

14. See Griffet, *Histoire du règne de Louis XIII*, 1:461.

15. On finances, see Bonney, *King's Debts*, 120–21, 126–27.

16. See Richelieu, *Papiers*, 1:208–9; *Mercure françois*, 11:925–26.

17. There is a good near-contemporary analysis of the peace in Vialart, *Histoire du ministère de Richelieu*, 1:203–8.

18. See Griffet, *Histoire du règne de Louis XIII*, 1:481, 649; and Richelieu, *Testament politique*, 99–100.

19. The sources do not tell us all we would like to know about motives and aims. See Bassompierre's short account, *Journal de ma vie*, 3:238–42; a much more extensive reconstruction by Siri, *Mémoires secrets*, vol. 35; Lublinskaya, *French Absolutism*, 278–81; and D. P. O'Connell, *Richelieu* (Cleveland, 1968), 92–96. I suspect, following Siri, that Louis was furious with the first draft in December 1625, but decided to call a council rather than recall and punish his ambassador for overzealousness. The council opted for changes rather than rejection, on the pragmatic recommendation of Richelieu, who stood between the extreme dévots and the anti-dévots (probably Marshals Schomberg, Créquy, and Bassompierre). A second, less unacceptable treaty was then negotiated by the ambassador in March 1626; and this time Louis called in the marshals while Richelieu was indisposed to say that it had been signed without his authorization and to tell them to talk with the cardinal. It is probable that, this time, the king's anger was feigned; and that Fargis had been told to negotiate a treaty that could be termed unauthorized, in order to cover up the fact that Louis had negotiated it unilaterally with Spain behind

the backs of his Italian allies. Bassompierre concluded his account with the revealing reflection that at the full council meeting "everyone took greater pleasure in blaming the worker than in undoing his work." When Savoy and Venice complained, Louis authorized a third round of negotiations, leading to the treaty confirmed in May.

20. Lublinskaya, *French Absolutism*, 278–81, commenting on historians' views of the treaty, concludes that it was "useful and advantageous to France." Elliott is more sober: "The Peace of [La Rochelle] with the Huguenots in February 1626, and the Peace of Monzon with Spain a month later, were disappointing short-term settlements to long-standing problems, and they revealed the persistent underlying weaknesses of the crown" (*Richelieu and Olivares*, 78). Cf. Elliott's *Olivares*, 256–57.

21. See Elliott, *Richelieu and Olivares*, chap. 3; Trevor Aston, ed., *Crisis in Europe, 1560–1660* (London, 1965); Geoffrey Parker and Leslie Smith, eds., *The General Crisis of the Seventeenth Century* (London, 1978); and Lublinskaya, *French Absolutism*.

22. The classic account of Richelieu's economic programs remains Henri Hauser, *La pensée et l'action économiques du Cardinal de Richelieu* (Paris, 1944). Mariéjol, *Henri IV et Louis XIII*, is still worth consulting. In general, historians have been mesmerized by the cardinal's schemes.

23. The Assembly of Notables can be followed in *Mercure françois* and Griffet, *Histoire du règne de Louis XIII*. It is analyzed by Bonney, *King's Debts*; Lublinskaya, *French Absolutism*; Tapié, *France in the Age of Louis XIII and Richelieu*; Major, *Representative Government*; and in Jeanne Petit's *L'assemblée des notables de 1626–1627* (Paris, 1936).

24. Richelieu's memoirs can be compared with the pro-Marillac version of the reform movement by Lefèvre, BN ms. fr. 14027, fols. 223r–27v. There are no changes in the manuscript copy, BN ms. fr. nouv. acq. 82–83. Hayden's statistical comparison of reform ideas, *Estates General*, 211–15, concludes that the Code Michau owed more to the Notables of 1626 and Richelieu's immediate concerns than to the Estates of 1614.

25. Arnauld d'Andilly, *Journal inédit, 1627*, 35; Molé, *Mémoires*, 1:478–82. Louis's letter, accompanying Marillac's personal note, may have been drafted by the keeper of the seals, but it certainly reflected the king's feelings. Marillac warned the judges that their monarch was very upset.

26. Blet, *Clergé de France*, 1:392; and Richelieu, *Papiers*, 3:274–76 (which has the king's covering letter, discovered by Grillon). Michel Houssaye, *La vie du cardinal de Bérulle* (Paris, 1874–75), 3:303–4, is typical of traditional scholarship, in writing: "At the instigation of his minister, Louis XIII called the bishops from the assembly to his camp at Surgères, and delivered this speech. . . ." This incident became engraved on the king's mind, for two years later he testily accused the clerics of going back on their word to continue the payments without the need of calling a new clerical assembly. Louis wrote to Richelieu: "I am writing you this letter in order to tell you what to

relay from me to the deputies who have gone to find you by my order, [namely] that I have no intention in making the request I made other than in keeping with their promise at La Rochelle that if I took that place, they would give me twice what they gave me then. . . . I would rather do without their help now even though I could in all fairness expect it, fully meriting it from the church and experiencing great need in the urgent necessity of my affairs. I leave it to the very first assembly being held to receive the effect of their good will" (AAE France ms. 244, fol. 8).

27. See Ranum, "Richelieu and the Great Nobility"; and Herr, "Honor Versus Absolutism."

28. Bassompierre, *Journal de ma vie*, 3:289; Arnauld d'Andilly, *Journal inédit, 1627*, 20; *Mercure françois*, 13:411. Chevallier, *Louis XIII*, has a good account. However, the Bouteville case has been most brilliantly studied in its broadest social, political, and ideological context by François Billacois, *Le duel dans la société française des XVIe–XVIIe siècles: Essai de psychosociologie historique* (Paris, 1986), esp. 247–75.

29. *Mercure françois*, 13:417–24.

30. See above, chap. 8.

31. See Richelieu, *Mémoires*, ed. SHF, 7:66; idem, *Testament politique*, 102; and above, chap. 8 (text and n. 17).

32. Bernard, *Histoire du roy Louis XIII*, 1:500; Arnauld d'Andilly, *Journal inédit, 1627*, 30–31; *Mercure françois*, 13:449–50.

33. Arnauld d'Andilly, *Journal inédit, 1627*, pp. 35–37.

34. AAE France ms. 2164, fol. 150.

35. See Chevallier, *Louis XIII*, 306–7.

36. See BN ms. fr. 4027, fol. 299r (abbreviated in Héroard, *Journal*, 2:305).

37. Contrast Richelieu's memoirs (which implicate in a "grand crime" almost the entire court, including the cardinal's collaborating minister Schomberg) with the 1643 tract *Le maréchal d'Ornano, martyr d'estat* (BN ms. fr. 18536, fols. 540–63); the views of the well-informed confidant of Louis and Anne, Beringhen, in Motteville, *Mémoires*, 21; and the main text and supporting documents in Jean Canault, *Vie du Maréchal J.-B. d'Ornano, par son secrétaire Jean Canault*, ed. Jean Charay (Grenoble, 1971). Siri, *Mémoires secrets*, 36:4–5, 13–17, 20–21, accuses Richelieu of manipulating everything and everyone so that he could retain power under either Louis or a future King Gaston. One need not accept this criticism in toto, but it should not be dismissed, either.

38. See *Mercure françois*, 12:413, and the accounts by Bernard, *Histoire du roy Louis XIII*; Griffet, *Histoire du règne de Louis XIII*; and Vaunois, *Vie de Louis XIII*.

39. The initial capitulation, dated 31 May and signed by Gaston, Louis, and Marie, is in AAE France ms. 782, fols. 151–53.

40. BN ms. Baluze 348, fols. 16, 21, 22, 43. This paternalistic side contrasts with the traditional picture of Louis as a relentlessly jealous and hostile brother, in Georges Dethan, *Gaston d'Orléans: Conspirateur et prince charmant*

(Paris, 1959). Before the Chalais conspiracy, Louis had helped Gaston prevent a duel by Ornano, saying "he wished to see this quarrel ended with good feelings and friendship" and bringing the rivals together in the great hall of the Louvre (Louis XIII, *Lettres*, 2:333–34, 373–74; *Mercure françois*, 12:428–30).

41. See Richelieu's memoirs for early July 1626; Arnauld d'Andilly, *Journal inédit, 1626*, 16, 17n.2, 35–37; and Siri, *Mémoires secrets*, 36:34–38.

42. See Richelieu, *Testament politique*, 161; and idem, *Mémoires*, SHF ed., vol. 6, including the editorial footnotes. Griffet, *Histoire du règne de Louis XIII*, 510–15, is a good corrective.

43. Claude Dulong, *Anne d'Autriche: Mère de Louis XIV* (Paris, 1980), 73–76, has a good defense of the queen's conduct. Martha Freer, *Married Life of Anne of Austria*, 1:125–49, is harsher; while Ruth Kleinman, *Anne of Austria*, 70, is speculative. Cf. Batiffol, *Richelieu et Louis XIII*, 150–51; Motteville, *Mémoires*, 22.

44. In addition to Héroard's record of the royal couple's sexual relations, there are traces of the supposed pregnancy after the Chalais affair in Richelieu's memoirs and in Arnauld d'Andilly's journal.

45. Tapié, *France in the Age of Louis XIII and Richelieu*, p. 177. For a sampling of Richelieu's gyrations on the Huguenots, see Richelieu, *Papiers*, 1:226–33; Griffet, *Histoire du règne de Louis XIII*, 1:479; AAE France, ms. 780 (Richelieu's correspondence), fol. 78; and Siri, *Mémoires secrets*, 33:704; 34:68, 103–4.

46. Bernard, *Histoire du roy Louis XIII*, 1:493.

47. See Vialart, *Histoire du ministère de Richelieu*, 1:356–57.

48. Letter of 5 September, in Richelieu, *Papiers*, 2:448.

49. Bernard, *Histoire du roy Louis XIII*, 2:19; Griffet, *Histoire du règne de Louis XIII*, 1:565–66.

50. Bernard, *Histoire du roy Louis XIII*, 2:28–30, 50; Griffet, *Histoire du règne de Louis XIII*, 1:566–68.

51. Vaunois, *Vie de Louis XIII*, 381.

52. See Bernard, *Histoire du roy Louis XIII*, 2:51; Griffet, *Histoire du règne de Louis XIII*, 1:574–76; and Chevallier, *Louis XIII*, 332–35.

53. Griffet, *Histoire du règne de Louis XIII*, 1:577.

54. Ibid., 1:624–25; and Chevallier, *Louis XIII*, 339.

55. See Arnauld d'Andilly, *Journal inédit, 1628–1629*, 72–77; Bernard, *Histoire du roy Louis XIII*, 2:108; Vialart, *Histoire du ministère de Richelieu*, 582.

56. BN ms. Baluze 348, fol. 55.

10. Alais, Mantua, and the Day of Dupes

1. For varying interpretations, see Georges Pagès's key article, "Autour du 'grand orage': Richelieu et Marillac, deux politiques," *Revue historique* 174 (1937); Tapié, *France in the Age of Louis XIII and Richelieu*, chap. 6: "The Misery of the People and the Glory of the State"; and Major, *Representative Government*, chaps. 14: "Richelieu and Marillac, 1624–1629," and 16: "The Triumph of Richelieu," pt. 1.

2. In 1933, when the duke of La Force began to collaborate on Hanotaux's turn-of-the-century *Histoire du Cardinal de Richelieu,* the editor asked of French policy making: "What was . . . the role of Louis XIII?" (see 3:vi). The author, unfortunately, did not share the editor's curiosity, but there are clues in Tapié, *France in the Age of Louis XIII and Richelieu;* Batiffol, *Richelieu et Louis XIII;* and Chevallier, *Louis XIII.*

3. Chevallier, *Louis XIII,* 367. Cf. Tapié, *France in the Age of Louis XIII and Richelieu,* 235: "The clash between the two [different policies] was sufficiently serious to give rise to hesitations in the king's mind and to battles within his conscience."

4. The date is usually set at 29 December 1628. But Arnauld d'Andilly's meticulous diary records that on the fourteenth Louis went from Versailles to his mother's Palais du Luxembourg, where he held a "great council at which the war of Italy was absolutely resolved" (*Journal inédit, 1628–1629,* 77).

5. Elliott, *Richelieu and Olivares,* 99, concludes that Richelieu "forced Louis to accept his own ordering of priorities." Cf. Griffet, *Histoire du règne de Louis XIII,* 1:650–53; Richelieu, *Papiers,* 3:587; idem, *Lettres,* 3:150–52, 179–213; Houssaye, *Cardinal de Bérulle,* 3:416–23. On the question of military leadership, Chevallier, *Louis XIII,* 355, suggests that Louis assumed from the La Rochelle experience that Gaston was unworthy of a high command, while Richelieu held out for the reason of state argument of keeping the heir content. I suspect that Louis wanted to lead right from the start, and that this was one of the times when Richelieu's rationality and Louis XIII's political instinct clashed.

6. See Vialart, *Histoire du ministère de Richelieu,* 1:497–98; Elliott, *Olivares,* 346, 360, 375–81.

7. BN ms. Baluze 348, fol. 63.

8. See BN Cabinet des Estampes, series Qb[1] (1629); and Richelieu, *Mémoires,* SHF ed., 10:278–79.

9. Griffet, *Histoire du règne de Louis XIII,* 1:664–65; Arnauld d'Andilly, *Journal inédit, 1628–1629,* 96, 98–105; Bernard, *Histoire du roy Louis XIII,* 2:151–52.

10. The king's correspondence is in BN mss. fr. 3828, fols. 37–38, 61, 75–76; 3829, fols. 7–8, 21. The cartoon is in BN series Qb[1], 27 May 1629. Griffet, *Histoire du règne de Louis XIII,* 1:669–71, summarizes the various explanations of what caused the Privas holocaust.

11. BN ms. fr. 3829, fols. 62–63.

12. Chevallier, *Louis XIII,* 349; Richelieu, *Lettres,* 3:410–11.

13. See BN series Qb[1] (1628–29).

14. See above, chap. 8.

15. Bernard, *Histoire du roy Louis XIII,* 2:193, is emphatic on the queen mother's major involvement in decision making in 1630. But involvement did not mean that she won the king over to her view unless he had reasons to do so: he did regarding his brother's marital future; he did not regarding his being in Savoy.

16. BN ms. Baluze 348, fol. 53.

17. See above, n. 5.

18. Louis's correspondence is almost a chronology of the affair.

19. Chaumont, 7 March 1629 (BN ms. Baluze 348, fol. 64).

20. Quoted in Chevallier, *Louis XIII,* 357.

21. Goulas, *Mémoires,* 1:6.

22. Vaunois, *Vie de Louis XIII,* 402, accepts the supposed pact.

23. Elliott, *Richelieu and Olivares,* 100.

24. Elliott, *Olivares,* 388. On the Habsburgs' military-political dilemmas, see ibid.; Robert Birely, *Religion and Politics in the Age of the Counterreformation: Emperor Ferdinand II, William Lamormaini, S.J., and the Formation of Imperial Policy* (Chapel Hill, N.C., 1981); and Jonathan I. Israel, *The Dutch Republic and the Hispanic World, 1606–1661* (Oxford, 1982).

25. Pagès, "Grand orage," 81; Topin, *Louis XIII et Richelieu,* 143.

26. Pagès, "Grand orage," 86.

27. BN ms. fr. 3828, fols. 18–19. Pagès, "Grand orage," 87–88, gives a slightly different reading of some words from the manuscript. I agree with him that the document must date from May, not July as the original archival conservator thought.

28. Pagès, "Grand orage," 80.

29. J. Humbert, *Le maréchal de Créquy, gendre de Lesdiguières (1573–1638)* (Paris, 1962), 172.

30. See Pagès, "Grand orage," 82–87.

31. Bernard, *Histoire du roy Louis XIII,* 2:193–95.

32. Ibid., 2:203–5; Arnauld d'Andilly, *Journal inédit, 1630–1632,* 25. Marillac's ill-fated allusion caused the king to retort: "If I went to the frontier wanting to cross it by myself, I would pass over and no one could stop me" (Batiffol, *Richelieu et Louis XIII,* 242–43).

33. See Arnauld d'Andilly, *Journal inédit, 1630–1632,* 27–38; Bernard, *Histoire du roy Louis XIII,* 2:207–11; and Vaunois, *Vie de Louis XIII,* 410–11.

34. Pagès, "Grand orage," 93.

35. AAE France mss. 244, fols. 9–10; 2164, fol. 9. Portions of these letters are also in Vaunois, *Vie de Louis XIII,* and Topin, *Louis XIII et Richelieu.*

36. Louis to Gaston, Lyon, 16 August. BN ms. Baluze 348, fol. 98.

37. Chevallier, *Louis XIII,* 369.

38. Batiffol, *Richelieu et Louis XIII,* 248.

39. Hanotaux and La Force, *Cardinal de Richelieu,* 3:264.

40. Richelieu, *Lettres,* 3:873–83.

41. Tapié, *France in the Age of Louis XIII and Richelieu,* 227–28, assumes that Louis's "thoughts and opinions elude us" during the late summer.

42. BN ms. Baluze 348, fols. 101–3.

43. I have used the Ormesson copy of Suffren's account in the Rouen Municipal Library, ms. Leber 5767, fol. 138. Bernard, *Histoire du roy Louis XIII,* 2:224–25, adds the king's apology "for his failings in governing his kingdom."

44. The quotation is from Burckhardt, *Richelieu and His Age*, 1:376, who miscasts Marie de' Medici's vote. Hanotaux and La Force, *Cardinal de Richelieu*, 3:283–84, have a more precisely documented account but leave the queen mother's role unclear, and the king's position is stated only in an official letter drafted by Bouthillier. Batiffol, *Richelieu et Louis XIII*, 259–60, states that the king left Richelieu to "examine the question" with Marillac, Bouthillier, and Marie de' Medici and that the council "majority" followed the cardinal's position.

45. Richelieu, *Lettres*, 3:968.

46. The letter is in ibid., 960–64. The editor has a long nota on the varying views of the councillors at Lyon and Roanne after the treaty arrived; Avenel ignores the king and lauds "the superiority of Richelieu over all those around him." I have followed the reconstruction of the 26 October meeting in Chevallier, *Louis XIII*, 376–77, while being more concerned to determine the monarch's own position.

47. Despite all our knowledge of the Regensburg and Casale negotiations, every historian gives a different version. Mariéjol, *Henri IV et Louis XIII*, has one of the fullest accounts. Elliott, *Olivares*, 401, notes that Olivares as well as Richelieu was furious at losing out to Ferdinand.

48. Arnauld d'Andilly writes: "Ever since Lyon, the queen mother had pressed the king relentlessly to dismiss the cardinal, saying that she could no longer abide him. Concerning this, she claimed that the king had begged her to wait until peace was made so that this would in no way prejudice his affairs, and [also] that he had deferred it until his return to Paris. On these grounds, she assured herself on the king's arrival in Paris that he could not help carrying out what she construed the requested delay to guarantee" (*Journal inédit, 1630–1632*, 121).

49. La Ville-aux-Clerc's eyewitness account is in Henri-Auguste de Loménie de Brienne, *Mémoires*, MP ed., 3d ser., vol. 3 (Paris, 1838), 52. Cf. Richelieu's recollection: "At Auxerre, the king divulged to the cardinal all the diabolical things the queen mother had said against him, and all the artifices she had employed to persuade [Louis]" (Hanotaux and La Force, *Cardinal de Richelieu*, 3:288).

50. Hanotaux and La Force, *Cardinal de Richelieu*, 3:288–89.

51. Bernard, *Histoire du roy Louis XIII*, 2:236–37, stressed Gaston's shift as the key to Marie's boldness two days later; but we need to weigh the fact that this king's historiographer was crafting a picture of the queen mother as the victim of bad influences around her rather than the initiator of the crisis.

52. See Arnauld d'Andilly, *Journal inédit, 1630–1632*, 121.

53. I agree on these points with Chevallier, *Louis XIII*, 379–81, 389, 395, who has the best reconstruction of a great event that will never be completely demystified. The accounts by Batiffol, *Richelieu et Louis XIII*, and Georges Mongrédien, *10 novembre 1630: La journée des dupes*, have met with serious criticism.

54. Arnauld d'Andilly, *Journal inédit, 1630–1632*, 122. Cf. Marillac's con-

temporary biographer, BN ms. fr. 14027, fol. 276r. Bernard records that the king "knew who the artisans of these divisions were, so that on leaving for his residence at Versailles he ordered the cardinal and the keeper of the seals, each one separately, to follow him. . . . The keeper of the seals was sent to lodgings at Glatigny, where the king said he would tell him his will the next day, and the cardinal was lodged at the château of Versailles beneath the king's chamber; and in the evening Richelieu went into council with the king" (*Histoire du roy Louis XIII*, 2:237).

55. On these actions, see Arnauld d'Andilly, *Journal inédit, 1630–1632*, 123–24.

56. Richelieu, *Lettres*, 3:969; Marvick, "Childhood History," 197 (a rebuttal of my critique).

11. Governmental Revolution

1. The thesis of a governmental revolution was first proposed in 1932 by Georges Pagès in his "Essai sur l'évolution des institutions administratives en France du commencement du XVIe siècle à la fin du XVIIe," *Revue d'histoire moderne* 7 (1932). It has been developed in Roland Mousnier's many publications. See also my *Revolt of the Judges*, chap. 2, "The Reign of Louis XIII: Governmental 'Revolution' and the *Officiers.*"

2. For these developments, see the journals of Arnauld d'Andilly; Chevallier, *Louis XIII*; and Batiffol, *Richelieu et Louis XIII*.

3. Bullion to Richelieu, 22 November 1630, quoted in Hanotaux and La Force, *Cardinal de Richelieu*, 3:316. Batiffol, *Richelieu et Louis XIII*, 285–86, puts the quotation in the first person.

4. Arnauld d'Andilly, *Journal inédit, 1630–1632*, 126.

5. Batiffol, *Richelieu et Louis XIII*, 282, 286.

6. Quoted in Hanotaux and La Force, *Cardinal de Richelieu*, 3:326.

7. Batiffol, *Richelieu et Louis XIII*, 293.

8. See Arnauld d'Andilly, *Journal inédit, 1630–1632*, 151–53. Cf. Bernard, *Histoire du roy Louis XIII*, 2:240.

9. For the flight, see above, chap. 8.

10. The above quotations come from Church, *Richelieu*, 208, 212–14, 306. I have altered the wording slightly for style. Donald A. Bailey's bibliographical articles on Matthieu de Morgues's pamphlets are an excellent guide.

11. See Batiffol, *Richelieu et Louis XIII*, 313.

12. See especially Griffet, *Histoire du règne de Louis XIII*, 2:362; Hanotaux and La Force, *Cardinal de Richelieu*, 401–2; Chevallier, *Louis XIII*, 465–68; and Tapié, *France in the Age of Louis XIII and Richelieu*, 308–10. At the time, Louis expressed the consolation he received from Father Arnoux's account of the condemned man's brave, repentant preparation for death: "I am sorry that it had to come to this, and it consoles me to hear your words about his virtue

in dying . . . as a good Christian." Vaunois, *Vie de Louis XIII*, 462–63, blames Richelieu for pursuing Montmorency out of jealousy and with "fierce pleasure."

13. On Michel de Marillac, see BN ms. fr. 14027, fols. 276–90; and Major, *Representative Government*, 571–81. Donald Bailey is working on a biography of Marillac that promises to rescue him from the shadow—and criticisms—of Richelieu. For Louis de Marillac, the standard account is Pierre de Vaissière, *Un grand procès sous Richelieu: L'affaire du maréchal de Marillac (1630–1632)* (Paris, 1924).

14. Marvick, "Childhood History," 162. Cf. Vaunois, *Vie de Louis XIII*, 455–58.

15. O'Connell, *Richelieu*, 240–44.

16. Church, *Richelieu*, 230.

17. Cf. my *Revolt of the Judges*, 59–63.

18. See Church, *Richelieu*, 209–11. Cf. a prior five-sheet letter by Louis to Gaston, BN ms. Baluze 348, fol. 110bis.

19. See Bernard, *Histoire du roy Louis XIII*, 2:256–61; Arnauld d'Andilly, *Journal inédit, 1630–1632*, 166–73.

20. See Hanotaux and La Force, *Cardinal de Richelieu*, 4:158–68; Arnauld d'Andilly, *Journal inédit, 1630–1632*, 167–68. On negotiations over the paulette, compare Mousnier, *Vénalité*, with Bonney, *King's Debts*.

21. Molé, *Mémoires*, 2:143–44. Cf. Mariéjol, *Henri IV et Louis XIII*, 393–96; and Moote, *Revolt of the Judges*, 41–43.

22. See Major, *Representative Government*, 532–49, 599–601; Sharon Kettering, *Judicial Politics and Urban Revolts in Seventeenth-Century France: The Parlement of Aix, 1629–1659* (Princeton, N.J., 1978); René Pillorget, *Les mouvements insurrectionnels de Provence entre 1596 et 1715* (Paris, 1975); and Mariéjol, *Henri IV et Louis XIII*, 400–402;

23. See Hanotaux and La Force, *Cardinal de Richelieu*, 4:319; Bonney, *King's Debts*, 164–65. On the intendancies, see also below, chap. 12.

24. See Major, *Representative Government*, 619, 635, 672. At times Major's interpretation of "Richelieu's policy" looks much like this traditional alternative: "Thus Richelieu . . . reverted to the Renaissance practice of trying to govern through the estates, assemblies of the clergy, and other duly constituted bodies" (p. 619).

25. The roles of all these individuals during the early 1630s are worthy of careful study. Major, *Representative Government*, and Hanotaux and La Force, *Cardinal de Richelieu*, touch on the ministerial infighting.

26. See O'Connell, *Richelieu*, 260–62; Elliott, *Richelieu and Olivares*, 119.

27. AAE France ms. 2164, fol. 12; Richelieu, *Lettres*, 4:269–70.

28. Arnauld d'Andilly traces Louis's travels in detail. The last word has not been written on Châteauneuf's sudden disgrace.

29. Elliott, in *Richelieu and Olivares*, brilliantly demolishes historians' untenable assumptions about the inevitability of the Bourbon-Habsburg war.

30. One can consult the standard works for French foreign policy at this time, but especially ibid., and Fritz Dickmann, "Rechtsgedanke und Machtpolitik bei Richelieu," *Historische Zeitschrift* 196 (1963). I am again indebted to Geoffrey Parker for a verbatim report of the original version, presented at a conference on the Thirty Years' War at Munich in 1984, of Hermann Weber's paper, "Vom verdeckten zum offenen Krieg: Kriegsgrunde und Kriegsziele Richelieus 1634–65," including Parker's notes on the lively and invaluable discussion that followed (especially comments by Roland Mousnier and John Elliott). The session revealed archival evidence that Louis XIII was pressing and Richelieu hesitating even while actively preparing for an open war. Also noteworthy is Mousnier's oral comment that "this is just one more example of how the major policies of Louis XIII's government were in fact the king's, and how the 'terrible' Cardinal often tried to moderate royal imprudence." Cf. above. chap. 8, n. 42.

31. See Tapié, *France in the Age of Louis XIII and Richelieu*, 330.

12. Warfare King, State, and Society

1. Mousnier, *Institutions de la France*, 2:489; Bonney, *Political Change*, 164, 173; and the table on increases in military manpower in Parker and Smith, eds., *General Crisis*, 14.

2. Cf. Lossky's comment on my article, "Two-headed Monarchy"; and Mousnier's comment on Weber's paper, cited above, chap. 11, n. 30.

3. AAE France ms. 2164, fols. 40–41, 64, 66–67.

4. My examples come from ibid., fols. 44, 89, 104, 121–22.

5. On the Caussin affair, compare Montglat, *Mémoires*, 59; and Chevallier, *Louis XIII*, 540–46.

6. AAE France ms. 2164, fol. 130.

7. On the difficulties Louis's ministers had with his close watch and mood swings on policy, see Ranum, *Richelieu*. A revealing ministerial correspondence that stretches from Richelieu's last months to the eve of Louis's fatal illness is contained in BN mss. Clairambault 384, fols. 160, 168, 171, 179, 256, 286, 288, 294; and 385, fols. 101, 103. Richelieu, Mazarin, Chavigny, Sublet, and Anne all worked for the Guise family's rehabilitation on behalf of Guise's widow; Louis, however, kept insisting that the Guise heir's "bad conduct" prevented royal exoneration of the family.

8. Mazarin's rise to favor with Louis XIII is still a mystery to us (though his contemporaries' writings make it clear he was the man commanding their attention, just as Richelieu had been in the years before his definitive entry to the royal council). See Georges Dethan's works, especially "Mazarin avant le ministère," *Revue historique* 227 (1962), on the time-honored thesis that Richelieu chose Mazarin as his successor.

9. Bonney, *King's Debts*, 176–77, states that state exactions from the venal officials amounted to 39 percent of total royal revenues in the early 1630s

and almost 25 percent from 1635 to 1639, tapering off somewhat after Bullion's death.

10. Bonney, *Political Change*, 43, 125.

11. Douglas T. Baxter, *Servants of the Sword: French Intendants of the Army 1630–70* (Urbana, Ill., 1976), 3–19, 61–85; Mousnier, *Institutions de la France*, 2:488.

12. Mousnier's many studies on the intendants should be read in conjunction with Bonney's full-dress study *Political Change*.

13. Marillac had stated in January 1630, that "the uniformity which the king desires to establish in his kingdom has caused him to refuse offers [by Burgundy's Estates to redeem the creation of élections and élus]." Had Louis personally held such a rigid position, then relented after Marillac's fall, only to turn to the intendancy in the mid 1630s? Contrast the views by Major, *Representative Government*; and Bonney, "Absolutism: What's in a Name?" *French History* 1 (1987), 112 (text and n. 93).

14. The connection between Louis's ministers and their commissaire past is shrewdly noted in Bonney, *Political Change*, 40–41.

15. See ibid.; and Major, *Representative Government*.

16. See the table on military expenses after 1635, in William Beik, *Absolutism and Society in Seventeenth-Century France: State Power and Provincial Aristocracy in Languedoc* (Cambridge, 1985), 283. Cf. Bonney, *Political Change*, 381: "In these years, the troops took what the estates refused to grant."

17. There is a good summary of these developments in Lavisse's monumental *Histoire de France*, and an allusion to the mortmain question in Barbara Diefendorf's *Paris City Councillors in the Sixteenth Century: The Politics of Patrimony* (Princeton, N.J., 1983). For a partisan position by a high contemporary cleric, see Montchal's fascinating memoirs.

18. Boris Porchnev, *Les soulèvements populaires en France de 1623 à 1648* (Paris, 1963), discusses the hidden taxes imposed on the nobles. See also Bonney, *Political Change*, esp. 354–55.

19. Yves-Marie Bercé, *Histoire des Croquants: Etude des soulèvements populaires au XVIIe siècle dans le sud-ouest de la France* (Geneva, 1974), 1:147.

20. Quoted in Tapié, *France in the Age of Louis XIII and Richelieu*, 385.

21. Ibid., 419–20; Chevallier, *Louis XIII*, 583–600. Jean-Marie Constant, *Les conjurateurs: Le premier libéralisme politique sous Richelieu* (Paris, 1987), is revisionist in stressing the ethical strain of Christian stoicism held by the great and lesser nobles who conspired against Richelieu between 1626 and 1642, but he admits that self-serving noble individualism became more predominant among a second generation of conspirators, climaxing with Cinq Mars. See below, chap. 14, regarding Louis XIII's possible involvement in Cinq Mars's plotting against Richelieu.

22. See my *Revolt of the Judges*, especially chaps. 3 and 4.

23. Hanley, *Lit de Justice*, 283–84, and tables.

24. Griffet, *Histoire du règne de Louis XIII*, 2:818–19, quoted in Church, *Richelieu*, 203.

25. See the doctoral dissertation by James H. Kitchens, "The Parlement of Paris during the Ministry of Cardinal Richelieu, 1624–1642" (1974); and shorter treatments by Shennan, *The Parlement of Paris*, and Moote, *The Revolt of the Judges.*

26. Contrast Porchnev, *Soulèvements populaires*, and Mousnier, *Peasant Uprisings in Seventeenth-Century France, Russia, and China*, trans. Brian Pearce (London, 1971) (the author's expression in the original French edition being the less complimentary *fureurs paysannes*). My favorite studies of the subject are Bercé's *Histoire des Croquants*, and *Croquants et Nu-pieds* (Paris, 1974), because his concept of *émotions populaires* avoids Mousnier's denigration of the poor and Porchnev's too neat class polarization. See also the critique of Mousnier by Michael O. Gately, A. Lloyd Moote, and John E. Wills, "Seventeenth-Century Peasant 'Furies': Some Problems of Comparative History," *Past and Present* 51 (1971).

27. Bercé, *Histoire des Croquants*, 1:389, 415.

28. See ibid., passim.

29. Madeleine Foisil, *La révolte des Nu-pieds et les révoltes normandes de 1639* (Paris, 1970), is a fine study in the Mousnier tradition. Contrast Porchnev's viewpoint in *Soulèvements populaires*, as well as the balanced discussion in Tapié, *France in the Age of Louis XIII and Richelieu*, 396–407, which retains Porchnev's emotional realism without his polemics.

30. The notion running through the intendants' correspondence that the lower orders could never think of rebelling unless their social superiors failed to hold them on a leash, like mad dogs, can be found in Bercé, *Histoire des Croquants*; and Ranum, *Paris in the Age of Absolutism* (New York, 1968).

31. See Tapié, *France in the Age of Louis XIII and Richelieu*, 407.

32. See Braudel and Labrousse, eds., *Histoire économique et sociale de la France*, 1(1):46–47, 77, 193–94. They estimate that in 1665 nonmilitary officialdom accounted for 15 percent of the gross national product.

13. *King and Culture*

1. See Roland Mousnier and Jean Mesnard, eds., *L'âge d'or du mécénat (1598–1661)* (Paris, 1985), notably Elizabeth Marvick's article, "Richelieu le mécène: perspectives psychologiques."

2. Bassompierre, *Journal de ma vie*, 3:286.

3. From an anthropological viewpoint, the monarchy in early modern France was the "sacred center" that gave meaning to society and culture as well as politics. My argument here is that Louis XIII's politics and personality added to that generalized function. See Clifford Geertz, "Centers, Kings, and Charisma: Reflections on the Symbolics of Power," in *Culture and Its Creators: Essays in Honor of Edward Shils*, ed. Joseph Ben-David and Terry Nichols Clark (Chicago, 1977); Clifford Geertz and Edward Shils, *Center and Periphery: Essays in Macrosociology* (Chicago, 1977); and Lynn Hunt, *Politics, Culture, and Class in the French Revolution* (Berkeley and Los Angeles, 1984), 87, incl. n. 3.

4. Cultural histories of Louis XIII's reign virtually ignore the king, often using Richelieu's ministry as a watershed. See, e.g., Jacques Roger, *Panorama du XVIIe siècle français* (Paris, 1962). Emile Magne, *La vie quotidienne au temps de Louis XIII* (Paris, 1942), scarcely relates elite culture to the king. Even the king's biographer, Batiffol, says very little about his connection with culture in *Le Louvre sous Henri IV et Louis XIII: La vie de la cour de France au XVIIe siècle* (Paris, 1930).

5. There is a nicely illustrated overview of the reign's art in François Gebelin, *Histoire de l'art français: L'époque Henri IV et Louis XIII* (Paris, 1969).

6. Kathryn Norberg, *Rich and Poor in Grenoble, 1600–1814* (Berkeley and Los Angeles), 20–21.

7. Philip T. Hoffman, *Church and Community in the Diocese of Lyon, 1500–1789* (New Haven, Conn., 1984), 72.

8. Quoted in Henri Daniel-Rops, *The Church in the Seventeenth Century*, (New York, 1963), 1:59. On La Fayette, see below, chap. 14.

9. Quoted in Mariéjol, *Henri IV et Louis XIII*, 372.

10. On St. Vincent de Paul, see Daniel-Rops, *The Church in the Seventeenth Century*, 1:13–74.

11. Quoted in Georges Duby and Robert Mandrou, *A History of French Civilization*, trans. James Blake Atkinson (New York, 1974), 306.

12. Norberg, *Rich and Poor*, 3.

13. Jean Danès, *Toutes les actions du règne de Louis XIII rapportées au surnom de Juste* (1643), 51.

14. Louis kept a close eye on the clergy. In 1637, Chavigny wrote to the French ambassador at Rome: "I gave an account to the king of the contents of your dispatch of 5 April, which I then showed to [Cardinal Richelieu]. His Majesty sends the attached memo with his instructions, and I add only this word concerning the forms you are to pass on to the Cordeliers and Recollets. . . . His Majesty forbids the monks to go to the General Chapter in Spain" (BN ms. fr. 4071, fols. 44–47).

15. I have used the published version of the vow from BN ms. Clairambault 383, fols. 34–39. Cf. Mariéjol, *Henri et Louis XIII*, 369n.1; Chevallier, *Louis XIII*, 547–48.

16. Quoted in Chevallier, *Louis XIII*, 558.

17. David Ogg, *Europe in the Seventeenth Century*, 7th ed. (London, 1959), 331–32.

18. See Church, *Richelieu*, 384–401.

19. On Saint-Cyran, see ibid., 401–4; and Mariéjol, *Henri IV et Louis XIII*, 374–76.

20. It was not in Louis XIII's stoical nature to ask God for personal help. His letters are a litany of submissiveness to divine providence—whether referring to his own aches and pains or asking bereaved subjects to accept the will of God. Compare with Richelieu promising to say a mass every Sunday if St. John would intercede with God to cure his migraine and bringing the relics of St. Fiacre from the monks of Meaux to cure his

hemorrhoids. See Louis's *Lettres*, ed. Griselle; and Mariéjol, *Henri IV et Louis XIII*, 368.

21. I thank Orest Ranum for this information. On Richelieu's building tastes at the Palais Cardinal and his artificially constructed town of Richelieu, see Ranum's critical comments in his *Paris in the Age of Absolutism*, 93–95.

22. There are some perceptive comments on the secular architecture of the period in David Maland, *Culture and Society in Seventeenth-Century France* (London, 1970), 31–35, 70–94.

23. On Louis and the beginnings of Versailles, see Héroard, *Journal*; the Journals of Arnauld d'Andilly; and Batiffol, *Louis XIII à vingt ans*, 636–74.

24. Roger, *Panorama*, 99–102, alludes to a "Louis XIII style."

25. See Batiffol, *Louis XIII à vingt ans*, 657–58, 671–74.

26. See Chevallier, *Louis XIII*, illustrations 10 and 11.

27. René Taveneaux, *La vie quotidienne des Jansénistes aux XVIIe et XVIIIe siècles* (Paris, 1973), 170.

28. Jacques Callot, *Les grandes misères de la guerre*, no. 18: "Distribution des récompenses," Musée Historique Lorraine.

29. Louis Auchincloss, *Richelieu* (New York, 1973), reproduces some of these.

30. Of course, there was meaning to this informality. When Louis let his boon companions engage in cherry pit-throwing contests, he cheered his current male favorite's team.

31. On life at court, see Batiffol, *Le Louvre*, 193–232; and Magne, *Vie quotidienne*, 50–90.

32. Maland, *Culture and Society*, 83.

33. AAE France ms. 2164, fol. 132.

34. See Dubois, *Mémoire fidèle des choses qui se sont passées à la mort de Louis XIII* (1643), in *Archives curieuses de l'histoire de France*, ed. L. Cimber and L.-F. Danjou, ser. 2, vol. 5 (Paris, 1834–40).

35. Antoine Adam's work on literature is dated. Contrast Ranum's *Paris in the Age of Absolutism*, chap. 8: "The Last Heroes," which links letters, society, and politics; Erica Harth, *Ideology and Culture in Seventeenth-Century France* (Ithaca, N.Y., 1983), which stresses a bourgeois counterculture vying with traditional aristocratic ideology; and Mark Bannister, *Privileged Mortals: The French Heroic Novel 1630–1660* (Oxford, 1983), which sees literature as reflecting the tensions between aristocratic liberty and national absolutism.

36. See, e.g., Maland, *Culture and Society*, 79: "Louis XIII encouraged no new [artistic] style, confirmed no trend, nor did he show much interest. To poets he appeared wholly antagonistic. When Richelieu died he cancelled the literary pensions he had granted, saying with brutal frankness, 'we don't need that any more' (Tallemant). Plays however he greatly enjoyed."

37. BN ms. fr. 3840 contains a notebook of the king's battle accounts. See Howard M. Solomon, *Public Welfare, Science, and Propaganda in Seventeenth-Century France: The Innovations of Théophraste Renaudot* (Princeton, N.J., 1972), 149; and Elizabeth Marvick, "Richelieu and the Testament Politique."

38. Tapié, *France in the Age of Louis XIII and Richelieu*, 275, quoting Richelieu, *Lettres*, 4:610; and Marvick, "Richelieu le mécène."

39. The royal censor's copy of *Le Prince*, complete with his marginal notes, is in the *Réserve* collection at the Bibliothèque nationale.

40. There is a good description of the homes of Rambouillet and her contemporaries in Ranum, *Paris in the Age of Absolutism*, 151–55.

41. According to Mlle de Gournay, as quoted in Harth, *Ideology and Culture*, 38.

42. See Maland, *Culture and Society*, 111, for the censure.

43. Pierre Chevallier's *Louis XIII: Roi cornélien* assumes the connection.

44. On Descartes's would-be conservatism, see Richard H. Popkin, *History of Scepticism from Erasmus to Descartes* (New York, 1964), 175.

14. The Intimate Louis

1. See La Rochefoucauld, *Le cardinal de La Rochefoucauld*, 384.

2. Tallemant des Réaux, *Historiettes*, 1:338. Motteville had more understanding of the king's love life in saying that, "accustomed as [Louis] was to bitterness, he was tender only in feeling heartache and heavy heartedness." (*Mémoires*, 32).

3. On the above, see AAE France ms. 2164, fols. 95–100, 102.

4. Hester W. Chapman says of this scenario that the king "desperately needed a mistress" (*Privileged Persons*, 79).

5. On the dénouement of the relationship, see especially BN ms. fr. 25054: "Escrit du R. P. Caussin de la Compagnie de Jésus sur la vocation de la R. Mère Louise Angélique de la Fayette, religieuse de la Visitation" (copy), a detailed though biased source; Richelieu's equally biased memoirs; and Motteville's more measured *Mémoires*.

6. BN ms. fr. 25054, fol. 16. Chevallier, *Louis XIII*, has a slightly different wording. See also Griffet, *Histoire du règne de Louis XIII*; and Motteville, *Mémoires*.

7. Motteville, *Mémoires*, 34.

8. Here was surely basic material for the plot of a woman spurning a courtier's love and leaving the world, which La Fayette's sister-in-law wove into *La Princesse de Clèves*.

9. See Caussin's letter after the fact to La Fayette, BN ms. fr. 25054, fol. 36.

10. AAE France ms. 2164, fols. 74–76.

11. BN ms. fr. 3747 contains Anne's intercepted correspondence. Richelieu's and Séguier's collected papers on the subject are in BN mss. fr. nouv. acq. 4334 and 10215.

12. Dulong, *Anne d'Autriche*, 119–20.

13. Kleinman, *Anne of Austria*, 98, has a judicious assessment of Anne's acts.

14. For the letters cited above, see BN ms. fr. 3747, fols. 3v, 11r, 17v–18r, 22r, 32r, 41r.

15. For evidence that Louis, not Richelieu, pressed the issue, see Kleinman, *Anne of Austria*, 96–97, incl. n. 40; and Chevallier, *Louis XIII*, 536, quoting Richelieu's briefing of the Venetian ambassadors: "It has already been six months since the king told me that the [queen's] valet now arrested was having private conversations at midnight and other unusual hours, giving rise to suspicions by the king. . . . Finally the king said to me, 'I can't stand it any longer; something has to be done.' He was arrested, and a letter was found in his clothes near his knee. That's how everything was discovered. . . . The matter was resolved, and I did what I had to."

16. Arnauld d'Andilly, *Journal inédit, 1630–1632*, 182.

17. BN ms. fr. 10215, 59, 65–66 (paginated copy).

18. For an analysis of the conception from Anne's perspective, see Kleinman, *Anne of Austria*, 107.

19. AAE France ms. 244, fol. 265.

20. AAE France ms. 2164, fols. 89–90.

21. BN ms. fr. 4071, fol. 303.

22. Motteville, *Mémoires*, 36.

23. Dulong, *Anne d'Autriche*, 148–49 (letter of Bullion to Richelieu).

24. I owe these perspectives to John B. Wolf and his biography of Louis XIV.

25. Early modern homosexuality is just beginning to be studied with sophistication, although there are promising leads in the collaborative work edited by Philippe Ariès and Andre Béjin, *Western Sexuality: Practice and Precept in Past and Present Times*, trans. Anthony Forster (Oxford, 1985). Jonathan Dewald, in an unpublished paper entitled "Individualism and Aristocractic Culture in Seventeenth-Century France" (presented to the Early Modern French Studies Group of Southern California in 1988, and in an earlier version at the Thirty-third Annual Meeting of the Society for French Historical Studies, Minneapolis, in 1987), argues that seventeenth-century French society was ambivalent, perhaps even divided, over gossip about possible homosexual liaisons between noblemen. Louis's relations with men are described in factual terms by Chevallier, *Louis XIII*, 437–55; while Vaunois, *Vie de Louis XIII*, and Chapman, *Privileged Persons*, deftly question the tradition of discussing Louis's sexual behavior within such rigid categories as homosexuality.

26. Tallemant des Réaux, *Historiettes*, 1:339. At the 1985 meeting of the Western Society for French History, a group of scholars that included Madeleine Foisil, Elizabeth Marvick, and Orest Ranum agreed that Tallemant's tales are very untrustworthy.

27. Historians have nevertheless been rather harsh on Saint-Simon. See, e.g., Vaunois, *Vie de Louis XIII*, 529–30.

28. See Bernard, *Histoire du roy Louis XIII*, 2:86. I thank Jeanne-Françoise Rouffianges for diagnosing the romantic element in this code.

29. AAE France ms. 2164, fol. 17.

30. See Louis de Rouvroy de Saint-Simon, *Parallèle des trois premiers rois Bourbons* (Paris, 1967), esp. 375–425.

31. Montglat, *Mémoires*, 81.

32. Goulas, *Mémoires*, 344; Tallemant des Réaux, *Historiettes*, 1:346–47. Chevallier, *Louis XIII*, 453–55, doubts Tallemant's sources, concluding from Louis' "horror of sinning" that his "homosexuality remained latent. It was expressed by outward gestures, doubtlessly stopping half way." But I suspect it would have been easier for Louis to "sin" with men than with women, where a natural child might have resulted and mortified him.

33. AAE France ms. 2164, fols. 126–28, 135, 141.

34. See Tapié, *France in the Age of Louis XIII and Richelieu*, 419–20.

35. Louis informed his advisor of every spat with Cinq Mars in 1642. See, e.g., AAE France ms. 244, fols. 312–13.

36. See Richelieu, *Lettres*, 4:921–24, memorandum to Chavigny and Sublet de Noyers.

37. Burckhardt, *Richelieu and His Age*, 3:434–35.

38. Avenel quotes and comments on the letter, dated 3 June, in Richelieu, *Lettres*, 6:926n.1. Cf. Burckhardt, *Richelieu and His Age*, 3:436; Chevallier, *Louis XIII*, 609–22.

39. Treasure, *Cardinal Richelieu*, 279–82; Vaunois, *Vie de Louis XIII*, 640.

40. Chevallier, *Louis XIII*, 598.

41. Some of the incriminating documents are copied in BN ms. Clairambault 385, fols. 9–15.

42. Ibid., fols. 17–18.

43. Chevallier, *Louis XIII*, 598.

44. On this last royal-ministerial contest of wills, see Richelieu, *Lettres*, 7:163–81. Louis's additional agreement on 20 November not to let any favorite interfere with statecraft and his delineation of the territorial demands he would insist on in a Bourbon-Habsburg peace were mere reiterations of past stands, not a capitulation to Richelieu's humiliating set of written demands.

45. The late William Church and I ran across two different copies of Louis's letter to Richelieu, instructing him to draw on Séguier's advice as the expert for such a proceeding.

46. Goulas, *Mémoires*, 1:399–400; Bernard, *Histoire du roy Louis XIII*, 2:469.

47. Quoted in Chevallier, *Louis XIII*, 623; and Marvick, "Childhood History," 164.

Conclusion: Louis XIII Beyond the Grave

1. See especially Antoine, *Journal de la maladie et de la mort de Louis XIII*, ed. Alfred Cramail (Fontainebleau, 1880), 25, 31, 33–38. There are several versions of Louis's outburst against his physician.

2. Quoted in Henri d'Orléans d'Aumale, *Histoire des princes de Condé* (Paris, 1863–96), 6:176. Contrast Antoine's sympathetic account, *Journal*, 44, with Montglat's "He was regretted but little," *Mémoires*, 137.

3. This reflection goes back to a conversation many years ago with Edward Gargan on the most valid ways of judging a historical personage's contributions.

4. Vialart, *Histoire du ministre de Richelieu*, 1:3.

5. Paul Hay du Chastelet, *Recueil de diverses pièces pour servir à l'histoire* (1639), 2.

6. Charles François d'Abra de Raconis, *Discours funèbre panégyrique et historique sur la vie et vertus, la maladie et la mort du roy très chrestien Louys le Juste* (Paris, 1643), 75.

7. Goulas, *Mémoires*, 1:449.

8. La Rochefoucauld, *Le cardinal de La Rochefoucauld*, 381.

9. Morgues, *Diverses pièces pour la défense de la royne mère du roy très-chrestien Louys XIII faites et reveues* (1637), preface. I have used the copy in the BN Réserve Lb³⁶ 3410 (1).

10. Thuau, *Raison d'état*, 135.

11. I owe this reference to Ronald S. Love's doctoral dissertation, "The Religion of Henry IV," 2:310–11.

12. Dupleix, *Histoire de Louis le Juste du nom* (Paris, 1643), 2, 4; Morgues, *Très humble, très véritable et très importante remonstrance au Roy* (1631), in *Diverses pièces*, 3–6, 10–11. The Venetian ambassador gave the most critical obituary on Louis XIII's political role, writing that he had exercised nominal rule (*pouvoir*) for thirty-three years, "but for the most part with what could be termed very limited personal authority [*puissance*]: in his first years because of the tutelage and authority of his mother; and in the last ones due to the domination of the late cardinal who in his capacity of minister went beyond the limits of ministerial authority" (dispatch of 15 May 1643, quoted in Aumale, *Histoire des princes de Condé*, 6:170).

13. Vialart, *Histoire du ministère de Richelieu*, 1:4.

14. Antoine, *Journal*, 45–46.

15. Charles de Montchal, *Mémoires contenant les particularitez de la vie et du ministère du Cardinal de Richelieu* (Rotterdam, 1718), 4.

16. Ranum, *Artisans of Glory: Writers and Historical Thought in Seventeenth-Century France* (Chapel Hill, N.C., 1980), 113.

17. I owe my knowledge of Louis XIV's curiosity about his father's exploits to Madeleine Foisil, and the other facts to John B. Wolf's biography of Louis XIV. Anne's approach was in line with the unsolicited advice of Louis XIII's cashiered tutor, Vauquelin des Yveteaux, whose *L'institution du prince*, 162, asked her to raise Louis XIV in the opposite fashion to the education imposed on Louis XIII by Vauquelin's successors. Jean Danès, *Toutes les actions du règne de Louis XIII*, pleaded in vain with the regent to have the new king imitate his father.

18. Mild and harsh versions of the views by Louis XIV's contemporaries were expressed, respectively, by Gatien de Courtilz de Sandras's bogus memoirs of d'Artagnan: "[Richelieu] forgot more and more that he was dealing

with his master, to whom he owed every respect"; and by the pro-Fronde physician Guy Patin, who called Richelieu a "red tyrant" and pointedly omitted Louis XIII from his list of great French rulers, which featured Louis XI, Louis XII, Francis I, and Henry IV. I owe the Courtilz de Sandras reference to Ronald Love; on Patin, see Thuau, *Raison d'état*, 159–65. See also the views of Tallemant des Réaux, quoted in my introduction.

19. Isaiah, 57:1–2.

20. See BN series Lb[36]: *Le roy triomphant ou la statue équestre de l'invincible monarque Louys le Juste* (Reims, 1637); *La Place royale ou la statue dressée à Louys le Juste* (Paris, 1639); and BN Cabinet d'Estampes series Qb[1] (1639): *Veue de la place royale où la statue du roi à esté placée*. James Leith first drew my attention to the pamphlet on the dedication of the Place Royale statue.

Bibliography

The following is an annotated list of the primary and secondary materials that most influenced the writing of this political biography, along with other helpful references for the subject. It is not meant to be a comprehensive guide to the vast literature on the age of Louis XIII. The initial English edition of Victor-L. Tapié's *La France de Louis XIII et de Richelieu*, entitled *France in the Age of Louis XIII and Richelieu*, trans. and ed. D. M. Lockie (London, 1974; New York, 1975), contains a magnificent bibliographical aid to the reign, composed of far more extensive scholarly footnotes, bibliography, and historiographical commentary than appeared in Tapié's French editions of 1952 and 1967. A still more recent paperback English edition, edited by R. J. Knecht (Cambridge, 1984), has a new but much shorter bibliography and regrettably drops Lockie's scholarly apparatus. See also William Farr Church's earlier and equally thorough labor of love, "Publications on Cardinal Richelieu Since 1945: A Bibliographical Study," *Journal of Modern History* 37 (1965): 421–44.

Louis XIII's Letters (major sources, with some overlap)

Archives du Ministère des Affaires Etrangères (*now* des Relations Extérieures) (AAE)
    Mémoires et Documents, France (France mss.) 244, 782, 2164
Bibliothèque de l'Institut de France (BIF)
    Collection Godefroy (ms. Godefroy) 268
Bibliothèque Nationale (BN)
    Fonds français (mss. fr.) 3818, 3828–29, 3843, 17487
    Collection Baluze (mss. Baluze) 323, 348
    Collection Cinq Cents de Colbert (ms. CCC) 98

Collection Clairambault (mss. Clairambault) 383–85

Collection Dupuy (ms. Dupuy) 92

Beauchamp, comte de, ed. *Louis XIII d'après sa correspondance avec le cardinal de Richelieu.* Paris, 1909.

Griselle, Eugène, ed. *Louis XIII et Richelieu: Lettres et pièces diplomatiques.* Paris, 1911.

———, ed. "Lettres de Louis XIII à Marie de Médicis." *Revue historique* 105–6 (1910–11).

Lacaille, Georges, ed. *Lettres inédites de Louis XIII à Richelieu.* Paris, 1901.

La Ferrière, Hector de. "Marie de Médicis et Louis XIII, d'après des lettres inédites." *Revue des sociétés savantes des départements* 3d ser., 4 (1864).

———. "Richelieu et Louis XIII d'après des lettres inédites." *Revue des sociétés savantes des départements* 4th ser., 2 (1865).

Louis XIII. *Lettres à la main de Louis XIII.* Ed. Eugène Griselle. 2 vols. Paris, 1914.

Thibaudeau, Alphonse, ed. *Catalogue of the Collection of Alfred Morrison* 1st ser., 1–6. London, 1883–92. (Contains massive correspondence of Louis, his family, ministers, et al., which I consulted mainly in the original form in the archives.)

Topin, Marius. *Louis XIII et Richelieu: Etude historique accompagnée des lettres inédites du roi au cardinal de Richelieu.* Paris, 1876.

There are also miscellaneous letters, diplomatic instructions, and catalogues of letters of the king in *Annuaire-bulletin de l'histoire de France* (1873); *Documents d'histoire* (1910–11); *Mélanges de la société des bibliophiles* (1903); *Revue rétrospective ou bibliothèque historique*, 2d ser. (1837); and a few letters of the king scattered in books of primary and secondary materials, for example in Aumale, Blet, Chanterac's edition of Bassompierre, Houssaye, and especially Vaunois, all cited below. On Louis's correspondence, as well as other primary sources, there are three distinctive standard bibliographies: Emile Bourgeois and Louis André, *Les sources de l'histoire de France: Le dix-septième siècle*, 8 vols. (Paris, 1913–35)—as thorough a discussion of primary political sources from the period as we will ever see; Edmond Préclin and Victor-L. Tapié, *"Clio" Introduction aux études historiques: Le XVIIᵉ siècle. Monarchies centralisées (1610–1715)* (Paris, 1949)—a penetrating historiographical as well as bibliographical analysis; and Alfred Franklin, *Les sources de l'histoire de France* (Paris, 1877)—a detailed inventory of major memoir and other documentary collections.

I have naturally focused my attention on letters actually written by Louis (as opposed to state letters signed by him and not necessarily expressing his considered opinion) and sought to determine as clearly as possible which of these were actually his in terms of patterns of thought and speech as well as handwriting. He both penned letters himself and dictated them to his personal secretary, who imitated Louis's hand flawlessly; yet anything in either hand can usually be considered the king's doing. My inferring that the early royal letters of Louis's personal reign after 1617 were his work differs from the view of Elizabeth Marvick; readers may wish to compare our interpretations. We await a balanced, representative edition of the monarch's correspondence; still better would be an edition setting Louis's letters and notations side by side with those of his leading ministers before and during Richelieu's ministry. It is unlikely that we will ever see the "complete and critical edition of Louis XIII's correspondence" for which the king's biographer Pierre Chevallier hopes.

Other Archival Sources

AAE France mss. 768–848 (mainly for ministerial maneuvers, often involving Louis XIII).

BIF mss. Godefroy 15 (Jesuits affairs: Fathers Coton, Arnoux, Caussin, Suffren; and ministerial correspondence on Jesuits); 56, 64, 67 (Marie); 269 (Jeannin, Luynes, Puysieux, La Vieuville, Buillion correspondence); 270 (Michel de Marillac to Richelieu); 283 (Châteaneuf, Tronçon); 284 (Jeannin, Bullion, Bouthillier); 310 (history of secrétaires d'état and sketches of individual secretaries' political maneuvers).

BN mss. fr. 3657 (Mangot); 3747 ("Lettres curieuses interceptées du Cardinal Infante et des ministres d'Espagne adressées à la Roine, Mme de Chevreuse, Mme du Fargis"); 3799 (Jeannin); 3800, 3804 (Concini); 3820 (La Vieuville); 4022–27 (the original of Héroard's famous diary about Louis XIII); 4071 (Chavigny); 4744 (state trials); 6556 (Bullion, Lesdiguières, etc.); 6644 (La Valette); 9354 (letters to Richelieu, many very revealing of how the minister and his creatures had to deal with a prickly royal master); 10215 ("Pièces relatives à l'affaire du Val-de-Grâce" [another copy of this dossier of Richelieu's is in mss. fr. nouv. acq. 4334]); 14027 (Nicholas Lefèvre, *Histoire de la vie de M. Michel de Marillac* [a copy with slight changes is in mss. fr. nouv. 82–83]); 15617 (Villeroy, Richelieu); 15617 (Brûlart de Sillery papers); 15620 (Patrocle correspondence; papers of the Sillery family); 16536 (state trials); 17487 (Louis and Marie correspondence; assassination of Concini); 17359 (Villeroy, Jeannin); 23200 (Richelieu papers collected by his secretary des Roches); 25054 ("Escrit du R. P. Caussin de la Compagnie de Jésus sur la Vocation de la R. Mère Louise Angélique de la Fayette Religieuse de la Visitation de la main de M. de Chaillot").

BN mss. fr. nouvelles acquisitions (nouv. acq.) 6210 (Sublet de Noyers, Chavigny, Bullion); 9735 (eighteenth-century studies of premiers ministres, secrétaires d'état, surintendants, etc., by Lancelot).

BN mss. Baluze 153–54 (Effiat); 214 (Marie, Richelieu, Luynes); 323 (Luynes); 333 (Effiat, etc., collected by Richelieu's secretary Charpentier).

BN mss. CCC 90 (Marie); 96 (letters to Luynes's cousin Modène); 97 (Luynes); 221 (Concini, Galigaï trial).

BN mss. Dupuy 581 (state trials); 351 (La Vieuville, d'Aligre).

BN mss. Clairambault 1132–33 (Luynes, La Vieuville).
BN Provinces de France ms. Périgord 6 (Concini).
Bibliothèque Municipale de Rouen ms. Leber 5767 (six unnumbered vols., comprising André Lefebvre d'Ormesson's papers).

Contemporary Image-making on Louis XIII

ROYAL HISTORIES

1609   Héroard, Jean. *De l'institution du prince.* Paris. (Republished in Héroard's *Journal,* cited below, vol. 2.)
1618   Bellemaure, sieur de. *Le pourtrait du roi.* Republished in *Archives curieuses de l'histoire de France.* Ed. L. Cimber and L.-F. Danjou. 27 vols. Paris, 1834–40. 2d ser. Vol. 1.
        Le Grain, Baptiste. *Décade commençant l'histoire du roy Louys XIII du nom* [1610–17]. Paris.
1622   Le Roy. *Remarques sur la vie du roy et sur celle d'Alexandre Sévère, contenant la comparaison de ces deux grands princes.* Paris.
        Les lauriers de Louys le Juste roy de France et de Navarre. Paris.
1624   Boistel de Gaubertin, Pierre. *Histoire des guerres et choses mémorables arrivées sous le règne très glorieux de Louis le Juste.* Rouen.
1631   Balzac, Guez de. *Le prince.* Paris.
        Dupleix, Scipion. *Histoire de Louis le Juste du nom.* Paris, 1643; first published 1631.
        Matthieu, Jean Baptiste. *Histoire de Louis XIII.* In Pierre Matthieu, *Histoire de Henri IV.* Vol. 2. Paris.
1633   Auvray, Jean. *Louis le Juste panégyrique.* Paris.
        Bernard, Charles. *Histoire des guerres de Louis XIII contre les religionnaires rebelles de son estat, 1618–1627.* (This work was later incorporated in Bernard's longer history of the king, cited below.)
[1633] *Les vertus du roy.*
1638   Charpy, N. *Le juste prince ou le miroir des princes en la vie de Louis le Juste.* Paris.
1642   Gombart d'Auteil, Charles. *Histoire des ministres d'estat qui ont servy sous les roys de France de la troisième lignée.* 2 vols. Paris, 1669; first edition 1642.
1643   Abra de Raconis, Charles François d'. *Discours funèbre panégyrique et historique sur la vie et vertus, la maladie et la mort du roy très chrestien Louys le Juste.* Paris.
        Amariton, Louis. *Oraison funèbre sur le tréspas de Louis le Juste XIII de ce nom . . . en l'église Sainct Estienne du Mont.* Paris.
        Bazin, Simon Thomas. *Oraison funèbre prononcée à Paris en l'église des jacobins réformez au service de Louis le Juste.* Paris.
        Danès, Jean. *Toutes les actions du règne de Louis XIII rapportées au surnom de Juste qui lui fut donné.*

Dubois. *Mémoire fidèle des choses qui se sont passées à la mort de Louis XIII.* Reprinted in *Archives curieuses de l'histoire de France.* Ed. L. Cimber and L.-F. Danjou. 27 vols. Paris, 1834–40. 2d ser. Vol. 5.

Le récit véritable des cérémonies faictes à Saint-Denis aux pompes funèbres et réception du très glorieux et invincible monarque Louis XIII, surnommé le Juste. Paris.

Vauquelin des Yveteaux, Nicolas. *L'institution du prince.* In *Oeuvres complètes,* ed. G. Mongrédien. Paris, 1921.

[1643] Antoine, garçon de la chambre du roi. *Journal de la maladie et de la mort de Louis XIII.* Ed. Alfred Cramail. Fontainebleau, 1880.

1646 Malingre, Claude. *Histoire du règne de Louis XIII (1601–1643).* Paris.

Bernard, Charles. *Histoire du roy Louis XIII, 1601–1643.* 2 vols. Paris.

1648 Dupleix, Scipion. *Continuation de l'histoire du règne de Louis le Juste.* Paris.

1656 Dinet, Jacques (retouched by Antoine Girard). *L'Idée d'une belle mort ou d'une mort Chrestienne de la fin heureuse de Louis XIII surnommé le Juste.* Paris. (See also the original Dinet account, *Derniers moments de Louis XIII,* in *Cabinet historique* 12 [1866].)

POLITICAL PAMPHLETS

1616 *Les veus d'un vray français au favory de la fortune.* Niort.

[1616?] *L'Italien français.*

Manifeste des personnes aux fidèlles français.

Résponse sur les calomnieux propos qu'un pédant a vomy contre un des grands de cest estat.

1617 *Dialogue du berger Picard avec la nymphe champenoise sur la fortune et gouvernement du marquis d'Ancre en Picardie.*

Le coup d'estat présenté au roy à Fontainebleau.

Le roi hors de page à la royne mère.

Les larmes de la France à ses enfans mutinez.

Les merveilles et coup d'essai de Louys le Juste.

Propos dorez sur l'authorité tyrannique de Concino Florentine.

Remerciment au roy de la justice exercée contre le maréchal d'Ancre et sa femme.

[1617?] *Le fléau des médisants.*

1618 Chiremont, Jean de. *Le combat de David contre Goliath au roy très-chrestien Louis le Juste.*

Les triomphes du très-chrestien roy . . . Louys le Juste.

1619 Framboisière, de la. *Panégyric du monarque des français et de la monarchie française.*

Le vray portraict de Louys le Juste présenté à sa majesté.

1620 *Le comtadin provençal.*

Le diable estonné sur l'ombre du marquis d'Ancre adressé à M. de Luynes.

1622 *Apologie ou response à la chronique des favoris.*

Recueil des pièces les plus curieuses qui ont esté faites pendant le règne du connestable [de Luynes] jusqu'à présent.

1623   *Dialogue du roy très chrestien Louys le Juste et de Monsieur son frère.*
La France mourante.

1624   *La disgrace des favoris.*
Le remerciement de la voix publique au roy.
Response à la voix publique.
Response au mot à l'oreille pour M. le marquis de la Vieuville.

1625   *Lettre de M. le Marquis de la Vieuville au roy.*

[1627?]   Bernard, Charles. *Cléobule ou l'homme d'estat.*

[1629?]   ———. *In Honorem Ludovico Decimi Terti.*

1633   *Lettre à M. le marquis de la Vieuville sur le sujet de sa disgrace d'avec M. le duc d'Orléans, frère du roy, et de sa retraite hors de la cour de Bruxelles.*

1637   Morgues, Mathieu de. *Diverses pièces pour la défense de la royne mère du roy très-chrestien Louys XIII faites et reveues.*

1639   Hay du Chastelet, Paul. *Recueil de diverses pièces pour servir à l'histoire.*
La Place Royale ou la statue dressée à Louis le Juste

[1639?]   *Lettre du père Caussin, Jésuite, confesseur de Louis XIII à Richelieu.* 1773 edition cited.

1643   Morgues, Mathieu de. *Pièces curieuses en suite.* (The second volume of the preceding compilation of Morgues's tracts; see Donald Bailey's bibliographical articles, below.)

1610–   *Mercure françois.* (Reprinted or summarized many royal and opposi-
1644   tion pamphlets in its annual issues; see below.)

Most of the above-listed pamphlets are in the Bibliothèque nationale Lb[36] series, for which there is a comprehensive bibliography in *Bibliothèque nationale: Catalogue de l'histoire de France.* 16 vols. Paris, 1855–95; 1968–69 reprint, vol. 1. The above list is a small sample of the immense number of partisan tracts published during Louis XIII's reign. I have consulted these and many more pamphlets, although not primarily for "facts" as was customary in the days of Louis Batiffol's massive publications on the reign. Nor am I able to determine (beyond a general impression) anything about "public opinion" from these materials or, in most cases, precisely who wrote or commissioned them. Instead I have read these fascinating propaganda pieces (and the "royal histories" listed above as well) to determine just what image of Louis XIII they were meant to convey. One hopes that it is obvious when a pamphlet was royal propaganda and crafted to give a favorable image of the king. The objective in many opposition pamphlets is less clear, but even in their case we can see how they drew on their image of the king to influence him, his advisors, and the court and country elements that made up the "public opinion makers" of the day. In between were pamphlets as well as public speeches, open letters, and other vehicles utilized by local communities, royal law courts, and so forth. They show that throughout the realm subjects were acquiring an image of their monarch and were quite adept at making his justice, piety, valor, etc. fit their own ideas of what he should do for the realm and their particular region or institution.

PICTORIAL REPRESENTATIONS

BN Cabinet des Estampes
Qb¹ "Histoire de France," 1601, 1610–43 (both originals and clichés). Includes medallions, portraits, cartoons, drawings of triumphal arches, "daily occupations of the king," contemporary depictions of various social groups, plus extensive inscriptions, poems, and explanations of allegories.
N² "Louis XIII" (clichés). Portraits of personages of the reign, from royalty to religious and literary leaders.

Godefroy, Théodore. *Le cérémonial françois.* 2 vols. Paris, 1649.

The Estampes are a wonderful complement to the often dry, one-dimensional pamphlets of the time in revealing the use of media to project certain images of Louis XIII.

REFERENCE WORKS

Bailey, Donald A. "Les pamphlets de Mathieu de Morgues (1582–1670): Bibliographie des ouvrages disponibles dans les bibliothèques parisiennes et certaines bibliothèques des Etats-Unis." *Revue française d'histoire du livre* 18 (1978).
———. "Les pamphlets des associés polémistes de Mathieu de Morgues. . . ." *Revue française d'histoire du livre* 27 (1979).
———. "Les recueils de Mathieu de Morgues. . . ." *Revue française d'histoire du livre* 33 (1981).
———. "The Pamphlets of Mathieu de Morgues, Marie de Medici, Gaston d'Orléans and Jacques Chanteloube: A Bibliography of Holdings in Selected Belgian Libraries." *Archives et bibliothèques de Belgique* 52 (1981).
Cioronescu, Alexandre. *Bibliographie de la littérature française du dix-septième siècle.* 3 vols. Paris, 1966.
Le Vager, Paul. *Les entrées solennelles à Paris des rois et reines de France . . . conservées à la Bibliothèque nationale: Bibliographie sommaire.* Paris, 1896.
Lindsay, R. O., and John Neu. *French Political Pamphlets 1547–1648.* Madison, Wisc., 1969.
Maumené, Charles, and Louis d'Harcourt. *Iconographie des rois de France.* Vol. 1, *De Louis IX à Louis XIII.* Paris, 1923.
Mazerolle, F. *Les médailleurs français du XVe siècle au milieu du XVIIe.* 3 vols. Paris, 1902–4.
Welsh, Doris V. *A Checklist of French Political Pamphlets 1560–1644 in the Newberry Library, Chicago.* Chicago, 1950.

The forthcoming publications of Jeffrey Sawyer stemming from his doctoral dissertation on the subject of pamphlet propaganda, faction politics, and the public sphere during the early years of Louis XIII's reign will add yet another dimension to our understanding of the ways in which the early modern French used image-making media.

Other Principal Sources

Anecdotes de la cour de France tirées de la bouche de M. du Vair. Appended to Marguerite de Valois, *Mémoires,* ed. Lalanne. Paris, 1858. (Du Vair's account contains a "Portrait du roi" by Louis XIII's preceptor, Nicholas Lefèvre, and his governor, Gilles de Souvré.)

Arnauld d'Andilly, Robert. *Journal, 1614–1620.* Ed. Achille Halphen and Edmond Halphen. Paris, 1857.

———. *Journal inédit.* Ed. Eugène Halphen and Jules Halphen. Paris, 1888–1909. (Separate volume pagination for 1620, 1621, 1622, 1623, 1624, 1625, 1626, 1627, 1628–29, 1630–32.)

Aubery, Antoine. *Mémoires pour l'histoire du Cardinal de Richelieu recueillis par le sieur Aubery,* 5 Vols. (Cologne, 1667).

Barozzi, Nicolo, and Guglielmo Berchet. *Le relazioni degli stati europei: Lettere al Senato dagli ambasciaturi Veneziani nel secolo decimosettimo. Francia.* Vol. 7 Venice, 1868.

Bassompierre, François de. *Journal de ma vie.* Société de l'Histoire de France ed. Ed. A. de La Cropte de Chantérac. 4 vols. Paris, 1870–77.

Bentivoglio, Guido. *Lettres sur diverses matières de politique et autres importans sujets.* Ed. Venerony and Minazio. Lyon, 1730.

Blanchet, Adrien, ed. "Un recit inédit de la mort du maréchal d'Ancre." In *Société de l'histoire de Paris et de l'Ile de France, Bulletin* 27 (1900).

Bourgeois [or Boursier], Louise. *Récit véritable de la naissance de messeigneurs et dames les enfans de France.* In *Archives curieuses,* Ed. M. L. Cimber and F. Danjou. 1st ser. Vol. 14. Paris 1837.

Brienne, Henri-Auguste de Loménie de. *Mémoires.* Michaud and Poujoulat ed. 3d ser. Vol. 3. Paris, 1838.

"Ce qui s'est passé lors de la consommation du mariage du roi." *Revue rétrospective ou bibliothèque historique, contenant les mémoires et documents pour servir à l'histoire.* Ed. M. J. Taschereau. Vol. 2. Paris, 1833.

Canault, Jean. *Vie du maréchal J.-B. d'Ornano par son secrétaire.* Ed. Jean Charay. Grenoble, 1971. (Includes many additional archival and published sources.)

[Chaulnes, Honoré d'Albert de Cadenet, duc de?]. *Relation exacte de tout ce qui s'est passé à la mort du mareschal d'Ancre.* Michaud and Poujoulat ed. 2d ser. Vol. 5. Paris, 1837.

Déageant, Guichard de. *Mémoires envoyez à M. le Cardinal de Richelieu.* Grenoble, 1668.

Dupuy, Pierre. *Histoire des plus illustres favoris anciens et modernes.* Leiden, 1659.

Estrées, François Annibal d'. *Mémoires.* Société de l'Histoire de France ed. Ed. P. Bonnefon. Paris, 1910.

Fauvelet-du-Toc, A. *Histoire des secrétaires d'estat.* Paris, 1668.

Fontenay-Mareuil, François Duval de. *Mémoires.* Michaud and Poujoulat ed. 2d ser. Vol. 5. Paris, 1837.

Girard, Guillaume. *Histoire de la vie du duc d'Epernon.* Paris, 1655.

Godefroy, Denys, with Jean Le Féron. *Histoire des connestables, chanceliers, et gardes des sceaux, mareschaux, admiraux, surintendans de la navigation, et généraux des galeries de France, des grands maistres de la maison du roy et les prévosts de Paris.* Paris, 1658.

Goulas, Nicholas. *Mémoires.* Société de l'Histoire de France ed. Ed. Charles Constant. Vol. 1. Paris, 1879.

Griselle, Eugène, ed. *Ecurie, vénerie, fauconnerie et louveterie du roi Louis XIII.* Paris, 1912.

———, ed. *Etat de la maison du roi Louis XIII.* Paris, 1912. (Includes the officers in the households of the rest of the king's family.)

———, ed. *Supplément à la maison du roi Louis XIII.* Paris, 1912.

Hermant, Godefroy. "Histoire de Beauvais: Les débuts du règne de Louis XIII." In *Louis XIII et Richelieu: Lettres et pièces diplomatiques,* ed. Eugène Griselle. Paris, 1911.

Héroard, Jean [or Jehan]. *Journal sur l'enfance et la jeunesse de Louis XIII (1601–1628).* Ed. Eudore Soulié and Edouard de Barthélemy. 2 vols. Paris, 1868.

Isambert, François-A., et al. *Recueil général des anciennes lois françaises depuis l'an 420 jusqu'à la révolution de 1789.* 29 vols. Paris, 1822–33.

La Porte, Pierre de. *Mémoires.* Michaud and Poujoulat ed. 3d ser. Vol. 8. Paris, 1839.

La Rochefoucauld, François de. *Mémoires.* Michaud and Poujoulat ed. 3d ser. Vol. 5. Paris, 1838.

L'Estoile, Pierre de. *Mémoires-Journaux.* Ed. G. Brunet et al. Vols. 7–12. Paris, 1875–96.

Fontenay-Mareuil, François Duval de. *Mémoires.* Michaud and Poujoulat ed. 2d ser. Vol. 5. Paris, 1837.

Malherbe, François de. *Oeuvres.* Grands Ecrivains de la France ed. Ed. M. L. Lalanne. Vols. 3–4. Paris, 1862.

Mercure françois. 25 vols. Paris, 1605–44. (An indispensable source for narrative events and royal [and opposition] image-making.)

Molé, Mathieu. *Mémoires.* Société de l'Histoire de France ed. Ed. Aimé Champollion-Figeac. Vols. 1–3. Paris, 1855–57.

Montchal, Charles de. *Mémoires contenant les particularitez de la vie et du ministère du Cardinal de Richelieu.* Rotterdam, 1718.

Montglat, François de Paul de Clermont, marquis de. *Mémoires.* Michaud and Poujoulat ed. 3d ser. Vol. 5. Paris, 1838.

Montpensier, Anne Marie Louis d'Orléans de. *Mémoires.* Michaud and Poujoulat ed. 3d ser. Vol. 4. Paris, 1838.

Montpouillan, Jean de Caumont de. *Mémoires.* In Jacques Nompar de Caumont, duc de La Force, *Mémoires,* ed. marquis de la Grange. Vol. 4. Paris, 1843.

Motteville, Françoise Bertaut de. *Mémoires pour servir à l'histoire d'Anne d'Autriche.* Michaud and Poujoulat ed. 2d ser. Vol. 10. Paris, 1838.

Ormesson, Olivier Lefèvre d'. *Journal.* Documents inédits ser. Ed. Pierre-Adolphe Chéruel. Vol. 1. Paris, 1860.

Pasquier, Nicolas. *Lettres.* In Etienne Pasquier, *Oeuvres.* Vol. 2, cols. 1053–1442. Amsterdam, 1723.

Peiresc, Nicolas-Claude de Fabri de. *Lettres à Malherbe.* Ed. Raymond Lebègue. Paris, 1976.

Pontchartrain, Paul Phélypeaux de. *Mémoires.* Michaud and Poujoulat ed. 2d ser. Vol. 5. Paris, 1837.

Richelieu, Armand-Jean du Plessis, cardinal de. *Lettres, instructions et papiers d'état.* Documents inédits ser. Ed. Denis-Louis-Martial Avenel. 8 vols. Paris, 1853–77).

―――. *Mémoires.* For the period preceding 1630: Critical Société de l'Histoire de France ed. Ed. H. de Beaucaire et al. 10 vols. Paris, 1907–31; for the remainder of the compilation: Michaud and Poujoulat ed. 2d ser. Vols. 7–9. Paris, 1836–39.

―――. *Les papiers: Correspondence et papiers d'état. Section politique intérieur.* Ed. Pierre Grillon. 5 vols. Paris, 1975–82; *Section politique extérieure.* Ed. A. Wild. Vols. 1– . Paris, 1982– .

―――. *Testament Politique.* Ed. Louis André. Paris, 1947.

Rohan, Henri de. *Mémoires.* Michaud and Poujoulat ed. 2d ser. Vol. 5. Paris, 1837.

Saint-Simon, Louis de Rouvroy de. *Oeuvres complètes.* Ed. René Dupuis et al. Vol. 1. Geneva, 1964. (Includes an account of the Day of Dupes.)

―――. *Parallèle des trois premiers rois Bourbons.* Paris, 1967. Also in the *Oeuvres,* above.

Siri, Vittorio. *Anecdotes du ministère du Cardinal de Richelieu et du règne de Louis XIII.* 2 vols. Amsterdam, 1717.

―――. *Mémoires secrets tirés des archives des souverains en l'Europe contenant le règne de Louis XIII. Oeuvre traduit de l'italien.* Vols. 7–36. Amsterdam, 1774–84.

Tallemant des Réaux, Gédéon. *Historiettes.* Ed. Antoine Adam. 2 vols. Paris, 1960–61.

Vauquelin des Yveteaux, Nicolas. *Oeuvres complètes.* Ed. G. Mongrédien. Paris, 1921.

Vialart, Charles. *Histoire du ministère d'Armand Jean du Plessis Cardinal duc de Richelieu, sous le règne de Louys le Juste, XIII du nom.* 2 vols. N.p., 1650.

Biographical References to Louis XIII

Ariès, Philippe. *Centuries of Childhood: The Social History of Family Life.* Trans. R. Baldick. London, 1962.

Baschet, Armand. *Le roi chez la reine ou histoire secrète du mariage de Louis XIII et d'Anne d'Autriche.* Paris, 1866.

Batiffol, Louis. *Au temps de Louis XIII.* Paris, 1903.

———. *La journée des dupes.* Paris, 1925.

———. *Le roi Louis XIII à vingt ans.* Paris, 1910.

———. *Richelieu et le roi Louis XIII: Les véritables rapports du souverain et de son ministre.* Paris, 1934.

Canu, J. *Louis XIII et Richelieu.* Paris, 1944.

Chapman, Hester W. "Louis XIII (1601–1643)." In *Privileged Persons: Four Seventeenth-Century Studies.* New York, 1966.

Chevallier, Pierre. "La véritable journée des Dupes: Etude critique des journées des 10 et 11 novembre 1630 d'après les dépêches diplomatiques." *Mémoires de la société académique de l'Aube* 108 (1978).

———. *Louis XIII: Roi cornélien.* Paris, 1979.

Crump, Lucy. *Nursery Life 300 Years Ago: The Story of a Dauphin of France, 1601–10.* London, 1929.

Dumas, Alexandre [fils]. *Les grands hommes en robe de chambre: Henri IV, Louis XIII et Richelieu.* Paris, 1877.

Erlanger, Philippe. *Louis XIII: Le stoïcien de la monarchie.* Paris, 1972.

Foisil, Madeleine. "Et soudain Louis 9 ans devint roi." *Historama* 14 (1985).

———. "Le Journal de Héroard, médecin de Louis XIII." *Etudes sur l'Hérault* 15 (1984).

Griselle, Eugène. "Louis XIII et les Jésuites." *Revue du Monde Catholique* (1901).

Guardin, J. M. *La médecine à travers les siècles.* Paris, 1865.

Guillon, Paul. *La mort de Louis XIII: Etude d'histoire médicale.* Paris, 1897.

Himelfarb, Hélène. "L'apprentissage du mécénat royal: Le jeune Louis XIII face au monde des arts et des lettres dans le journal d'Héroard." In *L'âge d'or du mécénat, (1598–1661),* ed. Roland Mousnier and Jean Mesnard. Paris, 1985.

Hunt, David. *Parents and Children in History: The Psychology of Family Life in Early Modern France.* New York, 1970.

Le magasin pittoresque. Vols. 2, 4. Paris, 1833–36.

Marvick, Elizabeth W. "The Character of Louis XIII: The Role of his Physician." *Journal of Interdisciplinary History* 4 (1974).

———. "Childhood History and Decisions of State: The Case of Louis XIII." *Journal of Psychohistory* 2 (1974).

———. "The Childhood of Louis XIII." *Proceedings of the Western Society for French History* 13 (1986).

———. *Louis XIII: The Making of a King.* New Haven, Conn., 1986.

———. "Richelieu and the *Testament politique:* An Attempt at Attribution."

Paper presented at the Twenty-seventh Annual Meeting of the Society for French Historical Studies, Bloomington, Ind., 1981. (Discusses the possible role of Louis XIII in the writing and objective setting of the *Testament politique*.)

Moote, A. Lloyd. "Louis XIII, Richelieu, and 'Two-headed Monarchy.' " *Proceedings of the Western Society for French History* 10 (1982).

Patmore, K. A. *The Court of Louis XIII.* London, 1909.

Romain, Charles. *Louis XIII: Un grand roi méconnu, 1601–1643.* Paris, 1934.

Rossignol, C. *Louis XIII avant Richelieu.* Paris, 1869.

Taylor, Ida A. *The Making of a King: The Childhood of Louis XIII.* London, 1910.

Todière, M. *Louis XIII et Richelieu.* Tours, 1851.

Vaunois, Louis. *Vie de Louis XIII.* 2d ed. Paris, 1961.

Wiley, W. L. "A Royal Child Learns to Like Plays: The Early Years of Louis XIII." *Renaissance News* 9 (1956).

Zeller, Berthold. *Le connétable de Luynes. Montauban et la Valteline.* Paris, 1879.

———. *Louis XIII: Marie de Médicis, chef du conseil (1614–1616).* Paris, 1898.

———. *Louis XIII: Marie de Médicis. Richelieu ministre.* Paris, 1899.

———. *La minorité de Louis XIII: Marie de Médicis et Sully (1610–1612).* Paris, 1891.

———. *La minorité de Louis XIII: Marie de Médicis et Villeroy (1612–1614).* Paris, 1897.

———. *Richelieu et les ministres de Louis XIII de 1621 à 1624.* Paris, 1880.

Other Secondary Studies

Several of the following studies contain important primary sources, notably royal and other correspondence.

Adam, Antoine. *Histoire de la littérature française au XVIIe siècle: L'époque d'Henri IV et de Louis XIII.* Paris, 1948.

———. *Grandeur and Illusion: French Literature and Society, 1600–1715.* London, 1972.

Albertini, Rudolf von. *Das politische Denken in Frankreich zur Zeit Richelieus.* Marburg, 1951.

Anis, Auguste-François. *Etude historique et littéraire: David Rivault de Fleurance et les autres précepteurs de Louis XIII.* Paris, 1893.

Anquez, Léonce. *Histoire des assemblées politiques des réformés de France (1573–1622).* Paris, 1859.

Arconville, Marie-G.-Charles Thiroux d'. *Vie de Marie de Médicis.* 3 vols. Paris, 1774.

Ariès, Philippe, and André Béjin. *Western Sexuality: Practice and Precept in Past and Present Times.* Trans. Anthony Forster. Oxford, 1985.

Aston, Trevor, ed. *Crisis in Europe, 1560–1660.* London, 1965.

Auchincloss, Louis. *Richelieu.* New York, 1973.

Aumale, Henri d'Orléans d'. *Histoire des princes de Condé*. Vols. 3, 4. Paris, 1863–96.

Avenel, Georges d'. *Richelieu et la monarchie absolue*. 4 vols. Paris, 1895.

Bannister, Mark. *Privileged Mortals: The French Heroic Novel 1630–1660*. Oxford, 1983.

Bardon, Françoise. *Le portrait mythologique à la cour de France sous Henri IV et Louis XIII: Mythologie et politique*. Paris, 1974.

Batiffol, Louis. *Autour de Richelieu: Sa fortune, ses gardes et mousquetaires, la Sorbonne, le château de Richelieu*. Paris, 1937.

———. *La duchesse de Chevreuse: Une vie d'aventures et d'intrigues sous Louis XIII*. Paris, 1913.

———. *Le Louvre sous Henri IV et Louis XIII: La vie de la cour de France au XVIIe siècle*. Paris, 1930.

———. *La vie intime d'une reine de France au XVIIe siècle: Marie de Médicis (1600–1617)*. 2 vols. Paris, 1906.

Baxter, Douglas Clark. *Servants of the Sword: French Intendants of the Army, 1630–70*. Urbana, Ill., 1976.

Beik, William H. *Absolutism and Society in Seventeenth-Century France: State Power and Provincial Aristocracy in Languedoc*. Cambridge, 1985.

———. "Searching for Popular Culture in Early Modern France." *Journal of Modern History* 49 (1977).

Bercé, Yves-Marie. *Croquants et Nu-pieds*. Paris, 1974.

———. *Fête et révolte: Des mentalités populaires du XVIe au XVIIIe siècle*. Paris, 1976.

———. *Histoire des Croquants: Etude des soulèvements populaires au XVIIe siècle dans le sud-ouest de la France*, 2 vols. Geneva, 1974.

Bergin, Joseph. *Cardinal Richelieu: Power and the Pursuit of Wealth*. New Haven: Conn., 1985.

Billacois, François. *Le duel dans la société française des XVIe–XVIIe siècles: Essai de psychosociologie historique*. Paris, 1986.

Bireley, Robert. *Religion and Politics in the Age of the Counterreformation: Emperor Ferdinand II, William Lamormaini, S.J., and the Formation of Imperial Policy*. Chapel Hill, N.C., 1981.

Bitton, Davis. *The French Nobility in Crisis 1560–1640*. Stanford, Calif., 1969.

Blet, Pierre. *Le clergé de France et la monarchie: Etude sur les Assemblées générales du clergé de 1615 à 1666*. Vol. 1. Rome, 1959.

———. "Richelieu et les débuts de Mazarin." *Revue d'histoire moderne et contemporaine* 6 (1959).

Bloch, Marc. *French Rural History: An Essay on Its Basic Characteristics*. Trans. Janet Sondheimer. London, 1966.

———. *The Royal Touch: Sacred Monarchy and Scrofula in England and France*. Trans. J. E. Anderson. London, 1972.

Blum, A. *Abraham Bosse et la société française*. Paris, 1924.

Blunt, Anthony. *Art and Architecture in France, 1500–1700*. 2d ed. Baltimore, 1970.

Bohanan, Donna. *The Nobility of Seventeenth-Century Aix-en-Provence: A Privileged Elite in Urban Society*. Baton Rouge, La. Forthcoming.

Bonney, Richard. "Absolutism: What's in a Name?" *French History* 1 (1987).

———. *Political Change in France Under Richelieu and Mazarin, 1624–1661*. Oxford, 1978.

———. *The King's Debts: Finance and Politics in France, 1589–1661*. Oxford, 1981.

Braudel, Fernand, and Ernest Labrousse, gen. eds. *Histoire économique et sociale de la France*. Paris, 1977–83. Vol. 1, pt. 1: *L'état et la ville* [1450–1660]. Ed. Pierre Chaunu and Richard Gascon. Paris, 1977. Vol. 1, pt. 2: *Paysannerie et croissance* [1450–1660]. Ed. Emmanuel Le Roy Ladurie and Michel Morineau. Paris, 1977.

Brémond, Henri. *Histoire littéraire du sentiment religieux en France depuis la fin des guerres de religion à nos jours*. 11 vols. Paris, 1967–68.

Brightwell, P. J. "The Spanish Origins of the Thirty Years' War." *European Studies Review* 9 (1979).

Buisseret, David. *Henry IV*. London, 1984.

Burckhardt, Carl J. *Richelieu and his Age*. Trans. Bernard Hoy, Edwin Muir, and Willa Muir. 3 vols. London, 1967–70.

Caillet, J. *De l'administration en France sous le ministère du Cardinal de Richelieu*. Paris, 1863.

Carmona, Michel. *La France de Richelieu*. Paris, 1984.

———. *Marie de Médicis*. Paris, 1981.

———. *Richelieu: L'ambition et le pouvoir*. Paris, 1983.

Charleton, D. G. ed. *France: A Companion to French Studies*. 2d ed. London, 1979.

Chartier, Roger. "A propos des Etats généraux de 1614." *Revue d'histoire moderne et contemporaine* 23 (1976).

Chartier, Roger, and Denis Richet. *Représentation et vouloir politiques autour des Etats-généraux de 1614*. Paris, 1982.

Châtelet, Albert, and Jacques Thuillier. *French Painting from Fouquet to Poussin*. Trans. Stuart Gilbert and James Emmons. Geneva, Switz., 1963.

———. *French painting from Le Nain to Fragonard*. Trans. Stuart Gilbert and James Emmons. Geneva, Switz., 1964.

Chéruel, Pierre Adolphe. *Dictionnaire historique des institutions, moeurs et coutumes de la France*. 2 vols. Paris, 1910.

Chill, E. "Religion and Mendicity in Seventeenth-Century France." *International Review of Social Sciences* 7 (1962).

Church, William Farr. "Cardinal Richelieu and the Social Estates of the Realm," *Album Helen Maud Cam* 2 (1961).

———. "France." In *National Consciousness, History, and Political Culture in Early Modern Europe*, ed. Orest Ranum. Baltimore, 1975.

———. *Richelieu and Reason of State*. Princeton, N.J., 1972.

Clark, S. "French Historians and Early Modern Popular Culture." *Past and Present* 100 (1983): 62–99.

Clarke, Jack Alden. *Huguenot Warrior: The Life and Times of Henry de Rohan, 1579–1638*. The Hague, 1966.

Cognet, L. *Le Jansenisme*. Paris, 1961.

———. *Les origines de la spiritualité française au XVIIe siècle*. Paris, 1949.

Collins, James B. *Direct Taxation in Early Seventeenth-Century France*. Berkeley and Los Angeles, 1988.

Constant, Jean-Marie. *Les conjurateurs: Le premier libéralisme politique sous Richelieu*. Paris, 1987.

Coope, R. *Salomon de Brosse and the Development of the Classical Style in French Architecture from 1565 to 1630*. London, 1972.

Corvisier, A. *Armies and Societies in Europe, 1495–1789*. Bloomington, Ind., 1979.

Cousin, Victor. "Le duc et la connétable de Luynes." *Journal des Savants* (1861–63).

———. *Madame de Chevreuse*. Paris, 1856.

———. *Madame de Hautefort*. Paris, 1856.

Coveney, P. J., ed. *France in Crisis, 1620–1675*. London, 1977.

Cruickshank, J., ed. *French Literature and Its Background*. Vol. 2, *The Seventeenth Century*. Oxford, 1969.

Daniel-Rops, Henri. *The Catholic Reformation*. Vol. 2. New York, 1962.

———. *The Church in the Seventeenth Century*. Vol. 1. New York, 1963.

Delamare, George. *Le maréchal d'Ancre*. Paris, 1961.

Deloche, Maximin. *Autour de la plume du cardinal de Richelieu*. Paris, 1920.

Delumeau, Jean. *Catholicism Between Luther and Voltaire*. London, 1977.

Dethan, Georges. *Gaston d'Orléans: Conspirateur et prince charmant*. Paris, 1959.

———. *Mazarin: Un homme de paix à l'âge baroque, 1602–1661*. Paris, 1981.

———. "Mazarin avant le ministère." *Revue historique* 227 (1962).

———. *Mazarin et ses amis*. Paris, 1968.

Dewald, Jonathan. "Individualism and Aristocratic Culture in Seventeeth-Century France." Paper presented to the Early Modern French Studies Group of Southern California, Los Angeles, 1988.

———. *Pont-St-Pierre, 1398–1789: Lordship, Community and Capitalism in Early Modern France*. Berkeley and Los Angeles, 1987.

Deyon, Pierre. *Amiens, capitale provinciale: Etude sur la société urbaine au 17e siècle*. Paris, 1967.

Dickmann, Fritz. "Rechtsgedanke und Machtpolitik bei Richelieu." *Historische Zeitschrift* 196 (1963).

Doucet, Roger. *Les institutions de la France au XVIe siècle*. 2 vols. Paris, 1948.

Duby, Georges, ed. *Histoire de la France urbaine*. Vol. 3, *La ville classique: De la Renaissance aux révolutions*. Ed. R. Chartier, G. Chaussinand-Nogaret, H. Neveux, and E. Le Roy Ladurie. Paris, 1981.

Duby, Georges, and Robert Mandrou. *A History of French Civilization*. Trans. James Blake Atkinson. New York, 1964.

Duby, Georges, and Armand Wallon, eds., *Histoire de la France rurale*. Vol. 2,

L'âge classique des paysans de 1340 à 1789. Ed. H. Neveu, J. Jacquart, and E. Le Roy Ladurie. Paris, 1975.

Dulong, Claude. *Anne d'Autriche: Mère de Louis XIV.* Paris, 1980.

Dupaquier, Jacques. *La population française du XVIIe et XVIIIe siècles.* Paris, 1979.

Elliott, John H. *Richelieu and Olivares.* Cambridge, 1984.

———. *The Count-Duke of Olivares: The Statesman in an Age of Decline.* New Haven, Conn., 1986.

Erlanger, Philippe. *The King's Minion: Richelieu, Louis XIII, and the Affair of Cinq Mars.* Trans. G. Cremonesi, and H. Cremonesi. Englewood Cliffs, N.J., 1972.

Fagniez, Gustave. *Le père Joseph et Richelieu (1577–1638).* 2 vols. Paris, 1894.

Ferté, Jeanne. *La vie religieuse dans les campagnes parisiennes, 1622–1695.* Paris, 1962.

Flandrin, Jean-Louis. *Families in Former Times: Kinship, Household, and Sexuality.* Cambridge, 1979.

Foisil, Madeleine. "L'écriture du for privé." In *Histoire de la vie privée,* vol. 3, ed. Philippe Ariès. Paris, 1986.

———. *La revolte des Nu-pieds et les révoltes normandes de 1639.* Paris, 1970.

Fouqueray, le père. *Le père Jean Suffren à la cour de Marie de Médicis et de Louis XIII d'après les mémoires du temps et des documents inédits, 1615–1643.* Paris, 1900.

Franklin, Alfred. *La cour de France et l'assassinat du maréchal d'Ancre.* Paris, 1913.

Freer, Martha Walker. *The Married Life of Anne of Austria.* 2d ed. 2 vols. London, 1865.

Gately, Michael O., A. Lloyd Moote, and John E. Wills. "Seventeenth-Century Peasant 'Furies': Some Problems of Comparative History." *Past and Present* 51 (1971).

Gebelin, François. *Histoire de l'art français: L'époque Henri IV et Louis XIII.* Paris, 1969.

Geertz, Clifford. "Centers, Kings, and Charisma: Reflections on the Symbolics of Power." In *Culture and Its Creators: Essays in Honor of Edward Shils,* ed. Joseph Ben-David and Terry Nichols Clark. Chicago, 1977.

Geertz, Clifford and Edward Shils. *Center and Periphery: Essays in Macrosociology.* Chicago, 1977.

Geley, Léon. *Fancan et la politique de Richelieu de 1617 à 1627.* Paris, 1884.

Giesey, Ralph E. *The Juristic Basis of Dynastic Right to the French Throne.* Philadelphia, 1961.

———. *The Royal Funeral Ceremony in Renaissance France.* Geneva, 1960.

Goubert, Pierre. *The Ancien Régime: French Society 1600–1750.* Trans. S. Cox. London, 1973.

———. *Beauvais et le Beauvaisis de 1600 à 1730.* 2 vols. Paris, 1960.

————. *The French Peasantry in the Seventeenth Century.* Trans. Ian Patterson. Cambridge, 1986.

Goy, Joseph, and Emmanuel Le Roy Ladurie. *Les fluctuations du produit de la dîme: Conjoncture décimale et domaniale de la fin du moyen âge au XVIIIe siècle.* Paris, 1972.

Greengrass, Mark. *France in the Age of Henri IV: The Struggle for Stability.* London, 1984.

Griffet, Henri [père]. *Histoire du règne de Louis XIII.* 3 vols. Paris, 1756. (Vols. 13–15 of Gabriel Daniel, ed. *Histoire de France depuis l'établissement de la monarchie française dans les Gaules.* 17 vols. Paris, 1755–57.)

Griselle, Eugène. *Profils de Jésuites du XVIIe siècle.* Paris, 1911.

Gutton, Jean-Pierre. *La sociabilité villageoise dans l'ancienne France: Solidarités et voisinages du XVIe au XVIIIe siècle.* Paris, 1979.

Hanley, Sarah. *The Lit de Justice of the Kings of France: Constitutional Ideology in Legend, Ritual, and Discourse.* Princeton, N.J., 1983.

Hanotaux, Gabriel, and duc de La Force. *Histoire du Cardinal de Richelieu.* 6 vols. Paris, 1893–1947.

Harding, Robert R. *Anatomy of a Power Elite: The Provincial Governors in Early Modern France.* New Haven, Conn.; 1978.

Harth, Erica. *Ideology and Culture in Seventeenth-Century France.* Ithaca, N.Y., 1983.

Hauser, Henri. *La pensée et l'action économiques du Cardinal de Richelieu.* Paris, 1944.

Hayden, J. Michael. "Continuity in the France of Henry IV and Louis XIII: French Foreign Policy, 1598–1615." *Journal of Modern History* 45 (1973).

————. "Deputies and *Qualités:* The Estates General of 1614." *French Historical Studies* 2 (1964).

————. *France and the Estates General of 1614.* Cambridge, 1974.

————. "The Uses of Political Pamphlets: The Example of the Estates General of 1614–15 in France." *Canadian Journal of History* 21 (1986).

————. "The Social Origins of the French Episcopacy at the Beginning of the Seventeenth Century." *French Historical Studies* 10 (1977).

Hayem, Fernand. *Le maréchal d'Ancre et Léonora Galigaï.* Paris, 1910.

Hepp, Noemi, and Georges Livet, eds. *Héroïsme et création littéraire sous les règnes de Henri IV et de Louis XIII.* Paris, 1974.

Herr, Richard. "Honor Versus Absolutism: Richelieu's Fight Against Duelling." *Journal of Modern History* 27 (1955).

Hickey, Daniel. *The Coming of French Absolutism: The Struggle for Tax Reform in the Province of Dauphiné, 1540–1640.* Toronto, 1986.

Hoffman, Philip T. *Church and Community in the Diocese of Lyon, 1500–1789.* New Haven, Conn., 1984.

————. "Taxes and Agrarian Life in Early Modern France: Land Sales, 1550–1730" *Journal of Economic History.* 46 (1986).

Houssaye, Michel. *La vie du Cardinal de Berulle*. Vols. 2–3. Paris, 1874–75.

Humbert, Jacques. *Le maréchal de Créquy, gendre de Lesdiguières (1573–1638)*. Paris, 1962.

Hunt, Lynn. *Politics, Culture, and Class in the French Revolution*. Berkeley and Los Angeles, 1984.

Huppert, George. *Les Bourgeois Gentilshommes*. Chicago, 1977.

Isherwood, Robert M. *Music in the Service of the King: France in the Seventeenth Century*. Ithaca, N.Y., 1973.

Israel, Jonathan I. *The Dutch Republic and the Hispanic World, 1606–1661*. Oxford, 1982.

Jackson, Richard A. "Peers of France and Princes of the Blood." *French Historical Studies* 7 (1971).

———. *Vive le Roi! A History of the French Coronation from Charles V to Charles X*. Chapel Hill, N.C., 1984.

Jacquart, Jean. *Le crise rurale en Ile-de-France, 1550–1670*. Paris, 1974.

Kantorowicz, Ernst H. *The King's Two Bodies: A Study in Medieval Political Theory*. Princeton, N.J., 1957.

Kermina, Françoise. *Marie de Médicis: Reine, régente et rebelle*. Paris, 1979.

Kettering, Sharon. *Judicial Politics and Urban Revolt in Seventeenth-Century France: The Parlement of Aix, 1629–1659*. Princeton, N.J., 1978.

———. *Patrons, Brokers, and Clients in Seventeenth-Century France*. Oxford, 1986.

Kitchens, James H. "The Parlement of Paris During the Ministry of Cardinal Richelieu, 1624–1642." Ph.D. diss., 1974.

Kleinman, Ruth. *Anne of Austria: Queen of France*. Columbus, Ohio. 1985.

Labatut, Jean-Pierre. *Les ducs et pairs de France au XVIIe siècle*. Paris, 1972.

La Bruyère, R. *La marine de Richelieu: Sourdis archevêque et amiral, 1594–1645*. Paris, 1948.

Lacroix, Paul. *Ballets et mascarades de cour de Henri III à Louis XIV, 1581–1652*. Paris, 1968.

La Rochefoucauld, Gabriel de. *Le cardinal François de La Rochefoucauld*. Paris, 1926.

La Varende, Jean de. *Anne d'Autriche, femme de Louis XIII 1601–1666*. Paris, 1938.

Lavisse, Ernest, ed. *Histoire de France depuis les origines jusqu'à la Révolution*. 9 vols. Paris, 1900–1911. (See also Mariéjol, Jean-Hippolyte.)

Le Clerc, Jean. *La vie du Cardinal duc de Richelieu, principal ministre d'état de Louis XIII*. 5 vols. Amsterdam, 1753. (Vol. 5 contains letters of Louis XIII.)

Lekai, Louis J. "Cardinal Richelieu as Abbot of Citeaux." *Catholic Historical Review* 42 (1956).

———. *The Rise of the Cistercian Strict Observance in Seventeenth-Century France*. Washington, D.C., 1968.

Leman, Auguste. *Richelieu et Olivares: Leurs négotiations secrètes de 1636 à 1642 pour le rétablissment de la paix*. Lille, 1938.

————. *Urbain VIII et la rivalité de la France et de la maison d'Autriche de 1631 à 1635*. Lille, 1920.

Lemoine, H. "Maisons religieuses fondées à Paris entre 1600 et 1639." *Bulletin de la Société de l'Histoire de Paris et de l'Ile-de-France* 32 (1942–43).

Léonard, Emile G. *A History of Protestantism*. Vol. 2, *The Establishment*. London, 1967.

Le Roy Ladurie, Emmanuel. *Les Paysans de Languedoc*. 2 vols. Paris, 1966. Abridged English edition: *The Peasants of Languedoc*. Trans. John Day. Urbana, Ill., 1974.

Le Vassor, Michel. *Histoire du règne de Louis XIII*. 10 vols. Amsterdam, 1700–1711.

Lightman, Harriet L. "Queens and Minor Kings in French Constitutional Law." *Proceedings of the Western Society for French History* 9 (1981).

Ligou, D. *Le protestantisme en France de 1598 à 1715*. Paris, 1968.

Livet, Georges. *La Guerre de trente ans*. Paris, 1963.

Lougee, Carolyn C. *Le Paradis des Femmes: Women, Salons, and Social Stratification in Seventeenth-Century France*. Princeton, N.J. 1976.

Lough, John. *An Introduction to Seventeenth-Century France*. London, 1954.

Love, Ronald S. "The Religion of Henri IV: Faith, Politics, and War, 1553–1593." Ph.D. diss., 1987.

Lublinskaya, Aleksandra D. *Frantsiya v nachale XVII veka 1610–1620*. Leningrad, 1959.

————. *French Absolutism: The Crucial Phase, 1620–1629*. Trans. Brian Pearce. Cambridge, 1968.

————. "Les assemblées d'états en France au XVIIe siècle: Les assemblées des notables de 1617 et de 1626." *Studies Presented to the International Commission for the History of Representative and Parliamentary Institutions* 31 (1966).

McGowan, Margaret. *L'art du ballet de cour en France, 1581–1643*. Paris, 1978.

MacLain, Ian. *Woman Triumphant: Feminism in French Literature 1610–1652*. Oxford, 1977.

Magne, Emile. *La vie quotidienne au temps de Louis XIII*. Paris, 1942.

Major, J. Russell. *Representative Government in Early Modern France*. New Haven, Conn., 1980.

————. "Fidelity and Clientage in Seventeenth-Century France. The Revolt of 1620: A Study of Ties of Fidelity." *French Historical Studies* 14 (1986).

Maland, David. *Culture and Society in Seventeenth-Century France*. London, 1970.

Mandrou, Robert. *Classes et luttes de classes en France au XVIIe siècle*. Florence, 1965.

————. *Introduction to Modern France, 1500–1640*. London, 1976.

————. *La France aux XVIIe et XVIIIe siècles*. Nouvelle Clio ser. Paris, 1970.

Mariéjol, Jean-Hippolyte. *Henri IV et Louis XIII (1598–1643)*. Vol. 6, pt. 2 of

Histoire de France depuis les origines jusqu'à la Révolution. Ed. Ernest Lavisse. Paris, 1905.

Martin, Henri-Jean. *Livre, pouvoirs et société à Paris au XVIIe siècle, 1598–1701.* 2 vols. Geneva, 1969.

Marvick, Elizabeth W. "Favorites in Early Modern Europe: A Recurring Psychopolitical Role." *Journal of Psychohistory* 10 (1983).

———. "Nature Versus Nurture: Trends and Patterns in Seventeenth-Century French Childrearing." In *The History of Childhood*, ed. Lloyd Demause. New York, 1974.

———. "Richelieu le mécène: Perspectives psychologiques." In *L'âge d'or du mécénat (1598–1661)*, ed. Roland Mousnier and Jean Mesnard. Paris, 1985.

———. *The Young Richelieu: A Psychoanalytic Approach to Leadership.* Chicago, 1983.

Mastellone, Salvatore. *La reggenze di Maria de' Medici.* Florence, 1962.

Méthivier, Hubert. *Le siècle de Louis XIII.* Paris, 1971.

Meuvret, Jean. "Comment les français du XVIIe siècle voyaient l'impôt." *XVIIe siècle* 25–26 (1955).

———. *Etudes d'histoire économique* Paris, 1971.

Michaud, Hélène. *La grande chancellerie et les écritures royales au XVIe siècle.* Paris, 1967.

Mongrédien, Georges. *Etude sur la vie de Nicolas Vauquelin.* Paris, 1921.

———. *10 novembre 1630: La journée des dupes.* Paris, 1961.

———. *Léonora Galigaï: Un procès de sorcellerie sous Louis XIII.* Paris, 1968.

Moote, A. Lloyd. "The *Annales* Historians." *Queen's Quarterly* 85 (1978).

———. "The Emerging French Intendants and Political Change." *Canadian Journal of History* 14 (1979).

———. "The French Crown Versus Its Judicial and Financial Officials, 1615–83." *Journal of Modern History* 34 (1962).

———. "The Preconditions of Revolution in Early Modern Europe: Did They Really Exist?" In *The General Crisis of the Seventeenth Century*, ed. Geoffrey Parker and Leslie Smith. London, 1978.

———. *The Revolt of the Judges: The Parlement of Paris and the Fronde, 1643–1652.* Princeton, N.J., 1971.

Moote, A. Lloyd, Michael O. Gately, and John E. Wills. *See* Gately.

Morcay, R., and G. Sage., *Le préclassicisme.* Paris, 1962.

Mousnier, Roland. *The Assassination of Henry IV: The Tyrannicide Problem and the Consolidation of the French Absolute Monarchy in the Early Seventeenth Century.* Trans. Joan Spencer. London, 1973.

———. "Comment les français du XVIIe siècle voyaient la constitution." *XVIIe siècle* 25–26 (1955).

———. "Le conseil du roi de la mort de Henri IV au gouvernement personnel de Louis XIV." *Etudes d'histoire moderne et contemporaine* 1 (1947).

———. *Les institutions de la France sous la monarchie absolue, 1589–1789.* 2 vols.

Paris, 1974–80. English edition: *The Institutions of France Under the Absolute Monarchy, 1598–1789.* Trans. Arthur Goldhammer and Brian Pearce. 2 vols. Chicago, 1979–84.

———. *Peasant Uprisings in Seventeenth-Century France, Russia, and China.* Trans. Brian Pearce. London, 1971.

———. *La plume, la faucille et le marteau.* Paris, 1970.

———. *La vénalité des offices sous Henri IV et Louis XIII.* Rouen, 1945; 2d ed. Paris, 1971.

Mousnier, Roland, and Jean Mesnard, eds. *L'âge d'or du mécénat (1598–1661).* Paris, 1985.

Mousnier, Roland, et al. *Le conseil du roi de Louis XII à la Révolution.* Paris, 1970.

Muchembled, Robert. *Popular Culture and Elite Culture in France, 1400–1750.* Trans. Lydia Cochrane. Baton Rouge, La., 1985.

Norberg, Kathryn. *Rich and Poor in Grenoble, 1600–1814.* Berkeley and Los Angeles, 1985.

Orcibal, Jean. *Les origines du Jansénisme.* 5 vols. Paris, 1947–62.

———. "Richelieu, homme d'église, homme d'état." *Revue d'histoire de l'église de France* 34 (1948).

Pagès, Georges. "Autour du 'grand orage' : Richelieu et Marillac, deux politiques." *Revue historique* 174 (1937).

———. "Le conseil du roi sous Louis XIII." *Revue d'histoire moderne* 12 (1937).

———. "Essai sur l'évolution des institutions administratives en France du commencement du XVIe siècle à la fin du XVIIe." *Revue d'histoire moderne* 7 (1932).

———. *Les institutions monarchiques en France sous Louis XIII et Louis XIV.* Paris, 1933.

———. *La monarchie d'ancien régime en France (de Henri IV à Louis XIV).* Paris, 1946.

———. *Naissance du grand siècle.* Paris, 1948.

———. *The Thirty Years War 1618–1648.* Trans. David Maland and John Hooper. London, 1970.

Pannier, J. *L'église réformée de Paris sous Louis XIII.* 3 vols. Paris, 1922–32.

Parker, David. *La Rochelle and the French Monarchy: Conflict and Order in Seventeenth-Century France.* London, 1980.

———. *The Making of French Absolutism.* London, 1983.

Parker, Geoffrey. *The Army of Flanders and the Spanish Road, 1567–1659.* Cambridge, 1972.

Parker, Geoffrey, and Leslie Smith, eds. *The General Crisis of the Seventeenth Century.* London, 1978.

Pavie, Eusèbe. *La guerre entre Louis XIII et Marie de Médicis 1619–1620.* Antwerp, 1899.

Petit, Jeanne. *L'assemblée des notables de 1626–1627.* Paris, 1936.

Perrens, François-Thommy. *L'église et l'état en France sous le règne de Henri IV et la régence de Marie de Médicis.* 2 vols. Paris, 1872.

————. *Les mariages espagnols sous le règne de Henri IV et la régence de Marie de Médicis, 1602–1615.* Paris, 1869.

Picot, Gilbert. *Cardin Le Bret (1558–1655) et la doctrine de la souveraineté.* Nancy, 1948.

Pierret, Marc. *Richelieu ou la déraison d'etat.* Paris, 1972.

Pillorget, René. *Les mouvements insurrectionnels de Provence entre 1596 et 1715.* Paris, 1975.

Pintard, R. *Le libertinage érudit pendant la première moitié du dix-septième siècle.* 2 vols. Paris, 1943.

Pithon, Rémy. "La Suisse, théâtre de la guerre froide entre la France et l'Espagne pendant la crise de Valteline (1621–1626)." *Schweizerische Zeitschrift für Geschichte* 13 (1963).

————. "Les débuts difficiles du ministère de Richelieu et la crise de Valteline (1621–1627)." *Revue d'histoire diplomatique* 74 (1960).

Popkin, Richard H. *History of Scepticism from Erasmus to Descartes.* New York, 1964.

Porchnev, Boris. *Les soulèvements populaires en France de 1623 à 1648.* Paris, 1963.

Prat, Jean-Marie. *Recherches historiques sur la Compagnie de Jésus en France au temps du P. Coton.* 5 vols. Lyon, 1876–78. (Vol. 5 contains primary sources.)

Ranum, Orest. *Artisans of Glory: Writers and Historical Thought in Seventeenth-Century France.* Chapel Hill, N.C., 1980.

————. "Courtesy, Absolutism, and the Rise of the French State, 1630–1660." *Journal of Modern History* 52 (1980).

————. "The French Ritual of Tyrannicide in the Late Sixteenth Century." *Seventeenth-Century Journal* 11 (1980).

————. "Guise, Henri III, Henri IV, Concini: Trente ans d'assassinats politiques." *Histoire* 51 (1982).

————. *Paris in the Age of Absolutism.* New York, 1968.

————. *Richelieu and the Councillors of Louis XIII: A Study of the Secretaries of State and Superintendents of Finance in the Ministry of Richelieu 1635–1642.* Oxford, 1963.

————. "Richelieu and the Great Nobility: Some Aspects of Early Modern Political Motives." *French Historical Studies* 3 (1963).

Richet, Denis. *La France moderne: L'esprit des institutions.* Paris, 1973.

Roger, Jacques. *Panorama du XVIIe siècle français.* Paris, 1962.

Rothrock, George A. "The French Crown and the Estates General of 1614." *French Historical Studies* 1 (1960).

————. *The Huguenots: A Biography of a Minority.* Chicago, 1979.

————. "Officials and King's Men: A Note on the Possibilities of Royal Control in the Estates General." *French Historical Studies* 2 (1962).

————. "Some Aspects of Early Bourbon Policy Towards the Huguenots." *Church History* 29 (1960).

Roupnel, Gaston. *La ville et la campagne au XVIIe siècle: Etude sur les populations des pays dijonnais.* 2d ed. Paris, 1955.

Rowen, Herbert H. *The King's State: Proprietary Dynasticism in Early Modern France.* New Brunswick, N.J., 1980.

Russell, Conrad. "Monarchies, Wars, and Estates in England, France, and Spain, c. 1580–c. 1640." *Legislative Studies Quarterly* 7 (1982).

Salmon, John H. M. *Renaissance and Revolt: Essays in the Intellectual and Social History of Early Modern France.* Cambridge, 1987.

———. "Storm over the Noblesse." *Journal of Modern History* 53 (1981).

———. "Venality of Office and Popular Sedition in Seventeenth-Century France." *Past and Present* 37 (1967).

Schalk, Ellery. *From Valor to Pedigree: Ideas of Nobility in France in the Sixteenth and Seventeenth Centuries.* Princeton, N.J., 1986.

Shennan, Joseph H. *The Parlement of Paris.* London, 1968.

Solomon, Howard M. *Public Welfare, Science, and Propaganda in Seventeenth-Century France: The Innovations of Théophraste Renaudot.* Princeton, N.J. 1972.

Soman, Alfred. "Press, Pulpit, and Censorship Before Richelieu." *Proceedings of the American Philosophical Society* 120 (1976).

Sutcliffe, F. E. *Guez de Balzac et son temps: Littérature et politique.* Paris, 1959.

Tapié, Victor-L. *The Age of Grandeur: Baroque Art and Architecture,* Trans. A. Ross Williamson. London, 1960.

———. "Comment les français du XVIIe siècle voyaient la patrie." *XVIIe siècle* 25–26 (1955).

———. *France in the Age of Louis XIII and Richelieu.* Trans. and ed. D. M. Lockie. New York, 1975.

———. *La politique étrangère de la France et le début de la Guerre de trente ans (1661–1621).* Paris, 1934.

Taveneaux, René. *Le catholicisme dans la France classique, 1610–1715.* 2 vols. Paris, 1980.

———. *La vie quotidienne des Jansénistes aux XVIIe et XVIIIe siècles.* Paris, 1973.

Tessereau, A. *Histoire chronologique de la Grande chancelerie de France.* 2 vols. Paris, 1710.

Thuau, Etienne. *Raison d'état et pensée politique à l'époque de Richelieu.* Paris, 1966.

Treasure, Geoffrey R. R. *Cardinal Richelieu and the Development of Absolutism.* New York, 1972.

Tyvaert, Michel. "L'image du roi: Legitimité et moralité royales dans les histoires de France au XVIIe siècle." *Revue d'histoire moderne et contemporaine* 21 (1974).

Vaissière, Pierre de. *Un grand procès sous Richelieu: L'affaire du maréchal de Marillac (1630–1632).* Paris, 1924.

Venard, Marc. *Bourgeois et paysans au XVIIe siècle: Recherches sur le rôle des bourgeois parisiens dans la vie agricole au sud de Paris au XVIIe siècle.* Paris, 1957.

Verlet, P. *Versailles*. Paris, 1961.

Vienot, J. *Histoire de la réforme française*. 2 vols. Paris, 1934.

Weber, Hermann. "Vom verdeckten zum offenen Krieg: Kriegsgrunde und Kriegsziele Richelieus 1634–35." In *Der dreißigjährige Krieg*, ed. Konrad Repgen. Munich, 1988.

Wolf, John B. *Louis XIV*. New York, 1968.

Wolfe, Martin. *The Fiscal System of Renaissance France*. New Haven, Conn., 1972.

Wolfe, Michael, "The Conversion of Henri IV and the Origin of Bourbon Absolutism." *Historical Reflections* 14 (1987).

Zeller, Berthold. *Henri IV et Marie de Médicis*. Paris, 1877.

Zeller, Gaston. *Aspects de la politique française sous l'ancien régime*. Paris, 1964.

———. *Les institutions de la France au XVIe siècle*. 2d ed. Paris, 1987.

Index

For Louis XIII, see the five main entries under his name, as well as subentries of entries on institutions, places, themes, and other persons (e.g., under Council, royal; Dutch Republic; Favorites, personal; Richelieu).

Abra de Raconis, Charles François de, 293
Acarie, Mme, 258
Aix, 230; Parlement of, 230
Alais (Alès): Grace of, 199–200, 203–4
Albret, Jeanne d' (queen of Navarre), 23, 121
Alès. *See* Alais
Aligre, Etienne d': chancellor of France, 167–69; keeper of the seals, 108, 113–14, 167
Alsace, 233, 235, 240, 242
Amboise, 53, 55, 83
Amiens, 103, 193, 242, 246
Ancre, marquis of. *See* Concini, Concino
Ancre, marquise of. *See* Galigaï, Leonora
Angers, 55, 112; Treaty of, 112–14
Angoulême, 110; Treaty of, 111
Anjou: Cardinal La Valette becomes governor of, 231; Marie de' Medici as governor of, 111–12
Annales historians, 6, 12–13, 15–16, 310n.28
Anne of Austria (queen of France): appearance and character, 84, 143; betrothal and marriage to Louis XIII, 48, 83–85, 142; and Buckingham, 147–48, 193–94; and Chalais conspiracy, 193–94; and Mme de Chevreuse, 103, 142, 146–49, 193, 223, 274, 279; and her children, 243, 277–83; and Day of Dupes, 221; and Mme du Fargis, 221–23; and foreign affairs, 132, 135, 143, 201, 278–81; and Gaston d'Orléans, 191; and the *Gazette*, 269; and her household, 142, 147–48, 222–23, 275, 332n.32; illness and miscarriages, 145–47, 194, 209, 223, 322n.19; and Mlle de La Fayette, 276–77, 280; and La Vieuville, 148, 280; and Marie de' Medici, 84–85, 147, 216, 332n.22; marital relations, 92, 126, 139, 141, 144–48, 193–94, 277–78, 281; regent for Louis XIV, 252, 282; regent for northern France, 332n.22; religious interests, 257, 259, 280; and Richelieu, 88, 159, 221, 223, 234, 280; secret correspondence crisis, 278–81, 354n.15
Ariès, Philippe, 10
Arles, 151, 242, 311n.19
Army of France: under Marie de' Medici, 51, 82; officers in, 31, 39; size and organization under Louis XIII, 198–99, 202, 210–11, 230, 239–40, 245. *See also* Lesdiguières: constable of France; Louis XIII, travels and military campaigns; Luynes, Charles d'Albert de: constable of France

383

Arnoux, Father Jean: confessor of Louis XIII and Luynes, 103, 105, 122; as a dévot leader at court, 110; Louis XIII's relations with, 110, 122, 124, 132, 138, 143–44; as Luynes's creature, 103, 105, 122

Arras, 244

Art and architecture, under Louis XIII, 256–67

Asterac, 250

Austrian Habsburgs: domains of, 24–25; and Edict of Restitution, 208; foreign policy after 1630, 232–36, 239–45; and Henry IV, 20, 39; and the Mantuan succession, 199–200, 207, 210–13, 232; and Marie de' Medici, 48; and Treaty of Regensburg, 212–17; and the Thirty Years' War from 1618 to 1630, 131–34, 179–80, 206–8, 212–13; and the Val Tellina, 134–35, 179–83. *See also* Ferdinand II

Avenel, Denis-Louis-Martial, 4, 288, 337n.33; quoted, 173, 218

Avigliana (Veillane), 162, 214

Avignon, 102, 110, 242

Bailiffs, 64

Balzac, Guez de, 270

Barberini, Francisco (cardinal), 180, 183

Barbin, Claude: and Déageant, 93, 102; imprisonment and exile, 101–2; Louis XIII's relations with, 91, 101–2; and Richelieu, 88, 101–2; superintendent of finances under Marie de' Medici, 87–88, 91, 101

Barradat, François de, 157, 165–66, 187, 283

Bärwalde, Treaty of, 232

Bassompierre, François de: ambassador to Spain, 134; and Assembly of Notables, 186; Bouteville and des Chapelles arrested by, 188; at council, 181; and Henry IV, 35; imprisonment and release, 223, 244; and Louis XIII, 82, 107, 111, 141, 148, 233, 245; and Louis XIII's building expenditures, 256

Batiffol, Louis, 9, 38, 223, 225, 323n.16, 333n.28

Baux, Les, 230

Bavaria, 133, 232–34, 240

Bayle, Pierre, 7

Béarn, 121–24

Beaumarchais, Vincent Bohier de, 107, 114

Bellegarde, Roger de Saint-Lary, duke of, 139, 207, 209, 230

Bentivoglio, Guido, 113, 122

Bergerac, 126

Beringhen, Henri (son), 222

Beringhen, Pierre de, 46–47

Bernard, Charles (historiographer of Louis XIII): Louis XIII's exiling of his mother blamed on Luynes by, 100–101; Louis XIII's massacres at Nègrepilisse and Privas rationalized by, 129–30, 293; Louis XIII's memory and intelligence noted by, 22, 161; and origin of Louis XIII's sobriquet, 96

Bérulle, Pierre de (cardinal): and Catholic Reformation, 159, 258; and Descartes, 271; and Henrietta Maria's marriage negotiations, 181; and Marie de' Medici, 168, 183; and Protestantism, 194, 201, 204; Richelieu's friendship with, 159

Beuvron, Jacques d'Harcourt, marquis of, 188

Béziers, Edict of, 230

Biron, Charles de Gontaut, duke of, 25

Blainville, Jean de Varignies de, 82

Blanche of Castile: regent for Louis IX, 41

Blaye, 123, 166

Blois, 55, 191; Gaston d'Orléans's expansion of the château, 263; Marie de' Medici's exile at, 100–102, 104, 109

Bohemia, 24, 48, 132

Bois-dauphin, Urbain de Laval de, 82

Bonney, Richard, 231, 348n.9, 349n.14

Bons Français: described, 45–46, 48, 178

Bordeaux, 82–84, 140; Parlement of, 88

Bouillon, duchy of, 233

Bouillon, Frédéric-Maurice de La Tour d'Auvergne, duke of, 251

Bouillon, Henri de La Tour d'Auvergne, duke of, 25, 30, 67, 86–87, 99

Bouteville, countess of, 188

Bouteville, François de Montmorency, count of, 158, 163, 187–89, 192

Bouthillier, Claude Le: career, 171–72; and Day of Dupes, 218; secretary of state for foreign affairs, 172, 212, 218, 227; superintendent of finances, 171, 245

Bouvard, Charles: physician to Louis XIII, 157, 291

Brantes, Léon d'Albert de (duke of Luxembourg-Piney): background, 80; and Concini's assassination, 94; favors and offices under Louis XIII, 103, 123, 149; loses royal favor, 171

Braudel, Fernand, 15, 310n.28

Breda, 242

Breisach, 242

Breitenfeld, battle of, 233

Brittany: and Chalais conspiracy, 191; Estates of, 55, 119, 250; Guémadeuc's lawlessness in, 119; Louis XIII at Estates of, 55; Richelieu as governor of, 230–31, 248; César de Vendôme as rebel governor of, 50, 52–55

Brosse, Salomon de, 262–63

Brûlart de Léon, Charles, 212–16

Brûlart de Sillery, Nicolas: chancellor under Marie de' Medici, 40, 44, 63, 75–76; death, 167; disgraced by Marie, 10; governmental role under Louis XIII, 99, 105, 108, 110, 113; Louis XIII banishes, 108, 113, 135

Buckingham, George Villiers, duke of: and Anne of Austria, 147–48, 193–94; and Huguenot wars with Louis XIII, 182, 193–96; Louis XIII's hostility toward, 195; minister-favorite in England, 89, 98–99, 103, 165

Buisseret, David, 29

Bullion, Claude: and Day of Dupes, 219; career noticed by Louis XIII, 130; as *commissaire* and supporter of intendants, 248; prevails over Servien, 337n.42; prevails over Sublet de Noyers, 250; Richelieu's confidant regarding the king's behavior, 209–10, 214, 221; superintendent of finances, 171, 245–46

Burckhardt, Carl J., 330n.45, 345n.44

Burgos, 83

Burgundy: Louis XIII's visits to, 299–30, 233; royal control of Estates of, 248

Cadenet, Honoré d'Albert de (duke of Chaulnes): background, 80; and Concini's assassination, 94, 321nn.27 and 29; favors and offices under Louis XIII, 103; Louis XIII continues to consult, after Luynes's death, 149; in Luynes's conciliar faction, 105

Caen, 113, 140

Calais, 134, 234

Callot, Jacques, 266

Candale, Henri de Nogaret de La Valette, count of, 82

Carcassonne, 230

Carmona, Michel, 8–9, 309n.19

Casale, 161, 200, 202, 207–17

Cascaveoux, revolt of, 230, 248

Castelnaudary: battle of, 225; Louis XIII at, 230

Castres, 179, 203

Catalonia, 240, 242

Catherine de' Medici (queen of France), 111

Catholic clergy of France (First Estate), 63–65; at Assemblies of Notables, 117, 184; and Estates General of 1614–15, 65–74; and financing Louis XIII's wars, 186, 249; and Huguenots, 20, 45–46, 121–22; Louis XIII's attitudes toward, as an estate, 186, 249, 340n.26, 351n.14

Catholic League: French, 23, 45; German, 132–33, 208, 232

Catholic Reformation, 45–46, 67, 257–59. *See also* Dévots

Caussin, Father Nicolas, 260; confessor of Louis XIII, 243, 262, 276–77, 285; and Mlle de La Valette, 276–77; Louis XIII's rule criticized in correspondence of, 293; and Richelieu, 243

Chalais, Henri de Talleyrand, count of, 189, 191–92

Chalais conspiracy, 182, 189–94

Châlons-sur-Marne, 246

Chambre de justice, 179, 246

Chambre de l'Arsenal, 228, 246

Chambres des comptes, 64, 99

Champagne, 39, 232–33; Barradat lieutenant general of, 165; Laffemas intendant in, 246

Champaigne, Philippe de, 265–66

Champigny, Jean Bochart de: first president of Parlement of Paris, 167, 171, 336n.38; superintendent of finances, 167; Louis XIII and Michel de Marillac praise, 336n.30

Chancellor of France. *See* Aligre; Brûlart de Sillery; Séguier

Chantal, St. Jeanne de, 258

Chapelles, François de Rosmadec des, count of, 187–89

Chapman, Hester W., 331n.11

Charles I (king of England): and marriage to Henrietta Maria, 135, 176, 181, 195; and Spanish marriage quest, 147; and Treaty of La Rochelle, 182

Charles IV, duke of Lorraine, 233–34

Charles IX (king of France), 111

Charles Emmanuel (duke of Savoy): relations with Louis XIII, 161–62, 202, 208–10, 212. *See also* Savoy, duchy of

Châteaudun, 227

Châteauneuf, Charles de l'Aubespine, marquis of: disgraced, 234; keeper of the seals, 171, 218; and Parlement of Paris, 229; Servien's friendship with, 218

Châtillon, Gaspard de Coligny, duke of, 128, 226

Chaulnes, duke of. *See* Cadenet, Honoré d'Albert de

Chavigny, Léon Le Bouthillier, count of: secretary of state for foreign affairs, 172; triangular relationship with Louis XIII and Richelieu, 172, 243–44, 281, 287–89; watches Gaston d'Orléans, 171

Cherasco, Treaty of, 232

Chevallier, Pierre: on Bourbon-Habsburg conflict, 329n.35; on Cinq Mars conspiracy, 288; on Day of Dupes, 345n.53; on Louis XIII as a Corneillian king, 9, 353n.43; Louis XIII's role in his government analyzed by, 9, 173, 326n.46; on Louis XIII's sexual preferences, 355n.32

Chevreuse, Claude de Lorraine, duke of, 141, 146, 230

Chevreuse, Marie de Rohan-Montbazon, duchess of (previously duchess of Luynes): assessment of Louis XIII, 193; background and first marriage, 103; escapes disgrace through second marriage, 146; head of Anne of Austria's household, 103, 142; involvement in Chalais conspiracy and flight, 191, 193; Louis XIII's changing attitude toward, 139, 141, 143, 146, 273–74, 331n.8; second disgrace and Châteauneuf's fall, 234; secret correspondence with Anne, 279

Christine (sister of Louis XIII and duchess of Savoy): and Anne of Austria, 143; and Louis XIII, 139, 144–45, 202, 241; and Marie de' Medici, 27–28; marriage to Victor-Amadeus, 109, 134, 144–45; regent for her son, 240–41

Church, William F., 308n.11, 330n.42

Cinq Mars, Henri Coiffier de Ruzé, marquis of: background and career, 285; and Cinq Mars conspiracy against Richelieu, 251, 286–89; courtiers' uncomfortableness with, 283; as personal favorite of Louis XIII, 244, 285–89

Clérac, 126–27

Clergy. *See* Catholic clergy of France

Code Michau, 185, 231

Coeuvres, François Annibal, marquis of (later duke of Estrées), 135

Cologne, 224

Commissaires, 231, 246–48. *See also* Commissions for state trials; Intendants

Commissions for state trials: and Chalais, 191; and Guémadeuc, 226; and Laffemas, 246; and Louis de Marillac, 227; and Montmorency. *See also* Chambre de justice; Chambre de l'Arsenal

Compiègne, 171, 223, 233; Treaty of (1624), 135; Treaty of (1635), 235

Concini, Concino (marquis of Ancre): assassination plot against and death of, 82, 92–95, 321n.25; and Barbin, 87, 91; career and offices, 44, 82, 87, 90–91, 103; grandee hostility toward, 82, 86, 89; and Henry IV, 90; Louis XIII's relationship with, 50, 80–81, 90–100, 320nn.21 and 22; 321nn.25 and 29; and Marie de' Medici, 44, 50, 89–94, 320n.18; marriage to Leonora Galigaï, 44, 90; Parlement of Paris and, 75–76, 95, 100; pamphlets about, 89, 95–96, 326n.48; popular hatred of, 50, 89–90, 99–100; posthumous reaction against, 95–100; and Richelieu, 86–88, 91, 102, 163

Condé, Charlotte de Montmorency, princess of, 118, 188–89

Condé, Henri II de Bourbon, prince of: biographical background, 50; Bouteville's execution opposed by, 188; and Concini, 82, 86; in the council of Marie de' Medici, 63, 65, 86; and Estates General of 1614–15, 65, 67–69; fights Habsburgs, 241; governor of Burgundy, 230, 248; and grandee opposition to Marie de' Medici, 50–55, 82, 86, 88; and Huguenots, 86, 105, 107, 122–23, 128–130; imprisonment by Marie de' Medici and Louis XIII (1616), 86–87, 118; and Louis XIII as boy king, 52–53, 56, 59, 67–69; and Montmorency's execution, 226; and Parlement of Paris opposition to Marie de' Medici, 75; released and restored to council by Louis XIII (1619), 104; Richelieu's relationship with, 86, 159, 216–17, 226, 283; role in Louis XIII's court and council (1619–22), 104, 107, 112–13, 122–

23, 128–30, 324n.24; second disgrace by Louis XIII (1622), 107, 324n.25; second recall by Louis XIII and favor after Day of Dupes, 191, 216–17, 223; and Soissons, 141

Confessors, royal. *See* Jesuit confessors of Louis XIII

Conjunctures: defined, 12. *See also* Economy, French

Constable of France. *See under* Lesdiguières; Luynes, Charles d'Albert de

Constant, Jean-Marie, 349n.21

Conti, Marguerite de Bourbon, princess of, 84, 209

Corbie, siege of, 241, 251

Corneille, Pierre, 9, 270–71

Coronation (*sacre*): of Louis XIII, 42–43; of Marie de' Medici, 39

Coton, Father Pierre: confessor of Louis XIII, 34, 47, 49, 82

Coucher, royal, 29, 81, 137; Concini's pun on, 91

Council, royal (membership and functioning): changes of 1626, 169–70; from Day of Dupes to death of Richelieu, 170–73; Louis XIII's introduction to as a minor, 44, 52, 58; Louis XIII's reliance on, 89, 102, 104–5, 137–38, 161, 166–67; with Luynes as minister-favorite, 98–100, 104–6; from Luynes's death to La Vieuville's disgrace, 106–9, 113–15; under Marie de' Medici, 44, 63, 87–88; after Richelieu's entry and La Vieuville's fall in 1624, 166–69; after Richelieu's death, 244–45

Council of Trent, 45, 67, 257

Cours des aides, 64

Court, royal. *See* Royal family households

Courtenvaux, Jean de Souvré, marquis of, 81–82, 148, 166

Courtilz de Sandras, Gatien de, 356n.18

Créquy, Charles de Blanchefort de, 202, 231

Croquants, revolts of, 240, 250, 253–54

Danès, Jean, 259

Darnton, Robert, 14

Dauphiné: Lesdiguières as governor of, 82; Soissons as governor of, 231; Talon intendant in, 250; taxation in, 250

Déageant, Guichard de: and Barbin, 93, 102; and Concini's assassination, 93–94; offices and influence, 93, 98, 105, 138, 321n.28; ousted from court, 170

Denmark: and Thirty Years' War, 179–80, 208

Descartes, René, 271–72

Dethan, Georges, 341n.40, 348n.8

Dévots: defined, 45; and Louis XIII's foreign policy, 178, 181–82, 199–200; and Louis XIII's wars against Huguenots, 122, 182, 194, 197, 199, 204. *See also* Arnoux, Father Jean; Bérulle, Pierre de; Catholic Reformation; Caussin, Father Nicolas; Marillac, Michel de; Suffren, Father Jean

Dieppe, 142

Dijon: municipal privileges curbed, 229–30; Parlement of, 230

Divine right of monarchs, 40, 43, 67

Dôle, 241

Don gratuit, 64, 186, 249. *See also* Catholic clergy of France

Dueling: and Barradat's disgrace, 57, 165–66; and Bouteville case, 158, 163, 185–89; and Chalais, 189, 191–92; decrees against, 118, 121, 185–86; and Guémadeuc case, 119–20; and Guise-Nevers dispute, 120; Henry IV's attitude toward, 25; Louis XIII's views on, 120, 157–58, 163, 187–89; under Marie de' Medici, 71; Richelieu's experience with, 157–59, 163, 187–89; and Schomberg family, 157–58

Dumas, Alexandre: interprets Louis XIII negatively, 2, 5–7, 33, 79, 308n.12; and Tallemant-Dumas tradition, 9, 11, 38

Dupes, Day of, 169; events of, 216–19, 221, 346n.54; governmental changes after, 171–72, 220–228; as a turning point in Louis XIII's reign, 199–200, 220

Dupleix, Scipion, 294

Duplessis-Mornay, Philippe de, 125

Dutch Republic: commerce and navy of, 181, 184; Eleven Years' truce with Spain, 48, 133–34; and Henry IV, 48, 131; and Louis XIII, 133–34, 176, 179, 181, 213, 232, 235; and Marie de' Medici, 48; war with Spain, 133–34, 201, 208, 242–43; and the Val Tellina, 134, 176, 179, 183

Economy, French, 12, 15, 184; Richelieu's reform ideas on, 184

Effiat, Antoine Coiffier de Ruzé, marquis of: career of, 169–70; at council meeting on Mantuan war, 211; credit policies of, 179, 246; as marshal, 170; at

Effiat, marquis of (*continued*)
Notables assembly of 1626, 184; and *pays d'états*, 226, 229–33, 247; superintendent of finances, 169–70, 179, 231–32
Elbeuf, Catherine-Marie de Vendôme, duchess of: childhood, 28; marries duke of Elbeuf, 144
Elbeuf, Charles de Lorraine, duke of: governor of Picardy, 230; marries Catherine-Marie de Vendôme, 144
Elections, 64, 226, 248, 349n.13; *pays d'élections*, 226, 229–31, 247
Eleven Years' Truce, 44, 133–34
Elisabeth (sister of Louis XIII and queen of Spain): childhood relations with Marie de' Medici, 27–28; betrothal and marriage to Philip IV of Spain, 48, 51, 81, 83; illness, 83; Louis XIII's relationship with, 81, 83, 139
Elliott, John H., 329n.35, 340n.20, 345n.47, 347n.29
Elus, 64, 226, 229–31, 247–48, 349n.13
England: and Charles I's marriage to Henrietta Maria, 135, 176, 181, 195; commerce of, 184; navy of, 195–97; hostilities with French monarchy, 123, 195–97; threat to northeastern France in 1620–21, 123; and Treaty of La Rochelle, 182. *See also* Buckingham; Charles I
Entrées, royal, 57, 140, 267
Epernon, Jean Louis de Nogaret de La Valette, duke of: governor of Guienne, 113, 123, 231, 250–51; Henry IV's assassination and, 40–41; loses influence over Marie de' Medici to Richelieu, 111; loses royal favor and governorship of Guienne, 250–51; Louis XIII's attitudes toward, 110–11, 123, 323n.18, 324n.21; in Marie de' Medici's ruling circle, 41, 44, 63, 68; military command at Metz, 110; and Parlement of Paris, 68; and War of the Mother and Son (1619), 110–11
Esplan, Esprit d'Alard d': personal favorite of Louis XIII, 107, 150, 327n.49
Estates General of 1614–15: cahiers of, 61, 73–74; and Code Michau, 185; composition of, 65–67; demands for and elections to, 50–55; Louis XIII's relations with, 67–74, 80; meetings of, 66–73
Estates of provinces. *See under* Brittany;

Burgundy; Languedoc; Normandy; *Pays d'états*; Provence
Evangelical Union, 132–33

Faret, Nicolas, 270
Fargis, Charles d'Engennes du, count of, 182–83, 221–23
Fargis, Madeleine de Sillery du, countess of, 183, 279–81
Favorites, personal (female). *See* Hautefort; La Fayette
Favorites, personal (male): Louis XIII's predilection for, 106–7, 148–50, 273–78, 281, 283; Louis XIII vows to exclude from political influence, 106, 284, 287; phenomenon of, 89. *See also* Barradat; Bassompierre; Cinq Mars; Courtenvaux; Esplan; Luynes, Charles d'Albert de; Saint-Simon, Claude de Rouvroy de; Toiras; Vendôme, Alexandre de
Ferdinand II (Holy Roman Emperor and Austrian Habsburg ruler), 131–32, 208, 211–13; Louis XIII's attitude toward, 131–32, 211. *See also* Austrian Habsburgs
Finances, French royal: under Barbin, 87–88, 91–92; under Bullion and Bouthillier, 171, 245–46; Déageant and, 105; under Effiat, 169–70, 179, 231–32, 246; under Henry IV and Sully, 44, 107; Jeannin and, 59, 105; under La Vieuville, 107–8, 114; under Marillac and Champigny, 167; under Schomberg, 105, 107, 167; and state budgets (1610–17), 59, 87–88, 91–92; and state budgets (1617–24), 105, 107–8, 114; and state budgets (1624–29), 179, 182, 186, 197–98; and state budgeting after 1630, 220–21, 228–32, 239–40, 245–55, 348n.9. *See also* Paulette; Venality of office
First Estate. *See* Catholic clergy of France
Florence, 19
Foisil, Madeleine, 13, 32, 38, 307n.7, 313n.36
Fontainebleau, redecoration of château of, 262
Fontenay-Mareuil, François Duval, marquis of, 104, 105, 150
Fortifications: of grandees in 1614, 52; of Huguenots, 130, 179, 197, 204; Louis XIII's views on razing, 55, 126, 182, 185–86, 197, 204; Richelieu and, 197; royal, 182

Foullé, Etienne: intendancy of, 250
Franche Comté, 24, 224, 240
Francis I (king of France), 263
François de Sales, St., 257–58
Fronde, 248, 251–52

Galigaï, Leonora (marquise of Ancre): and Barbin, 87; grandee, popular, and pamphlet hostility toward, 89–90, 99–100; head of household and closeness to Marie de' Medici, 44, 82, 90–91; marriage to Concino Conini, 44; Parlement of Paris and, 75–76, 100; trial and execution of, 100
Gallicanism, 45–46, 67–68
Gargin, Edward, 356n.3
Gascony, 250
Gaston (brother of Louis XIII and duke of Orléans): and Anne of Austria, 191, 193, 279–81; and the arts, 256, 263; character of, 251; birth of his daughter, 192, 194; childhood and governors, 36, 103; and Cinq Mars conspiracy, 287; and Day of Dupes, 217, 221, 345n.51; flights from France, 206, 224–25, 228, 230, 233; Louis XIII's attitude toward, 139, 190–93, 201–2, 205–6, 221–26, 283, 341n.40; Mantuan war supported by, 209; and Marie de' Medici, 190, 206–7, 217, 221, 235; Marie de Nevers's romance with, 206–7; marriage to Marguerite of Lorraine, 224, 234–35, 262; marriage to Marie de Bourbon-Montpensier, 168–69, 189–94; military role as rebel, 225, 233; military roles in royal army, 195, 197, 201, 205, 209, 343n.5; and Montmorency's fate, 226, 228; and Richelieu, 172, 207, 217, 221–25, 251; watched by Chavigny, 172
Gaston de Foix, 36
Gazette, 269
Généralités, 64, 247
Genoa, 161, 180
German princes, 39, 48, 208, 212, 232
Germany: and Edict of Restitution, 208; and Jülich-Cleves question, 39, 48; and Regensburg Diet and treaty, 212–17; and Thirty Years' War, 131–34, 179–80, 208, 212–17, 232–43. *See also* Austrian Habsburgs
Ginzburg, Carlo, 13
Goulas, Nicolas, 285, 293
Governors: Louis XIII opposes awarding of posts for money, 118; personnel changes among, 230–31, 234; role of, in provinces and towns, 50–51, 63; role of lieutenants general to, 51. *See also under specific persons and provinces*
Grandees (*les grands*): described, 49–50; at Assemblies of Notables, 117–18, 184, 186; and Chalais conspiracy, 189–93; and Estates General of 1614–15, 65, 67–69; Louis XIII's relations with (1617–24), 110–13, 118–20, 123; Louis XIII's relations with (1624–28), 186–93; Louis XIII's relations with (1629–30), 205–22; Louis XIII's relations with (1631–43), 222–32, 240, 248–51; revolts against Marie de' Medici, 49–60, 82–83, 86–88, 91, 93, 99; and Wars of the Mother and Son, 110–13
Grenoble: Louis XIII in, 210, 241; religious philanthropy in, 258
Griffet, Father Henri, 7
Grillon, Pierre, 4, 9
Grisons, 48, 131, 134–35, 180–83, 240
Guardin, J. M., 331n.11
Guémadeuc, Thomas de, 119–20, 157
Guienne: Epernon as governor of, 113, 123, 231, 250–51
Guise, Charles de Lorraine, duke of: 41, 82–83, 230, 334n.14
Guise, Louis de Lorraine (cardinal), 120
Guise family, 23, 209, 349n.7
Gustavus Adolphus (king of Sweden), 213, 233–34. *See also* Sweden

Habsburgs. *See* Austrian Habsburgs; Spanish Habsburgs
Hallier, François de l'Hôpital du (Vitry's brother), 82, 94, 98
Hanley, Sarah, 252, 314n.6
Hanotaux, Gabriel, 329n.35, 345n.44; and collaboration by La Force, 343n.2
Hardy, Alexandre, 270
Hautefort, Marie de: and Anne of Austria, 274–75; and Louis XIII, 268, 274–75, 278, 281, 284–85; in Marie de' Medici's household, 274; and Saint-Simon, 284
Hayden, J. Michael, 317n.10, 340n.24
Hay du Chastelet, Paul, 228, 293
Henrietta Maria (sister of Louis XIII and queen of England): and Catholic worship at English court, 181; and Louis XIII, 139, 193, 331n.17; and Marie de' Medici, 27; marriage to Charles I, 135, 176, 181, 195

Henry III (king of France), 20, 107, 113, 294
Henry IV (king of France): appearance and character, 21, 23, 29, 294; and Catholics, 20, 23, 45, 122; clemency of, 25, 37, 118; and Concini, 80, 90; death and funeral, 39–42; and his extended family, 28–30; extramarital relations, 28–29, 282; foreign policy of, 20, 39, 131, 134; and Huguenots, 20, 123; Louis XIII's relations with, 19–20, 22–32, 35, 283; Marie de' Medici's relations with, 19, 28–29, 39, 84, 90, 312n.16; and the paulette, 64
Héroard, Jean: Concini fails to secure dismissal of, 321n.26; *Journal* of, 4–5, 10, 139, 312n.11; Louis XIII's attachment to, 33, 313n.25; as Louis XIII's physician, 19–20, 31–34, 36, 54, 313n.26; Vauquelin's criticism of, 36
Hoffman, Philip T., 258
Holy Roman Empire. *See* Austrian Habsburgs; Ferdinand II; German princes; Germany
Holy Sacrament, Company of, 259
Households, royal family. *See* Royal family households
Huguenots: in Béarn, 121–24; and Edict of Nantes, 20, 46, 121; and Grace of Alais, 199–200, 203–4; Louis XIII's relations with, 46–47, 121–30, 179, 181–82, 194–205; under Marie de' Medici's rule, 46, 82, 86; national assemblies of, 46, 121, 124; and Treaty of La Rochelle, 182, 195; and Treaty of Montpellier, 130. *See also* Bouillon, Henri de; La Force; Lesdiguières; Rohan; Soubise; Sully
Hungary, 24, 48, 132
Hunt, David, 10, 311n.9

Ile de France, 103, 246
Intendants, 231, 246–48, 252–53
Italy: and Austrian Habsburg (Holy Roman Emperor's) formal suzerainty over the Grisons and Mantua, 134–35, 200, 207; Henry IV's alliances in, 48, 134, 330n.45; and Louis XIII, 108, 134–35, 161–62, 179–83, 199–202, 207–13, 240–41; and the Mantuan succession, 161–62, 199–202, 207–13; and Marie de' Medici, 48; Spanish possessions in, 24; and Val Tellina question, 134, 182–83, 240–41

Jansen, Cornelius, 261
Jansenism, 260–62
Jeannin, Pierre, President (in parlement of Dijon): Louis XIII influenced in council by, 59, 110, 132; superintendent of finances for Louis XIII, 59, 99, 105; superintendent of finances under Marie de' Medici, 59, 63, 76
Jesuit confessors of Louis XIII, 46, 138; Arnoux, Father Jean, 103, 105, 110, 122, 124, 132, 138, 143–44; Caussin, Father Nicolas, 243, 262, 276–77, 285, 293; Coton, Father Pierre, 34, 47, 49, 82; Maignon, Father, 223; Suffren, Father Jean, 215, 221, 223
Jesuit order (Society of Jesus): architecture of, 257–58; Henry IV and, 45; Louis XIII's childhood experiences with, 47, 49; Marie de' Medici and, 45–46; and Ravaillac's trial, 46; and theology, 260. *See also* Jesuit confessors of Louis XIII
Joseph, Father (François Joseph Le Clerc du Tremblay): and Louis XIII's policymaking, 1619–20, 122, 132; and Regensburg Diet and treaty, 212–16; and Rhineland policy of Louis XIII, 234; and Richelieu, 170, 177–78, 232. *See also* Tremblay, sieur de (Father Joseph's brother)
Jülich-Cleves dispute, 39, 48
Justice, royal: early seventeenth-century assumptions about, 13–14, 37, 56–57, 99–100, 310n.32; historians and Louis XIII's association with, 10–14; Louis XIII's concept of, as a child and adolescent (1601–17), 30–31, 37–38, 47, 56–59, 88–89, 320n.16; Louis XIII's concept of, during his personal reign (1617–43), 99–102, 116–20, 129–30, 150–51, 157, 227–28, 231, 292–97; and Louis XIII's acquiring of sobriquet "the Just", 56–57, 59, 73, 79, 96, 117, 316n.32; pamphlets on, 56–57, 72–73, 95–96, 130, 151, 177, 329n.32

Keeper of the seals. *See* Aligre; Châteauneuf; Mangot; Marillac, Michel de; Séguier; Vair

La Fayette, Louise de: in Anne of Austria's household, 275; enters Visitadine convent, 258, 277; and Father Caussin,

176–77; Louis XIII's relationship with, 274–78, 281, 288

Laffemas, Isaac: career of, 246–47

La Force, Jacques Nompar de Caumont, duke of: at Assembly of Notables of 1626, 186; fights Gaston d'Orléans's army in Luxembourg, 233; governor of Béarn, 123; loses favor at court, 123; made marshal, 129

La Meilleraye, Charles de La Porte, duke of, 230, 248

La Mothe-Houdancourt (marshal), 224

Languedoc: and Edict of Béziers, 230; Estates of, 230, 248; and Huguenot wars, 124, 128; Louis XIII at Estates of, 230; Montmorency as rebel governor of, 225–26; as a *pays d'états*, 226

La Porte, Suzanne de (mother of Richelieu), 159

La Rochefoucauld, François, duke of, 293

La Rochefoucauld, François de (cardinal): and Catholic Reformation, 122, 124; consulted by Louis XIII on dueling penalties, 158; grand almoner of Louis XIII, 122; place in royal council, 168

La Rochelle: closeness of Richelieu's bishopric of Luçon, 159; fortifications of, 130, 183, 197; and grandee revolt, 55; Huguenot national assembly at, 124; Louis XIII bypasses in 1622, 128; Louis XIII's attitude toward, 124, 195–97; and Treaty of Montpellier, 130; siege and capitulation of, 168, 184, 186, 194–200; Treaty of, 182, 195

La Trémouille, Henri, duke of, 86

La Valette, Bernard de Nogaret, duke of, 251

La Valette, Henri de Nogaret de (count of Candale), 82

La Valette, Louis de Nogaret de (cardinal): in council debate, 181; and Day of Dupes, 218; Epernon's son and Richelieu's creature, 181; governor of Anjou, 231; military role of, 242, 260

La Vieuville, Charles Coskaer, marquis of: Anne of Austria and, 148, 280; career of, 107–9; character, 63; escape and exile in Spanish Netherlands, 109, 280; fiscal policy as superintendent of finances, 107–8, 118, 176; foreign policy initiatives of, 135, 176, 181; Louis XIII relies on, 113; Louis XIII turns against and arrests, 109, 114,

135, 327n.50; *principal ministre*, 168; prosecution of financial coterie of, 179

La Ville-aux-Clercs, Henri-Auguste de Loménie de: family of, 337n.43; as secretary of state at Day of Dupes, 218, 337n.43

La Vrillière, Louis Phélypeaux de: as secretary of state at Louis XIII's dying, 291, 337n.43; family of, 337n.43

Le Fèvre, Nicolas: preceptor of Louis XIII, 47

Le Jay, Nicolas: first president of the Parlement of Paris, 171, 218, 229; Louis XIII's attitude toward, 167, 229, 336n.30; rebels against Marie de' Medici, 218; as Richelieu's creature, 167, 218

Le Mercier, Jacques: builds Palais Cardinal for Richelieu, 262; builds Louis XIII wing of Louvre, 264

Le Nain brothers, 266

Le Nôtre, Jean: landscape architect for Louis XIII, 267

Lerma, Francisco Gomez de Sandoval y Rojas, duke of, 104, 165

Le Roy, Philibbert: builds Louis XIII's hunting lodge/château at Versailles, 263

Les Baux, 230

Lesdiguières, François de Bonne, duke of: constable of France, 120, 125; converts to Catholicism, 125, 178; death of, 178; in council debate, 105, 130; governor of Dauphiné, 82; and Huguenots, 82, 125; and Louis XIII's views on dueling and religious toleration, 120, 125; named marshal general of French army, 125

Le Seq (secretary of Anne of Austria): dismissed and temporarily jailed by Louis XIII, 148

Le Sueur, Eustache, 266

Le Tellier, Michel: intendant and secretary of state for war, 245

Lettres de jussion, 64

Lever, royal, 25, 29, 81, 137

Limoges, 246

Limours, 160, 190

Lit de justice, 41, 63, 111, 185, 252

Livurdun, Treaty of, 234

Longueville, Henri II, duke of: governor of Normandy, 123; and grandee revolts, 86, 123

Lorraine, Charles IV, duke of, 233–34

Lorraine, duchy of: and Gaston d'Or-léans's flights from France, 206, 208, 223–24, 233; Louis XIII's invasions of, 233–35, 240–41; strategic location of, 206, 233

Lossky, Andrew, 161, 327n.1

Loudun, Treaty of, 86

Louis IX (St. Louis): and Blanche of Castile, 41; Bourbon dynasty founder, 36; Louis XIII compared with, 58–59, 113, 178; Louis XIII identifies himself with, 37, 122, 257; Louis XIII's name associated with, 36–37, 41, 47, 59

Louis XI: Louis XIII objects to being compared with, 229

Louis XII: golden age of past associated with, 71; Louis XIII associated with virtues of, 37, 41

Louis XIII, and Anne of Austria: betrothal and marriage, 48, 83–85, 142; and Buckingham, 147, 193–94; and Chalais conspiracy, 193–94; and their children, 282; and Day of Dupes, 221–23; and *Gazette*, 269; and her household, 142, 147–48, 222–23, 275, 332n.22; and Huguenot campaign of 1621, 126, 145; and their illnesses, 145–47, 215, 290; and Mantuan war, 209, 211; marital relations, 92, 126, 139, 141, 144–48, 193–94, 277–78, 281; and her regency powers in 1620 and 1643, 282, 332n.22; and her secret correspondence, 278–81, 354n.15

Louis XIII, biography: accession to throne and coronation, 39–43, 314n.8; betrothal and marriage to Anne of Austria, 48, 51–52, 76, 79, 83–85, 142; birth, 19–21, 24; breaks with his mother, 100–101 (1617), 170–71 (1631); childhood sibling relations, 22–23, 27–28, 36; children (Louis XIV and Philippe of France), 260, 273, 282–83; death of and transition to Louis XIV's minority, 258, 268, 291–92; education and upbringing, 22–38, 47, 58; illnesses (serious), 91–92, 170, 195, 199, 211–15, 291–92, 344n.43; moves from St-Germain to Louvre and male household entourage, 22–23, 32–35, 40; named Louis, 36–37; sobriquet "the Just" given to, 56–59, 72–73, 79, 95–96, 117, 130, 151, 177, 316n.32,

329n.32; status at his majority, 41, 51, 59, 61; status during his minority, 44, 51; vow to Virgin, 260–62

Louis XIII, historiography: by his contemporaries, 292–95, 356n.12; since his reign, 1–16. *See also* Avenel; Batiffol; Bernard; Chapman; Courtilz de Sandras; Dumas; Foisil; Fontenay-Mareuil; Guardin; Héroard; Hunt, David; Major; Marvick; Montglat, François de Paul de; Pamphlets; Ranum; Saint-Simon, Louis de Rouvroy de; Tallemant des Réaux; Tapié; Vaunois

Louis XIII, personality, 1–16, 22–23, 37–38, 58–60, 76–81, 137–51, 156–57, 160, 173, 273–97; appearance and physique, 21, 81–82, 84, 156, 265–66, 290; artistic interests, 22, 81, 256–72; attitude toward ceremonies, 23, 25–26, 30, 43, 140; dependence on others, 79–80, 106–7, 148–50, 165, 273–78, 281; emotional repression, 38, 59, 76–79, 139–46, 149, 226–27, 275–77, 281; health (as child), 21, 27, 31, 53–54, 56, 59; health (as teenager and adult), 81, 83, 111, 120, 129, 141, 156–57, 244; illnesses (serious), 91–92, 170, 195, 199, 211–15, 291–92, 344n.43; intelligence, 22, 161; magnanimity, 26, 37, 53, 56, 81, 151, 158, 197; marital interests, 22, 24, 35, 47, 52, 58, 80, 126, 140–41, 242–45; moodiness, 21–22, 27–28, 30, 140–41, 157, 172; parsimoniousness, 59, 70, 118; preoccupation with minutiae and mechanical undertakings, 22, 47, 80, 140–41; recreation, 22–24, 43, 54, 58, 80–82, 92, 138–41, 145, 267–69; sexuality (childhood), 31–32, 37, 58, 80, 84–85; sexuality (teenage and adult) and men, 102–4, 148–49, 283–86, 332n.25, 354n.25, 355n.32; sexuality (teenage and adult) and women, 80, 84–85, 144–48, 194, 273–82; speech and writing difficulties and manner (as child), 3–5, 21, 23, 27, 33–35, 56, 59; speech and writing difficulties and manner (as teenager and adult), 137–40, 146–47, 161–65, 269, 281, 286–89; vindictiveness, 26, 128–30, 141–42, 150–51, 157, 227–28, 310n.32

Louis XIII, travels and military campaigns (in chronological order): prior to Estates General (1614), 52–55; for his marriage (1615), 82–83; Wars of the

Mother and Son (1619–20), 110–13, 121; to Béarn and Calais (1620–21), 121–24; Huguenot wars (1621–22), 124–30, 145; siege of La Rochelle (1627–28), 195–98; Mantuan and Huguenot conflicts (1629), 199–205; Mantuan campaign (1630), 207–16, 229; against Gaston d'Orléans and Lorraine (1631, 1632), 230, 233–34; against Lorraine (1634, 1635), 235, 241; relief of Corbie (1636), 241; northern, eastern, and southeastern anti-Habsburg offensives (1638–39), 241; northeastern and eastern forays (1640–41), 241; siege of Spanish Perpignan (1642), 242, 287–89

Louis XIV: and Anne of Austria, 282–83, 295, 356n.17; attitude toward Louis XIII, 264, 291, 295; birth and infancy, 21, 282; christening, 283; education, 283, 295, 356n.17; Louis XIII's relations with, 282–83; and Mazarin, 283; minority and majority, 251–52, 282; Versailles construction by, 264

Louvigny, Roger, count of, 189, 191–92

Louvre palace: Concini assassinated at entrance of, 94–95; construction by Louis XIII and Louis XIV at, 262, 264; Louis XIII moves to, 35; Marie de' Medici finds unlivable, 264

Lucas, Michel: personal secretary of Louis XIII, 160, 170

Luçon, bishop of. *See* Richelieu, Armand-Jean du Plessis de

Lude, François de Daillon, count of, 103

Lunel, 230

Lützen, battle of, 234

Luxembourg, palace of, 90, 217; building of, 262–63, 265

Luxembourg, Spanish, 233

Luxembourg-Piney, duke of. *See* Brantes

Luynes, Charles d'Albert, duke of: background and character, 58, 80–81, 102–4, 148, 163; and Concini's assassination, 92–95, 100–101, 322n.30; and Condé, 80, 104; constable of France, 103–4; and Henry IV, 80; and Huguenots, 122–28; Louis XIII's childhood relationship with, 58, 80–81, 92; Louis XIII's marriage consummation and, 144; Louis XIII's personal relationship with (1617–21), 102–3, 106, 144–45, 148–50; Louis XIII's policies and, 100–102, 111–12, 118–20, 122–23, 127, 192, 323n.18; and Marie de' Medici, 80–81,

100–101, 104, 192, 323n.18, 326n.44; offices and favors under Louis XIII, 58, 80–81, 83, 98–106, 118; pamphlets for and against, 106, 323n.17; Richelieu's relations with, 102, 104, 110–11, 113, 163

Luynes, Mme de. *See* Chevreuse, Marie de Rohan-Montbazon

Lyon: Louis XIII at, 140, 209–15, 230, 241–42, 289; Cinq Mars's trial and execution at, 289; danger of plague at, 202

Machault, Charles: intendant in Burgundy, 248

Madrid: French royal palace of, 138; Treaty of, 134–35

Maignon, Father: confessor of Louis XIII, 223

Maine, Henri de Lorraine, duke of, 86, 99, 128

Mairet, Jean, 270

Maîtres des requêtes, 253

Major, Russell, 231, 308n.11, 347n.24

Maland, David, 352n.36

Malherbe, François de, 37, 269

Mangot, Claude: career of, 87–88; keeper of the seals, 88, 99, 101; secretary of state, 88

Mansart, François, 263

Mantua: siege of (town), 208, 211–12; duchy of, 166, 236. *See also* Mantuan succession; Nevers, Claude de Gonzague, duke of Mantua and

Mantuan succession, 161–62, 183, 199–203, 205–17, 232

Marca, Pierre de, 249

Marguerite of Valois (queen of France), 19, 21, 53, 56

Marie de' Medici: and Anne of Austria, 84–85, 147, 216, 221, 332n.22; appearance and character of, 21, 27; Blois exile and escape, 100–101, 104, 109; and Chalais conspiracy, 190, 192–93; Compiègne exile and flight from France, 170–71, 223–24; and Concini, 44, 50, 82, 89–94, 320n.18; and Condé, 59, 68–69, 86, 113; coronation of, 39; and her daughters, 27–28, 83, 109; and Galigaï, 44, 82, 90–91; and Gaston d'Orléans, 190, 206–7, 217, 224, 235, 345n.51; governor of Anjou, 111, 231; and Henry IV, 19, 28–29, 39, 84, 90, 312n.16; household of, 217, 222–23, 275; Louis XIII's relations with, as dauphin (1601–10), 27–32, 312n.12; Louis

Marie de' Medici (*continued*)
XIII's relations with, during his early personal rule (1617–24), 100–102, 109–115, 126, 128, 139, 142, 325n.32, 326n.46; Louis XIII's relations with, from his illness at Lyon to her death (1630–42), 215–16, 221–24, 244; Louis XIII's relations with, as a minor king, 44, 51, 58–60 (1610–14); Louis XIII's relations with, after royal majority (1614–17), 67–69, 76, 80–81, 84–85, 90–94; Louis XIII's triangular relationship in council with Richelieu and (1624–31), 168–71, 200–201, 207, 211–19, 221–24, 325n.28, 345n.49; Luxembourg palace built for, 262–63; Luynes and, 100–102, 104, 110, 112, 192, 326n.44; and Mantuan succession, 200–201, 209, 211, 214, 216, 243n.15; and Nevers as grandee rebel and duke of Mantua, 99, 200–201, 206; regent for northern France (1627–28, 1629), 205, 206; and Richelieu as her servitor (1610–24), 86, 88, 101–2, 104, 109–14, 163, 325n.32, 326n.46; and Richelieu as Louis XIII's servitor (1624–42), 168–71, 200–201, 207, 211–19, 221–24, 244; role of, after her reentry to Louis XIII's council (1622–24), 107–109, 113–14, 326n.44; rule of, as Louis XIII's head of council (1614–17), 61–63, 66–76, 80–94; rule of, as Louis XIII's regent (1610–14), 40–55, 59–60; and Val Tellina question, 181, 325n.28, 345n.49; and Wars of the Mother and Son, 110–13
Marillac, Louis de, 167, 196, 217, 223, 227–28, 327n.49
Marillac, Louise de, Mlle Le Gras, 227
Marillac, Michel de: background, 167; councillor of state, 336n.31; and Day of Dupes and his disgrace, 170, 217–18, 227, 346n.54; keeper of the seals, 169, 340n.25; La Rochelle siege and, 194, 196; Louis XIII's relations with, 167, 169, 184, 211, 217–18, 336n.30; Mantuan succession war opposed by, 201, 204, 209, 211, 216; and Marie de' Medici, 167–68, 216–18; state reform views of, 184, 211, 229, 231, 247, 340n.25; superintendent of finances, 167; and Val Tellina question, 181
Marillac family, 258

Marseille, 128
Martellange, Etienne, 257
Marvick, Elizabeth: on Day of Dupes, 218–19; on Héroard's journal, 4, 311n.11; and Louis XIII's character, 10–12, 38, 161, 227, 333n.26; and Louis XIII's upbringing, 31, 311n.9; and Richelieu's *Testament politique*, 333n.2
Matthieu, Pierre, 128
Mazarin, Jules (Giulio Mazarini): and Fronde, 252; as Louis XIII's minister, 244–45, 283, 288; Louis XIV's relationship with, 273, 283; as papal agent, 212, 214, 216
Medallions: and Concini's assassination, 95; after La Rochelle's surrender, 198; of Louis XIII's coronation, 43; at Louis XIII's majority, 56–57
Mentalité: defined, 12–13; under Henri IV, 12, 20; under Louis XIII, 13, 54, 184, 185, 220
Mersenne, Marin, 268, 271
Métezeau, Clement, 197
Méthivier, Hubert, 8
Metz, 110, 134, 229, 233, 246
Michau, Code, 185
Military affairs. *See* Army of France; Louis XIII, travels and military campaigns; Navy: French
Minister-favorite: phenomenon of, 89, 103–4, 165. *See also* Buckingham; Concini; Lerma; Luynes, Charles d'Albert de; Olivares
Ministers, French. *See* Council, royal; *and individual ministers*
Miron, Robert, 70
Modena, 236
Modène (cousin of Luynes): as minister, 105, 170
Molé, Mathieu, 224–25, 336n.29
Monceau, palace of, 244
Monheur, 128, 328n.29
Montauban, 33, 127–28, 179, 203–4
Montbazon, Hercule de Rohan, duke of, 52, 118, 135, 139–40
Montchal, Charles de, archbishop of Toulouse, 295
Montchrétien, Antoine de, 184
Montesquiou, baron of, 250
Montglat, François de Paul de Clermont, marquis of, 285
Montglat, Françoise de Longuejoue, baronness of: governess of Louis XIII, 19–21, 26–28, 31–34, 319n.24

Montmorency, Henri II, duke of: confiscation of wealth and château of, 231, 268; and Gaston d'Orléans, 225–26, 228; governor of Languedoc, 225–26, 229, 248; Louis XIII's closeness to, 182, 215, 226, 346n.12; military commands for Louis XIII, 182, 212; rebellion, trial, and execution, 225–26, 228, 230, 346n.12; and Richelieu, 226, 346n.12

Montmorency family: and Théophile de Viau, 269

Montpellier, 130, 140, 230, 242; Treaty of, 130

Montpensier, Marie de Bourbon-Montpensier, princess of Dombes: first wife of Gaston d'Orléans, 190, 192, 194

Montpouillan, Jean de Caumont, marquis of: at Béarn, 123, 321n.28; and Concini's assassination, 93–94, 321n.28; loses favor at court to Luynes, 103, 123, 150; Louis XIII's childhood friend, 47, 82

Monzon: Treaty of, 182–83, 339n.19

Moret, Antoine, count of: half brother of Louis XIII, 225

Morgard, Noël-Léon, 54, 316n.28

Morgues, Mathieu de, 224, 294

Mortmain, 249

Motteville, Françoise Bertaut de, 277, 353n.2

Moulins, 223

Mousnier, Roland, 317nn.7 and 10, 327n.3, 338n.46, 348n.30

Moyenvic, 233

Music: of Louis XIII, 256, 268–69

Nancy, 235

Nantes: Chalais's execution at, 192; Edict of, 20, 46, 57, 121; Louis XIII's visits to, 55, 57, 128, 192

Narbonne, 230, 242, 287

Navarre, 23, 121, 124

Navarreins, 123

Navy: English, 195–97; French, 184–85, 195; Dutch, 181, 242

Nègrepelisse, 128–30, 141, 227

Nevers, Claude de Gonzague, duke of Mantua and: Cardinal Guise's altercation with, 120; and Gaston d'Orléans's passion for daughter of, 205–6; as a grandee rebel against Marie de' Medici, 99; and Mantuan succession, 199–202, 206–7, 212–13, 232. *See also* Mantua; Mantuan succession

Nîmes, 230, 242

Nobility, French (Second Estate): description of, as an estate, 63–65; at Assemblies of Notables, 117, 186; at Estates General of 1614–15, 65–74; and military service, 63, 249–50; and monarchy, 63–65, 250–51. *See also* Grandees; *and individual noblemen and noblewomen*

Nobility of race and sword (*noblesse de race, noblesse d'épée*): defined, 63. *See also* Nobility, French

Nobility of the robe (*noblesse de robe*): defined, 63–64. *See also* Parlements, provincial; Paulette; Third Estate; Venality of office

Norberg, Kathryn, 258, 259

Nordlingen, battle of, 235

Normandy: Concini as lieutenant general of, 90, 93, 98; Estates of, 248–49; Longueville as rebel governor of, 123; Louis XIII crushes grandee revolt in, 112; Luynes's acquisition of Concini's posts in, 103; Nu-Pieds revolt in, 240–41, 250, 254–55

Notables, Assembly of: in 1617–18, 117–18, 140, 185; in 1626–27, 184–86, 340n.24

Nu-Pieds, revolt of: 240–41, 250, 254–55

Nurse, of Louis XIII (Antoine Joran, Mme Bocquet, known as Doundoun), 26, 31–32, 91

Offices, venal: *See* Paulette; Venality of office

Ogg, David, 261

Oléron, 179

Olivares, Gaspar de Guzman, count-duke of: and Louis XIII's skepticism about his desire for peace, 243; and Mantuan succession question, 201; as minister-favorite in Spain, 89, 98–99, 104, 165; and open war with France, 235; and Treaty of Monzon, 183

Oratory confraternity, 159, 258, 261, 270

Orléans, 54, 82

Orléans, Gaston d'. *See* Gaston (brother of Louis XIII and duke of Orléans)

Ornano, Jean-Baptiste d', count of Montlaur: and Chalais conspiracy, 190–92; after Concini's assassination, 97–98; governor of Gaston d'Orléans, 103; imprisonment and death, 190–91; Louis XIII's attitude toward, 118, 190, 192

Pagès, Georges, 8, 156
Palaces. *See* Royal family residences
Palatinate, 131–33
Pamphlets (including manifestoes and public letters): on Concini, 89, 95–96, 326n.48; on bons Français/dévots differences, 178; on divine right of monarchs, 40; and Estates General of 1614–15, 51, 54–58, 72–73; and foreign affairs, 178, 224, 261, 293; and Gaston d'Orléans's and Marie de' Medici's flights of 1631, 224; after Grace of Alais, 205; and Huguenot wars, 130, 198; contributing to La Vieuville's disgrace and Richelieu's favor, 109, 114; on Louis XIII as Louis the Just, 95, 130, 151, 177, 329n.32; against Louis XIII's imminent marriage, 82; on Luynes, 106, 323n.17; against Louis de Marillac, 227–28; against Richelieu, 224, 293; after storming of Susa, 202; treason laws on, 186–87; and state reform in 1625–26, 176–77
Papacy: and Bourbon-Habsburg war after 1635, 240–41; Dominican debate on authority over councils of, 46; and Mantuan succession, 202; and Val Tellina question, 180–83. *See also* Gallicanism; Ultramontanism
Paris: anti-Concini/Galigaï violence in, 90, 99–100, 320n.19; anti-tax riots by winesellers in, 222; population of, 40; reaction to Ravaillac's execution in, 46; reaction to siege of Corbie in, 241; salons of, 270
Paris, Parlement of: analysis of its public role, 74–75; and dueling, 187–88; edict of 1641 curbing powers of, 253; and Estates General of 1614–15, 68–70, 74–76; and fall of Concini and Galigaï, 93, 95, 99–100; and Fronde, 251–52; Gallicanism of, 67; and Gaston d'Orléans's and Marie de' Medici's flights of 1631, 225, 228–29; Gaston d'Orléans's second marriage nullified by, 234–35; and grandee agitations of 1614–15, 68, 75; Henry IV and, 25, 30; lits de justice in, 41, 63, 111, 185, 252; Lorraine awarded to Louis XIII as suzerain by, 235; Louis XIII's accession acknowledged and recorded, 41; Louis XIII's conflicts over finances with, 111, 185–86, 224–25, 228–29, 252–53, 255; Louis XIII's majority proclaimed at, 59; Richelieu's re-

lations with, 228–29, 252. *See also* Champigny; Le Jay; Molé; Paulette; Venality of office
Parlements, provincial: of Aix (Provence), 230; of Bordeaux (Guienne), 88; of Dijon (Burgundy), 230; of Pau (Béarn), 123; of Rennes (Brittany), 191; of Rouen (Normandy), 254–55; of Toulouse (Languedoc), 226
Parma, 236
Parthenay, 140
Partisans, 246
Patin, Guy, 356n.18
Pau, 123–24; Parlement of, 123
Paulette: created by Henry IV, 64; Parlement of Paris thwarts abolition of (1615), 70, 75; renewal disputes on, 221–22, 228–29, 317n.7, 327n.3; suspended temporarily (1618–21), 118; sustained despite Louis XIII's curbs on venal officials, 228–31, 253
Pays d'élections, 226, 229–31, 247. *See also* Elus
Pays d'états, 226, 229–31, 247
Peasants: and Estates General of 1614–15, 66; as percentage of French population, 66; revolts by, 253–54
Périgord, 253
Perpignan, 242, 287–89
Perron, Jacques Davy du, cardinal, 67
Phélypeaux-Pontchartrain family: as secretaries of state, 337n.43
Philip II (king of Spain), 15, 25
Philip III (king of Spain), 81, 104, 134, 143
Philip IV (king of Spain): Anne of Austria's correspondence with, 135, 279–80; Louis XIII comments on principles of, 211, 222; Mantuan succession involvement regretted by, 201, 208; marriage to Elisabeth of France, 81, 83; military campaigning of Louis XIII contrasted with behavior of, 201, 211; and Olivares, 134, 183, 201, 242; seizes archbishop of Trier, 236
Philippe de France (duke of Orléans): as second son of Louis XIII, 282–83, 291
Picardy: Cadenet (Chaulnes) as lieutenant general of, 103; Chevreuse replaces Elbeuf as governor of, 230; Concini as lieutenant general of, and governor of towns in, 90; Luynes as governor of, 103
Pinerolo, 210, 212–13, 217, 232, 242

Place Royale (Place des Vosges): Boute-ville duel at, 188; equestrian statue of Louis XIII at, 297; festivities of 1620 at, 145; Henry IV's architectural style of, 49, 263–64; Louis XIII's betrothal cele-bration at, 49, 267
Pluvinel, Antoine: Concini hostile to, 91; Louis XIII's equestrian instructor and deputy governor, 35–36, 91, 145; Richelieu's equestrian instructor, 158
Poitiers, 52, 55, 125
Poitou: Condé abandons rebel plan to control, 55; Louis XIII in, 53, 55, 124; Richelieu's family origins in, 158–59; Sully as governor of, 47
Ponts-de-Cé, battle of, 112–13
Popes. *See* Papacy; Urban VIII
Porchnev, Boris, 317n.10
Portugal, 24, 240
Pourbus, François, 265
Poussin, Nicolas, 266
Prague, Peace of, 235
Préaux, des: Louis XIII's deputy gover-nor, 36
Presidial courts, 64
Privas, 203–4
Provence: Cascaveoux revolt in, 230, 248; duke of Guise as governor of, 230; Estates of, 248; Vitry as governor of, 230, 241, 251
Provinces. *See specific provinces*
Provincial Estates. *See* Brittany; Bur-gundy; Languedoc; Normandy; *Pays d'états*; Provence
Puisieux, Pierre Brûlart, marquis of: as-sists Villeroy in council, 99; disgraced, 108; secretary of state for foreign af-fairs, 105, 107–8, 113, 324n.24; views on Huguenot and Habsburg chal-lenges, 108, 122, 130, 132, 135
Pyrenees, Peace of the, 241, 296

Quillebeuf, 129

Rambouillet, Catherine de, 270
Ranum, Orest: Louis XIII/Richelieu re-lationship discussed by, 4, 8, 156, 335n.16, 338n.46
Ravaillac, François, 40, 45–46
Ré, 179, 195–96
Reform, state: Assemblies of Notables and, 117–18, 184–85; and clergy, 186; and Code Michau, 185; Estates General of 1614–15 and, 70–76; Louis XIII's

views on, 117–18, 176–77, 179, 183–87, 236, 259; Michel de Marillac's views on, 184, 211; and nobility, 184–87; pam-phlets on, 176–77; Parlement of Paris and, 74–76, 185–86; Richelieu and, 177, 179, 183–85, 210, 338nn.1 and 5
Regency: powers of, 44. *See also under* Anne of Austria; Marie de' Medici
Regensburg: Diet of, 208; Treaty of, 213–17
Reims, 42–43
Renaudot, Théophraste, 269
Restitution, Edict of, 208
Retz, Henri de Gondi de (cardinal): death of, 324n.24; head of council, 105, 122; and Huguenot wars, 122, 129
Rhineland, 39, 48, 131–33, 209, 232–36
Richelieu, Alphonse-Louis du Plessis de (archbishop of Aix and Lyon; brother), 158–59
Richelieu, Armand-Jean du Plessis de (bishop of Luçon and later cardinal): appearance, background, and family, 88, 156, 158–59, 163, 266; and arts and learning, 262, 269–71; and Anne of Austria, 88, 159, 223, 234, 280; and Barbin, 88, 101–2; church posts and ti-tles of, 71–72, 88, 109, 113–14, 159; cli-entage of, 165–73, 181; and Concini, 86, 88, 102, 163; and Condé, 86, 191; conspiracies against, 189–92, 218, 227, 251, 286–89, 324n.24; council reentry and power of (1624), 109, 114–15, 163–64, 175–76, 325n.28; council role as *principal ministre*, 168; and Day of Dupes, 216–18, 221; death of, 244; and dueling, 157–59, 163, 187–89; at Estates General of 1614–15, 70–72; and favor-ites (female) of Louis XIII, 274–76; and favorites (male) of Louis XIII, 165–66, 285–90; and foreign affairs (1624–30), 181, 179–83, 199–202, 208–17; and for-eign affairs (1630–42), 232–36, 241–44; and Gaston d'Orléans, 172, 207, 217, 221–25, 251; as governor of Brittany, 231, 248; grand master of navigation and commerce, 184; health of, 156, 164, 173, 213, 234, 242; and Hugue-nots, 159, 175–76, 181–82, 194–97, 200, 202–5; Louis XIII's decision mak-ing, in collaboration with (1624–42), 155–73, 179, 199–204, 208–19, 229, 235–36, 244–45, 296–97, 286–89, 327n.49, 348n.30; Louis XIII's differ-

Richelieu, A.-J. du Plessis de (*continued*)
ences with, over policy and personnel
(1624–42), 163–65, 167, 173, 197, 202,
244, 286–89, 296–97, 336n.30; Louis
XIII's early relations with (1614–17),
70–71, 88, 101–2; Louis XIII's relations
with, during Richelieu's rise to political
favor (1619–24), 104, 109, 111–15, 164,
325nn.28 and 32, 326n.46, 327n.49;
Luynes's relations with, 102, 104, 110–
11, 113, 163; as Marie de' Medici's servitor (1615–24), 72, 88, 101–2, 104, 109–
14, 325n.32, 326n.46; Marie de' Medici's triangular relationship with Louis
XIII and (1624–1631), 168–71, 200–
201, 207, 211–19, 221–24, 325n.28,
345n.49; and the Marillacs, 167, 211,
216–17, 227, 327n.49; military roles of,
184, 195–97, 200–204, 208–13; and
Montmorency, 226; and parlements,
159–60, 228–29, 252; and religion, 155,
159, 181–82, 260, 351n.20; residences
of, 160, 190, 227, 262; and Saint-Simon,
166, 281; secretary of state for foreign
affairs (1616–17), 87–88, 91; on state
reform, 71–72, 177, 179, 183–85,
210, 248, 338nn.1 and 5; writings of
and for, 4–5, 109, 114, 160, 177–78,
332n.2
Richelieu, François du Plessis de (father):
158–59
Richelieu, Henri du Plessis, marquis of
(brother), 158–59
Rié, 128–29
Rivault de Fleurance, David: preceptor of
Louis XIII, 47, 90, 316n.36
Roanne, 216
Rohan, Henri, duke of: and grandee revolt against Marie de' Medici, 55, 86;
Huguenot military-political leader
against Louis XIII, 127, 130, 179, 203–
5; Louis XIII criticized and praised by,
150, 204–5; as royal commander in It-
aly, 204–5, 236
Romain, Charles, 9
Rouen: Louis XIII decides to raze fortifi-
cations near, 129; royal entrée and As-
sembly of Notables at, 117, 140; Parle-
ment of, 254–55
Roussillon, 242
Royal council. *See* Council, royal
Royal family households: of Anne of
Austria, 142–43, 147–48, 222–23, 275;

grandees' role in, 63; of Louis XIII, as
dauphin, 35; of Louis XIII, as ruler, 49,
90–91, 118; of Marie de' Medici, 217,
222–23, 275; offices of, 158; transition
from Henry IV to Louis XIII, 42
Royal family residences: of Gaston
d'Orléans, 263; of Louis XIII, 22–23,
35, 138, 160, 256, 262–64; of Marie de'
Medici, 262–63
Royal favorites. *See* Favorites, personal;
Hautefort; La Fayette; Minister-favorite
Royan, 128
Rubens, Peter Paul, 262, 264–65
Ruccellaï, Louis-Jean de, 105, 111
Ruel (Rueil), 160, 227

Sacre. See Coronation
Saint-André, 203
Saint-Cyran, Jean du Vergier de Hau-
ranne, abbot of, 260–62
St-Denis, 36, 42, 291–92
Ste-Ménehould, Treaty of, 51, 53
Saintes, 253
St-Germain, Declaration of, 249
St-Germain, *faubourg* of, 90
St-Germain-en-Laye: Barradat captain of
château of, 165; Louis XIII's childhood
at, 22–24, 28, 30–33, 35; Louis XIII's
death at, 291; Louis XIV's birth at, 282;
redecoration and landscaping of, 262
St-Jean d'Angély, 123, 126–27, 129
St-Omer, siege of, 241
Saintonge, 124
Saint-Simon, Claude de Rouvroy, duke
of: Louis XIII's personal favorite, 166,
214, 217, 278, 284–85, 291
Saint-Simon, Louis de Rouvroy, duke of
(son): 202, 264, 285
Saumur, 55, 124
Sauveterre, 170
Savaron, Jean, 72
Savoy, duchy of: anti-French alignment
with Habsburgs in 1629–31, 199–202,
208–17, 232; anti-Habsburg alliance of
1623 with France and Venice, 135, 179–
80; anti-Habsburg alliance of 1629 with
France, Mantua, Venice, and papacy,
203; anti-Habsburg alliance of 1635
with France, Mantua, Modena, and
Parma, 236; and Henry IV, 48; Louis
XIII's friendly relations with (1617–23),
133–35, 179; and Louis XIII's relations
with Christine, 240–41; and Mantuan

succession, 161–62, 199–202, 208–17, 232; and Marie de' Medici's rule, 133; and Treaty of Cherasco, 232; and Treaty of Madrid, 134–35; and Treaty of Monzon, 183, 339n.19; and Val Tellina question, 134–35, 179–80, 182–83. *See also* Charles Emmanuel; Christine; Victor-Amadeus

Saxe-Weimar, Bernard of, 242

Schomberg, Charles de (duke of Halwin; son), 149, 230

Schomberg, Henri de (count of Nanteuil): and council triumvirate of 1622, 107, 324n.24; and duels involving himself and his family, 157–58; on Habsburg-Bourbon relations, 107, 132; and Huguenot-royal relations, 107, 129; Louis XIII's closeness to, 105, 107, 167, 324n.24; returns to council as minister without portfolio (1624), 167; Richelieu's relations with, 167, 341n.37; superintendent of finances, 105, 107, 113, 135

Scrofula, royal power of healing: ceremonies by Louis XIII, 43–44, 54, 82, 137

Second Estate. *See* Grandees; Nobility, French; Nobility of race and sword

Secretaries, personal: of Louis XIII, 138, 160, 170

Secretaries of state: functioning of, under Louis XIII, 138, 160, 337n.43. *See also* Bouthillier; Chavigny; Déageant; La Ville-aux-Clercs; La Vrillière; Le Tellier; Mangot; Puisieux; Richelieu; Servien; Sublet de Noyers; Villeroy

Sedan, 25, 233, 241–42

Séguier, Pierre: Anne of Austria's secret correspondence investigated by, 280; made chancellor, 172; and Cinq Mars conspiracy trial, 286, 289; and intendants, 246, 248; keeper of the seals, 171–72; Louis XIII instructs, on crime and moral reform, 259; and Norman uprisings of 1637 and 1639, 241, 254

Seneschals, 64

Servien, Abel: background, 171, 248; dismissed in 1636, 172, 337n.42; and intendants, 248; secretary of state for war, 171

Sillery, the Commandeur de, 108

Siri, Vittorio, 341n.37

Smith, Lacy Baldwin, 308n.9

Social structures, 12, 15, 220

Society of Jesus. *See* Jesuit order

Society of orders, 63–66, 248

Soissons, Louis de Bourbon, count of: death in battle, 251; flight of, after Chalais conspiracy, 191; flight and rebellion of 1641 by, 241–42, 251; governor of Dauphiné, 231; princely supporter of and rebel for Marie de' Medici, 111, 123

Soubise, Benjamin de Rohan, duke of: as Huguenot military-naval leader against Louis XIII, 126, 128, 179, 181–82

Sourdis, François d'Escoubleau de (archbishop of Bordeaux and cardinal), 67–69

Souvré, Gilles, marquis of: fails to make his son a royal favorite, 81; governor of Louis XIII, 20–21, 27, 34–35; and Louis XIII's early attitudes toward Huguenots, 47, 67–68; Louis XIII's friendship with, 82

Spanish Habsburgs: Anne of Austria's correspondence with, 135, 143, 278–81; and Cinq Mars conspiracy, 251, 287–88; domains of, 24; Dutch war with, 133–34, 201, 208, 242–43; Eleven Years' Truce with Dutch Republic, 48, 133–34; and Franco-Spanish alliance against Huguenots, 183; and Franco-Spanish marriage alliance, 48–49, 51, 144; and Franco-Spanish relations after 1630, 232, 234–36, 239–45; Gaston d'Orléans's relations with, 223, 227–28, 251; and Henry IV, 20, 39; and Mantuan succession, 161–62, 199–202, 207–17, 232; and Thirty Years' War beginning, 133; and Val Tellina, 134–35, 176, 179–83, 207–8, 235, 240–41. *See also* Philip II; Philip III; Philip IV

Spanish Netherlands, 24, 103, 109, 123, 133–35, 223–25, 232, 240–41

Spinola, Ambrosio, 201, 207, 212

Structures, social, 12, 15, 220

Sublet de Noyers, François: background, 172, 248; Bullion outmaneuvers, 250; and intendants, 247–48; Louis XIII's relations with, 244–45, 287–89; Richelieu's creature, 172, 287; secretary of state for war, 172, 245

Subsistances, 250

Suffren, Father Jean: confessor of Louis XIII and Marie de' Medici, 215, 221, 223

Sully, Maximilien de Béthune, duke of: background of, as *gentilhomme*, 65–66;

Sully, duke of (*continued*)
dismissed by Marie de' Medici, 44, 46–
47; governor of Poitou, 47; Louis XIII
contemplates bringing back as superintendent of finances, 169; Louis XIII's
fondness for, 46–47; superintendent of
finances and confidant of Henry IV, 39,
44, 46, 50, 167
Superintendent of finances. *See under*
Barbin; Champigny; Effiat; Jeannin; La
Vieuville; Marillac, Michel de; Schomberg, Henri de; Sully
Susa, 168, 202, 207, 210, 217
Sweden, 208, 213, 233–35, 242–43
Swiss cantons, 48, 134. *See also* Grisons

Taille, 236, 245, 247, 250
Tallemant des Réaux, Gédéon: Louis
XIII's character interpreted by, 6–7; on
Louis XIII's sexuality, 85, 274, 283–86;
on Louis XIII's slashing of literary pensions, 269; Marvick's view of Louis XIII
and, 11, 38; Tallemant-Dumas interpretation noted, 9, 11, 38; trustworthiness
as a source, questioned, 354n.26
Talon, Jacques: intendant, 250
Tapié, Victor-L.: Louis XIII's character
and role in government analyzed by,
97–98, 255, 329n.37; Louis XIII's policies (1617–24) criticized by, 97–98,
327n.1, 329nn.35 and 37; on Louis
XIII's relationship with Richelieu, 8;
Richelieu's policy on Huguenots, as
viewed by historians, questioned by,
194
Tarrascon, 288–89
Tiers. See Third Estate
Third Estate: composition of, 63–65; at
Assemblies of Notables, 117–18, 140,
184–86; at Estates General of 1614–15,
65–67, 69–74; popular revolts among,
253–55. *See also* Paris, Parlement of;
Parlements, provincial; Paulette; *Pays
d'états*; Peasants; Venality of office
Thirty Years' War. *See under* Austrian
Habsburgs; Germany
Thou, François-Auguste de, 251, 287–89
Tiriot, Jean, 197
Toiras, Jean de Saint-Bonnet de: Casale
defended against Spaniards by, 202,
207, 210–11; military role against Huguenots, 181–82; personal favorite of
Louis XIII, 107, 150, 181–82; Richelieu
leery of, 182

Topin, Marius, 8
Toul, 233, 246
Toulouse: entrée of Louis XIII to, 140,
230; Parlement of, 226
Tours: Catholic riot in, 124; Louis XIII at,
55, 111
Traitants, 246–47, 253
Treasure, Geoffrey, 8, 288
Treasurers of France, 64, 247
Tremblay, sieur de: at Day of Dupes, 218;
governor of Bastille, 170
Trent, Council of, 45, 67, 257
Trier, 234, 236
Triumphal arches, 39, 140, 198
Tronçon, Louis: disgrace of, 160, 170;
personal secretary of Louis XIII,
108, 160
Tuileries palace gardens, 267
Turin, 241

Ulm, 132–33; Truce of, 132
Ultramontanism, 45–46, 67. *See also*
Papacy
Urban VIII (pope), 180, 241
Urfé, Honoré d', 270

Vair, Guillaume du: death of, 103, 127;
keeper of the seals for Marie de' Me-
dici until replaced by Mangot, 88, 99;
regains the seals under Louis XIII, 99;
role in council of Louis XIII, 105, 119
Val-de-Grâce, 257, 280
Valois monarchs, 20, 40. *See also* Charles
IX; Henry III
Val Tellina, 134–35, 176, 179–83, 207–8,
235, 240–41, 330n.45
Varin, Jean, 266
Vatan, Florimond de, 119
Vaunois, Louis, 9, 28
Vauquelin des Yveteaux, Nicolas: criticizes Louis XIII's education and upbringing, 36, 356n.17; preceptor of
Louis XIII, 31, 36, 47
Venality of office: definition and description of, 64; and Estates General of
1614–15, 70, 72–73; and new offices,
185, 245, 253; Louis XIII's attitude toward, 70, 118; Richelieu's views on,
159–60. *See also* Paulette
Vendôme, Alexandre de (half brother of
Louis XIII and Grand Prior of Malta):
background and family, 28; Chalais
conspiracy, and imprisonment and
death of, 190–91; friendship with